SÃO PAULO
in the Brazilian Federation
1889-1937

SÃO PAULO
in the Brazilian Federation
1889-1937

JOSEPH L. LOVE

STANFORD UNIVERSITY PRESS

Stanford, California   1980

Sources of photographs on pages 146–51: 1 and 3. Biblioteca Nacional, Rio de Janeiro. 2, 4, and 6. Instituto Agronômico do Estado, Campinas, São Paulo. 5, Museu do Café, Ribeirão Preto, São Paulo. 7–13. *O Estado de S. Paulo.*

Stanford University Press
Stanford, California
© 1980 by the Board of Trustees of the
Leland Stanford Junior University
Printed in the United States of America
ISBN 0-8047-0991-2
LC 78-66177

Published with the assistance of
the Andrew W. Mellon Foundation

For Jamie, Stevie, and Laurie

Preface

TO MY COLLEAGUES, Robert M. Levine and John D. Wirth, I am thankful for the opportunity to have worked so long and intimately in this collaborative undertaking. We remained in frequent contact with one another from the early conversations about a joint project to the last stages of editing. The volume outlines are similar, not only from chapter to chapter but, as far as feasible, within each chapter itself. Though we attempted to keep repetition at a minimum, each book necessarily draws on a common stock of information that was freely shared throughout the research and writing. Many tasks were shared, while others were assigned individually. Wirth and I compiled the code book for the collective biographies of the three state political elites; Levine and I designed the SPSS program for the comparative biographical study. We spent twelve months in 1969–70 in Brazil, and met three times. Later, Wirth and I spent a summer in Rio and Brasília, and Levine worked in the Public Record Office in London. We arranged to meet at least once a year after 1967.

Research funds for my work on São Paulo were provided by the U.S. Office of Education, and by two units at the University of Illinois at Urbana-Champaign: the Center for International Comparative Studies and the Center for Latin American and Caribbean Studies.

I am grateful to the following colleagues who kindly gave of their time to criticize drafts of the manuscript: Werner Baer, Paul Drake, Boris Fausto, Richard Graham, Michael Hall, Thomas Holloway, Frederic Jaher, Thomas Krueger, Robert Levine, Mauricio Solaún, and John Wirth. I want to thank Robert Shirley for generously sharing with me his research and data on the São Paulo judiciary. Thanks also go to my research assistants— Michael Conniff, Adalberto Marson, Amílcar Martins, and Santiago Romero, the first two of whom are now colleagues. Dorothy Osborne, an impeccable typist, did all drafts of the manuscript—and fast.

Of the staffs of the many off-campus institutions where I did research, I want especially to thank those of the Arquivo Público do Estado de São Paulo, of the Biblioteca Municipal de São Paulo, of the archives section of *O Estado de S. Paulo,* and of the Latin American Collection of the University of Texas at Austin. These were the places I kept going back to.

Readers will note changes in Portuguese orthography since the late nineteenth century. Conventionally, one cites author-title information as given on the title page, while using modern spelling for words, proper names, and places in the text. Until 1942, the milréis was the currency of Brazil. The conto, which is 1,000 milréis (written 1:000$000), was the largest monetary unit. On November 1, 1942, the milréis was replaced by the cruzeiro, one milréis (1$000) being equivalent to one cruzeiro (cr$1,00). Dollar equivalents are given in Appendix C.

JOSEPH L. LOVE

University of Illinois
Urbana-Champaign
September 1979

Contents

Six pages of photographs follow p. 145

Figures and Tables

Introduction

THIS IS ONE of three independent but coordinated studies on the regional dynamics of Brazilian federalism from the beginning of the Republic in 1889 to the establishment of the Estado Novo in 1937. The objective is to write comparative history from the regional perspective, that is, to pinpoint similarities and differences among three leading states, while identifying modes of interaction at the national level. The role of São Paulo, which is located in the Center-South, and which received the greatest benefits from export-led growth, is examined by Joseph L. Love. Politically powerful Minas Gerais, situated between the prosperous southern states and the impoverished Northeast, is analyzed by John D. Wirth. Pernambuco, the Northeast's most important state, is treated by Robert M. Levine as a case study in political and economic decline.

The period under study begins with the devolution of power from the centralized Empire to the states, and follows the course of the Union's gradual assumption of authority and responsibility over the ensuing half-century. Recentralization began well before the "Old Republic" (1889–1930) was abolished by coup d'état in 1930; it was formally and stridently proclaimed by the Estado Novo dictatorship, Getúlio Vargas's unitary regime from 1937 to 1945.

Our purpose is to bring together insights into the complex dynamics of state-level social and political structures, which have always been crucial in Brazil, but particularly during the nation's most decentralized phase, the years under study. Political events define the chronological limits of these studies, yet the coups of 1889 and 1937 and the very different constitutions that attended them are partly arbitrary benchmarks. Important political events in the states did not always mirror national events, nor did they bear the same meaning. Moreover, the neatness of this periodization is blurred by socioeconomic continuities that dilute the impact of what historians used to call "turning points." We refer both to the historic North-South shift in power and resources, which started around 1850 and rendered the Northeast an internal colony of the dynamic South, and also to the modernizing forces—social differentiation, urbanization, the growing internal market—which the political events overlay.

Though the issues of federalism are ostensibly a set of political problems, the economic, social, and cultural contexts receive extensive treatment in these books. This fact is evident from the format of the studies, which are organized on thematic rather than chronological lines. To calibrate change over time, however, each author used a chronology appropriate to his own state while relating regional events to those at the national level and those in the other states.

We also use the concept of political generations to order the several themes. Leaders born before 1869 were socialized under the Empire, with its centralized bureaucracy. Those born in the 20 years before 1889 knew the Republic as young men in the period of its greatest decentralization. Leaders in the third political generation came of age after 1910, when the impetus for a more integrated polity affected the military, fiscal, and economic policies of the nation and the states. The origins, career expectations, and experiences of these three political generations are discussed in Chapter 5. Generational analysis also informs the chapter on integration which follows it.

These volumes explore the regional dimensions of change, adaptation, and rigidities of the Old Republic and the initial phase of the Vargas government. Structural changes were extensive: in the economy, coffee and rubber exports reached their apogee and went into sharp decline; manufacturing underwent its initial surge in a complicated set of rhythms. For much of this period economic growth was largely dependent on exports and foreign capital, including investments in government bonds for infrastructural development. By the 1930's, Brazil had shifted its dependence in financial and economic affairs from Great Britain to the United States. This coincided with the acceleration of industrialization by import substitution.

Brazilian society likewise was transformed: the nation received a net inflow of between two and one-half and three million immigrants in the years 1889–1937, more than any other comparable period in its history. By the 1930's, internal migration was also greater than in any previous decade. Rapid urbanization and improvements in public health accompanied these population shifts. By 1940 the nation had two cities, Rio de Janeiro and São Paulo, with populations over one million, and 21 other cities with populations in excess of 100,000. In the cities the early labor movement was the crucible for anarchist and communist activity, only to be channeled and controlled from the top down by a government apparatus in the 1930's. In the complex interplay between federal and state units, government assumed new tasks not only in social control but also in social welfare, education at all levels (grossly neglected before 1889), and commodity marketing inside and outside the country. The period under study was also the classic age of banditry and messianism, principally but not exclusively in the Northeast, though both phenomena were vestigial by the time of the Estado Novo.

The political system established by the constitution of 1891 seemed anomalous in Latin America, even anachronistic in light of the centralizing tendencies in Mexico, Colombia, and Argentina. Yet a decentralized Republic suited the interests of powerful export-oriented groups, and the ancient patron-client system found its political expression in the *política dos governadores* by 1900. This system, directed by the president of the Republic and the governors of São Paulo and Minas Gerais, was an arrangement for the mutual support of incumbent elites at all levels of government. With a preponderantly rural population and low levels of political participation (only 1–3 percent of the population voted in federal elections before 1930), *coronelismo*—boss rule—prevailed in the countryside and made urban political groupings irrelevant until the 1920's. Without the moderating power of the Empire to remove incumbents from office, the Republic had no constitutional solution to the problem of entrenched establishments. Violence at local, state, and federal levels remained an indispensable tool in politics, sometimes involving the army, sometimes not.

In the 1930's Vargas consciously pursued a policy of deinstitutionalization of the most important state machines of the Old Republic— the Republican Parties of Minas Gerais, São Paulo, and Rio Grande do Sul. Meanwhile new antiliberal parties on right and left threatened the hybrid liberal-corporatist constitution of 1934. The Estado Novo dictatorship, outlawing all parties, was the culmination of the effort to depoliticize Brazil, as well as to centralize its government; yet success was limited, as our examination of the states reveals.

States are the units of analysis because they were the foci of political loyalty and political organization: there were no enduring national or multistate parties in the era in question. Even Pernambuco usually behaved as a politically self-centered region, despite its being the "natural" leader of the Northeast. In fact, Pernambuco's failure to marshal the Northeast as a bloc in Congress is an important theme in that state's history. Aspects of regionalism that did not follow state boundaries—markets, for example—are examined, but for the most part these books focus on the states.

We believe the three states covered were the logical choice for study, especially since Love had previously written *Rio Grande do Sul and Brazilian Regionalism*. In the era under examination, São Paulo and Minas Gerais were the economic, demographic, and political leaders, and only Rio Grande could hope to challenge their control of federal policies and institutions. Pernambuco was the most important state in Brazil's leading "problem" area—the poverty-stricken Northeast—and it provides a dramatic and, in many ways, representative case study of Brazilian regionalism from the "underside." Nonetheless, we realize that regionalism and its socioeconomic context cannot be fully understood without studies of other units, especially Bahia, Rio de Janeiro, and the old Federal District. Much remains to be done.

Region and regionalism are defined with reference to the problem at hand, which is to study politics and its social and economic bases over several decades. Thus, a region is defined as having the following characteristics:

1. It is part of a larger unit and interdependent with other regions that, together with the first, constitute the larger unit.

2. It has a definite geographic size and location, being politically bounded.

3. Each region has a set of component subregions, which are contiguous.

4. The region generates a set of loyalties on the part of its inhabitants, which vary in importance and intensity over time.

5. Loyalty to the region, however, is subordinated (nominally at

least) to loyalty to the larger unit—the nation-state—among the politically effective sectors of the region's population; this loyalty may also vary in importance and intensity.

Regionalism is here defined as political behavior characterized, on the one hand, by acceptance of the existence of a larger political unit, but, on the other hand, by the quest for favoritism and decisional autonomy from the larger unit on economic and social policies, even at the risk of jeopardizing the legitimacy of the prevailing political system. Thus the emphasis is not on regional peculiarities per se (e.g. folklore, patterns of dress and speech), but on those factors that can be demonstrated to affect the region's political, economic, and social relations with the other regions and the larger unit of government, in this case a nation-state.

Attitudes toward regionalism changed during the period under review. The hopeful modernizers of 1889 saw decentralization as a device to obtain a more efficient allocation of resources than could be achieved through the central government. By contrast, the authoritarian centralizers of 1937 blamed "selfish regionalism" for a host of social, economic, and political dislocations they vowed to set right by action at the center. Both groups thought of regionalism in policy terms, but reached radically different conclusions on its validity. Grounded in Brazilian historical experience, this prescriptive aspect of regionalism becomes part of the definition.

Regional elites believed their states were socioeconomic as well as political units which demanded allegiance. But when state was pitted against nation, their allegiances were ambivalent, as shown in the experience of São Paulo in the 1930's. Furthermore, their success in establishing the significance of the region was in doubt, or at least ambiguous. Outright failures occurred, notably in the case of Pernambuco, which could not establish political coherence. Exogenous market forces and the terrain channeled economic growth in ways the leaders of Minas did not want. Opportunities to live and work in Rio de Janeiro, the center of patronage and stylish city-state, eroded the regional ideal among Pernambucanos and Mineiros, in striking contrast to their Paulista counterparts. Above all, the interpenetration of manifold and complex structures across regional boundaries sapped regional coherence.

In holding to the regional ideal, however, the elites soon realized that regionalism was not necessarily incompatible with a strong federal government. State and nation were not necessarily antagonistic; they were part of a continuum along which the balance of forces shifted. Compartmentalized state economic policies were abandoned as early as the severe depression of the late 1890's. The elites soon came to measure and define regionalism in relation to other units and the central government. Shaping the terms of these relationships was in fact the essence of regional policymaking. Viewed this way, regionalism becomes more complex and significant than it would be if the problem were only that of nonviable states struggling against the centralizing tide.

Relationships changed as the nation became more integrated. By the time of World War I, elites were even less inclined to counterpose region to nation, although the aim of state policy was still to extract favorable terms. Thus the state elites welcomed integration when they could influence or control it, and on the whole accepted it when they had to. We devote considerable attention to the integration process, which began well before the 1930 Revolution.

In the Brazilian case, integration was the product of two congruent forces, namely, the interpenetration of social, economic, and political life across regional boundaries *and* the partial transfer of decisions and resources to a national level of political organization. We believe that the former reinforced, but did not directly cause, the latter. Thus we give attention to the interaction of congresses and meetings at state and national levels. Yet the ambiguities of the centralizing impetus are revealed in detailed case studies of state budgets and fiscal policies, and in our discussion of military forces.

Two concurrent kinds of relationships marked the integration process. One, on the horizontal dimension, occurred within and among groups based on common bonds, affinities, and shared interests. The other, structured vertically, was the process of interaction among unequals: clientelism is a prime instance. Having examined both types of social interaction, we found striking the weakness of group and interest associations and the persistence of vertical structures, though this varied by state. Furthermore, it is clear that the elites modernized selectively, minimizing social mobilization. By this yardstick Brazil was far from being a fully integrated society by 1937.

In probing the complex processes whereby the parts fit together, we also focus explicitly on the role of state policymakers—what they wanted, tried to get, and settled for. Though political integration was far from uniform or complete by 1937, we think our analysis of regional decision-makers is a way to understand what was achieved. By looking at the terms of interaction we hope to carry analysis beyond the vague proposition that the elites, in learning to cooperate, willed national integration.

Our initial hypothesis was that the states functioned as "halfway houses," pioneering in areas of social and economic legislation, and slowly ceding responsibilities to the federal government after World War I. It later became clear, however, that government responsibility at *both* state and federal levels was increasing down to 1930, and that some state responsibilities were still vigorous until 1937 and beyond. This is another way of saying that regionalism was not the antithesis of interpenetration and integration, which took place on all levels of government.

One of the most instructive aspects of the regional approach is the opportunity for comparison, and there are several topics for which comparative regional analysis is especially appropriate.

1. The political consequences of different patterns of economic growth are seen more clearly: Pernambuco in decline, Minas with a relatively weak economy, and São Paulo in rapid expansion developed different political strategies at the state and national levels.

2. The alleged causal links between the level of socioeconomic development and types of political organization are brought under triangulation, allowing for a better view of other factors affecting leadership and organizations.

3. Different center-periphery relationships are highlighted in these studies. Pernambuco tended to predominate among the Northeastern states, but was itself a satellite of the central government; Minas was on the margins of the Center-South; São Paulo enjoyed a rapidly expanding domestic market; all had their export links and contrasting patterns of international financial obligations.

4. Similarities and differences in identically defined political elites are thrown into relief by the comparative analysis of computerized biographical data.

5. The role of the states in fostering or impeding political and economic integration emerges from the comparative study of state militias, budgets, specialized congresses, and associational activity.

As histories of Pernambuco, Minas, and São Paulo, these studies are schematic, not exhaustive. The stress is on structures, parallels, and linkages, rather than on detailed narrative exposition, for which there is still need. We hope that some of the richness of a unique regional society emerges in each volume. Inevitably, each study reflects the type, amount, and quality of source materials and previous studies available to the individual authors, who are responsible for their own volumes. In sum, each study stands alone; but all three follow the same design, which is the product of collaborative effort.

It was our intention not only to illuminate the Brazilian past but also to make a contribution to the literature on social and political change. The three works are case studies of major subnational units during the early phases of modernization. In charting the strategies of the elites to promote or retard change and the political consequences of shifts in the economic base, we hope these volumes will be read by students of the processes of capitalist modernization as well as by those interested in the unique features of Brazilian history.

We also hope to contribute to the comparative literature on regionalism and federalism. The problems and perspectives of regionalism are far from dead in the United States, where such issues as revenue sharing and state vs. federal control of energy resources are widely debated. Furthermore, it seems clear that many of the world's underdeveloped countries are experiencing profound currents of regionalism (often reinforcing ethnic cleavages), as social mobilization brings new groups into the political process. One form this can take is separatism and civil war, as the recent tragedies of Bangladesh and Nigeria illustrate. There is also a possibility that regionalism will lead to a more creative definition of the nation, as may be occurring in parts of Western Europe. Finally, in Brazil itself the issues of federalism are by no means dead, and it has yet to be demonstrated that the allegiance of the masses to the nation-state of Brazil parallels those of political and economic elites.

R.M.L.
J.L.L.
J.D.W.

SÃO PAULO
in the Brazilian Federation
1889-1937

CHAPTER ONE

Man and the Land

WHAT IS IT that "can't stop," and into which "one more always fits"? Brazilians know that the answer, whether it refers to the state or its capital city, is São Paulo. From the frequency with which the phrases *São Paulo não pode parar* and *São Paulo: Sempre cabe mais um* are repeated, it is clear that most of São Paulo's inhabitants are wont to dwell on the most important feature of the state's story. And this emphasis is justified, for that story is above all one of growth.

Consider, for example, the exponential rate at which the capital city* has grown over the last century. In 1872 it had some 31,000 inhabitants; by 1970 Greater São Paulo was the eighth largest metropolitan area in the world, with 6,000,000 people in the city proper and 8,000,000 all together.[1] The state's demographic growth, though less vertiginous, has also been spectacular. From 840,000 persons in 1872, São Paulo grew to almost 18,000,000 in 1970, giving it a population almost equal to New York State's in that year. By 1970, 17 municípios in São Paulo had more than 100,000 inhabitants, and 80 percent of the state's population was regarded as urban.[2]

The federal censuses nearest the period under study—those of 1890 and 1940—show that the greatest absolute upsurge in population came after the birth of the Republic in 1889. In 1890 São Paulo had only 1,400,000 inhabitants, but by 1940 it claimed 7,200,000, an increase of

---

*Hereafter "capital" will refer to São Paulo city, and "São Paulo" to the state. The region around the capital will be called the Capital zone.

414 percent. In 1890, the state ranked third in population in the Federation (trailing Minas Gerais and Bahia), with 10 percent of Brazil's people; by 1940 it was first, with 17 percent. In the same period, the capital grew from 65,000 persons to 1,300,000, a twentyfold increase in 50 years, allowing the city to expand its share of the state's population from 4 percent to 18 percent.[3]

By 1940, many Brazilians would have agreed that São Paulo "couldn't stop." This chapter explores the giddy demographic and geographic expansion of that complex and aggressive frontier civilization. Its title, "Man and the Land," suggests several important themes, which we shall take up in turn: the land itself, its climate, geology, and topography; early efforts at settling that land; mass immigration in the heyday of coffee exports; the elimination of the Indians and the marginalization of the blacks; the relations of production in countryside and city; the state's unique public health program that helped attract immigrants from abroad and from other parts of Brazil; and, finally, the development of the state's 10 zones, most of which were defined by the westward advance of the railroad.

The Westward March

Geographically, São Paulo, though a heavily industrialized area, is part of the tropical world, with a capital that lies considerably closer to the equator than Cairo or New Delhi. Yet the state's latitude (19°46'30"S to 25°16'06"S) is a deceptive indicator of its climate. Though of São Paulo's area—250,000 sq. kilometers, less than 3 percent of Brazil's total—only a sixth lies south of the tropics, and though the Tropic of Capricorn runs a few miles north of the capital, most of the state consists of *planaltos* (plateaus) set high enough to mitigate the heat associated with tropical latitudes. Consequently, a geographer has estimated that more than 85 percent of the state enjoys a subtropical rather than a tropical climate, defined in terms of average daily temperatures.[4] The vast bulk of the population lives west of the escarpment defined by the Serra do Mar.* Rainfall is greatest along the tropical coastline (150 inches a year at Santos), but most of the state receives abundant quantities of rain (50 to 60 inches). Man's destruction of the virgin forest, however, has altered the

* For a map of the state, showing its principal rivers, its rail lines, and its zones, see p. 24.

climate: winters and springs have become drier and summers wetter, making the pattern of precipitation more typically tropical. Not only was land cleared to plant coffee, but trees were used extensively as fuel by sugar mills and railroads. The Araraquarense railroad, for example, even at a low point in its activity, during the early 1930's, required 10,000 cubic meters of firewood a month; and large estates kept forest reserves for fueling the engines that pulled coffee freight.[5]

But to note that deforestation has changed the climate is not to suggest that all the planalto area was once densely wooded—far from it. The basin in which the capital is located was originally a plains area—*campos* covered with tall grass and scrub vegetation. In this area, well above the coast, the climate is mild; average daily temperatures in the capital vary from 58° F in the winter to 69° in the summer, compared with a range of 66° to 78° at Santos, the state's principal port.

Just as the development of São Paulo is intimately linked with the expansion of the coffee industry, so coffee is linked with the famous *terra roxa* soil in which it thrives. Terra roxa is a "deep, porous soil containing considerable humus, which can be recognized by its dark reddish-purple color."[6] Its porosity permits coffee trees to sink deep roots and produce abundant and high-quality yields. Yet only 7 percent of the soil in São Paulo is true terra roxa, a type of soil that is always found with deposits of basalt.[7] The value of any soil, of course, depends in part on the crop for which it is intended, and though terra roxa is excellent for coffee production, it is inferior for cotton, the state's second-most-important commercial crop in the 1930's. A more common soil is the reddish clay of the crystalline uplands called *massapê* (not to be confused with the black massapê of the Northeast), which is also used for coffee planting.

The frontier has played a fundamental role in the development of São Paulo's economy and society, not only during the coffee era, but for the whole period from the sixteenth century through the 1930's. Indeed, six of the state's 10 zones were still frontier areas as late as 1880; and three, as we shall see, remained so well into the twentieth century. There were in fact two frontiers—a demographic frontier and a "pioneer" frontier behind it, directly linked to the international economy of the Atlantic basin. On the demographic frontier, where backwoodsmen pushed back or destroyed aboriginal tribesmen, land tenure was without legal title, and "law" usually depended on the pleasure of a powerful de facto landholder.[8]

The pioneer frontier, running just ahead of the railroad in our period, was shaped by the peculiar requirements of its *produit moteur*, coffee. First, coffee trees require a mild climate and certain types of soil, of which the best is terra roxa on high ground (to avoid frost). Second, coffee production requires the continual creation of new plantations, since the trees have a built-in obsolescence, leaching the soil of its nutrients after a few decades. These botanical facts and the economic desire to exploit them gave the pioneer frontier two characteristic features: the search for, and appropriation of, ridges of tablelands of terra roxa with the discovery of the value of that soil for coffee near Campinas in the 1870's; and the rapid commercialization of land with the recognition that production was subject to obsolescence because of soil exhaustion.

Legal land tenure prevailed on the pioneer frontier, where the concept of capitalist property rights accompanied the area's economic integration into an international economic system. Though land title issues could drag on for decades, the pioneer frontier inexorably moved westward, and so did the planters. *Fazendeiro* (planter) families bought virgin land for future operations, often in regions distant from their original estates. The Rodrigues Alves and Pereira Barreto families, for example, were rooted in the Paraíba Valley. The Pereira Barretos pioneered coffee development in Ribeirão Preto, the premier coffee county of the Mogiana zone, and the Rodrigues Alves family opened coffee plantations in São Manuel and Piratininga, respectively in the Alta Sorocabana and Alta Paulista zones.[9]

Though coffee was clearly the driving engine of São Paulo's development in our period, it was a recent crop compared with sugar and tobacco. Moreover, in the colonial era São Paulo was only a marginal producer in the Brazilian economy. The captaincy was important nevertheless in providing a strategic base for Portuguese imperial expansion; it was, in the laconic description of the historian Caio Prado Júnior, "a zone of passage."[10] São Paulo is uniquely endowed for a strategic mission, if such it was, for almost all its rivers flow toward the Brazilian interior; the proportion of its area drained inland is among the greatest of the Brazilian states.[11]

Colonial São Paulo is best known—both in formal historical studies and in the popular mind—for the phenomenon of *bandeirismo*, the collective actions of the slave raiders and trailblazers known as *bandeirantes*, based in the capital. Ranging thousands of miles across Brazil and neighboring Spanish America in the late-sixteenth and seventeenth centuries in expeditions called *bandeiras*, the bandeirantes, with their unquenchable thirst for slaves and gold and their daring exploits, are comparable in many respects to the conquistadores of Mexico and Peru. They raided Jesuit missions for Indian slaves in Paraguay and Rio Grande do Sul; they destroyed the rebel African community of Palmares in the Northeast captaincy of Alagoas; they opened the gold fields of Minas Gerais; and their descendants, in expeditions called *monções*, carried on the tradition in the gold camps of eighteenth-century Goiás and Mato Grosso, as well as exploring the Amazon Valley.

Twentieth-century Brazilian historians have pointed to the critical role of Paulista bandeiras and monções in defining Brazil's far-flung domains in Mato Grosso and the Amazon Valley, though a recent study argues that the Portuguese state also played an indispensable and hitherto insufficiently acknowledged part.[12] But if these historians have laid a foundation for the myth of the bandeirantes' almost Faust-like quest for adventure and opportunity, the mythmakers have accompanied the historians *pari passu*, linking São Paulo's current greatness with its "ancient" past. Cassiano Ricardo, author of *The Westward March* (1940), was perhaps the most successful of them, and even made something of a career of glorifying the bandeirante heritage.[13]

São Paulo de Piratininga, the Jesuit mission settlement destined to become one of the world's great metropolises, was a true "gateway to the backlands"—*boca de sertão*—in the sixteenth and seventeenth centuries. As elsewhere in the country, however, the initial Portuguese settlements were founded on the coast. The first site, São Vicente, was in fact on an island. Established between 1510 and 1516, it was quickly outgrown by Santos, founded two decades later on the same island, because of Santos's superior harbor. Efforts to found towns above the escarpment failed in the 1530's, but Jesuit missionaries managed to push their way inland to establish the village that became the capital in 1554. Located on the Tietê River, which flows northwestward into the Paraná, the town of São Paulo was the first permanent Portuguese site on the planaltos. Settlement then proceeded along the course of the river and its tributaries. The village of Parnaíba followed São Paulo in the sixteenth century. Three other villages—Itu, Mogi das Cruzes, and Jundiaí—were established in the opening years of the seventeenth century. In the 1630's new settlements fortified the Portuguese grip on the littoral—São Sebastião, Ubatuba, and Iguape. In the next decade colonization began along the

Paraíba, the only large river in São Paulo that empties directly into the Atlantic; São José dos Campos, Taubaté, and Guaratinguetá were all established in the 1640's, followed by Pindamonhangaba and Lorena at the turn of the century.

Sorocaba, founded to the west of São Paulo city in 1646, rapidly became a new boca de sertão. As the site of a fair where mules, horses, and livestock were sold, it was a point of contact between the ranchers of Mato Grosso and Rio Grande do Sul and the livestock buyers of Minas Gerais, Rio de Janeiro, and Bahia. The town "played the same role for eastern South America that Salta [in Argentina] played for the western part," i.e., it was a center for the mule trade and mule train traffic.[14]

From a staging, trading, and raiding base in the colonial period, São Paulo was transformed in the nineteenth century into an area of fixed, agriculture-based settlement, bringing the province its first landed elite. Although the myth of the 400-year-old families of São Paulo has some basis in fact, the large estates above the escarpment were almost all founded after the middle of the eighteenth century; the state's rural elite is thus closer to the vintage of Argentina's than Pernambuco's.[15]

São Paulo's first *fazendas* produced sugarcane, and the high-quality Cayenne variety reached the captaincy in 1809. By the second quarter of the nineteenth century, the major area of sugar production had moved above the escarpment, and by 1836 Itu and Campinas in the "west" were producing half the São Paulo crop. Colonization also proceeded north of Campinas during the sugar epoch, owing in part to the decline in gold production in Minas Gerais. Visiting Franca in 1819, the scientist Auguste de Saint-Hilaire asserted that all the inhabitants of the town were Mineiros.[16]

With sugar came a rapid increase in the province's slave population— an 80 percent rise, in fact, between 1813 and 1836, when the number of slaves reached 87,000. Yet in the early nineteenth century its sugar exports remained modest; Bahia alone sent abroad 20 times as much. By the 1830's, coffee had replaced sugar as the most important crop in the Paraíba Valley (sometimes called the "north" of the province), and by mid-century coffee had become São Paulo's main export.[17] Meanwhile, with a further decline of the mining economy of southern Minas Gerais, more Mineiros had crossed the border to found cattle ranches in the area around Mococa, Jaboticabal, and Ribeirão Preto; later these municípios would become bustling coffee producers. Coffee remained São Paulo's principal export crop after 1850, though many Paulista planters turned to cotton in the 1860's during the United States Civil War—only to yield again to the competition of the American South in the following decade.[18]

Given the excellence of terra roxa as a coffee soil, São Paulo's future as coffee empire and emporium was held in check by one thing only: lack of good transportation. The watershed, in this respect, came in 1867, when British engineers opened the so-called San Paulo Railway, an event that promised to drastically lower both freight charges and time-in-transit in moving coffee down the escarpment. Campinas, the coffee município par excellence, was connected to the rails five years later, and the time required to move coffee to the port was suddenly reduced from three to four weeks (by mule train) to a few days. Thereafter coffee tended to follow the terra roxa deposits on ridges along westward-flowing rivers; railroads tended to follow coffee;[19] and population and prosperity followed the railroads.

Forward-looking planters got the provincial government to aid the central administration in guaranteeing profit rates for rail companies, and they expanded their operations rapidly: São Paulo had 140 kilometers of rails in 1870, 1,200 a decade later, and 2,400 by 1890. In 1937, the state had 22 percent of the track in the country—7,400 kilometers, almost as much as Minas Gerais, a state with twice as much land.[20] Although Brazil's railway network has often been criticized for its lack of integration, São Paulo was fortunate in gaining a *regionally* integrated system. Moreover, on a square-kilometer basis, it is the most extensive system in all South America, save for the humid pampa area around Buenos Aires.[21] Railroads provided the chief means of conveyance westward throughout our period, and regions of the state are usually defined by the rail companies that opened them to settlement. It is probably no coincidence that the Paulistas' favorite image of their state in relation to the others is an engine pulling empty boxcars.

Railroads, of course, did not penetrate everywhere, and coffee had to be brought to rail terminals largely by oxcart as late as the 1920's. In that decade, however, a highway building program and the introduction of trucking made the road system a potential rival of the rails in its significance for the state economy. The cities of Rio de Janeiro and São Paulo were linked by a highway in 1928; and by 1937, São Paulo state had 48,000 kilometers of roads—the most of all the states and about one-quarter of Brazil's total.[22] In 1947 came the Via Anchieta, the modern highway connecting the capital with the port of Santos.

River transport also played a role in the coffee boom, linking the more remote plantations with rail stations; and some railroads ran auxiliary barge transport systems. Rivers in the nineteenth and twentieth centuries also provided the routes for the march of settlement, advancing wherever basalt beds containing terra roxa were found. As in colonial days, settlers (including scions of leading families) followed the course of the Tietê and other river systems, felling trees and opening plantations[23]—often in anticipation of the railroad's arrival.

After São Paulo entered the railroad era, Santos's only competition for primacy as a port city came from Rio de Janeiro itself. Santos exported 2,000,000 60-kilo bags of coffee in 1895, and after a major expansion of dock facilities two years later, foreign sales grew apace: 13,100,000 bags were exported in 1909, by which time the value of Santos's coffee sales was four and a half times the value of Rio's.[24] This achievement was made possible in part by the British-owned São Paulo Railway Company's completion of a double track down the escarpment in 1900. Furthermore, the first 260 meters of quays built in 1897 had grown to 4,720 by 1909. Some 1,000,000 metric tons of traffic were processed in 1901, 2,000,000 in 1913, 3,300,000 on the brink of the Depression in 1929, and more than 4,000,000 by 1938.[25]

Newcomers, Blacks, and Indians

The economic transformation of São Paulo brought in its wake a vast number of new developments in the local society. The racial and ethnic composition of the Paulista population changed profoundly after the fall of the Empire: a flood of immigrants poured in during the Old Republic (1889–1930), followed by heavy internal migration by Brazilians from other states in the next decade. As a consequence of the first phenomenon, São Paulo's Indian and black populations both rapidly lost ground.

The decline of slavery in the last half of the nineteenth century has been well studied, and here we need only touch on factors that laid a foundation for later events. For one thing, though it is true that the slaves as a percentage of the provincial population fell from a (censused) peak of 28 percent in 1854 to 9 percent in 1886,[26] it is also true that through all this period, coffee-growing São Paulo, with the most dynamic economy in the late Empire, was importing slaves from other provinces. Despite a tripling or quadrupling of slave prices in the 1870's and a two-conto tax on slaves entering the province after 1881, slavery remained an economically viable institution into the early 1880's, when some fazendeiros still claimed that the use of slave labor permitted an annual net profit of 50 percent.[27] The census figures reflect this trend. The absolute number of slaves in the province reached a maximum in the 1870's—175,000 were counted in 1872—at which time only neighboring Minas Gerais and Rio de Janeiro provinces had larger slave populations. By 1887, the year of the last slave count, the number of slaves in São Paulo had declined to 108,000, though Minas had almost twice that number. Yet here again the figures hardly tell the whole story, for as Robert Conrad has pointed out, while the total number of slaves decreased, as in all other provinces, the number of male slaves in São Paulo actually increased between 1874 and 1884.[28]

The substitution of European immigrant labor for slaves in São Paulo's coffee fields is also a well-researched topic, albeit a controversial one; some scholars see the influx of immigrant labor as an effect of the decay of the slave system and a solution to the planters' labor "problem," whereas others view it as a cause of abolition (see Chapter Two).[29] At any rate, by 1887 it had been demonstrated to the satisfaction of "western" planters around Campinas that immigrant labor was a viable substitute for slave labor; and by May of that year, some 60,000–70,000 Italians had been placed on São Paulo fazendas.[30] At a famous meeting in the provincial capital in December 1887, the most prosperous planters—chiefly from the new producing areas—agreed to call for the total abolition of slavery in Brazil in 1890.

Pronouncements by planters and politicians left no doubt why São Paulo sought immigrants—to plant, tend, and harvest coffee. Some Paulistas even professed to believe that colonos, as the foreign agricultural laborers were called, liked working for wages better than farming for themselves. In the words of the future President Manuel Campos Sales, speaking before the federal Senate in 1892, "The European immigrant prefers to be placed on the established plantations."[31]

Substituting European immigrants for slaves had been attempted as early as the 1850's. But these first efforts were regarded as failures: the immigrants had felt they were being treated as slaves, and the planters had complained of their workers' "indiscipline." Labor relations on the Vergueiro estate in Limeira, near Rio Claro, generated such a scandal in

Europe that Prussia prohibited the further recruitment of its nationals in 1859, and the Swiss government recommended the same policy to its federated cantons.[32] Meanwhile, spontaneous (nonsubsidized) immigration was held in check until the late 1880's by the profitability of slave labor and the cost of steamship passage from Europe to Brazil, which was sometimes twice as much as the fare to the United States.[33] But the falling costs of travel, a surplus population in southern Europe, the rising prospect of abolition, and the decision of Brazilian and Paulista authorities to subsidize immigrant transportation finally turned the trickle of foreigners into a flood. Some 2,300,000 (57 percent) of the immigrants who entered Brazil between 1888 (the first year their numbers exceeded 100,000) and 1935 came to São Paulo.[34]

The immigration subsidy program was designed to procure agricultural workers. The program, which provided free passage for immigrants who went into agriculture, was begun by the provincial government in 1884; the central and Paulista governments continued to subsidize plantation-bound immigrants well into the Republic. The program was such a success that federal subsidization temporarily ended in 1897, when the labor market became saturated.[35]

In the decade 1891–1900 São Paulo alone received more immigrants than Argentina; 1,130,000 foreigners came to Brazil in these years, and 700,000 of them made their way to São Paulo. By 1920, the population of the state was more than 18 percent foreign-born; but immigration virtually ground to a halt in the 1930's, and the figure declined to 10 percent in 1940.[36] Overall, Brazil attracted fewer immigrants than Argentina, and many who came to São Paulo left both the state and Brazil—an exit problem Argentina also faced. In the coffee-depression years of 1903 and 1904, and again in 1907, São Paulo actually experienced a net outflow of immigrants. But over the whole period 1885–1906 Brazil (and São Paulo in particular) had the good fortune to undergo economic expansion at the same time as Italy, a principal source of migrants, and Argentina and the United States, the major competitors for migrant workers, experienced depression.[37]

Just as the Paulista planters had no interest in attracting foreigners to their state who sought urban employment, so they tried to be selective in other ways. Reflecting European biases of the age—and perhaps influenced by the examples of the United States and Argentina—Brazilian and Paulista statesmen preferred Caucasian immigrants to Orientals and blacks. Ironically, it was the Paulista Francisco Glicério, himself a mulatto, who drew up a federal decree in June 1890 opening Brazil to all able-bodied workers "except indigents from Asia and Africa, who can be admitted only by the authorization of congress."[38] A clear anti-Chinese bias was present in São Paulo, though not universally held.[39] However, another federal decree, in 1907, quietly did away with the restrictions on geographic origins as São Paulo sought Japanese immigrants, who began arriving in 1908. By contrast, there was almost no dissent among Paulistas from the view that African immigrants were undesirable,[40] though the 1907 legislation apparently permitted their entry.

From 1882 through 1930, 2,223,000 immigrants came to São Paulo. Italians formed the largest single group, constituting 46 percent of the total and numbering just over 1,000,000.[41] The Italians, initially from the Po Valley and later from the Mezzogiorno, Sicily, and Sardinia, were also the first wave of newcomers to reach Brazilian shores. Prior to the Prinetti decree, which in 1902 forbade Italian nationals to accept subsidized immigration to Brazil because of the abusive treatment of their countrymen on Paulista plantations, most immigrants (to Brazil as a whole) came from the north of Italy. Thereafter southerners dominated, but for the entire period 1876–1930 northerners supplied over half the total to Brazil.

After the Italians, São Paulo's second-largest immigrant group in the 1882–1930 period were the Portuguese, who numbered 404,000 and constituted 18 percent of the total. Close behind them were the Spaniards, accounting for 17 percent. The rest of the immigrants (19 percent) were of various origins, including most notably Japanese; Syrians and Lebanese (both groups Turkish nationals before the First World War); Poles and Eastern European Jews (both groups Russian or Austrian nationals); Armenians (Russian or Turkish nationals); and Germans. The official subsidy program promoted the immigration of whole families, with the result that the majority of immigrants entering Santos came as families.[42]

That the planters should have their government underwrite immigration as early as 1884 in an era of laissez-faire economics indicates the breadth of vision that contributed to their growing lead over agricultural producers in the rest of the country. All the same, spontaneous immigration was sufficiently heavy by the late 1920's that the state government subsidy could almost be ended. By 1924–28, the proportion of subsidized immigrants, who in earlier years had made up as much as 94 percent of the total, had decreased to 29 percent.[43] In 1929, Governor Júlio Prestes reported to the state legislature that, following the virtual termination of the immigrant subsidy in 1927, the unsubsidized stream in 1928 had established a record. He could also confidently relate to the planter-dominated body that 87,000 of the 96,000 immigrants had gone into plantation agriculture.[44] The governor, however, neglected to mention three points: that there was an outflow of immigrants, which brought the net figure for 1928 down to 70,000; that Brazilian migrants were now beginning to arrive in sufficient numbers to make immigrant labor unnecessary; and finally, that subsidized immigration had not really ended.*

During the 1930's, in-migration definitively surpassed immigration as a contributor to São Paulo's demographic growth. National migrants had captured the lead for the first time in 1928, but the pattern became permanent only in 1934, owing to federal restrictions on immigration and the slump in international migration caused by the world Depression. Some 50,000 in-migrants had come to São Paulo under a state subsidy program by 1935,[45] but spontaneous migration was by then far more important. The 1940 census reveals that São Paulo received almost 500,000 more persons from other states than it sent out—a far greater net gain than any other state. The largest group in the gross total of 726,000 came from neighboring Minas Gerais, which contributed 349,000 migrants, followed by Bahia, with 153,000; meanwhile, 231,000 Paulistas had left the state, half of them migrating to the new coffee fields of northern Paraná.[46]

For the black and the mulatto, the influx of immigrants (and to some extent, of the in-migrants later) resulted in marginalization, and for the Indian, much worse. The racial composition of the state shifted sharply toward greater white predominance during the first half century of the Republic. Whereas almost 37 percent of the population had been identified as black or mulatto in the 1890 census, by 1940 the figure had fallen to 12 percent.[47] In some part this decrease appears to have been due to an excess of deaths over births among the black and mulatto population. Mortality statistics indicate such a trend for the capital in 1920–28 and for the state as a whole in 1932–41.[48]

São Paulo's social structure, like Brazil's in general, tended to locate

*With respect to the third point, a firm connected with the Japanese government was still bringing immigrants from Japan, and the São Paulo government continued to pay indirect costs as late as 1937. Furthermore, the state was still subsidizing overland transportation from Rio in 1928–29. Holloway, "Migration," p. 176; SP, Colleção das leis, 1937, tomo 47, v. 3: 1102. (For convenience, I hereafter refer to Brazilians from other states as immigrants and to their migration as in-migration.)

TABLE 1.1

*Educational Attainment by Racial Category of Paulistas
Above Ten Years of Age, 1940*

(Percent)

Race	Level completed			Representation in state population
	Primary	Secondary	Advanced	
White	92%	96%	98%	85%
Black	3	1	—	7
Mulatto	2	1	1	5
Asiatic	3	2	1	3

SOURCE: IBGE, *Recenseamento*, 1940. *Série regional*, 17(1): 6, 18.

NOTE: In calculating the educational percentages I have excluded persons in each racial category whose level of attainment was unknown.

blacks and mulattoes in the lowest strata. Education, a key element in social mobility, tells the story. As we see in Table 1.1, whites, composing 85 percent of the population in 1940, accounted for 92 percent of the students at the elementary level and 98 percent at the college level. Meanwhile, blacks and mulattoes, with 12 percent of the population, accounted for only 5 percent of primary students and a mere 1 percent of university students. These data, moreover, even slightly understate the disparity between the white and black groups, since the census from which they are drawn groups all persons of "undeclared" race with mulattoes.

Using the occupations of Paulista males in 1940 as an index of social class (Table 1.2), we can see how low the position of the black man was. Whites accounted for 96 percent of those in the liberal professions; blacks and mulattoes together, only 3 percent (one-fourth of their share of the total population). The black and mulatto groups did much better in public administration (11 percent) but were barely represented in the urban employer groups, with 3 percent in commerce and only 2 percent in manufacturing. Among the "higher-ranking" occupations in the table, blacks and mulattoes did best as agricultural employers (6 percent); but they also supplied far more than their share of farm and plantation laborers (20 percent).*

Such statistics imply, but hardly convey adequately, the degradation of

*In Table 1.1 we saw that the Asiatics (largely rural and mostly Japanese) were still underrepresented in educational attainment beyond the primary level in 1940. But as agricultural employers we see here that they ran far ahead of their 3 percent representation in the population.

TABLE 1.2
Select Occupations of São Paulo Males by Racial Category, 1940

Occupation	White		Black		Mulatto and undeclared		Asiatic	
	Number	Percent	Number	Percent	Number	Percent	Number	Percent
Employer								
Commerce[a]	11,261	95%	213	2%	64	1%	308	3%
Manufacturing	9,812	97	49	1	62	1	377	2
Agriculture	29,629	84	939	3	1,011	3	3,749	11
Professional	23,335	96	272	1	459	2	377	2
Public administration	44,982	89	3,255	6	2,340	5	69	—
Employee								
Commerce[a]	86,192	92	3,413	4	2,086	2	1,550	2
Manufacturing	267,609	89	18,869	6	11,831	4	1,242	—
Agriculture	436,713	78	73,724	13	39,557	7	9,890	2

SOURCE: Same as Table 1.1, p. 24.
NOTE: Percentages in this table and others that follow do not always total to 100 because of rounding.
[a] Commodities (*mercadorias*) only.

blacks and mulattoes as a group. Immigrants quickly took the jobs in the capital's newly opened factories, and blacks were generally relegated to the most dangerous, casual, and menial jobs outside industry. The sexual brutalization and overcrowding found in our own black ghettos were also present in São Paulo's capital; and there, as here, the black family tended to be matrifocal.[49] Yet in the 1920's and 1930's the blacks of São Paulo began to mobilize, and the capital became the focus of a national black movement. The best known organizations were the Centro Cívico Palmares (Palmares Civic Center), founded in 1927 and named after a seventeenth-century kingdom of rebel slaves, and the Frente Negra Brasileira (Brazilian Negro Front), founded in 1931.[50]

But if blacks were absorbed at the lowest levels of society, the Indians were not. The more fortunate were pushed back, and the rest destroyed, with the whites' every step westward. The Coroados (Kaingangs and Bororos) were exterminated in the twentieth century with the same ruthlessness as the Tamoios were destroyed or enslaved in the sixteenth. On a map published in 1868, a third of São Paulo was described as "lands occupied by wild Indians,"[51] and some portions of the state could still be so described well into the twentieth century. As elsewhere in the Americas, the killing of an Indian was accepted as a commonplace, and modern bandeirantes preferred to extirpate rather than enslave. Fighting often broke out near the railheads as agriculture penetrated the interior and land values soared. Techniques varied; firearms were used most frequently, but sertanistas (backwoodsmen) and bugreiros (redskin-killers) also poisoned the Indians' food and water supplies or induced epidemics by distributing the clothing of smallpox victims to unsuspecting tribesmen. The word genocide must be used in connection with campaigns that included the murder of pregnant women and small children. A Capuchin mission that went to the Campos Novos area near the Rio Peixe in 1904 to prevent the slaughter of Indians soon came into armed conflict with them; when the federal government's Rondon Commission (precursor of the Indian Protection Service) arrived in Campos Novos in 1911, there were no Indians left to protect.[52] Today, the state's few surviving Indian communities, by all recent evidence, are beset with the same problems of alcoholism and tuberculosis often found among their North American counterparts.[53]

Of course there were also Indian raids and counterraids against the frontiersmen, who, like the classical bandeirantes, often had Indian blood in their veins. Atrocities were most frequent on the demographic frontier, and the bulk of the region bordered by the Paraná, Paranapanema, and Peixe rivers was still beyond the law as late as the mid-1930's.[54]

Social Configurations

On the eastern side of the frontier, the overwhelming majority of the population was rural. As Table 1.3 reveals, nearly two-thirds of São Paulo's economically active population in 1920 was engaged in agriculture; and though the proportion dropped by 1940, more than half of the economically active workers were still agriculturalists. We observe that industry's share of the work force appears to have lost ground in this period, but this anomaly is simply an artifact of changes in census definitions: seamstresses and tailors were placed in the industrial sector in the 1920 census and in the services sector in 1940. Unfortunately, the data are not detailed enough to make an accurate correction, but Albert Fishlow estimates that by the 1940 standards, the Brazilian industrial labor force as a whole grew from 4 percent to 10 percent in the intercensal period. In São Paulo the number of industrial workers grew from 84,000 in 1920 to 273,000 in 1940.[55]

Yet if these data show a relative decline in the agriculturally active population, they also show that a majority of the Paulistas still earned their livelihood in the countryside throughout the period under study. Planters, as we have seen, wanted immigrants and migrants only as farmworkers. But could they block widespread homesteading under conditions of a constantly expanding frontier? The big estate was the typical unit on which coffee was produced, and it had preceded coffee, arriving on the plateau in the late eighteenth century as sugar culture ascended from the

TABLE 1.3
Economically Active Population of São Paulo and Brazil by Sector, 1920 and 1940
(Percent)

	São Paulo		Brazil	
Sector	1920	1940	1920	1940
Agriculture	63%	56%	70%	66%
Industry	18	16	14	10
Services	19	28	17	23

SOURCE: Villela and Suzigan, *Política do governo*, p. 291.

TABLE 1.4

Land Concentration in São Paulo and Brazil,
1920 and 1940

(Percent of total value of agricultural holdings)

Size category in hectares	São Paulo		Brazil	
	1920	1940	1920	1940
200+	70%	48%	63%	48%
400+[a]	55		50	
500+[a]		32		32
1,000+	32	21	37	21

SOURCE: DGE, *Recenseamento*, 1920, 3 (1ª parte): 6–7, 18–19; IBGE, *Recenseamento*, 1940. *Série nacional*, 3: 2, 130.

NOTE: Value of the land includes improvements and equipment.

[a] Category changed from 400+ to 500+ in the 1940 census.

littoral. By 1818 the big estate already predominated among the legally registered holdings in Rio Claro, which was to become the edge of the coffee frontier before the railroad penetrated the interior.[56]

Statewide evidence of land concentration (by the measure of value) is available only in the censuses of 1920 and after, and even these provide only indirect indicators.[57] In 1920, agricultural units of over 400 hectares (988 acres) accounted for only 8 percent of all the agricultural properties in São Paulo, but represented 55 percent of the value of agricultural lands. This crude measure understates concentration because of the multiple holdings of individuals, families, and corporations.

For many students of rural São Paulo, an estate of 200 hectares approaches the category of "large property."[58] Applying that broader definition to the data for 1920, we see in Table 1.4 that the value of agricultural properties was concentrated in smaller units in São Paulo than in Brazil generally. This was due in part to the fact that coffee estates tend to be smaller than cattle ranches. Indeed, though coffee plantations last only three decades, 2,000 trees can be planted in a mere two to three hectares.[59] And also by this broader definition, we see that in 1940 almost half the land in the state was still concentrated in relatively large units. On the other hand, by that time the value of properties had so shifted in the larger size categories as to bring the state squarely into line with the country as a whole—no "better," no "worse."

Employing a different indirect measure, available only for 1940, we learn that holdings were apparently more concentrated in São Paulo than in the country at large. For Brazil, the ratio of rural property owners to the agriculturally active population aged ten and above was 1 : 2.9, compared with 1 : 3.5 for São Paulo; São Paulo was in the "top" half of the states by this criterion of land concentration.[60]

Still a different measure of the concentration of rural wealth in São Paulo—more restricted, but also more striking—is the possession of coffee trees. In 1926, something over a score of fazendas had more than 1,000,000 trees each, and in 1931, before the partial breakup of the big estates, almost half of the 1.1 billion coffee trees in São Paulo were held in units having 100,000 trees or more.[61]

For all this, it would be incorrect to assume that planters uniformly opposed the opening of land to small farmers. Despite Campos Sales's judgment that immigrants wanted to be rural wage-earners rather than smallholders, state officials and leading planter groups had agreed by the beginning of the century that small farms had a role in the Paulista land tenure system. The coffee crisis of the years after 1896 offered an incentive to cut the wage bill: since large landowners had variable labor requirements (with demand rising at harvest time), small farms near large plantations could serve as labor pools for which fazendeiros did not have to provide year-long employment. Thus state-sponsored *núcleos coloniais* were viewed by Agriculture Secretary Cândido Rodrigues in 1900 as "labor nurseries."[62] Small farms near large plantations also had the advantage of providing a stable labor force in a system where the migration of workers from one estate to another was a constant problem for planters.

Still, Carlos Botelho, who was to become the Secretary of Agriculture in 1904, apparently believed that smallholdings were desirable for their own sake, as well as for the needs of planters, a view he expressed as early as 1902.[63] Accordingly, he and Governor Tibiriçá created an Agency of Colonization and Labor in April 1906. But though one of its purposes was to expand the settlement program on state properties, a program that appeared in the propaganda aimed at immigrants, the núcleos coloniais scheme never amounted to much.[64]

Nonetheless, many immigrants did obtain land. Indeed, by 1920 foreigners held 22 percent (by value) of the agricultural properties in São Paulo, and 12 percent in Brazil as a whole.* Since foreign ownership in

* DGE, *Recenseamento*, 1920: *Synopse do Censo da Agricultura*, pp. 20–21. None of the censuses from which the data in this paragraph are drawn distinguish foreign nationals from foreign-born immigrants.

São Paulo was heavily Italian, Portuguese, and Spanish, most of the 22 percent was probably in small properties (though there were a few giant estates owned by foreign companies). Of the coffee farms in 1932, foreigners owned 36 percent by value, with the Italians alone accounting for 20 percent. And similarly with all rural holdings in 1934–35: foreigners owned 34 percent by value, with the Italians in the lead at 17 percent.[65] By 1940, foreigners accounted for 36 percent of rural properties by value, and the Italians had 14 percent of the total.[66]

Enormously important as immigrants were in the rural economy, they also played a vital role in the development of the new industrial complex. In the capital they already accounted for eight of every 10 workers in manufacturing in 1893, and in 1920 they still composed a majority. In 1920, the first year for which statewide data are available, almost 40 percent of São Paulo's industrial workers were foreign-born, and an overall majority were probably immigrants or descendants of immigrants who had arrived since the 1880's.[67]

Women formed a large part of the industrial proletariat, and a clear majority in some industries. As early as 1872, more than 90 percent of the cotton textile workers in São Paulo were women. The employment of women and children prevailed through the 1930's in food processing and clothing and especially in textiles, where they were "substituted for adult males whenever possible because of their greater docility and lower wage costs."[68] Indeed, so overwhelmingly female was the textile labor force that adult male workers sometimes spurned jobs in the textile factories as "women's work."[69]

In 1919 the industrialist Jorge Street, speaking of Brazil as a whole—but presumably referring to his area of operations, Rio and São Paulo—claimed that half the workers in manufacturing were under eighteen years of age.[70] Perhaps this was an exaggeration, but it may have been true of the largest single industry, textiles. At any rate, such a statement helps explain the reluctance of employers to report children's true ages in the face of child labor laws.

Yet São Paulo's new industrial economy also afforded upward mobility for some. In 1962, a survey found that almost half of the founders or chief developers of the larger firms in the metropolitan area—those with 100 employees or more—were immigrants (most of whom, presumably, arrived in the era under study); that another 24 percent had foreign parents; and that 11 percent were grandchildren of immigrants. Thus fewer than 16 percent of the firms had been developed by Brazilians having native grandparents.[71] In some ways, the immigrant's success is not surprising, for half the state's residents in 1920 were first- or second-generation Brazilians.[72] Nor did immigrants have to make their way by competing with a powerful native urban bourgeoisie.[73]

There are no studies of social mobility in São Paulo during the period in question, but according to Bertram Hutchinson's analysis of the 1950's, social mobility in the capital was more of a "structural" than an "exchange" process, i.e., upward mobility was based on an expanding economy that created new middle- and upper-strata positions, rather than on a reciprocal downward mobility by privileged groups. One need not agree with Hutchinson, however, that such a process was less desirable than the greater upward and downward mobility (and hence the greater "fluidity") found in Great Britain in a similar survey in 1949. In the British case, after all, the net change was downward, whereas the trend in São Paulo was upward.[74] At any rate, Hutchinson's findings of limited "replacement" mobility for São Paulo city in 1957 might well apply in earlier decades of the century to both the capital and the hinterland. The exception of course would be the 1930's, when many coffee-based fortunes were lost.

The Health Issue

All social classes, especially urban ones, benefited from the state's public health programs. In this respect São Paulo provided firm leadership for the rest of the country. It established a comprehensive public health administration (in 1892); it required smallpox vaccinations of all its citizens before the federal capital did, as well as providing a model for Rio's public health program; and it even sent missions to other states to assist in vaccination campaigns.[75]

Public health measures nonetheless encountered serious resistance in the state legislature, and when opponents of such legislation failed to block it altogether, they managed at least to limit its effectiveness. The powerful rural groups that controlled the legislature were concerned not only about the cost of a public health program, but also about the possibility of interference in their own domains. They were apparently won over in 1892 and at later junctures by the compelling argument that if the state gained a reputation among potential immigrants as an unhealthful place to work, the coffee planters would lose their cheap labor supply[76]—a variation, perhaps, of the seventeenth-century theme "No slaves, no sugar; no sugar, no Pernambuco." All the same, the planter groups were able to restrict the state health agencies' jurisdiction to the cities, except during epidemics.

The first state sanitary code, promulgated in March 1894, was precise but unenforceable. The Sanitary Service and the sanitary code were altered several times; responsibility for public health programs oscillated between state and município authorities. In 1911 came a benchmark reform that largely limited the Sanitary Service's work to the capital, but at the same time made great advances in the control of epidemics, the gathering of health statistics, and the regulation of local health programs. A further reorganization of the service in 1917 authorized it to enforce the sanitary code in rural areas, but only on farms and plantations established after that date (except in times of epidemic). Despite such limitations, public health authorities were well funded, and the state's per-capita health expenditures compared favorably with contemporary outlays in the United States.[77]

Nor did the state confine its endeavors in public health to sanitation works and inspection programs. It was even more innovative in its funding of the research programs of the Bacteriological Institute, established in 1892 (as well as those of several other state-run laboratories). The institute, which flourished until 1914, was "the first center of science in Brazil to be organized along modern laboratory lines, and its work included the first systematic application of bacteriology and parasitology to public health in Brazil."[78] Another important research agency, founded in 1901, and after 1918 a renowned venom antidote center, was the Butantã Institute. Though the Osvaldo Cruz Institute in Rio later gained preeminence as the foremost medical research center in Brazil, the Bacteriological Institute and other laboratories in the state sent researchers to, and received them from, the Rio-based institution.

The first spectacular achievement of the São Paulo health program (apart from its success in ending an outburst of bubonic plague in Santos in 1899) was the elimination of yellow fever in Sorocaba and Ribeirão Preto in the early 1900's under Sanitation Director Emílio Ribas; again, this effort antedated the more celebrated work of Cruz in Rio. A serious and recurrent problem, yellow fever caused more than 14,500 deaths in São Paulo between the birth of the Republic and 1903; but not one death from that disease was recorded in the whole of the state in 1906.[79] Ribas's campaign was advanced by a major expansion of sewage systems and water mains under Governor Francisco Rodrigues Alves (1900–1902), who as President of Brazil in 1902–6 authorized Osvaldo Cruz's sanitation program in Rio. By 1920, more than half of São Paulo's 120 municípios had sewage systems of some sort, and almost all had public water supplies. In Pernambuco, by contrast, only 10 percent of the municípios then had public water supplies, and just one—Recife—had a sewer system.[80]

Government attempts to promote vaccination against smallpox began in São Paulo as early as 1874, though few people were affected by the program in the nineteenth century. The disease was brought under control shortly before the First World War. Trachoma, typhoid, and leprosy also were attacked with varying degrees of success. However, little was done in these years about tuberculosis, a major killer throughout Brazil.[81]

Victories over most epidemic diseases in São Paulo contributed to an impressive decline in the general mortality rates. In the capital, deaths per 1,000 population fell from 23 in 1894–1900 to 18 in 1901–10; and though the figure rose slightly in the following decade, chiefly because of the worldwide influenza epidemic of 1918, in which 6,800 inhabitants died, it then dropped significantly, to stand at 13 in 1940.* Considerable progress was made in controlling communicable diseases in particular; here the capital's death rate fell from 5 per 1,000 in 1894–1900 to 3 per 1,000 in 1911–20, excluding 1918, the year of the flu deaths.[82]

On the other hand, infant mortality remained high, and was virtually unaffected by advances in sanitation and the state's public health campaigns. In 1910, after Ribas's greatest triumphs, almost 162 children of every 1,000 born alive in the capital did not live out their first year. By 1940, the figure had dropped to 124, to give São Paulo city the lowest rate

---

*Blount, "Public Health Movement," pp. 153, 168–69; Nogueira, "Indices do desenvolvimento," p. 185. By 1960, mortality in the capital had fallen to roughly 8 per 1,000, and in the state as a whole to a little over 9, a level below the national average of the United States in 1959 (Nogueira, p. 186). Until the 1930's, lower mortality rates were reported in the interior than in the capital; however, since the interior's rates were uniformly higher than the capital's from 1930 to 1960—the 1940 rate for the interior was 19, pushing the state's rate up to 18 in that year—we may assume that incomplete reporting before 1930 accounts for the apparent differential.

among the country's seven major urban areas, including the Federal District. However, improvements were much slower to come in the interior, where infant mortality was almost half again as high as in the capital.*

As these figures make clear, in the early years of the century especially, most achievements in public health were limited to the capital. Conditions in the interior varied widely, not just in terms of health, but also in levels of prosperity. This unevenness is not particularly surprising when we consider the historical evolution of the several zones or regions of the state.

The Ten Zones

Regionalization is obviously a process defined by the problem under study. Pierre Monbeig, in his essay on the regionalization of São Paulo, considers physiography, period of settlement, communication grids, urban nodes, types of economic organization, and railroad networks as alternate bases for regional divisions. Another French geographer, Pierre Deffontaines, discerns 19 "natural" regions in the state. "Social" regions have been defined in a variety of ways, including the creation of noncontiguous zones found to have similar characteristics from data collected at the município level.[83]

Our central concern is political behavior over time, but there is unfortunately no altogether satisfactory way to define political regions in São Paulo. Congressional and state legislative districts had different seats (sedes), and official districts did not always correspond to de facto power domains. The Partido Republicano Paulista—the establishment party from 1889 to 1930—had no single pattern of regionally defined operations, and after 1905 it organized its activities within 10 zones for state elections and four for federal contests.

Most regionalization schemes dealing with the state's human population have been based on historical patterns of settlement, and within that framework the dominant theme has been the penetration of the railroad into the interior. Except for the four "old" zones—the area around the capital, the Paraíba River Valley, the underdeveloped south (Baixa Sorocabana), and the southern littoral—São Paulo's territory was populated

---

*Giorgio Mortara, cited in Villela and Suzigan, *Política do governo*, p. 258. Health care improved so greatly in the next 20 years that the state's infant mortality was more than halved, falling from 178 in 1940 to 77 in 1960. The capital's rate in 1960 was 62. Nogueira, "Indices do desenvolvimento," p. 192.

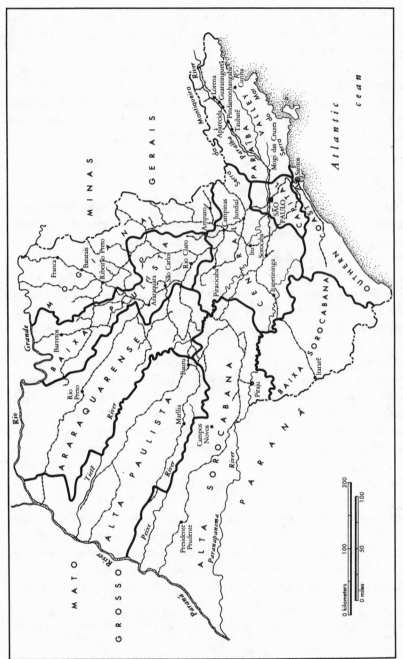

Fig. 1. São Paulo and its zones.

as coffee plantations and railroads pushed into the hinterland. With enthusiasm or reluctance—*faute de mieux* in the case of Deffontaines[84]—students of the development of Paulista society have usually adopted the regions carved out by railroad lines, a pattern that coincides with the regionalization used by the average citizen.[85] Of the several schemes of this sort, I have employed José Francisco de Camargo's 10-region system, which is worked out in much greater detail than the similar and more famous scheme of Sérgio Milliet. Moreover, Camargo's treatment is more sensitive to the weaknesses and strengths of historical census materials, and (unlike Milliet's study, which was published earlier) draws on the 1940 census, widely regarded as far more reliable than any of its predecessors at the federal level.

After the occupation of the four old zones, a process that was virtually complete by the middle of the nineteenth century, the peopling of São Paulo followed a roughly counterclockwise progression, beginning in the area immediately to the west of the capital, moving north to the Minas border, west to the Paraná River, and finally south beyond the state line into the rich coffee lands of northern Paraná.

The first region in the system adopted here is the metropolitan area of São Paulo city, the Capital zone, which encompasses eight municípios (of a total of 270 by 1940). The smallest of the 10 zones, it increased its share of the state's population from 5 percent in 1886 to more than 20 percent by 1940. By that time virtually all of its 1,500,000 inhabitants worked in the urban complex or were engaged in the provisioning of São Paulo city (e.g., in truck farming). Predictably enough, the smallest average agricultural properties were found in this zone in the 1934 census.[86] The abandoned coffee lands near the capital city had by then been dubbed *terra de japonês*, implying that only Japanese immigrant farmers could make such soil bear fruit. In fact, the Japanese had established produce farms in the zone as early as 1915.[87]

The capital proper is located on a series of hills overlooking the valleys of the Tietê River and its tributaries. The capital's higher elevations were more salubrious than most of the state's other, lower-lying population clusters, and the relatively healthful climate was one reason for its rapid development. Other factors are discussed in Chapter Three; here we will consider only the result—the dazzling increases in population. The city grew at the astonishing rate of 14 percent a year between 1890 and 1900

TABLE 1.5
Growth of São Paulo City's Population, 1872–1940

Year	Population	Intercensal growth rate	Annual (compounded) growth rate
1872	31,385	—	—
1890	64,934	107%	4.1%
1900	239,820	269	14.0
1920	579,033	141	4.5
1940	1,326,261	129	4.2

SOURCE: IBGE, Anuário estatístico, 1971, p. 42.

(see Table 1.5), mostly because of immigration, which reached its peak in this decade. Between those two census dates the capital added more new residents (some 175,000) than the Federal District, containing the city of Rio de Janeiro, though the District still had three times as many people in 1900.[88]

The city's population more than doubled between 1920 and 1940. One important reason for that growth was the rise in the number of industrial jobs. In 1907, the capital had just 15,000 industrial workers; by 1940, that figure had quintupled.[89] The population of municípios adjacent to the capital—in the process of becoming industrial suburbs—grew at an even faster rate than the city.[90] In the capital município itself, foreigners accounted for 35 percent of the population in 1920 and 22 percent in 1940; and 21 percent of the zone as a whole was still foreign-born as late as 1940, the highest proportion of all the zones.[91] In the circumstances, it is hardly surprising that by 1940 the first zone also had the lowest proportion of pretos (blacks) and pardos (mulattoes)—8.3 percent of the population, compared with 12.0 percent in the state as a whole.[92]

The Paraíba River Valley and the coast north of Santos form the second zone, sometimes called "the north" and here called the Paraíba Valley zone. The oldest region in terms of extensive and permanent settlement, it reached its peak as a coffee-growing area in the third quarter of the nineteenth century. The Paraíba Valley zone had the distinctive feature of being economically linked to the port of Rio de Janeiro rather than Santos, its coffee moving eastward on the Central do Brasil Railroad rather than southwest toward Santos. This zone had the largest population in every census from 1836 through 1886; it also had the largest slave population at mid-century, and still had the second-largest number of slaves (28,500) in 1886, two years before abolition.[93]

After 1886, however, the Paraíba Valley zone consistently lost ground in its share of the state's population, which fell from 28 percent to 7 percent in 1940.[94] The majority of the inhabitants were still rural in 1940, and as early as the 1920's ranching and subsistence farming had replaced coffee cultivation as the principal economic activities. The coffee output in the zone decreased from 1905 to 1920, and after 1920 the population also declined, as did the average size of agricultural properties over the years 1905–40.[95] An area clearly in decay after coffee had leached the soil, the Paraíba Valley offered little to immigrants; fewer came there than to any other zone, and less than 3 percent of its 1940 population was foreign-born. This fact, coupled with the zone's heavy representation of slaves in the nineteenth century, gave it the highest proportion of pardos and pretos in the state in 1940 (17 percent).[96]

In the 1870's and 1880's, the Valley's political leaders had tried to resist the growing power of the "western" planters around Campinas; in 1888 one senator from the older region even proposed that it be amalgamated with parts of Minas Gerais and Rio as a new province. Apparently the idea also had its supporters in Minas, where a state separatist movement broke out in the town of Campanha (some 220 kilometers northeast of São Paulo city) in 1892.[97] But even though the Paraíba Valley gained a rail link with the provincial and national capitals in 1877, decline followed, for the soil was becoming exhausted, as had already happened downriver in the Rio de Janeiro portion of the Valley. By the early 1900's, the coffee-growing areas in São Paulo's part of the Valley, like Vassouras in Rio Province before them,[98] were almost reduced to ghost towns and ghost plantations. In 1906 the novelist José Bento Monteiro Lobato described a Valley plantation thus:

Seen from afar, the fazendas are Escorials of an imposing aspect, [but they appear] woeful when one draws near them. Flanking the Big House [are] empty slave-compounds and stone coffee-drying terraces, with thriving broom-jute trees in the crevices. The owner is absent: he lives in Rio, in São Paulo, in Europe. Worn-out coffee plantations. Scattered sharecroppers. Only a handful of hookworm-ridden *caboclos* manage to subsist, like lizards on a rock . . . defenseless, unable to make the earth produce, unable to abandon the old homestead—true vegetables of flesh who neither flourish nor bear fruit.[99]

The "west" of which the Paraíba Valley planters complained is the Central zone in our scheme. This was the first region to be formed by railroads: the Paulista, Sorocabana (including the Ituana), and Bragantina lines. In the 1830's, the Central zone was still a sugar-producing region while the Paraíba Valley was already specializing in coffee; subsequently, the coffee-growing qualities of its terra roxa were discovered, and with the sharply reduced freight costs brought by the railroad, it was able to produce more than twice the Valley zone's output by 1886.[100] The município of Campinas was connected by rail to the British-owned trunkline at Jundiaí (and therefore to Santos) in 1872, by which time it could boast a population almost as large as that of the capital city. Campinas also had its cultural aspirations. It was the birthplace of the composer Carlos Gomes (1836–96), whom the city claimed as its own even though he spent most of his adult years in Italy and had his operas set to Italian lyrics. When Sarah Bernhardt visited the province in 1886, she performed for planters and their families in Campinas, as well as for audiences in the capital.

In the slave counts of 1874 and 1881, Campinas had the largest number of slaves of any município in the province, and the Central zone as a whole had the most among all the 10 zones in both years. Yet this was precisely the region where planters established that immigrant labor could profitably be substituted for slaves. By 1920, foreigners still accounted for 13 percent of the Central zone's population; the majority were Italians (61 percent).[101] As the frontier passed beyond the zone, and its coffee lands became increasingly less productive, its proportion of the state's population fell from 24 percent in 1886 (second largest) to 12 percent in 1940, though its population almost tripled in that period, reaching 849,000.[102] Furthermore, Campinas, Jundiaí, and Sorocaba, unlike the towns of the Paraíba Valley, attracted sufficient industry to keep the zone's overall economy from deteriorating. By 1940, smallholdings dominated the rural landscape, a development influenced to some degree by the fact that most of the state-sponsored núcleos coloniais were established in this zone.[103]

The fourth zone, Mogiana, was formed by a series of railroads feeding into the Mogiana line, which connected Campinas to Mogi-mirim in 1875 and to Ribeirão Preto in 1883. By 1887, the railroad had reached the banks of the Rio Grande, which forms the border between São Paulo and Minas Gerais. Ribeirão Preto, the coffee capital of the world in the years preceding the First World War, was the hub of the Mogiana zone. It was here that Henrique Dumont and Francisco Schmidt, two of São Paulo's "Coffee Kings" (so adjudged by the millions of trees they owned), made their fortunes, and a third, Geremia Lunardelli, got his start. Dumont was the son of an early-nineteenth-century immigrant, and Schmidt and Lunardelli were first-generation Brazilians.

The Mogiana zone experienced a virtual population explosion in the 1890's, to the point where it accounted for 20 percent of the people in the state in 1900. But its share dropped to 12 percent by 1940, and the population decreased absolutely in the 1930's. The Mogiana was the second zone to come into being because of the penetration of railroads, and its rural inhabitants, like those of the Paraíba Valley and the Central zones before them, were turning from coffee growing to ranching by the 1930's. Unlike the Central zone, though, the Mogiana did not have the compensating development of industrial activity, largely because of its greater distance from São Paulo and its less-extensive rail system. Yet of the whole immigrant and national migrant stream from 1901 to 1940, the Mogiana zone received the second-largest net figure—274,000 persons— and led the state in terms of relative growth in this respect for the period. The majority of the foreigners, as in the Central zone, were Italians. The Mogiana also had the largest number of blacks and mulattoes in the state by 1940, and proportionately the second-largest number (16 percent).[104]

The settlement of the fifth zone—the Baixa Paulista (named for the "lower" portion of the Paulista Railroad)—followed hard on that of the fourth. The region corresponds to the portion of the state served by the Paulista and São Paulo–Goiás rail lines, which were pushed ever northward to connect the major coffee-producing município of Rio Claro, São Carlos, and finally, in 1885, Araraquara. The município of Araraquara illustrates the delayed but meteoric effect that the arrival of a railhead could have on land prices as the countryside was cleared for coffee planting: in real terms, they increased seven and a half times from 1885–89 to 1890–94.[105] Material progress in the nearby town of São Carlos was so impressive that by the 1890's its boosters were calling it the "Princess of the West" and the "capital of the interior."[106]

The Baixa Paulista was the last of the zones to be settled in the nineteenth century, and was thus the last where the coffee-based slave regime held sway; it had 17,000 slaves in 1886, 11 percent of the provincial total. The Baixa Paulista, too, experienced rapid growth based on post-slavery immigration, benefiting from the same stream of Italian workers that fed the Mogiana and Central zones. But as the frontier moved on, its share of the state's population fell from 12 percent in 1900 to 8 percent in 1940, and by then, like the Mogiana, it had suffered an absolute decline in both population and coffee production.[107]

The next three zones—the Araraquarense, Alta Paulista, and Alta Sorocabana—are called the pioneer zones because they are still developing rapidly. Most of this development has taken place since 1921, when immigrants began to pour in to work the newly established coffee plantations. A full 70 percent of the 800,000 new arrivals in the state between 1921 and 1940 (both immigrants and in-migrants) went to one of these three zones. As a result, from less than 9 percent of the state's population in 1886, their combined share grew to more than 33 percent in the mid-1940's. By 1940 the three zones accounted for 70 percent of the state's coffee output, 61 percent of the cotton output, and almost 50 percent of the cattle herds. In 1920, their foreign-born population ranged from 14 percent in the Alta Sorocabana to 24 percent in the Alta Paulista. Furthermore, by 1937, foreign-born rural property owners held more than 30 percent of the agricultural land in both the Araraquarense and the Alta Paulista, the largest shares (by area) among the 10 zones; foreign ownership in the Alta Sorocabana was not far behind at 25 percent.[108]

As the last three zones to be occupied, the pioneer zones faced the same problems of violence and insecurity of land titles that had previously characterized the older zones. The *grileiro* (claim jumper) preceded the railroad, and the lack of clear title cost the state huge amounts of revenue; presumably tax evasion was a motive for keeping titles uncertain. One judge referred to the town of Presidente Prudente in the extreme west as "Grilópolis."[109] The arrival of the railroad tended to reduce (but hardly eliminated) the legal chaos by bringing in its wake the rule of law—judges and the state police.[110] Even so, as we shall see, the state proved itself altogether ineffective in preventing squatters from taking permanent ownership of public lands, and equally ineffective in establishing orderly procedures for distributing such lands to the private sector.

The first of the pioneer zones—the sixth in our scheme—is the Araraquarense, formed by the municípios served by the Araraquarense, Dourado, and Paulista railroads, all tied into the Paulista trunk line. The region was producing coffee by 1905, and 15 years later, the município of Rio Preto already had 127,000 inhabitants, though the rails had only arrived there in 1912. From 33,000 persons in 1886, the zone grew to nearly 1,000,000 by 1940, making it second only to the Capital zone in population. Italian nationals accounted for the largest contingent of foreigners in the year 1940, as they did in the Central, Mogiana, and Baixa Paulista zones.[111]

The seventh zone, Alta Paulista, is formed by the Paulista and Noroeste lines; it stretches northwest from Bauru, the only município in the region before 1913. The Sorocabana line reached Bauru in 1904, followed by the Paulista two years later. The town was the point of departure for the Noroeste railway, which moved westward into Mato Grosso—with predictable results. As late as 1910, the area around Marília was considered Indian territory;[112] by the 1930's, whole trainloads of migrants were arriving there daily. And Lins, some 65 kilometers to the north, was now on the frontier; like the departure points in the sixteenth century, it was referred to as a boca de sertão. From 1920 to 1934, the population of the Alta Paulista zone increased 350 percent; by the end of that period it already had a tenth of the state's population.[113] Again, the mushrooming growth was caused by a heavy flow of immigrants and in-migrants, who arrived in greater numbers here than in any other zone between 1901 and 1940 (310,000). But what in this case is even more remarkable is that 93 percent of them arrived after 1920. In that year, the largest group of foreigners were Spaniards; but they soon gave way to the Japanese, who accounted for more than half the foreign-born by 1940. As noted, by 1937 the foreign-born held more than a third of the agricultural land in the zone; by 1940 the figure had grown to 43 percent, the largest proportion (by area) in any zone.[114]

The eighth zone, served by the farther reaches of the Sorocabana railroad and therefore called the Alta Sorocabana, begins at Botucatu, where the rails arrived in 1889. The region extends westward to Presidente Prudente (connected by rail in 1919) and Presidente Epitácio on the Mato Grosso border (connected in 1922). Like the Alta Paulista, the Alta Sorocabana experienced a massive population increase in the twentieth century, becoming the home of a tenth of the state's population by 1940. In that year, the zone was still near its peak coffee outputs, though cotton production (by weight) had passed coffee in at least one município by the late 1930's. The Japanese were the largest group of foreign nationals in 1940.[115]

TABLE 1.6

Distribution of the Population of São Paulo
by Zone, 1886–1940

(Percent)

Zone	1886	1900	1920	1940
Capital[a]	6.1%	12.3%	14.3%	20.6%
Paraíba Valley	27.5	17.8	10.6	6.6
Central	24.3	18.2	16.4	11.8
Mogiana	14.6	20.4	17.7	11.7
Baixa Paulista	10.9	12.1	11.5	8.1
Araraquarense	2.7	6.5	12.7	13.2
Alta Paulista	—	0.3	3.0	11.9
Alta Sorocabana	5.9	5.2	7.4	10.1
Baixa Sorocabana	4.5	3.5	2.9	2.4
Southern Coast	3.5	3.7	3.5	3.6

SOURCE: Camargo, Crescimento da população, 1: 104.
[a] The capital município's share alone was 3.9% in 1886, 10.5% in 1900, 12.6% in 1920, and 18.5% in 1940.

The ninth and tenth zones—those formed by the "lower" portion of the Sorocabana railroad (Baixa Sorocabana) and the littoral from Santos southward—are "old" zones but were never major coffee-producing areas. The Baixa Sorocabana zone's agriculture is mixed; because most of the region is too cool for coffee growing, cotton became the most important commercial crop. Here the population grew by accretions rather than spurts. The zone attracted fewer foreigners and in-migrants in 1901–40 than any other except the Paraíba Valley, and in 1940 had only slightly more than 2 percent of the state's population.[116] The zone is important, however, from both an economic and a military point of view, because of its strategic location: the town of Itararé on the São Paulo–Paraná border, sits astride the only railroad to Rio Grande do Sul (called the Brazil Railway in our period).

The tenth and last zone—the Southern Coast—is a residual region having little internal cohesion.[117] It is here that the Portuguese first settled in the sixteenth century. The port of Iguape still had the largest population in the zone in 1886, but Santos overtook it in 1900, when it passed the 50,000 mark. In the latter years of the Empire, slaves in the zone were used principally as bearers and dockworkers in Santos and Iguape rather than as fieldhands; in any case they represented only 2 percent of the population in 1886. The dramatic growth of Santos's population began about that time, rising from 16,000 in that year to more than 10 times that number by 1940. By then, almost three-quarters of the people in the zone were urban dwellers. In 1940, it was second only to the Capital zone as an urban region and was also second in the proportion of foreigners in its population (17 percent).* A unique feature of the Southern Coast zone is that more than half of its foreign residents, in both 1920 and 1940, were Portuguese nationals.[118]

The rhythm of settlement in the 10 zones (see Table 1.6) varied with the fortunes of the state's economy. An indirect index to the relationship between economic and population growth is to be found in the number of municípios created during the various "boom" and "bust" decades for the period under study. (Old municípios were divided up as the frontier moved west and settlement grew denser; the numbers in the following tabulation indicate the *net* number of units established in the period.)[119]

Decade	New municípios	Decade	New municípios
1880–89	30	1910–19	32
1890–99	40	1920–29	55
1900–09	0	1930–37	4

As we observe, the two decades that saw the greatest proliferation of local governmental units were the 1890's and the 1920's; both were periods of soaring coffee sales. By contrast, a coffee depression in the opening years of the twentieth century brought município development to a complete standstill. The near-collapse of coffee exports in the 1930's also seems to be reflected in the number of new municípios formed in São Paulo in that decade.

Along with the increasing number of municípios came increasing urbanization. Spurred on by the coffee and cotton frontiers in the "new" zones and by industrialization in the Capital and Central zones, São Paulo had become Brazil's most urbanized state by 1940, according to one definition of urban communities, namely, municípios of 5,000 or more inhabitants. By this standard, 36 percent of São Paulo's population was urban, compared with a national rate of 22 percent.[120] In another approach to the problem, the geographer Moacir Silva, using a population of 50,000 as the lower limit of a "medium size" município in 1940, has classified Brazil's larger municípios in that year into five groups, as follows:

---

* Camargo's definition of urban: seats (sedes) of municípios and seats of their component *distritos de paz. Crescimento da população*, 1:82.

Large municípios	Medium-sized municípios
1. 1,000,000 +	4. 100,000–250,000
2. 500,000–1,000,000	5. 50,000–100,000
3. 250,000–500,000	

São Paulo city was the only unit in Brazil other than the federal capital in group 1; the country had no communities at all of the group 2 size at that time; and all those in group 3 were state capitals: Recife, Pernambuco; Salvador, Bahia, and Pôrto Alegre, Rio Grande do Sul. In the medium range, 18 communities fell into group 4, of which only two, Santos and Campinas, were in São Paulo, compared with four in Rio State, three in Rio Grande do Sul, and two in Minas Gerais. But in group 5 São Paulo had the largest number—19 of the nation's 98.[121] Ten of the 19 were in the three pioneer zones, against none at all in the Paraíba Valley, Baixa Sorocabana, and Southern Coast zones (though Santos, as noted, ranked in group 4). This fact, as much as any other, throws the rapid growth of the pioneer zones into sharp relief: 20 years earlier, none of the three new zones had a single município with as many as 50,000 inhabitants.[122]

An examination of município revenues for selected years tells a similar story—the decline of the Paraíba Valley and the rise of the three pioneer zones—though município revenues did not strictly follow population trends. As we see in Table 1.7, by 1920 two municípios from the new zones were represented in the top 12, as were two in 1938. Municípios in the Central zone did better, accounting for four of the top 12 municípios by 1938; and not surprisingly, in these years São Paulo city, Santos, and Campinas ranked one-two-three, just as they did in population in both 1920 and 1940. Perhaps the most striking development revealed in the table is the shifting fortunes of São Paulo city and Santos in the course of some 50 years: the increasing hegemony of the one and the important but deteriorating position of the other. From 1886 to 1938, the capital's share of total município income rose (irregularly) from 27 percent to 56 percent, and Santos's fell from 17 percent to 7 percent. Santos could count indirectly on foreign trade, but the capital could rely on imposts on burgeoning industrial and commercial activities. Urbanization as such only partly explains the capital's proportion of município revenues in 1938, for its percentage of the state's population in 1940 was only a third as large as its share of revenues two years earlier. The new role of the industrial economy in producing município revenues is underscored by the fact that between 1920 and 1938 São Bernardo, an industrial suburb of São Paulo

TABLE 1.7

São Paulo's Municípios Ranked by Income (Top 12), Select Years

(In round current contos)

1885–86			1896		
Município	Revenues	Zone	Município	Revenues	Zone
Capital	338	Capital	Capital	3,864	Capital
Santos	209	Southern Coast	Santos	1,997	Southern Coast
Campinas	82	Central	Campinas	1,049	Central
Taubaté	34	Paraíba Valley	Taubaté	442	Paraíba Valley
Mogi-mirim	29	Mogiana	Ribeirão Preto	428	Mogiana
Amparo	26	Mogiana	São Carlos	297	Baixa Paulista
Rio Claro	25	Baixa Paulista	Piracicaba	252	Central
Pindamonhangaba	23	Paraíba Valley	Amparo	248	Mogiana
São Carlos	21	Baixa Paulista	Sorocaba	236	Central
Itu	20	Central	Guaratinguetá	174	Paraíba Valley
Capivari	18	Central	Jaboticabal	174	Baixa Paulista
Limeira	18	Baixa Paulista	Itapira	165	Mogiana
Total for province	1,243		Total for state	13,423	

1920			1938		
Município	Revenues	Zone	Município	Revenues	Zone
Capital	25,563	Capital	Capital	150,601	Capital
Santos	7,085	Southern Coast	Santos	18,080	Southern Coast
Campinas	2,040	Central	Campinas	6,925	Central
Ribeirão Preto	1,256	Mogiana	São Bernardo	3,298	Capital
Bauru	921	Alta Paulista	Marília	3,103	Alta Paulista
Amparo	832	Mogiana	Ribeirão Preto	2,823	Mogiana
São Carlos	754	Baixa Paulista	Sorocaba	2,273	Central
Araraquara	718	Baixa Paulista	Piracicaba	2,066	Central
Taubaté	576	Paraíba Valley	Araraquara	2,057	Baixa Paulista
Sertãozinho	561	Mogiana	Jundiaí	1,900	Central
Jaú	553	Araraquarense	Rio Preto	1,652	Araraquarense
Sorocaba	497	Central	São Carlos	1,604	Baixa Paulista
Total for state	60,322		Total for state	269,769	

SOURCE: SP, Relatório (Commissão Central), pp. 192–93; SP, São Paulo, pp. 71–73, 83–86, 95–99.

NOTE: Since data are missing for some years for several municípios, the combined revenue totals are not complete.

city, replaced the erstwhile "coffee capital" of Ribeirão Preto as the state's fourth-largest revenue producer; no agriculturally based município ranked higher than fifth place by 1938.

With this we conclude our brief introduction to the São Paulo experience—a story of pioneering and prosperity, exploitation and extermination, and finally, a story of unparalleled growth. As the frontier moved west, both old families and newcomers wrested the soil from the Indians, and immigrants crowded into the cities as well. New communities sprang up in three zones almost entirely settled in the twentieth century, while the state capital was developing into what is now one of the world's largest cities. By Latin American standards, São Paulo's immigration and public health programs were brilliant (and related) successes. It was equally successful, after the virtual halt of immigration in the 1930's, in attracting enough Brazilians from other states to fill its labor needs. According to John Wirth, that achievement was envied by political and economic leaders in Minas Gerais, men who feared the loss of their (cheap) labor force. (In Pernambuco, in the view of Robert Levine, political leaders were probably relieved when wretchedly poor migrants began to leave the state in the late 1930's, if they thought about the matter at all.)

São Paulo was not only economically more advanced than the other states; it was economically better integrated because of its extensive rail network. The state had no problem comparable to Wirth's Minas, with its disparate regions, let alone Levine's Pernambuco, where the interests of the coastal zone were so frequently opposed to those of the interior. Indeed, most of São Paulo's zones were integrated into a single economy as they were created by the railroads, which followed the cultivation of coffee and brought new settlers. That coffee-based economy is the subject to which we now turn.

CHAPTER TWO

The Economy

BY THE 1880's, São Paulo already had the fastest growing economy in Brazil, and that leadership has never abated. In 1920, when the first national economic census was taken, the state accounted for more than two-sevenths of the agricultural and industrial output of the country—twice the share of the runner-up, Minas Gerais. In 1939, the first year for which gross domestic product figures are available by state, São Paulo again accounted for more than two-sevenths of the total. Moreover, it had also increased its lead over the other states, with more than three times the output of its nearest competitor, now Rio Grande do Sul.[1] São Paulo's preeminence was obvious in the export realm, where the state dominated coffee and later cotton sales, and obvious also in manufacturing by 1920. São Paulo was a leader as well in banking, though it was overshadowed in that sector by the Federal District.

Coffee pushed São Paulo into its preeminent position; industrialization has kept it there. These are the two great themes of this chapter. Of the two subjects, industrialization is the less well-studied; but it has begun to generate a literature that promises to be as large and full of controversy as that on the coffee sector, and I have included an evaluation of this material in my discussion. I shall also consider the essential support industries for both coffee and manufacturing, namely, commerce, banking, and transport.

Coffee

Coffee cultivation was where it all began. "The basis of Brazilian wealth," São Paulo Governor Júlio Prestes termed coffee in his campaign for the presidency in 1929.[2] That assertion was closer to fact than hyperbole, because coffee by that time accounted for more than 70 percent of Brazil's export earnings, and almost the whole of São Paulo's. *O café dá para tudo*—coffee takes care of everything—was a sentiment so ingrained in the Paulista mentality that it was still being heard in the streets of the state capital in the 1930's, when coffee prices and sales had plummeted to disastrous levels.[3] Some 35–40 percent (by value) of the country's exports between 1900 and 1910 already passed through Santos, the state port. With the collapse of Brazilian rubber exports in the following decade (because of cheaper labor and superior technology in the East Indies), coffee loomed even larger, pushing the figure beyond 50 percent in the years 1921–40.[4] Brazil thus became a one-crop economy as far as exports were concerned, and the fortunes of the coffee industry became even more central in determining the fate of the national economy. Since Brazil's terms of trade tended to follow international coffee prices and the value of coffee exports, the deterioration of the terms of trade in the 1930's kept per-capita income in the nation stagnant, even though manufacturing was thriving.[5]

Coffee exports were essential to the country in other respects. Brazil's ability to import obviously depended on its earnings from exports. Imports in turn affected domestic production: the nation's early industrial growth was dependent on both foreign capital and "social overhead capital" (e.g., transportation systems) paid for by profits accumulated from coffee exports.[6] Furthermore, as a net importer of capital in both the public and the private sector, Brazil needed a substantial export surplus to offset debt servicing and profits remittances abroad. Coffee was the keystone in the federal government's financial structure, just as it was in the state's. Indeed, it was largely due to a fall in the value of coffee exports that Brazil contracted the Funding Loan of 1898, the beginning of an unprecedented degree of foreign control of federal finances.[7] Thereafter foreign loans to both the Union and São Paulo were increasingly tied, directly and indirectly, to the fortunes of coffee.

Brazil's coffee boom was part of a worldwide phenomenon, namely, a tremendous increase in the trade in tropical products. In the 30 years preceding the First World War, the world's tropical trade doubled.[8] In some parts of Latin America the boom was accompanied by a growth of small farms, and smallholders dominated the coffee market in Colombia. In São Paulo, however, large-scale production continued to prevail. In

TABLE 2.1

Distribution of São Paulo's Coffee Production by Zone,
1905, 1920, and 1934

(Percentage by weight)

Zone	1905	1920	1934
Capital	0%	0%	0%
Paraíba Valley	5	4	2
Central	13	11	7
Mogiana	34	44	16
Baixa Paulista	21	16	11
Araraquarense	16	15	26
Alta Paulista	0	3	24
Alta Sorocabana	11	8	13
Baixa Sorocabana	0	0	0
Southern Coast	0	0	0

SOURCE: Camargo, *Crescimento*, 3: tables 107–8.

1920, the average coffee estate there was twice the size of an average Mineiro plantation; and according to a 1926 survey, more than 20 Paulista fazendas had over a million trees each.[9] Whether these large estates were intrinsically more efficient units of production is questionable.[10] At any rate, São Paulo's coffee estates were efficient to the extent that, unlike the country's rubber plantations, they were never really threatened by their East Indian competitors, despite the fame of Java coffee.* Brazil produced about two-thirds of the world's coffee from 1910 to 1920, and São Paulo produced 70 percent of this, or nearly half the world's total.[11]

Table 2.1 shows how coffee production shifted from zone to zone as the state's frontier moved westward in the twentieth century. We can easily observe here the trends discussed in Chapter One: the collapse of the Paraíba Valley, the decline of the Central, Mogiana, and Baixa Paulista zones, and the rapid rise of the three pioneer zones after 1920—especially the Araraquarense and Alta Paulista zones. (It is also worth noting that in these twentieth-century figures, the Capital, Southern Coast, and Baixa Sorocabana zones never produced as much as 1 percent of the state's output.)

The coffee economy had many rigidities, not a few of which derived

---

*The comparison between São Paulo and the Dutch East Indies is of limited value, though, not only because of the different soils, climatic conditions, and varieties of coffee in the two areas, but also because of a fall in the coffee output of Java and Sumatra as a result of disease in the early years of the century. In any case, Brazil's reduced share of the market over the long run was due more to its valorization policies than to inefficiency in production.

from the nature of the tree itself. A tree does not bear fruit for its first
four to six years, and its average bearing life is only 33 years, with a
decline in the yield after 20.[12] Though a number of soils in the state are
suitable for coffee, terra roxa is by far the best. Since terra roxa wears out
faster than most soils, fazendeiros were accustomed to keeping fresh land
ready on the frontier. Land in fact was a relatively cheap factor of production, except during the late 1920's, when speculation led to skyrocketing
prices: land prices in constant terms increased more than 30-fold between
1912 and 1927 in the Alta Paulista zone.[13]

Labor was a perennially expensive factor relative to land. Yet profits
were such in the closing years of the Empire that São Paulo could bid
away the slaves of other regions of Brazil. As late as 1883, an estate's slave
labor force was sometimes as valuable as its land (and coffee trees).[14] The
economic disintegration of the slave regime was unmistakably revealed
when bankers refused to continue to make mortgage loans based on
human collateral in 1886.[15]

The relationship between immigration and the abolition of slavery, as I
noted in Chapter One, is the subject of considerable debate. Warren
Dean argues that the current state of research favors the view that the
decline of slavery induced the introduction of immigrants, not the other
way around; and Robert Slenes has established that the reduction in the
number of slaves in the 1880's was gradual rather than catastrophic, a fact
that indirectly supports the idea of a labor crisis as the motor force, in the
sense that planters had time to develop an immigrant "solution." Yet
Slenes also states that "even in São Paulo it is likely that large numbers of
slaves did not abandon the plantation until the end of 1887 and the beginning of 1888," i.e., after the immigrants had already proved to be successful substitutes for slaves.[16] Thus immigration in late 1887 at least
hastened the end of the slave regime.[17] Michael Hall suggests that potential profits were so great in coffee-growing after the world price rise in
1886 that Paulista planters wanted all the workers they could get, free or
slave, Brazilian or foreign. In fact, the demise of slavery was accompanied
by an enormous increase in the demand for labor; in the years 1887–1913
alone, by Thomas Holloway's estimate, the number of workers employed
in São Paulo's coffee fields quintupled.[18]

Rural wages were relatively high, especially in comparison with the
wages in the poorer states of the country. Around 1910, an unskilled rural
laborer in Ribeirão Preto, the heart of São Paulo's coffee country, made

four milréis a day—almost three times as much as his counterpart in Açu, Rio Grande do Norte, one of the more prosperous municípios of that backward northeastern state.[19] In establishing a plantation, the labor costs in the early 1920's were as high as the cost of the land and other start-up costs together. The figure was even higher on a functioning plantation; labor accounted for roughly half the operating costs in the mid-1880's, and a bit more than that by the late 1920's. Yet in the first decade of the twentieth century, the coffee estates were estimated to make a profit of 9–15 percent annually; and an estimate for 1926–27 put the profits in the Araraquarense zone (good soil and a time of good prices) at 25 percent. In the circumstances, it is hard to take seriously the charge of Congressman Alfredo Ellis in 1902 that "a scum of [Italian] workers passes through the interior of the state, ensnaring the poor planter, who is tortured by the demands of the colonos."[20]

Transportation to the port was the second-largest item in the planter's annual budget, even though the spreading rail network after 1867 slashed freight charges from previously prohibitive rates. Transport costs from Campinas to Santos in 1863, before the arrival of the railroad, were more than 40 percent of the export price; the railroad perhaps decreased freight costs, on the average, to 20 percent of the price at the port. By the 1920's, freight charges amounted to a little more than a tenth of the planter's current costs.[21]

Whatever the profits, agriculture in Brazil was a risky affair, and credit was a recurrent problem for the fazendeiro. Rapid increases in the money supply, such as occurred in 1888, eased credit for rural interests; but until the 1920's, planters were consistently hard put for adequate mortgage credit, and banks refused to deal in short-term loans on crops. Season-to-season and year-to-year credit was initially supplied by the comissário, an agent who made the planter an advance on his crop, graded the coffee, and sold the stock to an exporter at Santos. The comissário commonly charged 3 percent for his services at the port, and 12 percent annual interest on short-term loans, a rate that persisted from the 1880's through the 1920's. This was apparently a far better rate than sugar planters could obtain in Pernambuco.[22]

In the two decades after the São Paulo Railway opened the coffee country of the planalto, the state's output expanded tremendously; but the comissário benefited even more than the fazendeiro, whose financial dependence on his agent in the port had now increased. Comissários began to acquire fazendas in significant numbers, probably as the result of defaults on their loans to planters. In the 1880's, the leading student of the coffee industry reported that few comissários were also fazendeiros; 40 years later, another coffee expert reported that few were not.[23] By that time, however, such agents probably had larger and richer firms than their predecessors.

New mechanisms for short-term credit appeared in the wake of an overproduction crisis in 1900–1905. Exporting companies, most of them foreign-owned, went into the agricultural lending business. (They were unintentionally aided by the federal government, whose financial austerity program under the Paulista presidents Campos Sales and Rodrigues Alves hurt marginal financial groups like comissários more than large banks.) As coffee stocks accumulated at the beginning of the century, a system of *armazéns gerais* (coffee warehouses) came into being, mostly built by export firms. These warehouses charged a fee for storage, and kept the stock until the planter or his agent ordered a sale. In 1905–6, the London-based firm of E. Johnston and Co., a dealer in Brazilian coffee since its organization in 1842, set up the Registradora de Santos and the Companhia Paulista de Armazéns Gerais; and a state law in 1906 guaranteed the company a 6 percent profit on these facilities.[24] In 1909 the two firms were consolidated under the control of Johnston's Brazilian Warrant Company. From the planter's point of view, one advantage of the warehousing system was that coffee warrants not only could be exchanged for cash when the coffee was sold, but also could be used as collateral against loans. In fact, Brazilian Warrant advanced loans at 9 percent against coffee deposited in its warehouses, thus undercutting the comissários by some 3 percent.[25]

Large-scale warehousing and the issuance of warrants were pioneered by Johnston's Edward Greene, who had joined the firm in Santos in 1891. He also persuaded the London office to enter the exchange speculation business, and to set up purchasing agents in the interior of the state to compete with comissários. In 1910, Greene returned to London as the director of E. Johnston.[26]

As Brazilian Warrant and other export houses expanded their credit operations in the interior, some comissários were put out of business by the larger resources of their competitors.[27] These firms also began to purchase the estates of bankrupt fazendeiros, as the comissários had done earlier. The number of coffee brokerage houses at Santos fell from 86 in

1920 to 45 in 1930, and to six, of which Brazilian Warrant was still one, in 1974.*

As the coffee industry grew larger, marketing practices necessarily changed. The Bolsa de Café, a state-regulated coffee exchange, began functioning in 1917. The exchange helped the state collect its export taxes, and provided foreign importers with a verification of the origin, quality, and type of coffee being shipped. On the export side of the trade, foreign firms at Santos already had control over the overwhelming bulk of coffee shipped abroad by the late 1890's. The American consul at Santos reported that less than 1 percent of the 6,000,000 bags exported in the year ending in June 1898 had been sold by Brazilian firms. According to another report, 87 percent of Santos's international coffee trade in the years 1895–1907 was in foreign hands. It was this dominance that allowed foreign firms to move into agricultural credit operations. Even in 1927, two-thirds of the coffee trade was still handled by foreign firms, though the decline may be significant.[28] In the 1930's, however, some foreign exporters made new gains at the expense of their Brazilian rivals, as the coffee market temporarily collapsed and cotton exports became more important. The Houston-based Anderson-Clayton Company, for example, which began to export cotton as well as coffee during that decade, grew steadily (to become the leading exporter of coffee in the 1960's). In any case, when the coffee market crashed in the 1930's, the bigger foreign firms were better equipped to survive the crisis than the small fry. Wille, which averaged only 10 percent of the coffee exports from Santos in the period 1925–30, averaged 17 percent from 1931 to 1938.[29]

One of the vital elements in the coffee trade, and perhaps the most complex, was the foreign-exchange system. Coffee producers calculated costs in Brazilian milréis but received "hard" dollars, marks, francs, and pounds for their goods. They consequently favored an ever-depreciating milréis. Although there were other interests who wanted an appreciating rate—including consumers and importers in São Paulo—the core of the opposition to rapid depreciation came from the federal treasury itself, which had to repay its extensive loan obligations in ever-more-expensive

---

*Lopes, "Comércio de café," p. 67. One key advantage Johnston–Brazilian Warrant held over its Brazilian rivals was its global view of market conditions, allowing it to speculate not only in exchange, but also in coffee stocks; this was equally true of its chief rival, the Theodor Wille firm, based in Hamburg. Fausto, "Expansão," pp. 212–13. Brazilian Warrant was a Brazilian-registered company in 1974, but it was still connected with E. Johnston, now American- and Brazilian-owned.

foreign currencies.[30] More often than not, until the 1930's, coffee interests got favorable foreign-exchange rates. In the 1890's, the falling rates made Brazilian coffee cheaper for importers in the consuming countries, helping Brazil to gain a dominant position in the world market; planters could make money as long as the rate of exchange fell faster than the international price of coffee, a condition then obtaining.*

Coffee was king in Brazil, and Brazil led the world in output. Having a near-monopoly on production, Paulista authorities, with the help of federal officials, were able to create a marketing scheme that tied the country to coffee ever more securely until the Depression. This was valorization, a neologism based on the word *valor* (value). Valorization was a producers' response to an oversupply crisis, a program that Georges Clemenceau, after a visit to Brazil, called a "coup d'audace sans parallèle."[31]

International coffee prices fell in 1894, and the first crisis of excess production occurred in 1896, when prices dipped again. In the meantime, easy credit during the Encilhamento, the financial boom of 1890–91, and high international coffee prices in the 1890's had encouraged extensive planting in São Paulo, and the maturing of these trees led to new levels of overproduction after 1902. The 1906–7 crop was predicted to be the largest ever—more than 20,000,000 60-kilo bags, in a period when international prices were half what they had been in the early 1890's. World consumption in 1905–6 was only 16,700,000 bags, and Brazil already had a 10,000,000-bag stock. Moreover, coffee was notoriously price-inelastic—that is, a fall in prices did not proportionally increase the level of world consumption.[32] Beyond all this, the planters found their position made still worse by the federal government's efforts to restore the value of the milréis vis-à-vis hard currencies. Brazil's earnings on foreign coffee

*Whether the exchange system had negative results for non-coffee-producing areas of Brazil has been the subject of debate. Nathaniel Leff has argued that though coffee interests sought falling exchange rates, on the whole, the value of the milréis was higher in the late nineteenth century than it would have been if cotton and sugar had set the rates instead: "The growth of coffee exports from the Southeast [Rio, Minas, and São Paulo] led directly to an accelerating decline in overseas sales of the Northeast's sugar and cotton [because these two commodities] required a lower sterling-milréis rate in order to export." "Economic Development," pp. 257–58. David Denslow has denied the validity of Leff's argument on both theoretical and empirical grounds, contending, among other things, that no other sugar-producing area of the world saw so great an external depreciation of its currency as Brazil between 1883 and 1913. Denslow also shows that Leff lacks evidence for his argument on a variety of other relevant issues. "As origens de desigualdade," especially p. 88. In any case, the political actors in our period were aware that Northeastern sugar and cotton producers wanted low exchange rates (see Chapter Six below).

sales fell 10 percent yearly between 1901 and 1904, the first such reversal in the history of coffee exports.[33]

Meanwhile, Paulista officials noticed that in the midst of this decline, the retail price of coffee in the consuming countries had tended to remain stable; furthermore, they observed that many foreign importers took advantage of the fact that coffee does not deteriorate much until it is roasted to buffer-stock, and were thus able to protect themselves against high prices in years of bad weather and short supply.[34] The possibility of stockpiling coffee at home was discussed in São Paulo as early as 1899, and a concrete plan for price maintenance and warehousing was presented by the Paulista delegation in Congress in 1903.[35]

At that moment, Brazil was indeed in a position to "valorize" coffee by intervening in the international market. Coffee interests assumed—correctly—that a decrease in the quantity offered would produce a price increase that more than compensated for the fall in volume.[36] Yet the success of the program over the long run was conditional on three things: first, that Brazil could maintain its dominant position in the world market; second, that consuming countries would not effectively retaliate; and third, that domestic coffee production could be limited in the face of artificially high international prices.[37] Though the last condition could not be met until after 1945, by which time Brazil no longer dominated the world market, expanding output did not invalidate the scheme in the short run.

Valorization was essentially simple: a foreign loan would be obtained to purchase coffee from planters and stockpile it; in years of bad harvests this supply would be released on the international market; and meanwhile all exported coffee would be taxed at a high enough rate to repay the foreign loan.

The dangers of valorization were recognized almost immediately—especially the likelihood of continued overproduction. The tocsin was sounded in Congress, and British embassy officials repeatedly predicted the ultimate failure of valorization.[38] On the positive side, coffee expert Augusto Ramos, who scouted the situation for the São Paulo government on a tour of competitor countries in Central and South America in 1904–6, found that they were in no position to take advantage of São Paulo's retention of part of its coffee stock.[39] Furthermore, retaliation by Brazil's leading customer, the United States, turned out to be minimal. Only twice, once in 1911–13 and again in 1926, did American government officials try to force Brazil's hand. In the first case, the issue of the "coffee trust" was settled by diplomatic negotiations, and in the second, a loan that Secretary of Commerce Herbert Hoover prevented São Paulo from obtaining in New York was quickly subscribed in London.[40]

Closely connected with valorization was the policy of manipulating the foreign-exchange rate to the advantage of coffee producers. Here the Paulistas needed the full collaboration of the federal government, and to obtain this they relied on an alliance with Minas Gerais and its representatives in Congress. The initial coffee support scheme, the Taubaté Convention of 1906, established by the states of Rio, São Paulo, and Minas, had explicitly called for a federal exchange-rate scheme to benefit coffee producers. The Exchange Bank (Caixa de Conversão), approved by a Mineiro-led Congress the same year, converted foreign currencies at a fixed rate that tended to remain below what the free market would have allowed; that is, drafts in foreign currencies bought more milréis than they would have fetched in a free market. The bank first pegged this rate at 27 pence per milréis; but after 320,000 contos had been exchanged, the rate was changed to 15 pence per milréis, a figure that has been called "nothing more than a general reduction of the nation's finances for the particular interests of coffee growers."[41] In a period when the milréis would have otherwise appreciated because of huge receipts for foreign coffee sales, a stable exchange rate of course aided coffee planters. The Exchange Bank lasted until the economic dislocations of the First World War forced its closing. In 1927, a new institution, the Stabilization Bank (Caixa de Estabilização), was founded with similar aims.

Three successful valorization programs were implemented following Taubaté: the first in 1907–8 by the state of São Paulo, a second by São Paulo in 1917, with federal backing, and a third in 1921 by the Union. In 1907, São Paulo borrowed £2,000,000 abroad, and the equivalent of 3,000,000 more in local currency from the federal government. But a bumper crop of 24,000,000 bags in 1906–7 almost brought down the fragile marketing edifice before it could be tested. A new infusion of money, in the form of a foreign loan of £15,000,000, refinanced the program in December 1908. The provisions for this huge loan, which nearly equaled the total outstanding foreign obligations of all the states combined in 1906,[42] set the standards for subsequent valorization programs. Coffee stocks were used as security. The federal government had to guarantee the loan, and was induced to do so by the Mineiro and Paulista delegations in Congress. Backing from Minas was bought with the agreement to include inferior grades of coffee (nos. 8 and 9) in valorization purchases, types largely grown in Minas Gerais and Rio de Janeiro.[43] The nominal interest rate on the loan was 6 percent, but service charges and discounts drove the effective rate up to 10 percent.[44] São Paulo state remained the legal owner of the stockpiled coffee, but an international syndicate of importers and bankers determined how and when it could be sold, and the state government was prohibited from enacting any coffee trade legislation without the syndicate's approval. The tax levied on the coffee shipped abroad, which had been three gold francs under the 1905–6 valorization plan, was raised to five per bag. Furthermore, an ad valorem tax of 20 percent on bags sold above a certain limit was introduced to guard against flooding the market. The Hamburg-based export house of Theodor Wille was to supervise the collection of the valorization tax. Thus in multiple ways the state government lost control of coffee marketing in 1908. Perhaps this outcome was inevitable, because foreign firms vertically integrated their operations in the coffee trade in the decade after 1896. In any event, the political behavior of Paulista statesmen was conditioned by this new economic and financial dependence.

It is difficult to say who ultimately bore the cost of repaying the valorization loans through the five-franc tax. Paulista authorities repeatedly asserted that the planters had to pay, and agricultural societies urged that the tax be minimized; but other sources claim that the exporters had to absorb it. For my own part, I doubt whether either group shouldered much of the burden; the importer and ultimately the consumer probably paid the greater share.[45]

The stock of the first valorization program was marketed over a 10-year period, and in 1917 São Paulo obtained a second valorization loan—this one from the federal government, since foreign capital was not available during the war. Stocks were exhausted again by 1920, and the following year a third valorization loan was subscribed abroad, this time by the federal government for £9,000,000. Stock operations and the collection of the valorization tax were now controlled by the Brazilian Warrant Company, which had replaced Wille as a result of the blacklisting of German firms during the war. By 1924, stocks had again been successfully disposed of. It has recently been argued that the three valorizations did in fact produce higher and more stable earnings and prices: "All three interventions resulted in improvements over what would have happened in the absence of market manipulation."[46] The problem was, however, that once in motion, the valorization juggernaut could not be stopped.

Valorization seemed to work well enough until the late 1920's. In 1924, the federal government returned the responsibility for the program to São Paulo, which set up a Coffee Institute to superintend financing and storage. But now more than ever, planters were allowed to translate high international coffee prices into high domestic receipts.[47] In other words, the federal government made no attempt to limit domestic profits through exchange-rate manipulations. In 1926, São Paulo's new state bank began to advance money on coffee stocks. Its purchase prices were set at a level that made coffee growing profitable even in older and less productive areas, despite the fact that new coffee lands were rapidly opening up. A tax on new plantings in 1902 had been largely ineffective,[48] and now there were no limitations at all. Furthermore, advances for stockpiled coffee in 1927 and 1928 were used to finance new plantings. On the positive side, the regulation of the entrance of coffee into the ports (arranged through an interstate agreement called the Second Coffee Convention) blocked exporter speculation on coffee stored in the armazéns gerais.

But the coffee market was careening toward disaster, an event that could only be averted or delayed by bad harvests, as happened in the case of the frost-devastated crop of 1917. Bumper crops, however, were delivered in three successive years—1927–28, 1928–29, and 1929–30. The British ambassador reported that

the [Coffee] Institute was still carrying dangerously large stocks when the fatal 1929–30 crop of 21½ million bags came into view. [Estimates were available in September 1929], and it speedily became certain that the supply of coffee in Brazil would be greater than the total *world* consumption for the third year in succession. . . . When in early October it was rumored that the São Paulo State Bank had ceased making advances on coffee, the crash immediately ensued.[49]

The rumor was untrue, but the directors of the Coffee Institute nonetheless resigned, and the long-expected fall in prices occurred. The coffee crisis thus materialized *before* October 24, 1929, "Black Thursday" on the New York Stock Exchange. By December, price levels stood at half the levels of the previous January.

The federal government, enamored of its plan to stabilize the milréis, refused to aid the institute with a loan of fiat money; President Washington Luís gambled that a sudden fall in coffee prices would expand sales. Since coffee was notoriously price-inelastic, the ploy was apparently based on the hope of speculative buying and stockpiling by importers. Meanwhile, government efforts to stabilize the exchange rate unfortunately facilitated the outflow of capital. The "policy" failed utterly. Although the state government obtained a foreign loan of £20,000,000 to alleviate the crisis, prices remained depressed, and 22,000,000 bags remained unsold at the end of 1930. In this, the first year of the Great Depression, the British embassy estimated that Brazil had lost a full year's earnings on coffee because of the fall in sales. Rural wages plummeted, and "many well-to-do persons . . . lost every penny of their fortunes."[50] Thus the failure of the valorization policy was compounded by bad luck, creating the worst overproduction crisis in history at the very time when foreign credit (on which valorization depended) and foreign sales both contracted sharply.

Another cost of valorization was the loss of control of coffee marketing to foreign lenders after 1908. In a sense, valorization was a vigorous response to foreign control—an attempt to wrest a larger share of the profits in the international coffee trade from foreign importers and wholesalers. But the financing arrangements instead gave exporters and foreign financiers even greater control. The effects of this change were immediate. Wille doubled its share of Santos's coffee exports in the very first year of valorization, and soon went on to become a major landholder and investor in industry.[51] By 1910, some of the largest coffee-growing operations were in foreign hands. The state's second-largest producer, the British-owned Dumont Coffee Company, controlled 4,000,000 trees. The immigrant Francisco Schmidt, a partner in land-dealing with the Wille firm, had almost 8,000,000, more than any other owner, individual or corporate, at that time. Foreign firms of course monopolized the international shipping and insurance operations associated with coffee: a Brazilian Warrant official was in the freight insurance business, as was Wille, which was also closely associated with a shipping company.[52]

The valorization program also contributed significantly to the foreign grip on Brazilian and Paulista finances. In 1916, a British financial expert asked, "Is it more valuable to be paid off [for valorization loans] or to still have control of the Coffee Tax?" He concluded that keeping control of Brazil's finances was more valuable.[53] Yet it would be erroneous to ascribe to valorization the whole responsibility for the increasing degree of foreign control, and indeed, as far as banking is concerned, the trend was checked by the late 1920's.

More directly assignable to valorization than foreign penetration of the economy was Brazil's loss of position in the international coffee trade in the 1930's. In the valorization years, Brazil had withheld coffee from the market; during the Depression, the country went further and undertook to destroy most of its stocks. Thus Colombia, the states of Central America, and European colonies in Africa, at no cost of warehousing or destroying their own crops, cut into the world market; they were "free riders." By 1937 Brazil's share had fallen below 50 percent.[54]

A final cost of valorization, the consequent distortion in Brazil's investment pattern and the country's misallocation of resources, is more difficult to assess accurately. In particular, it has been argued that more rapid industrial development and agricultural diversification might have been achieved if capital resources, domestic and foreign, had not been devoted so extensively to the protection of coffee.[55] Still, in the initial phase of valorization (1906–14) at least, before planters came to regard the market as ever expanding, higher prices for limited output seem to have diverted part of planter profits into industry.[56] Moreover, we have no way of knowing how much of the capital applied to valorization and coffee reinvestment would have found its way into "more productive" sectors. It is highly improbable that such massive international financing could have been obtained for any other purpose.

The Depression decade not only was a period of experimentation in limiting output, but also a period of experimentation in selling, bartering, and destroying coffee. In 1931, São Paulo's Coffee Institute turned over its responsibilities to the National Coffee Council (Conselho Nacional do Café), an interstate agency under federal supervision. New export taxes were placed on coffee to provide funds for the purchase and destruction of excess output, and prohibitive taxes were placed on new plantings in most areas. The destruction of coffee had been proposed as early as 1903, but was roundly rejected by the coffee interests. In the face of São Paulo's 18,000,000-bag stock in April 1931, however, that course of action did not seem so unthinkable, and may even have been the only realistic policy.[57] A centrally controlled National Coffee Department (Departamento Nacional do Café) replaced the council in 1934, and the government brought both the Treasury and the Bank of Brazil more forcefully to the aid of the coffee industry, a process discussed below.

The old foreign-exchange system was rapidly abandoned under Vargas. At the outset of the Depression, the coffee sector enjoyed an "automatic" benefit when capital flight and the end of gold convertibility for the milréis produced a devaluation of the currency; part of the coffee sector's losses could thereby be transferred to the population at large through rises in the prices of imports, while planter receipts in milréis rose.[58] The Vargas government, on the other hand, reversed four decades of foreign-exchange favoritism to coffee interests, and instituted a multiple-rate scheme designed to make international financial obligations less burdensome. The Economic Readjustment (Reajustamento Econômico), a program begun in April 1933, was conceived of as a form of compensation for an exchange system that discriminated against coffee; it canceled half the mortgage loans on coffee estates and limited interest rates on plantation mortgages. More than half of the Readjustment payments from 1934 to 1945 went to São Paulo, and the São Paulo State Bank reported in 1937 that only 29 of the 879 cases it had presented on behalf of the planters had yet to be resolved.[59]

When coffee prices failed to rebound, planters and farmers turned to other crops. Brazilian cotton exports grew from 2 percent of the value of exports in 1925–29 to 19 percent in 1935–39, while coffee's share fell from 72 percent to 47 percent. By 1936, São Paulo produced more than half of Brazil's raw cotton, and its cotton acreage increased from 117,000 hectares in 1933 to 1,314,000 in 1939, more than two-thirds the area devoted to coffee-growing in that year.[60] Just as non-Brazilian producers had long taken advantage of Brazil's coffee-support program, Brazilian agriculturalists now benefited from domestic price supports for cotton in the United States, a policy that raised international price levels. They also benefited from the new German demand for cotton on barter terms in the 1930's. In 1939–43, the domestic value of cotton grown in Brazil passed that of coffee. Cotton investment also indirectly aided industry, especially in São Paulo, whose textile mills were able to get 80 percent of their supply from growers within the state by 1937.[61]

Sugar likewise came up fast in the 1930's as an alternative to coffee, though most of the state's production was for the domestic market. In the middle of the Old Republic, São Paulo accounted for only 8 percent of the nation's output, but by the late 1930's, the state was competing with Pernambuco for first place in the Federation. Moreover, Paulista planters enjoyed lower freight costs than their Northeastern competitors, since the principal consuming areas were the cities of the Center-South. Indeed, in 1937, with a fifth of the crop by value, São Paulo temporarily replaced Pernambuco as the leading producer.[62]

In the same year the country's international coffee policy changed abruptly. No longer controlling the bulk of supply and failing to secure an international accord among sellers, Brazil at the outset of the Estado Novo abolished its duties on coffee and undertook a vigorous effort to expand exports. Virtually abandoning protection, the government tried to maximize receipts through lower prices and a larger volume of sales. Partly because of this program, but more directly because of the desire of the United States to ensure its wartime supply, an Inter-American Coffee Agreement was signed in 1942. The price of Brazilian coffee sold abroad (in constant terms) rose almost continuously thereafter until 1954.[63]

Commerce

Coffee's role in the economy of state and nation implied an overwhelmingly important position for Santos in Brazil's international trade. As noted above, Santos shipped more than half the value of Brazil's exports in the 1920's and 1930's—which is to say, 70 percent of all the coffee sent abroad passed through the port in those years.[64] Most of this coffee was from São Paulo, but it also included about a third of Minas's production, grown in the state's Sul region. After 1930, a rising share came from northern Paraná, the new coffee frontier.

São Paulo's coastwise trade with the other states—probably much more important than the trade by rail, though figures for interstate rail trade are lacking—steadily expanded from the 1880's through the 1930's. The value of coastwise "exports" relative to international exports increased from less than 4 percent in 1886–87 to some 14 percent in 1918–21, and to more than 25 percent in 1935–36. The value of the state's coastwise "exports" to other states also increased relative to "imports." In 1886–87, São Paulo's coastwise purchases from other states were worth twice as much as its sales to them. With the expansion of Paulista manufacturing, however, "exports" closed the gap, making especially rapid strides in the 1920's. By 1931, São Paulo was a net exporter to the other states, a position it maintained into the 1950's. In 1935 and 1936, its coastwise exports to other states were by value about half again as large as imports.[65]

It seems likely that this "export" surplus was paid for with capital flows to São Paulo. The 1930's, in any case, were the years in which São Paulo captured the national market for industrial goods, as Brazilians began to substitute Paulista manufactures for foreign products.[66] Regions of neighboring states became commercial satellites in the process of trade expansion. Prominent among these was the Triângulo zone of Minas, which by the mid-1930's was conducting about 95 percent of its trade with São Paulo. (The zone, however, had come under Paulista dominance 25 years earlier.)[67]

Commerce and industry, like agriculture and industry, were related in complex ways. Importers and consumers clashed with industrialists over the tariff issue and exchange policies, but many importers also became industrialists because they began either to process the raw materials they imported or to finish semi-manufactured goods.[68] Since many importers had already organized their own retail operations, as industrialists they had an excellent knowledge of market conditions.

Yet there were frictions between merchants and industrialists. Businessmen organized a mutual-interest association as early as 1884. This was replaced 10 years later by the Commercial Association of São Paulo, which is still active. As industry loomed larger in the state economy, an internal struggle took place over positions of leadership in the association. In 1928, a compromise slate was elected, giving industrialists a leading role for the first time.[69] This fact did not prevent the industrialists from setting up an interest group of their own, the Center of Industries, a few months later.

Industry

In 1970, São Paulo accounted for 57 percent of Brazil's total industrial output, by value, and nearly half the country's industrial jobs,[70] a concentration that has led some economists to characterize the state as a "Belgium in India."[71] The state clearly achieved this hegemony in the period under study. In 1907, the year of Brazil's first industrial census, São Paulo produced only 16 percent of the nation's industrial goods (by value); but by 1919 the figure had doubled, to 32 percent, and it rose to 43 percent in 1939.[72] The 1930's in fact witnessed a more rapid absolute increase in industrial development than any decade up to that time. Between 1933 and 1939, the number of manufacturing firms in São Paulo doubled, capital investment in industry more than doubled, and the value of output more than tripled. By 1939, industry had pulled abreast of agriculture as a contributor to state output.[73]

São Paulo's industrial preeminence has been attributed in the local mythology to the enterprising spirit of the Paulistas, dating back to the days of the bandeirantes.[74] Students of Brazil's economic history, on the other hand, have stressed other factors. Many, for instance, argue that São Paulo became the principal area of industrial growth primarily for reasons of geography. They note, for example, that São Paulo city's location made it a center of communications, outfitting, and distribution even in the colonial era; and by the twentieth century, its integrated rail network vastly increased its strategic effectiveness. Then, too, there is the state's extensive river system with its large hydroelectric potential. Inexpensive hydroelectric power was available by the first decade of the current century, and by 1939, São Paulo had well over half of Brazil's hydroelectric capacity.[75] The raw material for the state's major industry, cotton textiles, was also abundant locally by the 1920's. For other goods, the chief factor in the initial success of local firms producing for the consumer market was the weight-to-cost ratio, because freight charges up the escarpment made it profitable to produce heavy goods locally.[76]

Geography of course is the chief determinant of the climate, whose mildness may have contributed significantly to the industrial development of the planalto. Although the role of climate in economic development is hardly a fashionable subject of study among social scientists, it is certainly plausible that the climate helped attract the millions of immigrants from temperate zones; in turn, these immigrants provided the beginnings of a mass market, a measure of capital for industrialization, and the initial industrial labor force.[77] The accumulation of capital was also related to geography in the sense that planter profits were partly derived from rich coffee soils.[78]

Entrepreneurship is clearly a difficult thing to evaluate. Warren Dean approaches a mechanistic explanation when he asserts that the chief element in entrepreneurship in São Paulo was "the more intense operation of the market economy [than elsewhere], that is . . . the greater profitability of coffee and . . . the fuller use of money as a medium of exchange."[79] He argues convincingly that the Paulista planters turned industrialists had good luck in two major respects: first, they received their highest rates of return on coffee after slavery was moribund, and therefore did not sink their capital into slave labor; and second, they enjoyed relative freedom from foreign competition in developing the infrastructure necessary for the vertical integration of coffee production. Dean has

emphasized that the Paulista landowners were able to establish a transportation network, credit system, and initial industrial plant in part because the British, who were not major coffee consumers, did not monopolize Brazil's foreign trade, as they tended to monopolize Argentina's.
Nor did any other foreign nationality do so.[80] In addition, risk-taking was
minimized in a few areas, notably in the case of the railroads, where the
state was willing to grant lucrative monopolies and to buy out unprofitable
enterprises if necessary. But this argument is obviously limited, since the
vast majority of manufacturers did not obtain the guarantees the railroad
owners enjoyed.[81]

One important way in which entrepreneurship affected capital formation was through patterns of ownership. Railroads, banks, and import
houses were organized as joint-stock companies,[82] but manufacturing concerns usually were not; and even when they were, stock was seldom sold
outside the extended family.[83] In this respect, the planter bourgeoisie,
which dominated the railroad sector, seemed more innovative in capital
formation than the immigrant bourgeoisie, the other major group of entrepreneurs identified by Dean.

Planters preceded the immigrants as industrialists, first investing in
areas closely related to agriculture. Unlike many Latin American landowners, the Paulista coffee growers tended to consider land a factor of
production rather than an immutable demesne, and continually purchased new properties as old ones wore out. In the later years of the
Empire, they also tended to invest in railroads and in coffee-processing
machinery. Some of the most successful planters, such as Antônio Prado,
first went into banking and only later moved into branches of manufacturing not related to coffee.

The immigrants who became industrialists tended not to come from the
destitute masses that formed the bulk of the rural workers. Francisco
Matarazzo, creator of "the largest industrial complex in South America,"
for example, was the son of a lawyer and the largest property owner in
Castelabate, Salerno.[84] The younger Matarrazzo came to Brazil with a
modest amount of capital and began his career almost simultaneously as
an industrialist, merchant, and importer. His success, first in the lard
business and later in a broad range of industrial ventures, has been
ascribed more to commercial than industrial acuity. Matarazzo would
typically organize a chain of small retailers to distribute goods he produced to replace imports. As an importer, he began to finish foreign goods

in a process of vertical integration. Matarazzo also relied on his knowledge of immigrant consumption habits, and as a banker established a monopoly over immigrants' remittances to Italy, thus expanding his capital base.[85]

Foreigners representing overseas investors may not have played as important a role in São Paulo's industrial development as they did in Argentina's, but this is difficult to judge, for they remain a largely unstudied group. The Theodor Wille company went into manufacturing during the First World War because, by British war policy, its coffee had to be consigned to the Brazilian Warrant Company. The country's largest meat-packing plant, at Barretos, was foreign-owned. In cement, a capital goods industry, the most important firm in the 1920's was 70 percent American-owned. By 1940, the American investment in manufacturing in Brazil as a whole had reached $46,000,000.[86] In the statistics no distinction is made between temporary and permanent residents among the foreign-born, but some inferences are possible. In 1940–41, according to a state survey, more than two-fifths of the capital invested in São Paulo's industry belonged to foreigners or foreign-born persons. Only 12 percent of this belonged to Italians, and 2.5 percent to Portuguese, the largest- and second-largest nationality groups identified, with 5.5 percent belonging to various other specified national groups; 20 percent, however, belonged to unspecified "other" nationalities, presumably mostly Britons, Americans, Canadians, and Germans, who probably were not permanent residents.[87]

A "native" urban bourgeoisie apparently played almost no role in the state's industrial development. Dean asserts that "by 1930 there was not a single manufacturer of native-born lower- or middle-class origins, and only a very few appeared thereafter."[88] The immigrant-planter dichotomy, however, is not totally satisfactory. As noted, we lack information on the temporary foreign residents representing overseas firms. Moreover, several prominent manufacturers were neither planters nor immigrants, but expanded into industrial ventures after achieving success in commerce.*

The relationship between the growth of the international coffee trade and the growth of industry is complex, but the two were plainly linked. When coffee sales fell, the demand for industrial goods by consumers

---

*Such as Antônio Proost Rodovalho, Jorge Street, and Raymundo Duprat. All three were "native-born," though Street and Duprat were not of Portuguese stock, and Rodovalho only partly.

associated with the coffee sector (including colonos) also tended to fall, credit tightened up, and the outflow of immigrant workers and capital increased. At the same time, imported raw materials and machinery became scarcer, since exports governed the capacity to import; on the other hand, and for the same reason, competing foreign goods were also scarcer.[89]

When we distinguish between the building of industrial capacity and the growth of output, the rhythm is clearer. Capital imports tended to do well whenever international coffee sales did well.[90] But investment in industry—heavily dependent on these capital imports—was also affected by the milréis' value on the foreign exchange, and this was manipulated primarily on behalf of coffee producers. In the infrequent periods of appreciating or stable exchange rates, investment levels were high, and output, under the competition of cheaper foreign goods, was low (1924–26, 1932). When the exchange rate fell, output increased and capital imports dropped off (1921–23, 1927–31, 1933–39).[91]

The nature of Brazilian industrialization in this century, and especially the experience of São Paulo, has been the subject of intense debate by economists and economic historians during the last two decades. Most participants are associated either with the structuralist school, led by Celso Furtado, or with the neo-orthodox group, of which Carlos Peláez is the most prolific writer, though some analysts, mainly North Americans, have made important contributions without falling neatly into either school.[92]

The structuralist thesis, as advanced by Furtado, is that the Great Depression produced a weakening of Brazil's trade relations with the industrialized countries, and constituted a critical phase in the development of industry because of the process of import substitution; this was possible in part because of government action to maintain a high level of domestic demand. Omitting the government-action part of the thesis, a similar argument could be made about the effects of the First World War, which likewise saw rapid economic development because of a sudden expansion of output. Relying on a close examination of the data, Dean argues that it was capital already invested before the war that allowed output to grow so dramatically during the conflict, a time when capacity could not expand because of the absence of a capital goods industry and the interruption of foreign investment. This line of reasoning has been carried further by Peláez and Wilson Suzigan, who flatly assert that the war had a net negative effect on industrial development because of the lack of capital formation, and because of falling terms of trade (and therefore falling real income) during the war.[93] In a broader context, the neo-orthodox economists stress the distortions in profitability rates produced by valorization, and argue that, on balance, capital formation in industry was hurt by this interference with market forces.[94]

Wilson Cano, a structuralist, would go back still further in time, to the transfer of capital from coffee to industry beginning in the turn-of-the-century crisis. He also argues that the profits as a result of expanded industrial output during the First World War were invested in new capacity in the postwar period, and that the number of plants in São Paulo increased substantially during the war. Cano's chief interest lies in the concentration of Brazilian industry in São Paulo, and he points to the state's rise to virtual hegemony in industrial production between the economic censuses of 1907 and 1919, when output in cotton textiles grew 325 percent in São Paulo, compared with only 60 percent in the rest of Brazil;[95] meanwhile, as noted above, the state's total share of the value of Brazilian manufactured goods doubled. Besides the previously mentioned advantages São Paulo enjoyed in developing its industry, Cano notes that the going rate of pay for an adult male worker in manufacturing was lower there than in the leading competing units (the Federal District and Rio Grande do Sul) because of the state's large rural labor pool.[96] He also notes that the state had achieved a high degree of agricultural diversification into food crops by the First World War, and so did not have to spend its income on imports of food.[97]

Reaping large profits from the wartime boom, manufacturers in the 1920's placed orders overseas for capital goods; this decade was an era of slow growth of output but rapid growth of capacity.[98] Despite an initial drop in output with the advent of the Depression, production in São Paulo had almost reached the 1929 level again by 1933.[99] But the collapse of the international coffee market in that period brought in its wake a decline in the terms of trade, impeding capital formation. Thus, though relative prices of imports rose and production levels recuperated in the early 1930's, capital formation once again lagged.

After 1933, industrial output grew rapidly, except for the textile industry, which was faced with the problem of obsolescent plant. In the first half of the decade, the fuller use of the capacity acquired in the 1920's repeated the pattern of the First World War and the postwar years. In the period 1935–39, output and capacity rose together—apparently for the first time—as São Paulo and Brazil began to acquire a capital goods industry. Over the whole decade, the value of São Paulo's production rose about twice as fast as that of the rest of the country.[100]

The "traditional" light industries—chiefly textiles and food processing —accounted for only 57 percent of São Paulo's output by 1939, down 13 percentage points from 1919. Basic industry (metallurgy, tools and parts, electricity, and transport) almost doubled its share in the same period— from 9 percent to 17 percent. In the seven years from 1933 to 1939, metallurgy grew at an annual rate of 24 percent, transport at 39 percent, and overall industrial production at 14 percent.[101]

Structuralists, noting how rapidly São Paulo's manufacturing sector recovered from the initial shock of the Depression, argue that the directors of federal and state coffee policy inadvertently aided in this process. The first boost came from a £20,000,000 British valorization loan to São Paulo in 1930, before the fall of Washington Luís. The loan prevented the bankruptcy of the coffee sector in a period of federal inaction, and the foreign currency produced was used to finance debt service, not imports that could have competed with domestic manufactures.[102] Later, under Vargas, the federal government anticipated Keynesian countercyclical policies, albeit quite unintentionally. Though about half the coffee program was financed by taxes, some of the tax burden was passed on to the foreign consumer; the other half was financed by a deficit budget, which sustained purchasing power for manufactured goods in the vital coffee sector (including the colono population). Furthermore, one structuralist notes that though international coffee prices fell 70 percent between 1929 and 1939, domestic coffee prices, in real terms, fell only 35 percent, thus cushioning the loss of income in the coffee sector.[103]

Coffee subsidies in the 1920's probably hurt industry by distorting profitability rates otherwise determined by market forces. Nevertheless, government monetary, fiscal, and exchange policies in the early 1930's stimulated industrial development more than the subsidy policies impeded it. Monetary policy was expansionist; fiscal policy was based on deficit spending (despite government declarations of a contrary intent); and exchange policy kept the losses in milréis in the coffee sector below those in hard currencies, thus helping preserve income and demand in a period when foreign manufactured goods were not available because of low foreign-exchange earnings.[104]

Throughout our period, however, the government played only a limited role in the development of manufacturing, especially in the way of direct and conscious policy. Even in the heady nationalism of the 1930's, manufacturers did not enjoy the subsidies from state and central governments that railroad entrepreneurs had benefited from in the late Empire and early Republic. Furthermore, tariff protection was fitful. The tariffs of 1890 and 1900, which set effective barriers against foreign competition because they were collected partly in gold, were principally designed to obtain revenue, not to shelter infant industries.[105] By the late 1920's, the federal government began to respond more readily to manufacturing interests, and replied to the plaints of a Paulista textile industry in crisis with higher duties on foreign goods.[106] Yet manufacturers were still on the defensive against attacks from coffee planters in the Estado Novo era. Producers of burlap sacking for the coffee industry in São Paulo even had to defend themselves against (false) charges that foreign sacking was considerably cheaper; and few planters were interested in supplying the industry with jute, its raw material.[107] Again and again in the 1920's and 1930's, the São Paulo textile industry's propagandists found themselves trying to lay to rest the charge that manufacturing was an "artificial industry."[108]

The net effect of Vargas's tariff policies in the early 1930's is still being debated;[109] but even on the eve of the Second World War, there was no consistent policy of tariff protection,[110] though multiple exchange rates did benefit industry after 1931. The impact of the government's monetary policies on industrial development is more clear-cut; the expansionist measures of the 1890's, 1914–15, and the early 1930's, and the consequent loosening of credit, aided industrial growth substantially, though industry simply reaped spinoff benefits of policies designed for other purposes.[111]

The absence of a development bank and the existence of a poor domestic credit system are still further evidence of the feebleness of the central government's interest in industry.[112] But there were other important impediments to industrial growth—most notably restricted consumer markets; the near-absence of a capital goods industry until the late 1930's; and the lack of an adequate transportation network outside São Paulo, which made expansion of the market more difficult and kept the costs of imports of domestic raw materials high. In textiles, at least, there were also failings in entrepreneurship by the 1930's. In 1937, the state textile association's answer to a potential "overproduction" crisis was not to lower prices and sell a larger volume at less profit per unit, but to maintain a ban on the importation of modern textile machinery, and even to prohibit the manufacture of looms in Brazil.[113] The industrialists' image among consumers, moreover, was never very favorable because of high prices and shoddy goods, and possibly also because of the manufacturers' repressive labor policies.[114]

Banking

São Paulo's credit facilities can hardly be called negligible, even if they did not meet all the needs of industry. In fact, the state's banking business grew dramatically during the era under study. In constant terms, the combined deposits of banks located in São Paulo grew nearly 46 times between 1894 and 1937.[115] As a banking center, São Paulo took first place among the states, though in 1936 it still had a slightly smaller share of the nation's total deposits than the Federal District (35 percent and 36 percent, respectively), partly because the Bank of Brazil's headquarters were located in the federal capital. Virtually all the banking business in São Paulo was concentrated in the metropolis: in January 1938, the combined assets of all banks with headquarters elsewhere amounted to 2 percent of those in São Paulo city.[116]

The big money in Paulista banking, especially during the Old Republic, was in buying and selling foreign exchange, and this trade of course revolved around coffee. The capital was a "banks' selling market," and Santos a "banks' buying market"; that is, banks sold drafts primarily in São Paulo city, and their branches in Santos bought the coffee bills—a business that amounted to several hundred million dollars annually by the mid-1920's. The Bank of Brazil, exempted from stamp taxes on draft transactions, dominated the exchange market.[117]

Compared with coffee, industry received little attention from Brazilian banks, public and private alike. Matarazzo relied on foreign banks for loans in the early years of the Republic,[118] and a state-affiliated bank established in 1909 was exclusively concerned with agricultural transactions. The State Bank, organized in 1926, was authorized to make industrial loans from its inception, but agriculture remained its chief concern. In 1931, the Minister of Finance, Osvaldo Aranha, privately asserted that its sole purpose was to lend to planters.[119] The Bank of Brazil had no special division for industrial loans until 1937, and even then significant lending to manufacturers had to wait another four years.[120] The bank's "favoritism" to São Paulo in both public and private realms in the 1930's is detailed in Chapter Eight.

Before the 1920's, agricultural mortgage credit was a difficult proposition because of the relatively low cost of land as a factor of production and the limited life of the coffee estates. Mortgage credit in the 1880's was supplied primarily by the Bank of Brazil and the Banco de Crédito Real de São Paulo, and many of the best fazendas were mortgaged.[121] But foreign banks and the vast majority of private domestic banks were unwilling to enter the mortgage business, so that this form of credit remained a major problem for most planters. In the coffee depression at the beginning of the century, the Banco de Crédito Real barely escaped bankruptcy because of its losses on mortgages.[122] In 1904, the Tibiriçá government authorized the creation of an agricultural credit bank, guaranteeing a 6 percent annual profit to the firm that would accept the offer. A French concern took advantage of the opportunity, organizing the Bank of Mortgage and Agricultural Credit under state auspices in 1909; this operation became a model for a similar bank established in Minas Gerais two years later. In 1926, the São Paulo government took over the French bank, and supplied most of the capital for a new institution, the Bank of the State of São Paulo. Yet even at that late date it was the only significant rural mortgage bank in the state.[123]

All the same, the Paulista planter's mortgage problems were far less severe than those of his counterparts in other states; São Paulo in fact accounted for nearly three-fifths of the value of all Brazil's agricultural mortgages in 1909.[124] Again comparing Ribeirão Preto and Açu, Rio Grande do Norte, at about this time, we find that though the cost of land in the Paulista município was four times higher, many of the estates had been purchased with mortgage loans, whereas in the northeastern município such loans were simply nonexistent.[125]

Although by statute the State Bank could make loans to commercial and industrial groups, its single most important responsibility was the support of valorization operations; and the Secretariat of Agriculture and the state Coffee Institute were its chief shareholders. The bank borrowed £1,250,000 from Lazard in 1927 for loans on rural and urban property, but took out £5,000,000 the same year expressly to cover coffee operations.[126] It advanced money to planters and comissários against coffee as collateral, in addition to making mortgage loans. In the early 1930's, as a consequence of mortgage failures during the Depression, the bank found itself the owner of a "great number" of fazendas. It managed to sell these off quickly, however; in 1934 alone it disposed of 55 estates, containing millions of coffee trees. Some of the fazendas it sold were subdivided into small properties.[127]

The Bank of the State of São Paulo was the most important Paulista bank in 1937, measured by total assets. It was followed by the São Paulo branch of the Bank of Brazil and two private Brazilian-chartered banks; yet eight of the top 15 banks were foreign-based.[128] Most of the foreign banks had set up operations in the first two decades of the Republic; typically, as noted earlier, they were closely tied to the export trade. In addition, two of the largest export firms—Theodor Wille and Brazilian Warrant—became important lenders, having assumed major financial responsibilities as collectors of the valorization tax.

Assessing the importance of foreign firms in the banking business depends partly on what measure one uses to weigh their influence, but it is clear enough that their role had declined by the end of our period. From 78 percent of the value of all transactions in 1913, their share dropped to 33 percent in 1927. Foreign banks controlled "the major share" of the commercial discount business at the outset of the First World War but later lost it.[129] Though the foreign banks' reduced role by the late 1930's was probably due in good part to the coffee industry's paralysis during the Depression, local banks had managed to gain some ground on them earlier, with the growth of the coffee sector in the 1920's. The assets of domestically chartered banks in the state at the beginning of 1938 were two and a half to three times greater than those of foreign concerns.[130]

Yet despite their relative decline, foreign banks retained a large stake in São Paulo, and scurried to protect their interests in the tumult of the 1930's. In October 1932, the British Bank of South America and the Bank of London and South America asked the Foreign Office to "hold [the Vargas government] responsible for any loss suffered by British Banks" if the bonds issued by the São Paulo rebel government were repudiated. (The central government, however, immediately assumed the obligations, making any Foreign Office action unnecessary.)[131]

Inevitably, perhaps, foreign banks—especially the major international lenders—acquired powerful representatives in the upper political and financial circles of São Paulo. Numa de Oliveira, banker, politician, and president of the Clube Atlético Paulistano, represented Schroeder and Rothschild; and Wallace Simonsen, brother of the industrialist Roberto

Simonsen and himself a leading banker and coffee financier, was a local partner of Lazard Frères.[132]

Transportation

No less critical than banking to the development of industry and agriculture was the transportation system. Until the late 1930's, and then again during the Second World War because of gasoline shortages, São Paulo's economy moved by rail. Railroads did not "create" São Paulo as an economic and political unit as they did Argentina, but they played an indispensable role in its development from an area of secondary economic significance to one of overarching importance. Before the rail age began with the opening of the São Paulo Railway to Jundiaí in 1867, coffee could not profitably be grown west of Rio Claro, and two-thirds of the province either had a subsistence economy or was beyond the frontier.

As we see in Table 2.2, trackage increased an average of 1,300 kilometers a decade from 1870 to 1920, and then slowed down. Though only some 300 kilometers were added between 1930 and 1937, the amount of freight hauled in that period increased by more than 50 percent—from less than 10,000,000 metric tons in 1930 to 16,000,000 in 1937.[133] The composition of the freight changed too; cotton and industrial goods began to compete with coffee.

Brazil's railroads, like those of many other countries, were built with government support. In São Paulo, the subsidization initially took the form of an imperial guarantee of 5 percent annual profit, plus a provincial guarantee of an additional 2 percent. In the last 30 years of the nineteenth century, two lines prospered at near-fabulous levels—the São Paulo Railway and the Companhia Paulista de Estradas de Ferro. Others, however, such as the Sorocabana and Ituana lines, had to be continually subsidized.[134]

Railroads were generally profitable, even if for the state's lines as a whole costs rose relative to profits from 1895 to 1930.[135] Returns on capital invested were protected not only by government guarantees, but also, after 1893, by the legal right of companies to raise their rates as necessary as a hedge against falling exchange rates.[136] Moreover, profits could run as high as 12 percent for two consecutive years before a rate reduction was required.

The first company organized in São Paulo, and the one that achieved the greatest financial success, was the São Paulo Railway. The Barão de

TABLE 2.2
Growth of Railroads in São Paulo, 1870–1937
(Kilometers of track)

Year	Track	Year	Track
1870	139	1910	4,825
1880	1,212	1920	6,616
1890	2,425	1930	7,099
1900	3,373	1937	7,420

SOURCE: Nogueira de Matos, "O desenvolvimento," p. 381; IBGE, *Anuario estatístico*, 1939/1940, pp. 235–36.

Mauá, a famous Brazilian entrepreneur, was one of its earliest enthusiasts and planners, but in the end it was financed and constructed by the British; hence its local nickname the Inglesa. The shortest of the state's railroads—even in 1937 it had only 247 kilometers, counting the double track on its main line—it alone traversed the steep escarpment until that year. This monopoly meant that virtually all coffee freight in the state had to pass through the Inglesa's "funnel" down to Santos. Consequently, the São Paulo Railway was "the most profitable British railway enterprise in Brazil or anywhere else in Latin America." It paid annual dividends of at least 10 percent in the 1880's and at least 12 percent between 1902 and 1913, and averaged 11 percent over the 55 years 1876–1930.[137] The directors of the Inglesa were hardly unaware of the relationship between profits and monopoly. In 1909, they mobilized Rothschild and Schroeder to put pressure on state and federal governments not to allow another company to build a line to Santos.[138]

The Companhia Paulista, organized by planters in the Rio Claro area in 1868, began operations four years later, and pushed toward the northwest over the years as it bought out feeder lines. By 1881, it had completely repaid its debt to the London bankers who financed it. In the 1890's, the Paulista's dividends averaged 11 percent a year; and by 1900, its profits were 49 times greater than they were in 1872 (the year it reached Campinas).[139] Even in the heart of the Depression years, it was still earning money. An admiring British ambassador wrote the Foreign Office in 1935 that "of the few lines run by Brazilian public companies by far the best is the Paulista, which is operated by a group of hardheaded São Paulo businessmen." In fact the Paulista even surpassed the Inglesa in profits in 36 of the 48 years from 1890 to 1937.[140] Other railroads succeeded less brilliantly. The Sorocabana, eventually the longest line in São Paulo, had to be taken over by the state government in 1891. The state leased it to a Franco-American concern from 1907 to 1919, but had to assume direct control thereafter because of low profit rates.

The railroads continued to be the principal carriers of both freight and passengers through the period under study, but by the end of the First World War, the best-equipped coffee estates were using trucks and cars on their internal road networks; and by the 1920's, trucks were replacing ox-carts to move coffee to rail stations.[141] São Paulo had a state road development plan as early as 1921; it did not, however, create a state highway department until 1926, two years after Minas.[142] By 1937, São Paulo had the largest road network in Brazil—some 48,000 kilometers, almost a quarter of the nation's total. However, only 103 kilometers were paved, and two years later 90 percent of the state's network still consisted of "unimproved dirt roads."[143] The cities of São Paulo and Rio de Janeiro were connected by highway in 1928. Superhighways from São Paulo city to Rio and Santos were built soon after the Second World War, but the completion of a continuous paved highway from São Paulo to Pôrto Alegre had to wait until 1960. Meanwhile, São Paulo was relatively well supplied with trucks and automobiles. In 1937, a third of the nation's passenger cars were registered in São Paulo, as were 44 percent of the trucks.[144]

The great majority of Brazil's large ports were financed by foreign loans or foreign direct investment, but like most of São Paulo's railroads, the port of Santos was a wholly Brazilian enterprise. Led by such men as Cândido Gaffrée and Eduardo Guinle, the Cia. Docas de Santos used not only Brazilian capital, but also Brazilian contractors and engineers.[145] The Santos contract was awarded in 1888, but shipping was frequently bottlenecked until the completion of the first 260 meters of docks in 1898 and the laying of the Inglesa's second track in 1900. Some 1,000,000 metric tons of traffic passed through the port in 1901, 2,000,000 by 1913, and more than 4,000,000 by the late 1930's. The docks were congested during the boom years of the 1920's, in part because of the Inglesa's inability to move all the freight down the escarpment. According to the Commercial Association of Santos, more money was lost from congestion at the port in 1924–25 than the state government collected by all its taxes in that period. Yet even with the completion of another rail line down the escarpment in 1937, 90 percent of the traffic was still in the hands of the Inglesa in 1940.[146] A related problem was the inefficiency of the Brazilian coastal merchant fleet, which constituted the country's only nationally integrated transport system till after the Second World War.[147]

The commercial airline business was still in its infancy in the 1930's, and was only to burgeon during the war: Brazil's air freight tonnage increased ninefold between 1940 and 1945.[148] In the era under study, São Paulo lagged behind Rio Grande do Sul (where VARIG, now Brazil's national line, was created in 1927); but a state-subsidized company called Viação Aérea de São Paulo (VASP) was founded in 1934. Regular airline routes linked São Paulo's larger towns with the rest of the country by the late 1930's, though the airports of the Federal District and Rio Grande both had a greater volume of passenger traffic and freight in 1937.[149]

The years embracing the coups d'état of the Republic and the Estado Novo saw the consolidation of São Paulo's domination of the national economy. Coffee production and its attendant export trade reached their apogee and began a decline, but the shift to manufacturing was decisive in ensuring São Paulo's future economic hegemony. Other sectors of the economy—non-coffee agriculture, commerce, transportation, and banking—all grew with unprecedented strides. This growth propelled São Paulo further and further ahead of the other states. In the process, the state also pulled into its trading orbit large sections of neighboring units, and it conquered the national market for manufactured goods before the 1930's had ended.

Government intervention in the economy in these years was largely restricted to meeting the needs of the Treasury and agriculture, though the effects of given policies were sometimes beneficial to industry. Conflict between the various sectors of the economy, which might have allowed industrialists to push their demands for government support more forcefully, was muted by a pattern of overlapping ownership in all the fields reviewed here—manufacturing, transportation, commerce, banking, and agriculture.

These years also saw an extensive foreign penetration of key sectors of the economy. The phenomenon was most obvious in the domains of finance and exports, and valorization was one of its causes. Yet there is some evidence of an incipient "desatellization" in banking and the export trade in the years after the First World War. This important issue requires far more extensive research; e.g., to learn whether the desatellization was more apparent than real, because of the nominal domestication of foreign capital,[150] and whether a "resatellization" occurred in the late 1940's (and if so, to what degree), when foreign imports began to pour into Brazil again as a result of the uncontrolled expenditure of wartime credits. But as for the years of our own concern, there is no question that the foreign presence had a profound effect—not only on the economy, but also on Paulista political behavior, the subject of Chapters Four and Six. As we shall see in the next chapter, foreign influences also suffused São Paulo's society and culture.

CHAPTER THREE

Society and Culture

INSATIABLE IN HIS greed and lust, a man who, with boundless energy, scoured near-impenetrable jungles for a purpose he had perhaps forgotten: thus did the essayist Paulo Prado describe the bandeirante in 1928, in a manner reminiscent of Joseph Conrad's self-destructive Kurtz in *Heart of Darkness*.[1] For half a century, few literate Paulistas had doubted that their collective psychology had been inherited from the bandeirantes, but most writers and speakers emphasized the positive aspects: the bandeirante had pushed back the frontier; he had applied his energies to productive ends; he had perceived and seized his opportunities; and he had pointed the way to the future for the Brazilian nation. It had fallen to his modern descendants to accept their destiny in leading the country.

Forty years before the appearance of his nephew's sketch, Martinico Prado, the Republican propagandist, had appealed to regional pride and the bandeirante heritage in an attack on the imperial regime before São Paulo's provincial assembly. Arguing that the "hauteur and independence of the Paulista character" had been demonstrated in the election of Amador Bueno as "king" of São Paulo in 1640, the elder Prado went on to say that São Paulo now represented for Brazil what Paris did for France: "The brain that thinks [and] the arm that executes [the brain's commands]."[2] As if that was not brash enough, a Paulista delegate at the 1891 Constituent Assembly made it clear to other Brazilians what he thought about regional income disparities: if São Paulo was wealthy, it was because Paulistas worked hard; if northerners wanted to abolish poverty, they should go and do likewise. In 1922, Júlio Mesquita Filho, son of the publisher of the daily *O Estado de S. Paulo*, wrote of São Paulo's irresistible imperialism, as opposed to the "inertia" of neighboring states.[3]

Some writers, such as Alberto Sales (brother of President Campos Sales) argued that São Paulo and southern Brazil were "whiter" than other areas of the country, and implied that this alleged characteristic was associated with cultural and economic superiority. At least one of Sales's contemporaries, however, Joaquim Godoy, not only flatly rejected that thesis, but praised the race mixture that had resulted in the bandeirantes —a view that was later to win out as semiofficial ideology.[4]

Many outsiders subscribed to the Paulistas' image of themselves as the enterprising, opportunity-seeking heirs of the bandeirantes. The Dutch coffee expert van Delden Laërne, for example, was struck by the Paulistas's irritating but understandable sense of superiority. They "have justly earned the epithet of the Yankees of Brazil," he wrote in 1885. "Without a doubt they are more pushing, plucky, and self reliant than the Mineiros or Fluminenses. . . . But on the other hand they are much more proficient in the science of humbug."[5] Paulistas were inevitably accused of only being interested in money—a charge that caused propagandists to retort, as Vivaldo Coaracy did in 1931, that "Brazil, as always, hopes that São Paulo will [now] get to work."[6]

It is no coincidence that the Paulista self-image crystallized in the last quarter of the nineteenth century, for that image was inextricably linked with the expansion of the coffee frontier. The process of pushing back the frontier and converting the land behind it into private property—this, more than anything else, is what shaped São Paulo's society, what gave Martinico Prado and his generation their breezy confidence in their state's claim to preeminence in Brazil. And so, if we are to chart the growth and articulation of Paulista society, it is with the westward march of the coffee frontier that we must begin.

Frontiers and Settlement

As noted in Chapter One, São Paulo has two frontiers—the demographic frontier and the "pioneer" or economic frontier behind it, connected to the international economy of the Atlantic basin. The "pioneer" frontier in a capitalist system implies the full alienation of land and its transfer to private ownership, not just squatters' rights (or *posse*, in Portuguese).[7] Yet one land law after another in São Paulo resulted in the ex-post-facto legalization of land acquired by *posse*.[8] The state took over the public domain from the central government under the 1891 Constitution, and set up a land office in 1892. Eight years later, the state tried to require that public land be purchased, but subsequent legislation indicates that *posse* continued to be the major means of acquisition. Governor Washington Luís's statute of 1921 limited the amount of land that could be acquired by each applicant and required proof of cultivation for land obtained without charge, but it also legalized all *posses* held for at least one year before the law's implementation (thus inviting last-minute squatting before the law was declared in effect). The occupation of land by squatters continued unchecked, however, and in the 1930's, *posses* were still apparently the major means of acquiring land in frontier areas.[9] By 1934, landowners and squatters between them claimed 7,900,000 hectares of arable land not yet under cultivation—nearly a third of the state's total area. Thomas Holloway believes the state's inability to control the alienation of the public domain was due primarily to the sheer abundance of land.[10]

But the government's weakness cost the state money—not only in lost income from land sales, but also in lost taxes. The sacrifice in tax monies was especially significant when the rural land tax (*imposto territorial*) became a more important source of revenues in the 1930's.[11] Beyond the simple matter of revenues, the state's recognition of squatters' rights left the field open to land speculators and grileiros, who faked titles for themselves and fraudulently sold government land to others. Men of this stripe often anticipated the railroad as it moved westward, expecting land prices to shoot up. Sometimes there was collusion between lawyers, judges, and surveyors to defraud the state or dispossess lower-class squatters. One judge in fact took 80 percent of the land as his cut for legalizing a claim. Occasionally, legal owners were even forced to hand over their land titles at the point of a gun.[12] The rich had more subtle means of obtaining large blocs of frontier lands by working through state bureaucracies.[13]

Yet powerful fazendeiros did not hesitate to resort to legal tricks or force, or some combination of the two, to obtain new frontier properties. This eventuality was evident to a representative of the Japanese government, who informed his superiors, in 1919, that there were many Japanese nationals working their own land between Bauru and the Mato Grosso border in the Alta Paulista zone; but that as *posseiros* (squatters), they risked losing everything without the assistance of a lawyer.[14] In the

1930's and 1940's, some of the smaller posseiros lost their lands when the state renewed its efforts to legalize claims.[15]

Posseiros of modest means, powerless and inarticulate, left few records of their despoilment. However, the fictional account of Hernâni Donato in *Chão Bruto* (Raw Earth) probably represents the essentials of the process of claim-jumping against lower-class backlanders. In that work, one early pioneer in the Alta Sorocabana zone tells this tale:

When my old lady died and I went down to Salto Grande to register her death, I took the opportunity to list my claim with a notary's office. They gave me a deed covered with seals and blackened with the ink of rubber stamps. But I don't get it. Now they say it's not valid anymore, and that Captain Paulo is the owner, because he has a deed like mine. His is newer, with a lot more seals and stamps, and signed by I-don't-know-what bigwig there in the state capital; mine, on the other hand, only has the signature of a poor backcountry notary. And they say that one of these days Captain Paulo is coming gun in hand, to clear the road and set me walking on it.[16]

In the same novel, Captain Paulo evicts another farmer with what was presumably a typical use of the carrot and the stick. Maneco and his family, who have inhabited a small farm for five years and possess a deed to it, are suddenly told by four of the captain's *capangas* (armed enforcers) to clear out by nightfall, because the land now belongs to him. The leader, Piaçaba, making sure he is not in the line of fire of his three mounted henchmen, says: "What do you think we are? Bandits? You have a deed from the notary, don't you? Hand it over." With this demand, Maneco is proffered a payment far below the market value of the land. He contemplates both resistance and suicide, but finally submits.[17] (Probably the only atypical element in the novel is that the victims had a deed.)

By the late 1940's, the rural inhabitants of Bofete (also in the Alta Sorocabana zone) thought of the good old days as the *tempo de posse*, when everyone could have his spread. In a famous community study, they remembered that the first settlers were followed by "the rich fazendeiros, and because the *caboclos* [backlanders of mixed race] were ignorant, the fazendeiros bought land cheaply from some, and threw others out by force."[18] By the middle of the twentieth century, the caboclos of Bofete, who had begun as squatters, were *parceiros* (sharecroppers); but even this precarious hold on the land seemed to be in jeopardy, for the parceiros tended to become colonos or *camaradas* (unskilled farmhands) as the land became more commercialized.[19]

Money amassed through claim-jumping and land-grabbing was "laundered" over a generation or two. "Behind every great fortune, there stands a crime," wrote Balzac. The writer José Bento Monteiro Lobato put it another way for São Paulo: "To have a grileiro among one's grandparents . . . will be a source of pride for our future millionaires."[20]

Grileiros formed the vanguard for a society on the move. They were just ahead of the railroad and the state government; and the early years of "law and order," incorporating the new territory into the polity and economy, have been termed the "civilization of the *delegado*" by Mário de Andrade.[21] The delegado was a police officer of the São Paulo government with a detachment of the state's Força Pública to back up his orders. The frontier delegado was often fresh out of law school, a *bacharel* who had to adjust quickly to the absence of student bohemia and chorus girls, and to the brutality of the frontier. In Menotti del Picchia's novel *Dente de Ouro* (Gold Tooth), a twenty-two-year-old bacharel arrives in Rio Preto (Araraquarense zone) to tame the frontier by getting rid of horse thieves and other backlands malefactors—but not successful grileiros. On learning of a brawl and cruel murder, the protagonist shouts, "Balls! And for this a man spends five years in a law academy!" In fact, however, such men knew well that they provided a vital link between the power structures of countryside and city, and Menotti's hero is the son of a ruined fazendeiro.[22]

On the frontier grileiros were followed by, and sometimes merged with, established families. Elite families, as well as colonos and *caipiras* (the native posseiro, sharecropper, or smallholder, usually of mixed race), changed residence in succeeding generations, or even more often, as the frontier expanded. The powerful Almeida Prado, Toledo Piza, and Silva Prado families, for example, moved steadily westward along interfluvial plateaus to appropriate fertile virgin lands as the rail network expanded. Magnates like Jorge Tibiriçá and Carlos Leôncio Magalhães bought and sold one huge estate after another.[23] Urban and rural elites became closely linked by intermarriage through their mutual interest in the coffee trade. In the countryside, many merchants became fazendeiros.[24]

To what extent planters left the countryside to reside in the capital as they grew wealthy is not clear. The most successful planters in Rio Claro set up their residences in the capital in the 20 years after the arrival of the railroad, but most of the fazendeiros in nearby São Carlos moved only to the county seat, and alternately made their homes in town and country. Even those who moved to the capital from São Carlos remained involved in the local community until the 1930's.[25]

At the opposite end of the rural social hierarchy stood those who worked the land, and at the bottom, former slaves. São Paulo's freedmen were marginalized in the new rural order, often becoming camaradas on the fazendas, or moving just beyond the pioneer frontier to clear land for advancing estates, and then moving on. The camarada probably spent less time on a given plantation than a colono. Freedmen also served as capangas to keep immigrant workers in line.[26]

Colonos and Caipiras

Colonos formed most of the new rural proletariat. They were shipped from Santos to the Immigrant Hostel in the capital, where authorities were so concerned about an urban "leakage" of the labor supply that the hostel was a kind of prison; the exit ticket was a colono contract. Some, however, beat the game by breaking away from the group as soon as it arrived in Santos and making their way to the capital, where they were protected by friends or relatives from their village or province in the old country.[27]

Contracts at the hostel reflected the price of coffee and the size of the labor pool available to planters. There immigrants could bargain for the best wages and working conditions. Though many fazendeiros violated their contracts, the situation improved after 1906, when the state created a watchdog institution, the Agency of Colonization and Labor. This unit was charged with enforcing contracts and had an effective weapon against violations by the employer: it could deny him access to the Immigrant Hostel, São Paulo's most important marketplace for rural labor.[28]

Planters almost universally assumed that the European immigrant was a more efficient worker than the native Brazilian, often an ex-slave in the early years of the Republic. Others concurred. The American agronomist Eugene Davenport bluntly expressed his dismay at the low quality of São Paulo's native agricultural labor in 1891, three years after abolition.[29] We know, from Dean, that in 1905 the Brazilian workers of Rio Claro had a higher rate of productivity than the Italian immigrants,[30] but his data do not reveal anything about the productivity of ex-slaves. In the Old Republic, planters occasionally experimented with workers from other states. Carlos Leôncio Magalhães, owner of millions of coffee trees in the Baixa Paulista zone, found Cearenses unsatisfactory workers in 1920 because of their poor health; he preferred colonos and above all the Japanese. Of 19 Paulista fazendeiros surveyed by the Sociedade Nacional de Agricultura in 1925, nine considered Brazilian workers "undesirable" and ten approved of them with reservations. Planters cited the indolence, ignorance, and poor health of the Brazilian workers as their reasons.[31]

Italian immigrants in the 1880's and 1890's were reminded in a hundred ways that they had come to the coffee fields to replace slaves. A report on São Paulo's agriculture by a Mineiro investigator in 1888 stated that immigrants were often temporarily "housed" in old slave compounds. Like slaves, these colonos could not enter or leave the plantation without the owner's permission.

There was only one important rural strike in São Paulo before the First World War.[32] Considering that the real income of Italian colonos had been steadily declining in the face of sustained inflation, the relative calm in the countryside attests to the degree of planter social control. In the 1890's, fazendeiros frequently let wages fall into arrears. Beatings were not uncommon; and this was one of the abuses that provoked the Italian government's decree of 1902 prohibiting Italian nationals from participating in Brazil's subsidized immigration programs. Summing up the indictment against planter abuses of immigrant colonos from the 1880's, Michael Hall writes: "For over thirty years, [Italian] consular personnel and travelers . . . were unanimous in strongly recommending that their compatriots not come to work in the coffee fields of São Paulo."[33] Action by the Italian government may have helped bring about the creation of the Agency of Colonization in 1906.

Dissatisfaction with conditions on a given plantation usually led to a move elsewhere—to another plantation, to a town, or often to another country. The fact that 686,000 of the 1,553,000 immigrants who came to São Paulo between 1882 and 1914—that is, 44 percent—chose to leave the state is striking if indirect evidence of the quality of rural working conditions.[34] In 1905 and 1906, years of crisis in the coffee sector but years of good rural wages, between a third and a half of those who left went to Argentina. The exodus was still greater in 1907, a year of net emigration from São Paulo. In part this was because the crop looked poor and the demand for rural labor was limited, but many colonos must also have been enticed by the fact that they could translate their 1906 wages into gold (and Argentine pesos) at a good exchange rate.[35]

In any event, the overall rate of immigrant departure from São Paulo needs to be put into perspective. One scholar, for example, has estimated that the "repatriation" rate for the United States before 1907 may have been over 30 percent, and was as high as 53 percent for Argentina.[36] Even taking into account the fact that some who departed from Argentina were seasonal agricultural workers who migrated between the northern and southern hemispheres, São Paulo probably did not do much worse than Argentina; and in 1911, the Italian government also temporarily prohibited subsidized immigration to that country.

At any rate, when a colono in São Paulo moved, he was far more likely to head for another plantation than to leave the country or take up residence in the capital. Over the 35-year period 1895–1930, fewer than half the colonos on one prosperous fazenda in the Baixa Paulista zone stayed as long as six years, i.e., one cycle of bringing coffee trees to maturity. According to the state's Director of Colonization, 40 percent to 60 percent of the colonos left their fazendas each year (circa 1907?), but this figure seems exaggerated. Possibly as a defensive reaction, planters began to lure colonos away from each other's estates.[37] Since rural strikes were hard to organize or ineffective, changing jobs was apparently the colonos' best defense against exploitation.

Children over seven as well as women accompanied the men into the coffee groves. On the big estates, a large colono family could tend 10,000 trees, at the rate of 2,000 per adult worker. Hookworm was common because colono families worked barefoot. In 1919, by one account, even the children of "successful" immigrants frequently had no elementary schooling, and as late as 1930 two American observers reported that "since the children are very useful, it is not often that the parents or the fazendeiros themselves insist that they go to school."[38] Colonos had to rise at dawn and work until sunset or even later, and were required in the 1880's to have lights out by 10:00 P.M. They were subject to wage reductions, fines, and other forms of exploitation. Often forced to buy their goods at inflated prices at the company store, the colonos had to resort to credit; and to secure this debt they had to pledge the cereal crops and farm animals on which their families subsisted.[39]

Despite all this, some colonos apparently managed to save money. They had three possible sources of cash income. Besides their regular pay for the care of the coffee trees throughout the year, they got piece rates at harvest time, and some worked as needed as day laborers on the fazenda, though often salaried Brazilian labor gangs did this work on the big estates.[40] Moreover, the colonos paid nothing for their housing (the houses provided by the plantation were of masonry and stucco, with brick floors and tile roofs) and had their own plots for garden crops. A report in 1901 estimated that a colono family could save 38 percent of its total cash income; that accords, in broad terms, with a 1911 report on the Ribeirão Preto area, which revealed considerable savings among the Japanese colonos there. Though Dean provides details on the exploitation of colono laborers, he also concedes that the Italian immigrants he studied seem to have achieved a higher standard of living than they had known in Europe.[41] Since employment was seldom slack in frontier regions, colonos often had the opportunity to seek new employment, legally or illegally, elsewhere in the countryside or in the towns.

But how many colonos managed to acquire their own land? Thomas Holloway and Michael Hall, looking specifically at the Italian immigrants, have reached quite different conclusions. Hall, who notes that the real income of colonos fell between 1884 and 1914, and emphasizes the obstacles to their becoming landowners, finds that in 1905, after "twenty years of mass migration . . . it is quite possible that only 6 percent or even less of the land owned [by area] was held by Italians."[42] Holloway, on the other hand, establishes that many Italians did receive land. In part, the disparity in these conclusions can be explained by the fact that Hall's study ends in 1914, whereas Holloway's ends in 1934, after the coffee crisis and the partial or complete breakup of many big estates. Holloway believes that by 1934, 250,000 immigrants and their descendants may have been members of rural property-owning families on farms above minifundium size, assuming five members to a family. As for how the immigrant group alone fared, I doubt whether the "success" rate among the first generation was better than one in eight.[43]

In any case, the achievement of immigrant landowners needs to be set against the fact that half the state was beyond the frontier when mass immigration began. Furthermore, Dean points out that immigrants were a privileged sector of the agricultural proletariat during the Old Republic, and that "discrimination was a precondition for mass migration."[44] Thus their success may say little about the economic mobility of rural lower-class Paulistas and migrants from other states, most of whom arrived in São Paulo after the bulk of the foreign population. It seems likely, as Dean implies, that immigrant "success" was achieved at the expense of native rural workers. However, Dean's judgment that "it cannot be

TABLE 3.1

Land Tenure (by Area) and Population Share of the
Foreign-Born in São Paulo by Zone, 1934

(Percent)

Zone	Share of land	Share of population
Capital	24%	27%
Paraíba Valley	10	3
Central	25	8
Mogiana	15	10
Baixa Paulista	27	12
Araraquarense	31	13
Alta Paulista	31	21
Alta Sorocabana	25	13
Baixa Sorocabana	9	3
Southern Coast	20	21
State average	25%	15%

SOURCE: Camargo, *Crescimento da população*, 2: table 52; 3: table 125.

claimed that . . . 'many' immigrants achieved landownership" is not valid for the 1930's, as Holloway demonstrates. [45]

As we see in Table 3.1, the foreign-born were most successful in acquiring land in two of the three pioneer zones—the Araraquarense and the Alta Paulista. Moreover, in 1934, relative to their share of the population (admittedly a crude indicator, because it includes an urban component), they did better than the native population both in the state as a whole and in every zone but the Capital zone. That foreigners did as well as they did in the Paraíba Valley and Central zones can probably be ascribed to their willingness to buy worn-out coffee lands; in the new western zones their properties were more likely virgin soil.

Finally, in considering the foreign-born population's acquisition of land, it should be recalled that the breakup of coffee fazendas in the 1930's occurred in the context of economic disaster; and in that situation, colonos suffered too, especially the majority who did not become landowners. On one of the largest and best-run estates in the country, the British-owned Fazenda Cambuhy (part of the Brazilian Warrant Company's holdings), colono wages dropped to barely more than a third of their pre-Depression peak by 1931, and many immigrant families on the estate "must have known hunger." The rise in infant mortality there in 1933 "was probably in part due to malnutrition." [46]

Two immigrants, Francisco Schmidt and Geremia Lunardelli, were nonetheless renowned for their coffee wealth long before the Depression. Schmidt, born in 1850 in the Palatinate, arrived in Brazil at age seven; his parents were colonos on several estates, and he claimed to have been one himself, presumably as a child. Though illiterate, Schmidt made a fortune as a merchant and then became a coffee planter. He bought his first fazenda—apparently at a cheap price—soon after abolition, in Ribeirão Preto. By 1914, he possessed 10,000,000 coffee trees, and employed 11,000 colonos in the Ribeirão Preto area. For a time he was also a political boss, but because of his German background, he lost his influence in Ribeirão Preto during the First World War. Schmidt apparently felt that the rural labor system was a just one. Once, when asked by a representative of the Italian government to raise wages during one of the few strikes on his estates, he laconically replied, "I too was a colono. My colonos and I will fulfill the contract." [47]

Lunardelli was born in Venetia 35 years after Schmidt, and began his career in São Paulo as a small-town merchant, not as a colono. He too got his start in coffee-planting in Ribeirão Preto, but moved on to open new estates in Catanduva in the Araraquarense zone and Bauru in the Alta Paulista. By the early 1930's, he had moved still farther west in the "pioneer" Alta Paulista to Araçatuba, where he had a 53,000-hectare estate with 5,000,000 coffee trees and 2,000 head of cattle. He had also purchased virgin lands in Paraná State in 1924, anticipating the future movement of the coffee frontier. Lunardelli managed to maintain his estates during the Depression, in part by switching to the cultivation of cotton and rice. In 1943, he still had 10,000 rural workers in his employ. [48]

The life of the caipira was similar to the colono's but probably more primitive.* For an important report on caipira life in 1891–92 we are indebted to the American agronomist Eugene Davenport, of the University of Michigan, who was employed by the fazendeiro Luís de Queiroz to re-

---

*Although there are many ethnographic studies of local communities of São Paulo, few of them stretch back into the years before 1940. Of the lives and thoughts of individual slaves and ex-slaves we know almost nothing. The scores of narratives and autobiographies of slaves in the United States recorded in the decades before and after the Civil War have no counterparts in Brazil. And in contrast to the literally thousands of narratives collected in the United States in the 1920's and especially in the 1930's (see Rawick, ed., *American Slave*), we have no first-hand recollections of any of Brazil's ex-slaves, so far as I know. This neglect of the personal history of the Brazilian slaves contrasts sharply with the attention devoted (by amateurs) to the genealogies of members of the country's ruling classes. (One worshipful student of President Campos Sales even professed to trace his subject's lineage, generation by generation, back to the founder of the Merovingian dynasty. Gurgel, *Genealogia*, p. 3.)

organize a local agricultural school in Piracicaba (in the Central zone). Though Davenport himself was frustrated in his mission by the political turmoil of the Deodoro and Floriano years, his work eventually bore fruit with the establishment, in 1901, of an agricultural college; it was later named the Luís de Queiroz Institute. It was there, on the Queiroz estate in Piracicaba, that Davenport lived and reported on social conditions in an area as yet little affected by European immigration. He found a two-class society: "Literally there were no middle-class people." Laborers on the Queiroz fazenda subsisted almost exclusively on black beans, supplemented occasionally with pieces of sugarcane they cut in the fields. The daily routine was dull, broken on Sunday by a Portuguese-style bullfight in which the bull survived, but was allowed to gore a horse to death.[49]

On the position of women, Davenport noted:

Women have no standing as such. "A man marries to get a good servant," in the words of Mrs. Queiroz, who was a remarkable woman, well educated and much travelled both in Europe and Asia, as well as the United States.

[Local residents] were all nice to Emma [Davenport's wife], not because she was a woman but because she was mine. They would have been equally nice to my horse or my dog. Except for Mr. and Mrs. Queiroz, I do not remember seeing a man and his wife on the street together. . . . One of the greatest difficulties of the [Protestant] missionaries was to induce their converts to allow the wife at the table.[50]

The position of small-town women remained distinctly subordinate even after the Second World War in at least one caipira-populated município in the Central zone. In 1947–48, according to Donald Pierson, the women in Araçariguama, where there had been little immigration, were still segregated at social functions, were not free to go where they pleased, and were expected to obey their husbands. However, these traditional patterns seemed to Pierson to be breaking down as more and more contacts were made with the expanding metropolis.[51]

Urban Progress

Araçariguama was a sleepy village, to be sure, and hardly comparable to the rich coffee municípios, with their large immigrant populations and frontier mentality. There, society was perhaps more receptive to change, and clearly marked by a respect for material progress and a sense of civic pride. For inhabitants of Campos Novos in the Alta Sorocabana zone,

Salto Grande was the place to "drink civilization" after the railhead reached that town in 1909. With the subsequent rise of economic activity in Campos Novos, civilization followed in the form of newspapers (1910, 1912) and even electric lighting (1913).[52] By 1913, there were a half dozen newspapers, as well as 17 societies and clubs of various sorts, in Ribeirão Preto (Mogiana zone), where the railroad had arrived in 1883 and electric lighting in 1899. A successful campaign against yellow fever in the town was carried out in 1903. In this, the world's coffee capital around 1910, a Corsican immigrant and former waiter began importing European prostitutes for his bordellos as early as 1895.[53] Like Ribeirão Preto, São Carlos, a coffee-growing município in the Baixa Paulista zone, was flooded with immigrants. The railhead reached the community in 1885, and five years later telephones were being installed in the city and a few even on the larger estates. Electric lighting arrived in 1892, and in 1914, electric streetcars.[54]

The most dazzling transformations occurred, of course, in the capital, fueled by the massive population growth discussed in Chapter One. Juergen Langenbuch has distinguished three phases in the city's physical growth: the "premetropolitan" phase, 1875–1915, when a belt of small rural properties around the city was subdivided for urban development; the "early metropolitan" phase, 1915–40, marked by the growth of the periphery and a fuller differentiation of industrial-working-class and bourgeois-residential zones, made possible by the development of mass transportation; and, from 1940 onward, the full-scale "metropolitanization" phase, with an intensification of earlier processes, the determination of new areas of growth by superhighway grids and axes, and "vertical" growth in the form of skyscrapers in downtown areas.[55]

Hilly areas of the city were more salubrious than lower regions, where property values were correspondingly lower. Topography made for a low density of habitation, burdening the transport system, public works programs, and utilities networks. Furthermore, the rate of urbanization was so rapid as to constitute a major problem in itself; the city doubled in area, for example, between 1899 and 1909. Services consistently lagged behind as the city expanded. Inadequate transport facilities between grain mills and centers of consumption played no little part in the lower classes' support for the military rebellion in the city in 1924.[56]

In 1892, the state government agreed to channel the Tietê and Tamanduateí rivers flowing through the city, and to set up a sanitation commission to deal with the malarial Tietê floodplain. Work did not begin on the floodplain until the turn of the century, but in the meantime the pestilential Anhangabaú Valley was cleaned up and channeled; the Viaduto do Chá had already spanned the valley in 1892, and a second viaduct crossed it in 1913.[57]

Gas lighting arrived in the city in 1872, and electric lighting followed in the 1880's, though the area serviced was minuscule until 1900. These facilities were provided by foreign investors, but the company that made São Paulo's new water and sewer systems the best in all Brazil was a local one, organized by Paulista capitalists in 1877. The per-capita water supply expanded tenfold between 1891 and 1894, as the state government intervened. But even so, water shortages cropped up now and again as the city grew.[58]

Mule-drawn trolleys appeared in 1872, the same year the gas company was founded; they began to yield to electric streetcars in 1900, the same year as electric lighting began to replace gas lighting on a significant scale. São Paulo's first hydroelectric station followed in 1901. All of these services proved more or less inadequate as the city's population burgeoned. Moreover, by the First World War, all city utilities and services were foreign-owned, except for telephone service and streetcleaning.[59]

The city's revenues would have been the envy of any other Brazilian município except the Federal District, but the demand for services far outstripped income. Though the city's revenues almost doubled between 1893 and 1904, the amount spent on public works alone increased almost seven times.[60] The tax base from the 1880's to the First World War never expanded as rapidly as the population, and that base was small. In 1903, roughly 9,000 people in a population of some 250,000 paid the tax that provided the largest single share of revenue, that on industries and professions.[61] Even though the state assumed responsibility for providing sanitation and lighting, the inexorable demand for public facilities pointed to the solution of foreign borrowing (a theme we will return to in Chapter Eight). Partly because association with the state government was important for direct income as well as for borrowing prospects, the city's public works, at least before 1914, tended to grow during periods of prosperity in the coffee industry (since more than half of the prewar state revenues derived from the coffee export tax).[62]

The relationship between altitude and healthfulness, and the consequent differences in property values from hill to valley and plain, led directly to the geographic segregation of social classes in the capital. Though most immigrants headed for the rural areas, some settled in the capital; even in 1886—just before mass immigration began—the foreign-born accounted for a quarter of the city's population. By 1893, as the first wave of Italians streamed in, the proportion rose to more than half. Anti-Italian riots broke out in 1896, but immigrants kept pouring into the city, some directly from the docks at Santos, others from the plantations. By 1920, the foreign-born represented 52 percent of the city's industrial labor force, though Brazilians formed a majority of the industrial workers in the state as a whole.[63] The district of Brás, in the lowlands east of the old city center, became the most important residential area for the working class; by 1910 or so, it contained about a third of the city's population. The district's representatives on the city council were especially militant in trying to get the city government to provide public services of the same quality as those the affluent residents enjoyed.[64] In 1917, workers actually took control of Brás during a general strike.

Upper-class Paulistanos (as the capital's inhabitants are called) built their homes on the eastern hills of the central spine running through the city; the first "completely new aristocratic neighborhood," Campos Elíseus (Champs Elysées), dates from 1879. In the 1890's, Higienópolis (Healthtown), on the flanks of the central spine, became the most fashionable residential area. But the Avenida Paulista, which followed the maximum elevation of the central spine, was already challenging Higienópolis as the most desirable neighborhood by the turn of the century. The Avenida Paulista was traversed by the elegant Avenida Angélica, bordering Higienópolis. These two avenues tended to be the residences of the industrial elite of immigrant origins. Jardim América, dating from 1910, was the first garden suburb for the well-to-do.[65]

The wealthier fazendeiros began to build themselves city homes as early as the 1870's and 1880's. They soon joined with other members of the upper classes in establishing a Jockey Club (1875) for their amusement. Another favorite gathering place for the "society" of the capital was Guarujá, a suburb of Santos, which became the Paulistas' answer to Rio, the cynosure of other state elites. The Prado family began investing in Guarujá as a resort area in 1892. In 1910, Georges Clemenceau found it a delight, conveniently located only 20 minutes by tram from the bay of Santos.[66]

Other diversions for the elite included the performances of foreign theatrical and musical troupes. An Italian opera company played the capital city in 1874. Sarah Bernhardt performed there in 1886—and also, as noted, in Campinas, a sign, perhaps, that the cultural supremacy of the capital was not yet assured. Such hegemony probably came in the 1890's; it was certainly well established before 1918, a year that saw the transfer of the exclusive Colégio São Luís, a Jesuit preparatory school, from Itu to the Avenida Paulista.[67]

Immigrants too could scale the heights of the Avenida Paulista, as Francisco Matarazzo proved; and if we may judge by Ignazio Silone's *Bread and Wine*, word of a few successful immigrants' palatial homes on the Avenidas Paulista and Angélica even spread to remote villages of the Abruzzi, where some migrants to São Paulo had originated. In Plínio Salgado's novel *The Foreigner*, an immigrant industrialist, reflecting on the distance from Brás to Higienópolis, has no doubt that "the distance could be overcome. It was a condition of the bourgeois Republic."[68] True enough—for small numbers—and success for the few in Higienópolis may have helped legitimize the system for the many who remained in Brás.

Family and Class

At the apex of the urban social pyramid were the elite families, who moved about easily between their rural and urban residences. The "400-year-old family" (*quatro centão*) in São Paulo is largely a myth, though many families do date back to the colonial era.[69] The Silva Prados, for example, arrived from Portugal in the early eighteenth century. But many of the leading families, such as the Mesquitas and the Rodrigues Alveses, extend back no further than the early nineteenth century. In most cases, however, marriage ties in a thin elite, separated from the masses by a social chasm, provided a means for dressing up unadorned family trees. New sugar or coffee fortunes brought "family" in their train, in the style of Calogero Sedàra in Giuseppe di Lampedusa's *The Leopard*: "His family, I am told, is an old one or soon will be." Yet the myth was important: "A Paulista of 400 years would never pass unnoticed in the crowd in the Rua da Direita" (in the capital's business district), wrote the journalist Joel Silveira in 1945.[70]

The extended family, or *parentela*, was traditionally an important part of the lives of all social groups. Even in 1948, Pierson found a young woman in Araçariguama who could recall without effort the names of

166 consanguinial and affinitive relatives. In the capital, however, lower-class families tended to be organized in nuclear units by the 1960's, though the extended family continued to thrive among the upper classes.[71]

The internal dynamics of upper-class families in Brazil, as elsewhere in Latin America, are poorly understood. Darrell Levi's dissertation on the Silva Prados is one of the few professional studies of an elite family in Brazil. The following discussion is based on his findings.

The founding father of the family was Antônio Prado, a Portuguese immigrant who came to São Paulo in the opening year of the eighteenth century and invested in mining during the Minas gold rush. His descendants were merchants and sugar planters. Already in the 1700's the family's pattern of intermarriage with other important families had begun —Morais Leme, Queiroz Teles, Pereira de Queiroz. Marriage between cousins was common, and a small number of given names appeared from generation to generation. The third Antônio Prado (Barão de Iguape) was a capitalist, sugar merchant, tax farmer, and mule- and slavetrader. One of his illegitimate children, Veridiana, whom he married to his half-brother, was the mother of Antônio Prado (the fourth), Eduardo, and Martinho Júnior (Martinico), who figure in this book. Veridiana became the family matriarch, after separating from her husband; her *chácara* was a literary salon, and she knew and was admired by the Portuguese novelist Eça de Queiroz. She was one of the first Paulistas to hire a French governess for her children; and her sons received part of their educations in Europe, as did Antônio's sons Paulo, the essayist, and Antônio Prado Júnior. (Except for legal training, higher education abroad was fairly common within the social elite in the late nineteenth century, and though most young men went to Europe, some Paulistas chose to study in the United States.[72])

Intermarriage among the Prados and related families was less common by the late nineteenth century, though it was still frequent in the most important branches of the family. In addition, interrelated families often appeared on the boards of directors of Prado business ventures.[73] As an indication of the value the old families attached to their names, consider the case of Armando Prado, the bastard son of Eleutério (uncle of Eduardo, Martinico, and Antônio) by one of Eleutério's black cooks. Though illegitimate and a mulatto, Armando was still a Prado: he was valedictorian at the São Paulo Law School, and was a member of the political elite studied in this work.

By the Estado Novo era, and probably earlier, the oldest families were only one element in the capital's chic society, the so-called *grã-finos*, which also included a smart set with new money and a circle of small-town professionals with intellectual or social gifts (though Joel Silveira noted, in 1945, that one of this circle's "sonneteers" had published his only collection in 1912; fortunately, *"grã-finismo* [wasn't] very demanding"). São Paulo for the grã-finos was the Jaraguá, a bookstore cum tearoom, based on European models, and hot spots like The Roof and the Jequiti.[74]

The urban middle sectors in São Paulo were probably not very different from the rural elite in their values and aspirations,[75] but they were the closest thing Brazil had to a European bourgeoisie—certainly closer than the traditional bureaucratic stratum that staffed the patrimonial state in Rio de Janeiro. The reason why the Modern Art movement made such a triumph in the state capital, thought the poet Mário de Andrade, was that "there was a classic bourgeoisie to be shocked."[76]

São Paulo city's haute-bourgeoisie impressed some foreigners, and Paulistanos too, as vulgar and garish. Much of the criticism was directed at the immigrant nouveau riche; the lavish wedding reception Matarazzo threw for his daughter Filly was sneered at in some circles.[77] And though the French writer Louis Mouralis professed to admire São Paulo in the early 1930's (complete with 6:00 P.M. traffic jam), he dubbed the city "Babbitt-town." One could indeed find dry martinis in the Hotel Esplanada, he noted, but "the refinements of a breeding borrowed from European societies, flaunted with ostentation, have the effect of an unintended caricature, and in no way conceal the sentiments of a primitive crudeness. One quickly gets the impression that in [the hotel cocktail lounge] everything is false, except the jewels."[78] The anthropologist Claude Lévi-Strauss, reminiscing on the Brazil of the 1930's in *Tristes Tropiques*, was only slightly less condescending toward the Paulistano bourgeoisie than his compatriot.[79]

That bourgeoisie was increasingly composed of comparatively new arrivals. A study of the social mobility of São Paulo city in the 1950's showed that immigrants and the children of immigrants had greater ambitions to rise in the social order than the Brazilians of older origins.[80] In the first generation (those who arrived during the Old Republic), a number of Italian immigrants had risen on the social scale by becoming wholesalers of foodstuffs (e.g. grain dealers) and had frequently received their early commercial experience as fruit vendors or greengrocers in the capital or as *mascates* (peddlers) in the interior of the state. The last-named occupation was an especially important background for future wholesalers, because it provided contacts with buyers and suppliers and a knowledge of market conditions.[81]

All sectors of the bourgeoisie tended to share the civic pride that manifested itself among the grã-finos in a professed dislike for the city of Rio.[82] That attitude, whether feigned or not, was probably healthier than the intense desire to move to the federal capital, so characteristic of the social elites of Pernambuco and Minas Gerais. But civic pride among the Paulistanos easily slipped into boosterism, and many were sure that the future of urban Brazil lay with their city, not Rio de Janeiro. In 1935, the young Lévi-Strauss was assured by local boosters that São Paulo city was growing at the rate of one new house per hour.[83] And despite certain crudenesses and contradictions—Mário de Andrade called the city a "Gallicism bawling in the wilderness of America"—the capital was also the center of Modernism, Brazil's most important artistic movement in the 1920's and 1930's. In cultural matters, as in other respects, São Paulo city dominated the state far more obviously than Belo Horizonte dominated Minas Gerais.

Though the city could not compete with Rio in terms of physical beauty, wealthier Paulistanos preferred (or professed to prefer) to vacation in Guarujá. Furthermore, since the bourgeois Paulistano's self-image included a certain earnestness about life, he would probably have expressed contempt for the attitude of Senator Gilberto Amado, the ex-provincial of Sergipe and convert to Carioca ways: "I don't trust anyone who, if he can, doesn't go to the beach."[84]

Most of the capital's inhabitants clearly did not have to concern themselves about when and where to vacation. Industrialization created a large new proletariat whose wages were far below a level that would permit a workingman to provide the bare necessities for wife and children. Like their counterparts in the colono family, the women and children of the industrial proletariat often contributed directly to the family's income. Dean points out that in 1919, according to the reckoning of a government agency, the food bill alone for a family of seven was four times what the average worker made in São Paulo city. Sheldon Maram reaches similar conclusions using data for the same year.[85]

A cost-of-living index for São Paulo city from 1913 to 1934 indicates that the prices workers had to pay for goods and the wages they received repeatedly moved past one another, with wages (based on 1913 figures) doing best from 1928 to 1931.[86] Yet a survey of the working-class's scale of living in 1934 revealed that conditions verged on misery. The median monthly income of 221 families (averaging 5.4 members) was 320 milréis, or U.S. $22.40, in April–May 1934. More than half that income was spent on food alone, and rent took another 20–25 percent. More than a quarter of the families were undernourished in terms of calorie intake, and fewer than 3 percent got enough milk. For the vast majority, charcoal was the only source of energy in the home, and nearly half the families lived in either one- or two-room dwellings. Only eight of the 221 families had private bathrooms.[87]

Textile workers in Rio and São Paulo, before the partially successful strikes of 1919, typically worked nine and a half to 12 hours a day, six days a week, and sometimes seven. Children were often badly exploited and even physically abused. In one of the worst instances, children as young as eight years old worked a 12-hour day in Matarazzo's Mariângela plant in 1907. A 1901 survey revealed that even five-year-olds were being used in some factories, and later documents show that the employment of children under ten was "frequent." Children were sometimes treated cruelly by older workers, and young boys were subject to homosexual abuses. The state's Lei Sanitária of 1917 prohibited work by children under twelve, and night work by anyone under eighteen, but enforcement was poor. Fines were often applied to workers in the early years of the century, and even to child workers, with the proceeds reverting to the factory owners.[88]

Against such exploitation, workers organized and struck, though the overall picture is hardly one of smashing success, partly because of government support for employers. In 1906, local, state, and even federal forces were called out to quell the rail workers' strike against the Companhia Paulista; the president of the company was the tycoon Antônio Prado, who also happened to be the mayor of the capital and thus in control of the city's police force. Employers used agents provocateurs on occasion to stir workers to violent action; and federal legislation to expel anarchists was enacted from time to time at the initiative of Paulista congressmen. Victories by determined strikers were sometimes followed by the deportation of "ringleaders" and the firing of "troublemakers," and then by the revocation of concessions (the eight-hour day, for example, was won and then lost again in the years after 1907 and in 1920).[89] This is the context in which the unionization of workers and the frequency of strikes must be considered (see Chapter Seven).

The first federal welfare legislation for workers was enacted in 1919, with a workmen's compensation plan for accidental injury and death. In the early 1920's Brazilian workers received two weeks' paid vacation under legislation sponsored by President Bernardes. São Paulo employers were "appalled" when they discovered Bernardes intended to enforce the law, but they generally managed to circumvent it until the Vargas years.[90] More important because of the precedent it set was the federal Elói Chaves Law of 1923, which gave railroad workers retirement and survivors' pensions. This statute, drafted by a Paulista congressman, was later applied to a wide variety of other workers and became the basis for Brazil's social security system.

Labor's major gains, however, came about through the paternalist reforms of the Vargas era. In November 1930, São Paulo's workers got a 40-hour work week. A succession of other laws followed over the next decade. The competition for jobs was reduced with the closing of the immigration gates in 1934. By 1943, workers could take satisfaction in the enforcement of paid holidays; more effective legislation regulating the conditions under which women and children could work; a minimum wage law; and an expansion of social security benefits.[91]

Still, the working class, for all the harshness of its life, had its diversions even in the early years of the century. Before the First World War, workers in Brás and Belenzinho already had their own adaptation of soccer, the fashionable sport for which upper-class Paulistanos had established exclusive clubs at the end of the nineteenth century. The working-class version was rough, and some players even went armed to the matches. Italian, Spanish, and Portuguese immigrants participated, often basing their teams on the factories where they worked. (In Recife, by contrast, the lower classes did not take up soccer until the 1940's.)[92] Working-class families, as we shall see, also flocked to movie houses before the war.

Immigrant groups, including both proletarians and the upwardly mobile, valued their native cultures; and the "tongue of Dante" was prized not only by Italians who spoke the national language, but also by southerners who spoke dialect. The Teatro Colombo in Brás was inaugurated in 1908, with an Italian company performing a work by Paolo Giacometti. Brass bands frequently paraded through Brás, playing Italian military

marches and patriotic songs (often out of tune), the emblem of the patron
of their native village borne proudly aloft. Italian cuisine was popular
in the city almost immediately, and macaroni and polenta later invaded
the caipira diet as well.[93] Language was also affected. A "macaronic"
Italo-Portuguese slang heard on the streets of the capital was soon sati-
rized in mock-epic poems by Juó Bananére ("Giohnny" Banana-man).[94]

Cultural Institutions and Agents

The polyglot city was linked to the countryside by a good communications network. The first revolution in Brazilian communications was ush-
ered in by the telegraph, which often advanced into the interior side by
side with the railroad. Brazil's first line was laid in 1852 between Rio and
the summer capital, Petrópolis; and by 1875, Campinas, São Paulo, and
Santos were linked into a national network extending from Rio Grande do
Sul to Pernambuco. By then, Brazil was connected by cable to the United
States, Europe, and all the South American republics of the southern cone.
From the beginning, the central government was interested in telegraphy
for military reasons, with the result that by 1929 the second- and third-
largest networks were found in Mato Grosso and Rio Grande do Sul, respectively. The largest network was in Minas Gerais; São Paulo ranked
only fourth, though it had more lines per square kilometer than Minas.[95]

Telephones came to the state capital in 1884. By 1895, there were 680
instruments in the city, and calls could be placed to Santos. By then,
too, as noted earlier, rich planters were introducing telephones on their
fazendas. There were 5,000 telephones in the state by 1907 and 10,000
by 1913. By 1937, São Paulo city alone had 45,000, more than any other
state capital, though only half as many as the Federal District.[96]

The press likewise made rapid gains in the years under study. From the
1890's onward, new publications were launched at an ever-quickening
pace, to the point where almost 500 journals and papers were founded in
the decade 1920–29.[97] In 1912, São Paulo had by far the largest number
of periodicals in the Federation (including the Federal District); and this
was still true in 1930. In that year, the state was second only to the district
in the number of persons employed in journalism.[98]

From 1911 to 1929, the number of daily newspapers in São Paulo
nearly doubled, to a total of 66, the largest number in all of Brazil's constituent units, and more than twice as many as in the Federal District.[99]

Circulation figures for these dailies are sparse, but their distribution probably increased enormously over the course of the Republic. *A Província de S. Paulo* (subsequently *O Estado de S. Paulo*) had a circulation of 4,000 in 1888. *Correio Paulistano*, by contrast, had a daily printing of only 1,800 copies in 1890, the year in which it became the official organ of the Partido Republicano Paulista, the establishment party. In 1935, the capital had eight dailies with a circulation of 20,000 or more. The largest paper, *O Estado*, printed 90,000 copies on weekdays and 105,000–110,000 on Sundays. No paper in Rio, and presumably none elsewhere in Brazil, had a circulation of more than 80,000.[100] But São Paulo city's dailies had a decided advantage: a rail network that allowed them to reach readers in many backcountry towns on the day of publication.[101] By the late 1930's, they were able to extend their distribution still farther with the establishment of regular air routes to several towns in the state's interior and even more distant points.[102]

From the middle years of the Old Republic, the capital's dailies ran detailed news reports about communities in the interior of the state. Thus local newspapers did not have the same weight in São Paulo's regional culture as they did in Minas Gerais, just as culture in general was more thoroughly dominated by the state capital in São Paulo than in Minas. In fact, most of the Mineiros in both the Sul and the Triângulo got their out-of-town newspapers from São Paulo, not Belo Horizonte.

Each major immigrant community had one or more newspapers of its own in São Paulo, though Portuguese-language papers were predominant even in the age of mass immigration. In 1911, only 11 of the state's 211 newspapers were not published in Portuguese; four of these were in Italian, four in Arabic, and one each in French, German, and Spanish. But several of these papers had a substantial following. Of the eight dailies in the capital in 1935, two were large foreign-language papers: *Fanfulla* (Italian) had a circulation of 35,000 and the *Diário Alemão* (German), a circulation of 20,000.[103]

For the illiterate, mass communications came later, with the introduction of the cinema and the radio. In 1937, São Paulo had more than a quarter of Brazil's 887 cinemas, placing it far ahead of Minas and the Federal District, the units with the next largest numbers.[104] Motion pictures were immensely popular. The working-class districts had neighborhood cinemas as early as 1911. In one movie house in Belenzinho, each show was introduced by a band playing Italian marches, and in the early years, three feature films (usually from Italy or France), plus several short subjects, were strung together in a single showing, lasting five hours. Entire families attended, bringing sandwiches and bottled water.[105] Soon after the outbreak of the First World War, Paulistanos were viewing Pathé newsreels of "The European Conflagration."[106] By the mid-1930's, when the capital had over 30 movie houses, one indication of the cinema's popularity was that advertisements for a new feature film could occupy as much as half a page in a nine-column newspaper.

Regular radio broadcasting began in Rio in 1920, and São Paulo got its first station in 1924. A year earlier, towns in the interior as far from the capital as Araraquara were linked to radio in Rio by relay transmitters. By 1937, São Paulo had 28 of Brazil's 63 radio stations, by far the largest number; 18 of these were located outside the capital. Not surprisingly, the state also had by far the largest number of sets in the country: 153,000, or 44 percent of the national total.[107]

In the mid-1930's, most of the air time on the capital's stations was devoted to recordings of music; half-hour segments featured the music of Brazil, Italy, the United States, Argentina, Portugal, and other countries. Songs from films were especially popular, but jazz, operas, and symphonies were also aired. Radio serials had yet to be introduced, but sportscasts had made a debut. At 7:30 P.M. came the federal government's daily news and propaganda segment, the "Hora Nacional." Most, but not yet all, stations carried the half-hour program.

As in radio broadcasting, São Paulo was a leader in the field of education. At the end of the Empire, however, the Paulistas were in the same sorry state as the Brazilians in general, which is to say, overwhelmingly illiterate. The Empire bequeathed the Republic a national literacy rate of 15 percent (figure for 1890, all ages); and São Paulo's rate was 1 percent below the national average. Excluding the Federal District, which had virtually no rural education problem and therefore is not comparable to the states, São Paulo then ranked tenth among Brazil's constituent units. But by 1920 it had jumped to second place among the states, with 30 percent literacy for all ages, trailing Rio Grande do Sul, with 39 percent. São Paulo was still in second place in 1940 (with 52 percent literacy among those over age five), and this despite the huge numbers of migrants it received from other states between the two census years.[108]

In 1872, Brazil had only 151,000 pupils in primary and secondary schools in a national population of more than 10,000,000—or one pupil for every 68 inhabitants, compared with one in five or six in the United States. São Paulo, with a ratio of 1 : 74, ranked in the bottom half of the provinces.[109]

São Paulo improved its position considerably in the final phase of the Empire, with 26,000 students for a pupil-to-population ratio of 1 : 47 in 1886, compared with a national ratio of 1 : 75 at the end of the regime.[110] But its largest gains were still in the future: the enrollment in state-supported primary schools more than doubled between 1907 and 1912, when the number of pupils reached 124,000; and that figure tripled before the end of the First Republic. In 1929, the state's combined public and private primary-school enrollment was near the half-million mark. The ratio of all primary-school children to population in that year was 1 : 13. Over roughly the same period, the number of primary schools increased almost fourfold, from 2,400 in 1910 to 8,200 in 1930.[111]

These figures reveal that São Paulo's "success" in diffusing education lies in the second half of the Old Republic. We will consider how that success was accomplished after a brief look at the earlier period. Under the Empire, a provincial law of 1874 instituted compulsory education for all girls aged seven to eleven and all boys aged seven to fourteen (except slaves, of course), but enforcement was apparently not seriously contemplated by the lawmakers. Moreover, the province's single Normal School, sponsored by the provincial government, led a fitful existence. Apparently most of the primary teachers were men until the Republic. One of the people responsible for a change in this situation was Marcia Browne, an American school administrator who helped reorganize São Paulo's Normal School in 1894, and also helped establish "model" schools run by the state.[112]

The early Republic also witnessed the establishment of new professional schools in the capital. Under the Empire, there were only a half dozen such institutions of all sorts (law, medicine, engineering) in the whole country, among them the São Paulo Law School, founded in 1827. In addition to upgrading the Normal School, the state subsidized a new Polytechnic School in 1895. In 1896, Mackenzie College, founded by Methodists from the United States, added an engineering division and also set up Brazil's first business administration school. A college of pharmacy and dentistry followed in 1899. The only institution of higher education outside the capital was the aforementioned college of agriculture established at Piracicaba (Central zone) in 1901. A school of medicine was established in 1913; until then, most Paulista physicians had taken their degrees in Rio.

It was in the field of primary education, however, that São Paulo made the most innovations, setting a model for the rest of the nation in the latter half of the Old Republic. São Paulo educators introduced the *grupo escolar*, a primary school with graded classes and trained teachers. The state government emphasized urban education, and children were ideally to have six or seven years of primary education (in classes with 40 children of the same sex) in urban areas, compared with only three or four years in rural ones. In 1918, 59 percent of the children in São Paulo's grupos escolares were promoted to the next grade; in Bahia, by contrast, only 9 percent were promoted in the early 1920's. São Paulo's system gradually became the standard for other states, and many of them copied its statutes on education.[113]

The end of the First World War saw a wave of educational reforms in São Paulo, stimulated in part by the new sense of patriotism propagated by the Liga Nacionalista, an elite group whose leaders came from the law school. In São Paulo, as in other parts of Brazil during the second decade of the twentieth century, intellectuals and professionals became aware of the crippling problem of disease among lower-class Brazilians, and Liga spokesmen argued that literacy was essential for the diffusion of proper notions of hygiene.[114] The Liga Nacionalista also promoted Scouting to instill values of hygiene, discipline, and patriotism.

The Liga program found official support in the administration of Governor Washington Luís (1920–24) in the person of Antônio Sampaio Dória, Director of Public Education, who conducted a census of the state schools in 1920, the first in Brazil's history. Dória discovered that illiteracy was even greater than had been suspected, and that fewer than a third of the children in the state attended classes. An education reform law was passed that very year, with the goals of immediately eliminating illiteracy among school-age children, improving the health of the rural population, and inculcating patriotism. The law replaced the four-year compulsory system with a two-year crash program, in which the schools were set on double shifts in order to equip the largest possible number of children with basic reading skills. Despite attempts to hold this reform within the initial budget, the state's education expenditures increased 22 percent (in constant terms) in Washington Luís's term.[115] From 1920 to

1924, public-school enrollment rose from 195,000 to 267,000; in roughly the same period, average daily attendance climbed from 50 percent to 61 percent. Combined public and private primary-school enrollment rose 44 percent during the Washington Luís administration.[116]

In part, this program was designed in the interest of the planters, on the premise that the construction of more schools in the countryside would encourage rural residence; but the influence of fazendeiro-dominated politicians in the schools was diminished by the new statewide administrative apparatus that was created to enforce the law. In any case, planters allowed "hundreds of new schools" to be built on their fazendas.[117] Washington Luís's successor, Carlos de Campos, however, dismantled the program in 1925, in part because he felt that the aim of achieving basic literacy for the masses was too ambitious for a two-year program. He also relaxed the attempts to enforce school attendance, and returned the control of school appointments to local political leaders.[118]

Congruent with planter interests was the virtual neglect of secondary education in the early years of the Republic. Pierre Denis, visiting São Paulo in 1907, judged that if the state was to gain a middle class, "the question of secondary education is today one of extreme gravity." He noted that there were only three public secondary schools in the state, and that the one in the capital had just 145 students in a total population in excess of 300,000. But here too there was an awakening to a problem and a response in the latter years of the First Republic. São Paulo educators hosted the first national congress on secondary education in 1911. As for numbers, the percentages plainly reflect the state's increased emphasis on the upper grades; thus, whereas secondary students accounted for only 2 percent of the school enrollments in 1910, by 1929 the figure had reached 7 percent. In the same years the number of school-age children enrolled doubled.[119]

By the 1920's, the Paulistas' pioneering methods had caught the attention of educators and political leaders all over Brazil. A primer for rural pupils by the Paulista Thales de Andrade was adopted in many states. The Paulista Manuel Lourenço Filho was invited to Ceará to reform that state's schools in 1922, and José Ribeiro Escobar was invited to Pernambuco in 1928 to undertake a similar mission.[120] As President of Brazil (1926–30), Washington Luís brought the young Paulista educator Fernando de Azevedo to Rio to reform the methods of instruction in the schools of the Federal District. The composer Heitor Villa-Lobos returned from Europe in 1930, got involved in musical education in São Paulo, and was invited to Rio by Anísio Teixeira, who continued Azevedo's work in the Federal District after the Revolution of 1930.[121]

Azevedo himself was by then back in São Paulo, pursuing his efforts to translate his educational theories into practice. In 1933, he drew up a new Code of Education for the state. Meanwhile, disturbed by the Catholic Church's campaign to institute religious education in all the schools in the country, he, Lourenço Filho, Teixeira, and other self-styled Pioneers of the New Education had issued a manifesto calling for free, nonsectarian education.[122]

In 1934, Azevedo helped Governor Armando Sales Oliveira and Júlio Mesquita Filho launch the University of São Paulo, in a sense Brazil's first real university.[123] Many of the ideas of the Pioneers' manifesto were repeated in the founding decree. One of the innovations inspired by the Pioneers was to provide university education for future secondary teachers, a program that constituted "a tremendous boost in prestige for the entire educational system."[124] The university emphasized the social sciences, and young but extremely promising European scholars were recruited for faculty positions, among them Fernand Braudel and Claude Lévi-Strauss.[125] Meanwhile, the influence of North American social scientists was felt at the Free School of Sociology and Politics, an institution founded in 1933 by Roberto Simonsen and others and designed to teach members of both the traditional elite and the middle classes how to deal with new ideologies and social forces. (The school's founders had in mind the social unrest in the capital since the outset of the Depression.)[126]

The university reforms of the 1930's were carried out by men who were trying to combat the new influence of the Catholic Church in education and other fields. The "religiosity" of a regional culture is difficult to measure satisfactorily, and there are few indexes for our era. Most of the available data for the period 1889–1937 cluster around 1910. In that year, São Paulo had one Catholic seminary student for every 13,000 inhabitants, placing it seventh among the states; the Federal District and six states had none at all. By the measure of Church sacraments, again in 1910, São Paulo ranked tenth of 21 units in the proportion of last rites, tenth in marriages, and tenth in baptisms.*

*DGE, Annuario, 1: 252, and 3: 135, 136, 138, 937. There were many more lower-form seminarians than higher-form seminarians in São Paulo and the other states; this may

These data suggest that São Paulo's regional culture did not display the "hyper-religiosity" ascribed to the cultures of Antioquia, Colombia, and Nuevo León, Mexico, two other areas of Latin America that experienced rapid economic growth in the period under examination and were not national administrative centers.[127] The charge was seldom made explicitly, as it was of the Antioqueños, that São Paulo's economic and political leaders were "New Christians" (descendants of converted Jews). However, Paulo Prado briefly alluded to such a thesis in his *Retrato do Brasil* (Portrait of Brazil), published in 1928. Nine years later, in a scurrilously anti-Semitic tract, the Integralist writer Gustavo Barroso alleged that several leading political figures in São Paulo were Jews or "semi-Jews," including former Governor Armando Sales. Barroso hoped to expose some kind of ominous link between the large Jewish banking houses of Europe and their local agents and defenders, but most of his charges were pure fantasies.[128]

São Paulo had a dynamic Church hierarchy, whose activities are discussed in Chapter Seven. The Church and its archbishop were the butt of satirical poetry as late as the 1920's,[129] but São Paulo's middle classes experienced a partial recatholicization in the 1920's and 1930's, an expression, perhaps, of their growing conservatism in the face of a changing world order. Despite the position of the Pioneers of the New Education, São Paulo's delegation at the Constituent Assembly of 1933–34 went along with the Vargas government's introduction of religious instruction in public schools, though a Paulista, the Socialist (and Protestant pastor) Guaraci Silveira, was the leading opponent of the measure in the parliamentary debates.

Silveira represented a growing but still tiny religious community in São Paulo. In 1910, far less than 1 percent of the people in the state were professed Protestants, and despite some gains over time, the overwhelming majority of the population was and is Catholic. In 1940, still only a little more than 2 percent of the Paulistas were Protestants. In

---

imply that many of the lower-form students were simply getting a Catholic secondary education. For the secular seminarians in the higher forms (*cursos maiores*), São Paulo had 1 per 104,000 inhabitants, ranking 10th among the states; no data are given on numbers of priests. See *ibid.*, 3: 937. The 1940 census gives no data on seminary students, but does provide figures on persons who had completed seminary training. In that year, São Paulo had 1 clergyman per 6,000 inhabitants, ranking 4th among the nation's 21 administrative units. Unfortunately, the data do not give Catholic priests as a separate group. See IBGE, *Recenseamento*, 1940. *Serie nacional*, 2: 67, 91.

that year, as in 1910, they were less well represented in the state than in Brazil as a whole.[130] The Protestants' efforts at conversion were almost certainly hampered by the fact that most of the denominations excluded godparenthood, a basic form of solidarity in traditional Brazilian society. Perhaps the greatest social impact of the American and British Protestant missionary effort was in secondary and higher education, of which the most successful institutions were Mackenzie College and the associated American School, established in the capital in 1871.

In an age of materialism whose values held sway in São Paulo at least until the late 1920's, those who crafted the products of "higher" culture had little interest in religion, at least as a source of artistic inspiration. In many respects, São Paulo city was the locus of the most important cultural developments in Brazil during the 1920's and 1930's. Certainly the central event of the period was São Paulo's Modern Art Week, held in February 1922. That event, and the larger Modernist movement it represented, were conditioned in part by the rise of nationalism in Brazil during the First World War, but also by the Brazilians' sense of being out of things, the feeling that there was a new and revolutionary European world of art that they had to discover and assimilate.

Nationalist themes had been in the air as the war in Europe raged, and the São Paulo–based reviews *Revista do Brasil* (1916) and *Brazilia* (1917) turned this mood into a call for the conscious creation of a national culture. *Revista do Brasil* was inspired by the Futurist poet Filippo Marinetti and his insistence on masculinity and vitality as traits of authentic national cultures; this theme was picked up and repeated by the Liga Nacionalista from its founding in 1917.

Thus nationalism as such had foreign as well as domestic roots, but Modernism had some local precursors. The most important of these was the writer Monteiro Lobato, who in 1915 published *Urupês*, a collection of stories about the caipira Jeca Tatu that painted an unromanticized picture of Brazilian peasant life; in 1932, the novelist (and future Integralist leader) Plínio Salgado was prompted to remark that "Jeca Tatu is the national spirit."[131] Yet if Monteiro Lobato was a forerunner of Modernism, he displayed a curmudgeonly resistance to the new trends in art. Though he was willing to acknowledge Anita Malfatti's considerable talent, he denounced her 1917 exhibit, an event now regarded as the beginning of Modernism.[132]

The vehicle for the propagation of futurism, Dada, cubism, and expressionism was Modern Art Week, an event that brought together outstanding young painters (Malfatti, Tarsila do Amaral, di Cavalcanti), musicians (Villa-Lobos, Guiomar Novais), and writers (among them Mário and Oswald de Andrade, Salgado, and Alcântara Machado). The events in the Municipal Theater had as one objective *épater le bourgeois*. That playful spirit, perhaps the most celebrated characteristic of the Modernist movement, continued to pervade the circles of the Sociedade Paulista de Arte Moderna into the early 1930's.[133]

Much has been made of the fact that the "revolutionary" Modern Art Week occurred in the year that also saw the founding of the Brazilian Communist Party, the first tenente rebellion, and the beginning of the Catholic intellectual movement (through the Centro Dom Vital); but Art's message was ambiguous, and recent research has shown that the correspondence between Modernism and politics is mostly drawn from statements by the movement's participants years after the events in question. Furthermore, the establishment press's reaction to Modern Art Week was not hostile, but on the contrary, generally favorable, and the PRP's *Correio Paulistano* led the way.[134]

Even in the 1920's, during the more purely aesthetic phase of the Modernist movement, its members emphasized the relationship between the capital city, with its European orientation, and the supporting hinterland. Oswald de Andrade's *Memórias sentimentais de João Miramar* (1924) was a cinematic montage of impressions of São Paulo city and the centers of culture in Europe, but several rural scenes appear as well. One is framed in a routine report by the semiliterate foreman of a coffee estate; another vignette, called "Far-West," could be either a Hollywood Western or a scene from real life on the São Paulo frontier—more likely the latter. Mário de Andrade, the other high priest of Modernism, like (the unrelated) Oswald, was born and bred in the capital, and also wrote on rural life in São Paulo.[135]

The ambivalence of Modernism—its contradictory leanings toward regionalism, nationalism, and cosmopolitanism in art—typified São Paulo's higher culture in general. Perhaps such countervailing tendencies helped give rise to humorous but anxiety-tinted formulations. I think, for example, of Mário de Andrade's "the imperious cry of whiteness within me," which recalled not only the poet's mulatto ancestry, but the ambivalences of Brazil's creole culture. Or consider Oswald de Andrade's celebrated "Tupi or not Tupi" (in English), a triple entendre appropriately appearing in the mock-nativist "Anthropophagic Manifesto." (The author reminds his readers that Caeté tribesmen, a branch of the Tupi family, ate the first bishop of Brazil in 1552.)

In some ways, regionalism helped produce a new appreciation for Brazil at large. Mário de Andrade and Paulo Prado sparked an interest among Mineiro writers in the eighteenth-century art and architecture of Minas Gerais when they organized a motorized pilgrimage to Ouro Preto in 1924. Modern Art Week likewise influenced Gilberto Freyre's decision to hold a congress on northeastern culture in 1926.[136]

In *Macunaíma* (1928), Modernism broke openly with its Europeanizing tendencies, as Mário de Andrade "gleefully brought together Indian legends, folk proverbs, obscenities, [and] stereotypes shaped into popular satire."[137] In the 1930's, the Modernists moved in different directions— Plínio Salgado and Cassiano Ricardo to the Right, Oswald de Andrade to the Left. But nationalism remained a common and increasingly compelling theme, pushing aside competing allegiances to regionalism and cosmopolitanism, which had attenuated nationalism among the Modernists in the early 1920's. In 1935, Mário de Andrade, as director of São Paulo's Department of Culture, sought to "contribute to the psychological unification of Brazil," in the words of the poet Manuel Bandeira, by building a bridge between popular and formal art; the Estado Novo terminated the experiment.[138]

Thus ends our survey of São Paulo's society and culture, a civilization whose dynamism and ambivalences were related to a moving frontier, European immigration, and the rise of a new metropolis, and not least to the economy and culture of the North Atlantic basin. Movement was a basic feature—economic transformation, geographic relocation, social mobility—in a way unimaginable (and probably undesired) in Minas Gerais, where, according to John Wirth, the population had a fixed, small-town sense of place, within a well-defined social order. Because of frontier opportunities and the powers of attraction of São Paulo city, the strength of zonal loyalties was far weaker in São Paulo than in Minas, with the possible exception of the Paraíba Valley—though even there, prominent fazendeiros invested in virgin lands in frontier zones. Nor was there in São Paulo the sense of insularity, of peripherality within in Brazil, that Robert Levine has identified in Pernambuco, for São Paulo was challenging the federal capital for national leadership in culture, as well as in economic affairs.

São Paulo's cultural leadership within Brazil was probably considered self-evident by Paulistas no later than the 1920's, and notions of leadership easily slipped into notions of hegemony. Aspirations to hegemony also frequently underlay the Paulistas' political behavior, which is considered in the following chapter and in Chapter Six. Mineiro politicians repeatedly argued that Minas and São Paulo had to direct the nation by acting in concert, but when the Paulistas discussed leadership, there was a tendency to omit Minas. Self-assurance led to swagger.

CHAPTER FOUR

State Politics: Men, Events, and Structures

IN THE EARLY YEARS of the Republic, São Paulo's leadership was nowhere more obvious than in the political sphere, where the clearest indication was the state machine's control of the presidency for the 12 years
after 1894. This, the first of three chapters dealing with politics and politicians, presents the basic facts and features of São Paulo's political culture. The material is divided into four sections. The first, "Republicans
and the Empire," deals with the rise of São Paulo's Republican Party and
its opportunism in provincial politics in the 1870's and 1880's. The second, "Mainstream Politics," provides a brief survey of major political
events (including factionalism) during the period 1889–1937, focusing
on the establishment party and its principal opponents and successors in
power. "Structures," the third section, concerns institutions and persistent configurations of political import—state agencies, formal and informal patterns of dominance, organized interest groups, and "marginal"
but enduring political forces. The final section, "Representation and Elections," first deals with São Paulo's formal representation and electoral
power at the federal level, and then offers an interpretation of the state's
voting statistics—often regarded as meaningless—for the Old Republic
and the early Vargas years.

Republicans and the Empire

Paulista leadership at the federal level began with a time of testing for
São Paulo's Republican Party. No other provincial Republican organization could match the experience of the Partido Republicano Paulista in

the last two decades of the Empire. Brazilian Republicanism was born in 1870, but the most important event in its development that year may not have been the Republican Manifesto or the institution of the Third Republic in France: for São Paulo, at least, it was probably the publication of *A Província*, by Aureliano Tavares Bastos, a widely respected essayist and former member of Parliament. Citing the precedents of the newly created federations of Argentina, Canada, and Austria-Hungary, Tavares called for a federal monarchy in Brazil. He argued forcefully for administrative decentralization, provincial autonomy in politics and administration, provincial control of banking and immigration policies, and the decentralization of revenues.[1] This program had a powerful appeal for São Paulo's coffee planters, a nineteenth-century agricultural elite with bourgeois instincts. From Tavares's formulas, it was but a short step to substituting the ideal of a republic for the monarchy, and an explicitly federal republic was the goal of the signers of the Republican Manifesto of December 1870 in Rio. When the Paulistas organized a provincial Republican Party in 1873, they emphasized that the new regime would serve São Paulo.

Paulistas of various political persuasions had chafed at what they considered the neglect of the province by the imperial government. São Paulo entered its classic export phase with the completion of the Santos–Jundiaí railway in 1867, but revenues in the 1870's were totally inadequate to meet the provincial government's responsibilities for road construction and maintenance, public health, and education.[2] Despite its lack of passable roads and other public works, São Paulo was one of three imperial provinces that never received direct financial aid under the Empire.[3] In 1886–87, São Paulo contributed eight times as much to the central treasury as it received back in outlays. Politically the province was unable to remedy this state of affairs, for it was clearly underrepresented in the imperial parliament by the 1880's.[4] The Republicans of São Paulo called for a distribution of revenues that would allow the province to meet the requirements of the expanding export economy, and for political autonomy to maximize São Paulo's economic potential.[5]

One feature of the PRP distinguishes it from its counterparts: its skillful opportunism on issues such as separatism, the abolition of slavery, and (initially for a few) even the substitution of a republic for the monarchy. In these matters, the Paulistas may have been influenced by the example of the conservative wing of the Republican Party in France, whose leader

Léon Gambetta chose to call his program "opportunism," clearly intending no pejorative connotation. At all events, Paulista Republicans shared with Gambetta the belief that republican government had to support established interests.

One of the few issues on which the PRP never compromised was decentralization. The question of how far to pursue that goal, however, was a matter of hot debate. Some Paulista Republicans even threatened to set a separatist course for their province if a federation was not achieved. For a time, this group included Manuel Campos Sales, future President of the Republic. Economic and racist arguments were made for separatism by Republican ideologists such as Alberto Sales (Campos Sales's brother), but the party never officially adopted separatism as an explicit threat.[6] On balance, separatism emerges as a specter used to haunt imperial statesmen rather than a sincerely pursued objective. Here, as in other areas, opportunism was at work.

A more glaring instance of opportunism was the PRP's stance on slavery. Though the Paulista Republicans had rejected abolition in a conclave in 1872, they skirted the issue at the party's organizing congress the following year at Itu (where slaveowning planters predominated).[7] Slavery was declared to be a "social issue" that had to be solved "by the whole nation"—but on a province-by-province basis. Obfuscation was intentional in such language, though the delegates at Itu made one thing clear: that slaveowners would be compensated for financial losses. One vocal abolitionist, Luís Gama, left the party, though another, Bernardino de Campos, remained,[8] and the PRP now began a policy of deliberate ambiguity on the most important issue of the day, a policy it would maintain for 14 years.

For the Republicans, as for other Paulista politicians, the abolition issue was indissolubly linked with the immigration question. In 1885, Prudente de Morais, Brazil's President from 1894 to 1898, emphasized in his maiden speech in the imperial parliament that Paulista planters of all political hues would not abandon slavery without an alternate source of cheap labor.[9] After 1884, the provincial assembly provided free passage for immigrants who went into agriculture; and in 1888, the Republicans successfully promoted a new bill to bring more immigrants to São Paulo's coffee fields.[10] On the immigration issue, Republicans were closely allied with western planters of the Conservative Party. Indeed, they were more than closely allied, at least in the case of two of the Prado brothers: one,

Martinico, was the chief Republican spokesman on the issue and a founder of the Immigration Promotion Society; the other, Antônio, was a leader of the province's Conservative Party.

The men who controlled A *Província de S. Paulo*, a publication that was closely associated with the Republican Party, even extended their opportunism to the central issue of the form of government (though this was not true of the party itself). A *Província* initially defended all the PRP's major programs except the proclamation of the Republic, viz., gradual abolition under provincial auspices, with indemnification; decentralization; the election of governors; and the separation of Church and State.[11] At election time, Republicans were perfectly willing to make trade-offs with the monarchist party when that suited their interests. (In this sort of thing, to be sure, the Liberals and Conservatives showed themselves to be fully as opportunistic as the Republicans. Indeed, as early as 1881 dissident members of the Conservative Party, led by João Mendes de Almeida, attacked Antônio Prado for collusion with Republicans.)[12]

In the mid-1880's, a foreign observer described the Republican Party in São Paulo as a group drawn from both the landed and the non-landed sectors of society and composed of "talented men, who desire to make a career, and who support or oppose the governing party, as may best advance their own interests."[13] If the Paulista Republicans made any contribution on the moral plane, it was to resist the temptation to be reabsorbed by the Liberal Party on its return to power in 1878 after 10 years of opposition—as they might easily have done, since many of them had been Liberals and the two parties had many similar ideological features.[14]

Among Republican groups in Brazil, opportunism was almost a unique option for the Paulistas, because of their electoral strength in the province; in most provinces, even in the late 1870's and the 1880's, Republicans were simply ignored. The PRP was rooted in the richest agricultural area of Brazil, the Central zone of São Paulo, and its adherents included some of the province's most prominent planters. In 1877, three Republicans won seats in the 36-man provincial assembly—the first Republican victory anywhere in Brazil—and all three had support from the Liberal Party (out of power at the time).[15] The Republicans lost their seats in 1878. Electoral ups and downs ensued until 1881, when Republicans benefited by the introduction of the Saraiva electoral reform law, which required candidates for the national parliament to run for specific district seats. This stipulation allowed Republicans to concentrate on two districts of São Paulo, the seventh, incorporating parts of the Central, Mogiana, and Baixa Paulista zones, and the eighth, incorporating parts of the Central, Baixa Paulista, and the Araraquarense zones—all in the pioneering "west." In 1881, six Republicans won seats in the São Paulo Assembly in races that were based on the same districts established by the Saraiva Law.[16]

In the 1884 runoff elections for the imperial parliament, Republicans and out-of-power Conservatives each backed the other's candidates. As a result, Campos Sales of Campinas won in the seventh district, and Prudente de Morais of Piracicaba won in the eighth. Together with Alvaro Andrade Botelho of Minas, they were the first (and only) Republicans elected to parliament. Theirs was a short-lived victory, however, for in a special election the next year, the Conservatives withdrew their support, and both Paulista Republicans lost their seats.[17] All the same, four Republicans won places in the provincial assembly in late 1887.

The strategy of the Paulista Republicans was clearly to collaborate with the monarchist party in opposition—the Liberals in 1877 and the Conservatives in 1884. But this strategy was turned against them in the last imperial election of 1889, which saw their defeat in the seventh and eighth districts through the collaboration of the Liberals and the Conservatives. These groups drew together out of a common fear that the monarchy was near its end, and may have used fraud to carry those districts, as the Republicans believed.[18] At any rate, in that election Republicans accounted for one-fourth of the voters in São Paulo (a larger share than in any other province) in a highly restricted electorate—about 1 percent of the province's population.[19]

As the Republican Party matured in the final years of the Empire, its major problem remained the internal tension over abolition. The chief compromiser in the PRP was Francisco Glicério, also a fence-straddler on separatism, and a man who would later reveal his talents at political orchestration in organizing the first national Republican coalition, the Partido Republicano Federal. A mulatto himself, it was Glicério who kept a number of abolitionists in the party while he worked with the slave-owning planter group.[20]

The Republicans needed all of Glicério's talents, for they had tied their destinies in large part to the planters of the west (the Central zone and its northern fringes in our regionalization scheme). Many of the party leaders came from that area, if not from the planter group itself. Glicério, like Campos Sales, hailed from Campinas, the heart of the new west; Prudente de Morais resided in Piracicaba, João and Jorge Tibiriçá in Itu, Bernardino de Campos in Amparo, and Martinico Prado in Araras. In 1871, there were more Republican clubs in the Central zone than in any other.[21]

Indeed, it was precisely because of the Republican strength in the west that Campinas was the seat of the party's executive committee in the 1870's; and that is also why Itu was chosen as the site of the official organizing convention in 1873. In fact, the only delegates at Itu other than those from the capital and Rio were from the west.[22]

To some extent, the ideological differences among the Republican, Liberal, and Conservative parties yielded to regional cleavages within the province. As I noted earlier, one of São Paulo's senators, a member of the Conservative Party, was so irate at the government's "favoritism" of the west in its railroad-building and immigration-subsidy programs that he advocated the creation of a new province embracing the Paraíba Valley (including part of Rio Province) and southern Minas Gerais. He noted unhappily that the powers in all three Paulista parties opposed his bill. Certainly there was electoral collaboration between Republicans and Conservatives who promoted immigration in the west.[23] Yet official favors for the region were probably more the result of economic realities and mutual interest than any attempt by conservatives to co-opt Republicans.

The demise of slavery in São Paulo was the opportunity the Republicans had been waiting for. The crisis came in 1887, when the Central zone and its fringes in the west witnessed repeated slave uprisings while the rest of the province remained quiet.[24] Since the disorder and violence interfered with immigration,[25] such disturbances hastened the collapse of slavery in the Central zone, in São Paulo, and in Brazil as a whole. In March 1887, the São Paulo assembly voted a 400$000 tax on all slaves in the province, but the bill was not approved by the governor. Meanwhile, immigration in the west was succeeding brilliantly, and by May some 60,000–70,000 Italian colonos had been placed on São Paulo fazendas.

Once the rural labor problem was resolved, Paulista Republicans, like Fernand Braudel's man of action, chose to "take advantage of the weight of the inevitable,"[26] and moved quickly to dress up their image on the abolition issue. In May 1887, two fervent abolitionists were elected to the executive committee of the PRP, Vitorino Gonçalves Carmilo and Bernardino de Campos, who became its president. In a meeting in July, party leaders declared that no Republican could still own slaves on the centenary of the French Revolution (July 14, 1889).

In September 1887, planters of all parties in Campinas, under Glicério's guidance, promised their slaves liberty provided they would continue to work for their masters until the end of 1890. The death sentence of slavery in São Paulo was read at the founding of the Emancipation and Labor Organization Society in December 1887, under the presidency of the Marquês de Três Rios of Campinas. The event was attended by political leaders of all three parties and the province's most powerful planters, and the date adopted in Campinas (December 31, 1890) was now set as a deadline for abolition in the whole of São Paulo. Planters thus imposed abolition on themselves, in the hope that the freed men would remain on their estates. After 1887, the provincial police refused to help planters capture runaways, and total abolition had almost been achieved in the western municípios by January 1888,[27] four months before the imperial Golden Law freed all slaves. Antônio Prado's critical role as Minister of Agriculture in bringing about nationwide abolition is well known, and equally well established is his interest in the immigration program, the central issue for the planters of the west. São Paulo took out its only foreign loan during the Empire (£749,000 in 1888) explicitly to subsidize immigration.[28] Before abolition in May 1888, political leaders throughout the province had apparently been won over, since the assembly unanimously passed legislation providing the wherewithal to supply São Paulo with 100,000 more immigrants.[29]

Republicans, it is widely assumed if not proven, profited politically by abolition, as disgruntled planters apparently turned away from the imperial parties that passed abolition without indemnification in Parliament. Republicans were "blameless," since none had been elected for that session. They were quick to take advantage of the situation in the weeks after abolition by intensifying their campaign against the "Third Reign," i.e., the succession of Isabel, the Princess Regent, to the throne of Pedro II.[30] The Third Reign may have been a code word to brand Isabel as an abolitionist in the minds of planters, since it was she who gave final sanction to the law terminating slavery.

In any case, the end of slavery and the success of the immigration program accelerated a trend toward an ideological convergence of the three parties in São Paulo. In 1887, the Paulista Liberals had been sharply divided by the struggle over abolition, and their party was reported to be without a program in the first half of 1888. In June of that year, the party adopted Tavares Bastos's federalism; this act, coming when it did, shows that the Liberals were echoing the Republican program. A month later, Liberal leaders approached the Republicans about political collaboration. At the same time, they named their new party organ *O Federalista*. From then on, until the end of the Empire, they defended federalism in increasingly strident terms.[31]

The Conservative Party was also turning away from its traditional support of Crown and centralism, and in February 1889, party chief Antônio Prado declared for provincial autonomy. By September, according to *O Federalista*, he was awaiting the "advent of the Republic."[32] Conservative and Liberal leaders moved toward unity with the Republicans on the so-called Motion of São Borja, a movement to poll all Brazil's município councils on whether the monarchy should continue after the death of the ailing Emperor. The Conservative Antônio Prado and the Liberal Manuel Albuquerque Lins, on behalf of their blocs in the provincial assembly, supported the Republicans in censuring Governor Rodrigues Alves for his punishment of the município governments that endorsed the Motion. Liberal and Conservative leaders in 1888 were reported as having unanimous views, presumably meaning support of virtual autonomy for the province on immigration and fiscal policies.[33] The Liberal leader Rodrigo Lobato may not have been joking when he remarked in the São Paulo assembly in 1888 that "there is nothing so much like a Republican as a monarchist."[34] There were clearly strong overlapping economic interests among leaders of the three parties.*

The PRP played a significant role in the overthrow of the Empire,

---

*Consider, for example, the party affiliations of the men who set up the Banco do Comércio e Indústria de São Paulo at the end of 1889. Among the founders were J. B. Melo Oliveira, a Republican propagandist who served on the PRP executive committee in the late 1890's and early 1900's; Elias Pacheco Chaves, former member of the Conservative Party executive committee; the Barão de Jaguara, whose brother had been on the Conservative committee; and Antônio Souza Queiroz, a member of the Liberal Party committee. All three served on the Republican executive committee of 1891. Other founders were two ex-Conservatives who enjoyed long careers in the PRP—Antônio Prado and João Alvares Rubião Júnior. Note also that the chief founders of the Immigration Promotion Society were Martinico Prado, the Republican leader, and Antônio Queiroz Teles, a Conservative Party leader and governor of São Paulo, 1886–87. Ribeiro and Guimarães, *História dos bancos*, p. 325; Hall, "The Origins of Mass Immigration," p. 84.

though the coup d'état that terminated it was essentially a military operation. Indeed, the Paulistas were the only group outside Rio de Janeiro to participate. Glicério was one of the five plotters in Rio on November 11, and he was present four days later when Marshal Manuel Deodoro da Fonseca overthrew Pedro. Campos Sales worked with military officers in São Paulo city, and other PRP leaders were apprised of the conspiracy.[35]

In the wake of the coup, Glicério emerged as Minister of Agriculture in the provisional government, and was soon able to impose Paulista immigration policies at the national level. In anticipation of this, perhaps, São Paulo's Conservative and Liberal party chiefs, Prado and Augusto Machado, quickly announced their support for the new regime. The PRP in turn welcomed former monarchists into the Republican fold, and though most Liberal leaders declined to run as PRP candidates for the federal Constituent Assembly in 1890, some Conservatives did so. Among them was Francisco Rodrigues Alves, who had persecuted Republicans as governor in 1888. Opportunism was an ongoing policy—for all concerned.

Mainstream Politics

Among the various province-wide Republican parties, the PRP was without a doubt the most seasoned and cohesive in 1889. Yet its hearty welcome to former monarchists and its new power engendered divisions that developed into an open split as the Constituent Assembly completed its work in February 1891. Appointed governor by Deodoro, Jorge Tibiriçá nonetheless backed Prudente de Morais and the other congressmen who increasingly opposed the policies of the dictator-turned-President after the Constitution was approved.

Meanwhile, Américo Brasiliense, signer of the Republican manifesto of 1870 and grand old man of the party, made known his willingness to serve under Deodoro, though he had declined to do so in November 1889. In March 1891, Deodoro removed acting Governor Tibiriçá from office in order to eliminate what he and the Barão de Lucena, his "prime minister," considered the hostility of the Paulistas in Congress toward ex-monarchists; Brasiliense got the job.[36] The elderly Brasiliense was far from hostile to former Liberals and Conservatives, and quickly engineered a coup within the party. He dissolved the executive committee and filled most of the seats on the new committee with former monarchists. This sectarian move of course distressed the "Historical" Republicans, i.e., those who had joined the PRP before the Empire fell. (Brasiliense's attitude toward ex-monarchists paralleled that of Minas's Governor Cesário Alvim, who was consolidating power at home while younger and possibly more radical men served their state in the federal Congress.[37]) The "out" group in São Paulo, led by Glicério, Bernardino, Prudente, and Campos Sales, won only a third of the seats in the state Constituent Assembly elections. (In Congress, however, this faction still had enough prestige to lead the opposition to the President.) Meanwhile, with Deodoro's support, Brasiliense was elected governor by the state Constituent Assembly in July 1891 and proceeded to consolidate power. The assembly passed a law in late 1891 requiring that elections to that body be held at large, thus bypassing local political strongholds and strengthening the role of the governor. Brasiliense was indirectly aided in his effort by a tripling of state income under the new federal division of revenues. But he made the fatal error of supporting Deodoro's attempted coup against Congress in November; a near-even division in the State Assembly showed the unpopularity of the Marshal's action. A successful uprising in Rio Grande do Sul encouraged Historical Republicans and military groups in Rio in their conspiracies against Deodoro, and a naval revolt on November 23 brought the dictator down.

Marshal Floriano Peixoto, who succeeded to the presidency, now abetted those military units and political factions that had opposed the coup in ousting the implicated governors. On December 15, 1891, after a series of violent confrontations, Brasiliense was deposed by his former colleagues in the PRP.[38] He was allowed to resign in favor of his legal successor, José Alves de Cerqueira César, lieutenant governor and brother-in-law of Campos Sales.[39]

With the aid of Bernardino, Campos Sales, and Júlio Mesquita (publisher of what was now O Estado de S. Paulo), Cerqueira César dissolved the state legislature and reorganized the party. In Rio, Bernardino served as a link with Floriano, while Campos Sales worked with the army. Victory for the "restored" but purged PRP was certain in the 1892 assembly elections, for the same reason as it had been assured for Brasiliense's candidates: the resurgent Historical Republicans could count on the backing of the President, the governor, and the incumbent party.[40] The PRP executive committee, which had dominated party affairs in the imperial era, was once again completely reconstituted, with Prudente de Morais as president; the other members were Bernardino, Mesquita, Cesário Mota, Glicério, Carmilo, and Rodrigues Alves. All save the last were Historicals, and the former imperial governor had stood with his fellow congressmen against Deodoro's putsch; he was now serving as Floriano's Minister of Finance.[41]

The new establishment in São Paulo contrasted sharply with its counterpart in Pernambuco, where ex-monarchists dominated state politics. Not a single Historical Republican was elected governor there (though one, Alexandre José Barbosa Lima, was appointed from Rio). In São Paulo, nine of the governors under the Old Republic were Historicals, and only two were former monarchists (Rodrigues Alves and Albuquerque Lins). In Minas Gerais, ex-monarchists and Republicans in the establishment party reached a compromise by 1898, but the ex-monarchists came out on top.

After 1892, there were no more intraparty revolutions in São Paulo, and the PRP virtually monopolized public office till the fall of the Old Republic. This pattern of continuity contrasted sharply with the repeated upheavals in Pernambuco, and indeed in most states. Before the appearance of the Partido Democrático, a formal opposition party organized in 1926, the PRP was only shaken by rifts, most of which proved to be ephemeral. There were *dissidências* in 1901, 1915, 1923–24, and 1937; and less important splits in 1897, 1907, and 1910. The rifts of 1901, 1907, 1915, and 1923–24 involved the selection of the governor; all the others were related to presidential politics.

Francisco Glicério, who should have known, is credited with having said "To join the opposition in this country is a downright act of insanity,"[42] but such wisdom did not prevent him from bucking the PRP in 1910 with the support of the federal government and the boss of the Senate, the Gaúcho José Gomes Pinheiro Machado. The various splits involved clashes of personality and sometimes zonal competition for patronage and public works, of course; but a few also reflected conflicts of interest between economic sectors, and there were even doctrinally inspired cleavages.

The 1901 division, though temporary, produced the Prudente de Morais—Cerqueira César dissidência, as President Campos Sales blocked Cerqueira's bid to become governor.[43] Though Cerqueira was himself a brother-in-law of the President, the rift to some extent followed family lines; at least six of the dissident leaders were related to at least one other leader.[44] At the ideological level, the 1901 split was a reaction to Campos Sales's *política dos governadores* (the practice of mutual support by incumbent groups at the federal, state, and local level), and the related phenomena of a political massacre in Mato Grosso and gubernatorial interference in São Paulo's local politics.[45] The split may also have reflected the discontent of commercial and industrial interests associated with the party. The dissidents favored doing away with export taxes, the state transit tax, and all interstate tariffs. They also proposed to increase the federal government's power to regulate commerce; denationalize the merchant marine (because it could not handle the existing volume of freight); and limit the purchase of property by foreign corporations.[46]

Banking interests in 1901, by contrast, seem to have been well provided for, if the composition of the executive committee in that year is any evidence. Of the five recognized party *chefes* at that time—Bernardino, Rodrigues Alves, Campos Sales, Cerqueira César, and Prudente[47] —two of the three survivors in power had banking interests. So did all four of the executive committee members linked to those chefes: Antônio de Pádua Sales and Rubião Júnior were associated with the Banco do Comércio e Indústria; Lacerda Franco and Bernardino, with the Banco União; Frederico de Abranches, with the Banco de São Paulo; and Campos Sales, with the Banco do Crédito Real. All were currently or would soon be officers of their respective banks.[48]

The 1907 split pitted Albuquerque Lins, the protégé of the incumbent governor, Tibiriçá, against Campos Sales in the contest for governor. This division was of the ideological sort, centering on the refusal of the former President and architect of the Funding Loan to go along with Tibiriçá's valorization program.[49] Following Lins's victory by a vote of 54 to 40 in the PRP convention, a pro-Lins opposition took over a number of municípios where the local establishment had made the wrong choice; in most cases, however, the latter group made peace with the governor, and the newcomers merged with the previous incumbents or were ousted.[50] The closeness of the vote and its aftermath were indicative of the deep differences of thinking within the party on the valorization program and its consequences for state and federal finances. Still, at both the state and the federal level many of the losers in 1907 retained their posts, including such important figures as Glicério, Joaquim Lopes Chaves, Antônio Dino Bueno, Pádua Sales, Rodolfo Miranda, and Alvaro da Costa Carvalho. Thus the party held together. In any event, Tibiriçá's victory in imposing Albuquerque Lins was welcomed by most of the planters and commercial and banking groups associated with the coffee economy.

The 1915 rift saw the reemergence of the 1901 dissidents (Adolfo da Silva Gordo, Cincinato Braga, José Alves Guimarães Júnior, Júlio Mesquita) in opposition to Governor Rodrigues Alves's attempt to impose a successor. This action was a partial repudiation of "oligarchic democracy," or rule by the executive committee; the move seemed to parallel and reinforce the política dos governadores in the minds of the dissidents, who accounted for a quarter of the votes at the party convention in 1915.

The 1923–24 split again involved a gubernatorial election, with a cruder power play by the incumbent, Washington Luís. This time a largely new group temporarily broke away, headed by two members of the executive committee, former governor Altino Arantes Marques and Olavo Egídio Souza Aranha, a prominent banker. It also included Alvaro Carvalho (whose career in the Senate had been ended by Washington Luís) and the Rodrigues Alves clan, into which Carvalho had married. They were later joined by Rafael Sampaio Vidal, who served as President Artur Bernardes's Minister of Finance until 1924. His defection suggests that the dissidents may also have been prompted to break with the PRP because of its acquiescence in the decision, midway in the Bernardes administration, to reverse the falling exchange rate and end federal valorization. In any event, all these men were linked by common business interests.[51]

Of the federally related breaks, by far the most important was the fateful 1891–92 triumph and defeat of Américo Brasiliense, which permanently eliminated most of the ex-monarchists from power. This was the most thoroughgoing political rupture of the whole period. In 1897, Glicério and Rodolfo Miranda broke away in the struggle between President Prudente and Glicério's Partido Republicano Federal; and both Glicério and Miranda supported the Minas-backed candidate Hermes da Fonseca against Rui Barbosa, the choice of the PRP in the presidential race of 1910. But after those splits, they found it easy enough to reinsert themselves into the power structure. During the Hermes years Glicério and

Miranda at least offered the PRP a conduit to Pinheiro Machado and the President.*

Factional divisions within the PRP were offset in great measure by the continuity provided by the party's executive committee, a body that stood between the governor and the coronéis.† The committee's authority derived from the power of the party chefes (or their representatives) who sat on it.[52] Through the chefes, the committee also represented various zonal interests, and served the brokerage function of distributing patronage, including public works.[53] Furthermore, it legitimized the transition of power from one governor to the next. In the early years of the Republic, at least, it could also "intercede" with the state legislature, and, in consultation with the governor, it decided on PRP nominees for state and federal offices.[54] In the 1890's, it played an important if informal role in governing the state.[55]

Although the party did not offer a means of livelihood for any significant salaried group—Max Weber's professionals who live off politics—it did have a permanent headquarters and a professional secretary whose salary allowed him to devote full time to party affairs.[56] The PRP had organizational cohesion and discipline, and was clearly something more than an elaborate network of parentelas and clientelas; yet it had this side to it, too, and party divisions, such as the 1901 and 1924 splits, were heavily influenced by patterns of family solidarity. The PRP was an intermediate case between a modern "horizontally" organized, functionally or ideologically cohesive party and a "vertically" organized clientele network.[57]

In theory, município directorates elected the executive committee, and picked their own district candidates for state and federal office; the committee supposedly just added up their nominations (indicações) to determine the winner.[58] In practice, however, the chefes on the committee told their respective directorates how to vote.[59]

---

*In 1930, when the Paulistas and Mineiros were again on opposite sides in a contested presidential race, the PRP held together as a political bloc, but the fact is hardly surprising: Washington Luís's incumbency as chief executive (and the presumed extension of Paulista power through the election of Júlio Prestes) made the contest different from the 1910 race, when the PRP dissidents could count on the support of President-presumptive Hermes da Fonseca.

† Unfortunately, our knowledge of the party's functioning can only be approximate, since its archives were lost when the party headquarters were burned during the revolution of 1930.

The "schism" of 1901 did not cause any changes in the organization of the party, but the PRP was restructured in 1913, at least in part because of the external threat posed by the ambitions of Senators Rodolfo Miranda and Pinheiro Machado. A convention of município directorates in November elected nine of the most prestigious chefes to the committee (expanding its membership by three) in a near-unanimous vote. The convention then unanimously endorsed the actions of the incumbent executive committee and the governor regarding the presidential succession of 1914.[60]

The elections of the committee by the directorates were annual events until 1916, when a four-year term was introduced to coincide with the gubernatorial term. This change followed the split in the party over the nomination of Altino Arantes for governor in the 1915 PRP convention, and probably resulted from Governor Rodrigues Alves's desire to secure his successor a cooperative executive committee. Four years later, the committee met with state and federal deputies to select the PRP gubernatorial nominee for the 1920–24 term; a unanimous endorsement resulted, and this unanimity was preserved until the end of the Old Republic. In 1920, the committee was formally elected in a party convention, but it soon became self-perpetuating: in 1922, the members replaced one of their number by "inviting" a substitute on their own authority.[61]

In April 1925, apparently for the first time, the executive committee named candidates for state representatives without first consulting the município directorates, even as a formal gesture. Furthermore, those directorates, originally chosen by local party members, were by now being appointed by the executive committee. There was a slight relaxation of central control in 1928.[62] This brief bow to local control may have been a reaction to the new Partido Democrático's emphasis on the autonomy of its município branches.

By this time, however, the PRP's executive committee itself had already lost most of its power to the governor. Rodrigues Alves chose Altino Arantes for governor in 1915; Arantes chose Washington Luís in 1919; and in 1923, Washington Luís ran roughshod over the committee to impose Carlos de Campos (son of Bernardino) as his successor.[63] Washington Luís consolidated the governor's power in 1923–24, it seems, just as Artur Bernardes had in Minas Gerais by 1919 in his struggle with the PRM committee, with the result that by the late 1920's, the governor of São Paulo had immense power, presiding over a vastly expanded exec-

TABLE 4.1

Turnover of the Executive Committee of the Partido Republicano
Paulista by Five-Year Periods, 1890–1929

Period	Total number of members	New members	New members as percent of total
1890–94	25	21	84%
1895–99	16	10	63
1900–1904	14	5	36
1905–9	11	3	27
1910–14	10	1	10
1915–19	15	4	27
1920–24	11	1	9
1925–29	14	7	50

SOURCE: Derived from Appendix B.
NOTE: New members are defined as those who entered the committee for the first time each year after 1890, the base year. Francisco Glicério and Campos Sales, who were on the 1889 committee but off the following year, are counted as new members in 1892 and 1893, respectively.

utive branch and a greatly increased state budget, with all the patronage this implied. In constant terms (1912 = 100), state government expenditures increased by two-thirds between 1910–19 and 1920–29.[64]

An additional reason—possibly—for the decline in the prestige of the PRP executive committee is the fact that its membership tended to change very slowly after its consolidation under Cerqueira César in 1892. Table 4.1 shows the small number of new members admitted to the committee after 1900.

Of the total man-years of service on the committee through 1930, the generation born before 1869 accounted for 93 percent, and the succeeding generation for the other 7 percent.[65] Over the whole of the First Republic, Historical Republicans had an almost two-to-one edge over men who had adhered to the Republic. Given the welcome that the Historicals had extended to former monarchists at the outset of the new regime, it seems likely that adherents would have done much better had not so many been discredited by Brasiliense's decision to go along with Deodoro's abortive coup d'état. (In Minas, where the Historicals were much weaker, some of the supporters of the aborted 1891 coup did manage to make a comeback.)

In any case, after 1891 the PRP monopoly of power was never seriously challenged until the last four years of the Old Republic, when the Partido Democrático was formed. (This lack of competition was perhaps to be expected, since the state's Força Pública could block federal intervention, the only means by which opposition groups came to power in other states.) The PD had a fair share of predecessors, however, beginning with the Liga Nacionalista (1917), which was not a party but a movement appealing to youth, authority, and patriotism. The Liga was succeeded by the emphemeral Mocidade, Evolucionista, and Popular parties. The formation of a "liberal" opposition party in 1926, significantly *not* organized on the spur of the moment for an impending contest,[66] grew primarily out of the demands for a secret ballot and honest elections. In the PD manifesto the founders, including Francisco Morato and the now-ancient Antônio Prado, denied that Brazil (with the possible exception of Rio Grande do Sul) had real political parties, and clearly implied that the PRP was held together only by its leaders' common desire to exploit the resources of government. The manifesto affirmed the PD's support of agriculture, made a vague reference to the need for social welfare measures, and neglected to mention industry.[67] But other factors, less obvious than frustration over electoral sham, seem to have figured in the birth of the PD, notably the dissatisfaction of major coffee and commercial interests with the PRP's sanctioning of the federal government's abandonment of valorization in 1924, and the Republican Party's failure to incorporate a younger generation into its upper echelons.[68] There is no question, certainly, that the PD represented powerful interests. For an opposition party, it had an unusual characteristic—the ability to raise money. The Democrats were able to collect dues and contributions similar in magnitude to those of the PRP.[69]

The PD was clearly a bourgeois-liberal party; but the seeming impossibility of achieving power by electoral means left it in a state of ambivalence on revolutionary strategies. Its official song was dedicated to Luís Carlos Prestes, leader of the famous rebel band in the backlands of Brazil from 1924 to 1927. Yet the PD participated in local, state, and federal elections from its birth through 1930, always blaming its defeat on fraud. Its leaders were certainly less inclined to join an armed revolt than was Joaquim Francisco Assis Brasil, head of the Partido Libertador, its sister party in Rio Grande do Sul.[70] The Democrats won three seats in the federal Chamber in 1927, but lost all positions (amid the usual denunciations of fraud) in 1930. In the intervening period, they made some gains at the local level in the second- and third-most-populous municípios, Santos and Campinas, though not in the capital.

As participants in Vargas's Liberal Alliance and the conspiracy to bring him to power after his defeat in the campaign of 1930, the Democrats, led by Francisco Morato, expected to take charge of São Paulo upon the Gaúcho's assumption of power. But the Vargas coalition also included young military rebels of the 1920's, known collectively as the *tenentes* (lieutenants), who wished to maintain an authoritarian regime while carrying out economic and social reforms, and Vargas seemed to favor that path in 1930–32. The decision turned out to be a misguided one, the result of an overestimation of the tenentes' strength and the Democrats' weakness.

Initially, the Democrats thought elections for a constituent assembly would quickly follow the triumph of the revolution. But Vargas was absorbed in the economic and financial crisis, and preferred to delay elections, as the tenentes urged; moreover, to the dismay of the Democrats, he appointed João Alberto Lins de Barros, a tenente from Pernambuco, to the São Paulo interventorship. Excluded from important offices in the central and state governments, the Democrats by February 1931 were attacking the "foreign" interventor and his policies, perceived as pro-labor. By April, all PD members had resigned from official posts down to the município level. The following months saw the sustained inability of the central government to deal effectively with the coffee crisis, quarrels among tenente and anti-tenente military commanders in São Paulo, and efforts by tenentes to build a political base in the state at the expense of both the PRP and the PD. Democrats feared the worst from Miguel Costa, a Força Pública rebel in the 1924 uprising, now João Alberto's secretary of security. Costa's Legião Revolucionária (Revolutionary Legion) was actively seeking to recruit the São Paulo working class to the tenente cause in a populist authoritarian movement.[71] The replacement of João Alberto and Miguel Costa in July 1931 only temporarily diminished tenente influence in São Paulo.

More than 15 months after the triumph of the revolution, Vargas had not set a date for Constituent Assembly elections, and in mid-February 1932, the Democrats formed a United Front with their former enemies, the Perrepistas (PRP-ists). The Front paralleled the alliance between the two Gaúcho parties that had backed Vargas's revolution; both groups in Rio Grande do Sul were now disturbed by his pro-tenente posture. The dictator's concessions to the "Constitutionalists" in February and March were offset by tenente maneuvers, further alienating Vargas's allies in Rio Grande. Finally, on May 14, Vargas announced that elections for a constitutional convention would be held one year later. But it was too late to satisfy United Front leaders in São Paulo, emboldened by dissatisfaction with Vargas in Minas as well as in Rio Grande. On May 23, they convinced the current interventor, Pedro de Toledo, a veteran diplomat and a Paulista, to appoint a pro-Constitutionalist cabinet in defiance of the dictatorship.

The new state government quickly took steps to dismantle the Partido Comunista Brasileiro (Brazilian Communist Party). Meanwhile, a mob attacked Miguel Costa's Legião Revolucionária headquarters in protest of his pro-Vargas stance, and four students were killed. This gave the United Front the martyrs—known by their initials, M. M. D. C.—who would soon symbolize the cause of revolt. In photographs of the famous rally against the Provisional Government on May 23, most of the participants look to be of a middle-class background; but by July, the Constitutionalist cause had become something of a popular movement as well. With a heady appreciation of their power, United Front leaders resolved that Vargas and the tenentes would not control São Paulo again.

If it came to war, the Paulistas believed they could rely not only on their Força Pública, but also on political and military support from Constitutionalists in Rio Grande and Minas.[72] They were also conspiring with General Bertoldo Klinger, commander of federal troops in Mato Grosso. The replacement of a pro-Constitutionalist Minister of War by a tenente-backed general and Klinger's dismissal from his command on July 8 precipitated the conflict: United Front leaders proclaimed Toledo governor and took Miguel Costa prisoner.

In the crisis, the state governments of Rio Grande and Minas threw their military and political weight behind Vargas, despite internal dissension, and Klinger arrived in São Paulo without his troops. Inside the state, federal commanders sympathized with the conspirators, but these army units were regarded as unreliable, at least by the American consul.[73] Thus the responsibility for São Paulo's military operations fell largely on the shoulders of the state's Força Pública.

There is surprisingly little analysis of the civil war of 1932, given the enormous memoir literature (mostly by Paulistas) on the subject.[74] One persistent theme among United Front leaders during the conflict was the possibility of a workers' revolution, despite the success of the São Paulo government in suppressing the PCB in May. According to the British Consul, the state's rebel leaders were "obsessed with a fear of a Communist uprising" during the conflict.[75] Though the capital's working class on the whole was probably less than enthusiastic about the restoration of a constitutional government (implicitly under Paulista tutelage), the cause was popular in the interior.[76]

Rather than attacking an enemy over whom it had a strong advantage in morale by moving toward Rio along the tracks of the Estrada de Ferro Central, the Paulista command adopted a defensive strategy.[77] Here the previous experience of the Força Pública seems to have played a decisive role: it had successfully employed such a strategy in 1893–95 and 1912; and its mettle had not really been tested in 1930, for President Washington Luís had resigned shortly after rebel troops from the south reached the São Paulo border.

There was more fighting in 1932 than in 1930, but still more maneuvering on widely separated fronts, extending hundreds of kilometers. Estimates of the casualties vary, but the overall total was possibly as high as 2,100 killed and 7,600 wounded, compared with roughly 2,000 dead and wounded in the revolution of 1930.[78] The most famous casualty was Colonel Júlio Marcondes Salgado, commander of the Força Pública, who was killed in August in an absurd twist of fate—a bomb produced in São Paulo exploded while he was inspecting it. The ardor of the upper classes was unsurpassed, though few of their sons apparently went to the front. Members of the *jeunesse dorée* eagerly enlisted, only to find that they preferred the pleasures of the capital city. In the words of the United States military attaché:

While morale was high among these [upper-class] volunteer troops, discipline was weak. Thus young men unaccustomed to taking orders from anybody found themselves under command of an abrupt and perhaps uncouth military police officer with definite ideas regarding drill and prompt obedience of orders. The young aristocrats therefore abandoned camp and returned to the Paulista capital for a few days of rest and recreation, after which still-unquenched enthusiasm led them to enlist in another patriotic battalion and repeat the experience. This procedure apparently was not considered desertion and no attempt was made to punish absentees. But it hardly made for efficient organization.[79]

The Paulistas capitulated at the end of September. Despite the central government's generous terms, the collapse of the revolt was a profound humiliation for São Paulo's leaders, and resulted in a second military occupation. Yet the war strengthened the alliance between the PD and the PRP, at least temporarily. Vargas's military interventor (and uncle by marriage) was Valdomiro Castilho de Lima, who with João Alberto's aid, tried to establish a Planters' Party (Partido da Lavoura), using the power and patronage at the disposal of an interventor imposed by conquest. Valdomiro Lima managed to gain the support of ruined planters and a few still wealthy ones who had formerly been closely associated with the Coffee Institute.[80] Meanwhile, Miguel Costa backed the interventor by trying to organize the working-class vote into a tenente-controlled Socialist Party.

For the 1933 elections of the Constituent Assembly, the PD and PRP joined forces in a Single Ticket coalition (Chapa Unica), defending liberal democracy and traditional federalism. The Economic Readjustment, Vargas's scheme to cancel half the planters' debts (announced in April), did not seriously weaken the Single Ticket at the polls in May. The coalition in fact accomplished an unheard-of feat in Republican politics: it beat the party of the government, winning 17 of the 22 seats in the São Paulo delegation. São Paulo was the only place in the country where an interventor lost in 1933. And this, as the American consul wrote, "in spite of the Federal Interventor's official machine, with its thousands of officeholders, and the copious expenditure of funds of the Coffee Institute in favor of the Farmer's Party [Partido da Lavoura]."[81]

In 1934, the Democratic wing of the Single Ticket dissolved the PD and formed a broader-based party, the Partido Constitucionalista, which included two other groups—Ação Nacional (National Action), a reformist minority in the PRP, and the Federação dos Voluntários (Volunteers' Federation), a group of veterans of the 1932 war who supported federalism. The PC's program was essentially the same as the Single Ticket's: to defend state autonomy and constitutional government. Numerically, PD leaders of the previous years did not dominate the new party: three-fourths of the PC's executive committee members during its short lifetime (1934–37) had not served on the PD committee (see Appendix A).

The PC, with its leader, Armando de Sales Oliveira, in the interventorship, was not above putting pressure on firms that owed money to the state to contribute to the party's coffers.[82] It triumphed easily in 1934, winning 53 percent of the vote and taking 21 of São Paulo's 34 congressional seats, while the PRP garnered 39 percent of the vote and swept the remaining 13 seats. In the new unicameral state legislature, the PC won 31 seats, against 22 for the PRP and one apiece for the Proletarian Coalition and Brazilian Integralist Action (the fascist party).[83] Armando

Sales thereupon became a constitutional governor, elected by his majority in the legislature.

Despite the PC's successes, its ideological stance was now defensive in the face of rising challenges from new groups on the Right and the Left. Its founders stated, in the party's initial manifesto in February 1934, that Paulista liberalism was based on "a social system in which the family and property are cornerstones"; they vaguely defended "Christian education," and spoke of their desire to satisfy the "just aspirations" of practically everybody—lavoura (planters and farmers), industrialists, merchants, and workers. The manifesto called on São Paulo to "orient" Brazilian politics. In the elections of October 1934 the appeal was more crudely bairrista (regionalist): "Everything for São Paulo."[84]

Whatever their fears of "extremists," the two bourgeois-liberal parties, the PC and the PRP, were very much in charge, even during the Red scare following a 1935 Communist uprising in Rio and the Northeast. Oligarchic democracy was alive and well in São Paulo, and there was no perceptible threat of a rightist or leftist takeover. In the statewide município council elections of 1936 (the last contest before the Estado Novo coup), the PC received 53 percent of the vote and the PRP 34 percent —almost nine-tenths of the total between them. The Integralists, the third-largest political force in the state, got less than 4 percent of the vote, in what were probably honest elections. Even in the capital city, where more "modern" parties might have been expected to do best, the PC and the PRP together won 19 seats, and the Integralists only one. No other party was represented.[85]

At the national level, the political scene was changing rapidly in 1936, as Vargas manipulated threats from the Left and the Right to destroy the center. The President monitored, fostered, and exploited divisions within the two principal parties in São Paulo.* By June 1937, he had also taken over military equipment destined for the state's Força Pública and intervened in Mato Grosso and the Federal District. By October, Vargas was able to oust Governor José Antônio Flores da Cunha in Rio Grande do Sul, whose state police constituted the last military obstacle to a coup d'état.

---

*He had even spied on Valdomiro, his uncle by marriage, but apparently with justification, since Valdomiro, after his political defeat in May 1933, participated in a plot against Vargas. See unsigned police reports of Jan. 10 and Jan. 16, 1933, in AP, pasta 2, lata 4; and Dulles, Vargas, p. 125.

During June, the PRP split openly over the party's support of Pedro Aleixo, Vargas's candidate for president of the federal Chamber. The dissidents included both the PRP chefe, Sílvio de Campos (son of Bernardino and brother of Carlos), and the PRP leader in the Chamber, Roberto Moreira. This minority also backed Armando Sales as President for the next term (1938-42); but he had little chance of getting the regular PRP's support after Campos shot an editor of the *Correio Paulistano*, the PRP organ, following its publication of a confidential letter concerning Sales's candidacy. [86] Political tension mounted in mid-July when a Marxist immigrant attempted to shoot the Integralist leader Plínio Salgado during a party parade in the capital.

The approaching presidential elections also split the PC into two factions, one led by Sales and Paulo Nogueira Filho (who dispensed state patronage) and the other by Senator José de Alcântara Machado. The latter group, made up of former PRP members, was favored by Governor José Joaquim Cardoso Melo Neto, [87] a Sales protégé who was now responding to cues from Vargas. Even the Communists were divided on the presidential race; the São Paulo branch opposed the decision by the national leadership to back José Américo de Almeida, Armando Sales's chief rival. [88]

The man responsible for releasing the Communists and other leftists from prison in mid-1937 was the Minister of Justice, José Carlos Macedo Soares, a former Constitutionalist. At the beginning of that year he had resigned his post as Foreign Minister, encouraged by Vargas to run for President; Vargas hoped to get PRP backing for Macedo Soares so as to split the São Paulo vote. [89] Though the would-be candidate failed in his bid to win significant support, both the PC and the PRP were now divided anyway, and Vargas invited him back into the federal government. As Minister of Justice, Macedo Soares helped Vargas prepare the Estado Novo coup, apparently in the belief that he would be appointed interventor of São Paulo. [90] The American Embassy had been tipped off to the coup in advance, [91] and the imminence of such a move was no secret to Brazilian politicians. Armando Sales made public but bootless pleas for the army to block the action. After the proclamation of the Estado Novo, Cardoso Melo Neto was allowed to stay on as interventor until April 1938, when he was replaced, not by Macedo Soares (who had in fact resigned before the coup), but by Ademar Pereira de Barros, a newcomer from the ranks of the now-extinct PRP. The young Ademar, whose only previous official post had been state assemblyman, was regarded as the dictator's surrogate in São Paulo rather than a representative of São Paulo's interests.[92] The British Embassy commented that "the President may have wished to supersede [Cardoso Melo Neto] with a man of lesser capacity, who will be more amenable to himself."[93] Consequently, by 1938 Vargas had achieved in São Paulo what he had accomplished five years earlier in Minas Gerais by appointing Benedito Valadares interventor: the imposition of his own political creature.*

Executive authority in São Paulo had been gaining strength since the early 1920's, and federal executive authority had likewise been expanding since the constitutional amendments of 1926. The years 1930–37 were a period of "deinstitutionalization" of the party structure of the Old Republic, as the Vargas government moved toward a corporatist state. Simply put, businessmen and other groups turned away from the Paulista parties when they ceased to be effective vehicles for advancing their interests. The industrialists, for example, though they had enthusiastically backed the Constitutionalist Revolution in 1932, began to swing to Vargas's side in the mid-1930's when it became obvious that neither of the mainstream parties in São Paulo offered good access to an increasingly powerful central government that preferred to listen to corporate groups, rather than politicians, on economic matters.[94]

Yet Ademar de Barros, like Benedito Valadares, did not remain a creature of the dictator. He used the power of state government to build his own political machine, taking advantage of the fact that São Paulo's revenues grew faster than those of the central government during the Estado Novo, just as they had in the Old Republic. Thus the administrative decentralization demanded by the Republicans in the 1870's was not reversed by the political centralization of the Estado Novo.

Structures

The Republic of 1889 brought important changes in the ground rules of politics. Revenues shifted significantly from the federal administration to state and local governments. Furthermore, there were many more elective political offices than under the Empire, and suffrage also expanded markedly.[95] A problem the Old Republic never managed to solve

---

*Valadares, like Valdomiro Lima, was a relative of Vargas's by marriage. But Valdomiro's efforts to manipulate São Paulo for the dictator had failed.

was how to provide for the orderly replacement of incumbent groups in positions of power at federal, state, and local levels, now that the Moderating Power was gone. During the Third Republic in France, the historian Alphonse Aulard wrote, "How beautiful was the Republic under the Empire!" In São Paulo the equivalent phrase was the oft-repeated remark, "It wasn't the Republic of my dreams."

In *Os donos do poder*, Raymundo Faoro sees Brazilian history as a struggle between the power of the central government and the local or private power of the landed elite. This pattern seems to fit São Paulo well enough in the Empire.[96] However, during the First Republic it was not the federal government, but the state government, that increasingly restricted the power of the rural seigneurs, in part because its revenues grew faster than federal revenues.

The state's power expanded steadily throughout the Old Republic,[97] but it grew most markedly under Governors Jorge Tibiriçá (1904–8) and Washington Luís (1920–24). Tibiriçá not only introduced valorization under the aegis of the state government, but otherwise won the planters' backing by supporting agricultural research, establishing immigration-boosting programs, and laying the legal groundwork for a state bank that would supply credit to planters.[98] Governor Tibiriçá also modernized the state administration, with something less than enthusiastic support from the landowners, by vastly strengthening the state police force (Força Pública) and establishing a career civil police. Beyond all this, Tibiriçá's acquisition of the Sorocabana Railroad in 1905 had two important consequences for the politics of São Paulo: it marked the beginning of the state's dependence on foreign loans (because domestic credit was insufficient for its public works and valorization programs), and it gave the state (or its ruling party) control over transportation in the Baixa and Alta Sorocabana regions.[99]

Washington Luís, another modernizing governor, was able to carry out a thorough judicial reform, which professionalized the São Paulo judiciary and made it much less dependent on local power. A law of November 17, 1921, established entrance examinations for the judiciary; instituted a regular promotion system; and forbade a *juiz de paz*, usually an untrained dependent of a coronel, to substitute for a *juiz de direito*, a state official with certified legal training. Still more important, perhaps, the law greatly increased the salary of the juiz de direito.[100]

In the same year, 1921, Washington Luís pushed through the legislature a land law that began to regularize the process of distributing public lands. He also initiated a highway building program that put a new transportation network entirely in the hands of the government—as railroads and water transport were not.[101]

The Força Pública provided the muscle for the state government. Its professionalization began with a reorganization in 1901, and it was then that the name Força Pública was adopted. The major changes came, however, in 1906 with Tibiriçá's much-criticized decision to bring in a foreign military mission.[102] Tibiriçá had been born in France of a Brazilian father and a French mother, and his choice of foreign instructors was doubtless influenced by the fact that his uncles were French army officers.[103] Thus São Paulo was to have an explicitly military as well as a civil police. Colonel Paul Balagny's instructors began training the Força Pública a full 12 years before another French mission arrived to train the federal army.

One of the most important steps toward professionalism was a raise in pay. In 1900 the commanding officer of the force, holding the rank of colonel, earned only a little more than half the salary of a director of a state normal school. By 1912, he was making more than the director, and by 1925, twice as much. From 1910 onward, the Força's officers were consistently paid as well as or better than their counterparts in the federal army.[104]

Other improvements in the Força were made over the years; these included a military hospital, a social insurance program, and a primary school for enlisted men, who were often illiterates or foreigners.[105] Clemenceau, visiting Brazil in the middle of the Old Republic, thought the Força Pública's quarters were better outfitted and more hygienic and comfortable than those of the French army.[106] In the 1920's, artillery and an air arm were added, and tanks were introduced in 1931. After 1925, the Força got most of its officers from a proper officers' candidate school rather than from the ranks.

The Republican government more than doubled the police force between 1889 and 1892, to an authorized strength of 4,000 men. More men were authorized in the late 1890's, during the millenarian revolt against the Republic at Canudos, Bahia. The force was subsequently reduced until the arrival of the French mission, when its numbers began to move upward again, first slowly, than rapidly. A peak level of 14,000 men was reached in the mid-1920's, following the 1924 rebellion of federal and state troops in São Paulo against President Bernardes. By 1928, however, the Força had been reduced to 8,500 men, and it was kept at roughly this size through the 1930's, despite the political turmoil of that period.[107] São Paulo had Brazil's most expensive state police force, but the Paulistas could well afford it. In real terms (1912 = 100) the expenditures for the Força Pública almost doubled from 1889–90 to 1900, with another rise of more than 50 percent by 1910. Absolute expenditures (deflated) hit a peak in 1930. In the subsequent years, however, there was a rapid rise in expenditures on the state-controlled civilian police force, which was separate from the Força Pública. In 1936 and 1937 the state spent more on the police than the Força.[108] (The reasons for this change are discussed in Chapter Eight.)

Like the federal army, the Força Pública was politically divided after 1922,[109] and its professionalization was probably a direct cause of its officers' participation in the 1924 rebellion; modernization had its ideological side effects.[110] Yet the rebellion was quelled in six weeks, and the chief remedy applied to the Força's malady was to boost the authorized troop strength.

The Força Pública was by no means all spit and polish. On the frontier some of its personnel were as lawless as the bandits they were pursuing. An egregious example was José Antônio Oliveira, known as Tenente Galinha.[111] Barely literate, Galinha had enlisted in the provincial police force in 1888, had twice deserted, and had frequently been disciplined; yet he provided the services the state wanted on the frontier, and reached the rank of lieutenant in 1909. Galinha's conduct was little affected by the French mission. Famous for bravado more than bravery (at times he would cower before desperate outlaws in shootouts),* Galinha and his men eliminated many dangerous bandits on the coffee frontier, sending the severed ears of their quarry back to the capital. But they also raped the wives of law-abiding but powerless caipiras, massacred gypsies, and mercilessly beat innocent men and women who in any way had displeased them. Galinha distrusted the legal system, which was undergoing rapid change at the apogee of his career, and he preferred to save the state legal costs by executing his captives on the spot. Ironically, he survived all the risks to life and limb in his forays through the interior of the state, only to be murdered in his own bed by his wife's lover in 1913.

The Força Pública was occasionally used as a lever in politics, both

---

*Among other things, galinha means chicken-hearted, and Oliveira willingly adopted the term as a nom de guerre.

before and after the 1906 reform, and the threat of its deployment was always present.[112] It was sometimes used to assist the army and at other times was arrayed to discourage federal intervention in São Paulo. It was also used for "social control." Tibiriçá sent it out against strikers in 1906; and Governor Arantes did the same in the general strike of 1917.

In political terms, Tibiriçá's reform of the non-military police and the judiciary in 1905–6 had major consequences for one group only—the coronéis. Under the system he inherited only the state chief of police and a dozen of his top officials, all in the capital, Santos, and Campinas, received salaries; the district officers, or delegados, and their subdelegados, though nominally under the chief's control, served in a purely honorary capacity and were thus financially dependent on the local coronel. Tibiriçá made São Paulo the first state to boast a career police force. Under his program, all delegados and subdelegados became full-time state employees; regular promotion and rotation systems were established; and the delegados in the most populous municípios were required to hold law degrees.[113]

The state government had other important powers that could be used for political leverage. Most important was the power to dispose of the public domain in a state where two-thirds of the surface area in 1891 was described as *terras devolutas* (unoccupied government lands).[114] In fact the state remained rather weak in this field (as the Empire had notoriously been);[115] and until the Washington Luís law of 1921 there was no orderly procedure for the transfer of land to private owners. But even this law manifestly failed to solve the problem. As long as landholders in frontier areas (and to a lesser degree elsewhere) did not have clear title to property the threat of punishment by the state government was a useful tool for political discipline;[116] this was especially true after the 1921 judicial reform.

Another power of the state was its freedom to create, eliminate, and change the size and shape of municípios. The organization of new municípios tended to follow changes in demographic patterns, but the state government sometimes used its power to block the creation of municípios for political ends.[117] *Municipalismo*—the demand for a greater degree of local autonomy—had emerged in São Paulo under the Empire, and a *municipalista* convention in 1896 met in the capital to protest the "autocracy" of the state government.[118] Municipalista sentiment was still alive in the 1930's, when the cause was defended (in demogogic fashion) by the Integralists. They identified the município with the extended family and wanted to counterpose it to state power. On the whole, however, municipalismo was associated throughout the period with coronel rule and never won a large following.

Still another source of power for the state was its ability to authorize loans. This power existed even before the State Mortgage Bank opened in 1909. In 1900, for example, Francisco Glicério and Washington Luís, then prefect of Batatais, published a letter in the PRP organ, *Correio Paulistano*, charging that only those who voted with the PRP executive committee could receive loans from the Banco de Crédito Real.[119] This "disciplinary" power, however, was relatively small until the government got into large-scale mortgage lending with the organization of the State Bank in 1926.

For all the state government's power, however, the coronéis were an indispensable part of the PRP machine.[120] The link between coronelismo and party bureaucracy was typically provided by a regionally based PRP chefe, a "supercoronel" who sat on the executive committee or was represented on it. A few chefes had lines of authority that stretched deep into the interior along the railroads and the areas they serviced. In the 1920's Fernando Prestes and Ataliba Leonel wielded power as far as 300 kilometers from their home municípios.[121] Their suzereignty extended westward along the tracks of the Sorocabana Railroad, which reached the Mato Grosso border in 1922. Both men also directed the last of the private armies in the state, at a time when they had already disappeared in Minas Gerais. Unlike the notorious coronel Horácio de Matos in Bahia, however, Prestes and Leonel always fought on behalf of the state government—together in 1924 and 1930, and Leonel alone (after Prestes's exile) in 1932. But these men were exceptional. Leonel's private military power was related to his control over a frontier area, the Alta Sorocabana zone, and Prestes's stronghold at Itapetininga was situated on the strategic rail route to Rio Grande do Sul: he had succeeded in establishing himself as a military force against a threat of attack from the south during the Federalist rebellion of 1893–95.

In general, as the power of the governor grew, the power of the party chefes decreased. Moreover, the state was not uniformly dominated by regionally based chefes; powerful local coronéis ruled in a few enclaves. For a brief period in 1909–10, for example, the coronel of Ribeirão Preto, Joaquim Cunha Junqueira, a member of an old and powerful family, successfully defied the state machine; but he did so with support at the federal level. It is probably no accident that this município (in the Mogiana zone) was also the biggest coffee producer in the opening years of the century.[122] Occasionally a local man could bypass the regional PRP chefe and go directly to the top of the party, if he had the right connections; one coronel was able to short-circuit the powerful Ataliba Leonel because he was a compadre of Governor Júlio Prestes.[123]

Coronelismo in São Paulo was least restrained by the state government on the frontier. There the coronel dominated public employment and civic life in the classic pattern of rural bossism. Control of land title validation, at least in the first instance, was probably the greatest power of the frontier coronel, since the juiz de paz was under his authority. Even after the judicial reform of 1921, pressure from the powerful regional party chefes, if not from the coronéis, could occasionally prove effective in swaying the juiz de direito.[124] In the sertão, which more or less meant the fringe of Portuguese-speaking settlement beyond the railhead (the demographic frontier), the coronel might typically be a self-educated lawyer (rábula, literally shyster) or a self-styled physician (curandeiro, healer). Closer in, on the rail-connected coffee frontier, he was often a wealthy merchant.[125] Mutual support between the executive committee and the coronel was the rule, though on some occasions the state leadership let rival coronéis fight it out.

In São Paulo city, the ward boss had come into being as well. One of the most notorious PRP vote-fixers, the powerful and brutal José Molinaro, boss of the Bom Retiro district, was killed on the steps of the capitol in 1928. O Estado de S. Paulo, disdainfully describing Molinaro as "without any social standing," did not bother to print an obituary notice. Even the Correio Paulistano (the PRP organ) gave him a mixed review. In its obituary, written by a state assemblyman, Molinaro was praised for his aid to the humble and his "obedience to hierarchy," but he was also described as a "self-made man," who was hated by some, and who was not "a man of fine worldly behavior." His demise followed hard on an insult he had directed at the family of a former Italo-Brazilian associate.[126] Molinaro would have been a key figure in the politics of many cities of the United States at the time, or even in Brazil's Federal District,[127] but in his heyday the capital supplied less than 20 percent of the state's vote. The ward boss in São Paulo city was to come into his own only after the Second World War.

São Paulo's level of economic development, plus the power of the state government, may have served to mitigate the crudest forms of coercion associated with bossism. But the frontier—like frontiers everywhere—provided ample opportunity for violence, as desperate men fought for land beyond the reach of the law, even though they expected its arrival in a matter of years. Political assassinations and murders by powerful local bosses did occur. In 1897, Araraquara gained the nickname Lynchaquara in places as far away as Mato Grosso and Minas Gerais, after Colonel Teodoro Carvalho was acquitted of the murder of several northeasterners there;[128] yet the very fact that its reputation traveled so far may indicate that such premeditated crimes (as opposed to election-day brawling) were uncommon enough to cause a scandal. On the other hand, São Paulo had its full share of vote fraud, and the forms it took were no different from the practices elsewhere in Brazil—cheating on totals, illegally registering illiterates, voting the dead, buying ballots. And there, as in the other states, when all else failed, intimidation and violence were brought into play.[129]

In the early 1930's, Interventor João Alberto began to undermine coronel (i.e., PRP) influence by centralizing administrative authority and appointing município prefects, under powers granted him by the Provisional Government. He also set up a Department of Municipal Administration in March 1931 to supervise local finances. Coronelismo of course was muted when there were no votes to deliver. In 1936, a degree of control was returned to the local level, when prefects were chosen in contests regulated by extensive federal legislation. These elections were generally regarded as being fairly conducted,[130] but the state retained an important tutelary power through the Department of Municipal Administration.

Organized interest groups, as one might expect, worked through the executive committee and the state government rather than the coronéis. Most of the effective formal pressure groups active in the period under study were associated with agriculture; these and other groups are treated in detail in Chapter Seven. One of the first was the Immigration Promotion Society, which was so successful after 1887 in getting both the Paulista government and the central government to adopt its policies that it went out of business in 1895. Another early interest group was the Commercial Association of São Paulo city, which officially dates from 1894, but actually grew out of an organization established a decade earlier. For this group in the early years and still more for its counterpart in Santos, the coffee trade was overwhelmingly the central interest.

Fazendeiros as such were surprisingly slow to organize a powerful association, and only the coffee crisis of the late 1890's and early 1900's finally brought them to action. An important step came in 1899, when a congress of planters demanded federal and state aid in the form of long-term loans. Organization for more concerted efforts came with the founding of the Sociedade Paulista de Agricultura in 1902, a year of huge crops, low prices, and high exchange rates. (The Society had a predecessor, the Centro da Lavoura Paulista, organized in the 1890's, but it never had many members.) It was the SPA, formed by the state's most powerful planters and comissários, that sponsored the valorization program adopted in 1906–8. It virtually dictated coffee policy under Governor Tibiriçá, and its members served as state secretaries of agriculture and (federal) Ministers of Agriculture after the ministry was reestablished in 1909. The price planters had to pay for extensive state support under valorization was greater control by the state over local political affairs. Throughout the period (but especially after 1926), they were also probably induced to remain loyal to the PRP through the state's control of mortgage loans, and eventually of land titles.

Other agricultural associations rose to challenge the SPA at different times on such matters as taxation, non-coffee agriculture, and valorization arrangements. The most important was the Sociedade Rural Brasileira, founded in 1919. Agricultural associations worked together to support federal backing for valorization in 1921, but the cleavages within the agricultural sector were intensified, and new alignments arose after the 1929 crisis. Despite the lack of a united front in the 1930's, the planters still received major benefits from the state and federal authorities, not the least of which was the federal government's cancelation of half their mortgage debts under the Economic Readjustment. (But again the fazendeiros had to pay a price for these favors; and now the "cost" was not only increasing loss of control of politics and administration at the local level, but central government control of coffee pricing and marketing, and hence production.)

Industrialists were far less successful in bringing pressure to bear during this era. Textile mill owners founded an association in 1919, but industrialists as a whole remained largely without influence until 1928, when they broke away from the Commercial Association to form the Center for Paulista Industry. Only in the late 1920's did the federal government begin to respond to the textile industry's demands for greater protection, but no consistent policy for the protection of industry in general emerged in the Vargas government during the 1930's. Nor did the Bank of Brazil or the State Bank extend significant amounts of credit to industrialists. As late as 1928, São Paulo's powerful Sociedade Rural Brasileira opposed Roberto Simonsen's thesis that Brazil should industrialize,[131] but coffee was discredited as the mainstay of the Paulista economy in the following decade. This development opened opportunities for planter-industrialist cooperation on a broader scale, as coffee growers began to turn to cotton. The shift away from coffee, however, had one unwelcome consequence for industrialists and merchants. After 1936 they had to bear a larger share of taxation, as the revenue base moved from a reliance on export duties to an assessment on sales and consignments, a 1 percent turnover tax on all transactions.

By and large, organized pressure groups during the First Republic stayed within the PRP fold, since it was obvious that the Republicans had no intention of ever surrendering power. Yet minority representation was a nagging problem for the PRP. In the 1890's, when Republican leaders still regarded the federal regime as besieged by monarchist plotters, Campos Sales had privately opposed allowing even dissidents in the PRP to hold political and administrative posts.[132]

The federal Constitution called for minority representation, and the initial state legislature attempted to carry out that aim simply by following the imperial Lei dos Terços (in effect 1875–81), which provided for minority parties to hold a third of the seats in the state legislature. But this law did not effectively guarantee a place for minorities in the state government,[133] and they had little chance to be elected until, in 1905, Governor Tibiriçá sponsored a law that introduced a proportional voting system for the state Chamber and Senate. As a measure of the powerful states' attitude toward the federal government, it is noteworthy that Tibiriçá, like his counterparts in Minas Gerais and Rio Grande do Sul, refused to enforce the federal Rosa e Silva Law of 1904, with its cumulative voting provisions to safeguard minority representation in state elections. Voting procedures in São Paulo were refined in 1907 and again in 1909.[134]

The opposition in São Paulo, as in other states, had an impact only when it was able to find support in the federal government. It was thanks to federal backing, for example, that Rodolfo Miranda, the head of the São Paulo branch of Pinheiro Machado's Partido Republicano Conservador, was able to bully the PRP into letting him control five of the state's 22 seats in the federal Congress in 1912. Miranda, who had tried to divide the PRP by threatening to run for governor, used his leverage with Pinheiro and President Hermes da Fonseca to raise the specter of federal intervention, then taking place in Bahia, where General Sotero de Menezes was bombing the state capital. Yet Miranda's "victory" merely gained him the seats that would have gone to the largest minority in any case.[135]

As I have noted, formal challenges by minority parties to the PRP were almost meaningless before the organization of the Partido Democrático in 1926. Two groups, however, made attempts in the 1890's—Catholics and monarchists. Both aimed their slings at the federal government more than the state, though the PRP was the most important political party behind the regime at the time. At a national conference in São Paulo in 1890, the country's bishops denounced the separation of Church and State and the Republic's institution of civil marriage and lay education.[136] In the same year, a Catholic Party, with the backing of a few former imperial politicians, was the only group to formally contest PRP hegemony in the elections for the Constituent Assembly. It was swamped at the polls.[137]

At that time, Pope Leo XIII still had not "legitimized" the French Republic with his policy of *ralliement*.[138] In France, the recatholization of the middle classes began early in the Third Republic, and affected intellectuals in the last years of the Belle Epoque. This trend had political significance in Brazil by the 1920's, especially in the Federal District and Minas Gerais. In São Paulo, both the PRP and the PD by the early 1930's were more receptive to the Church's demands for a role in public education. At the 1933–34 Constituent Assembly, the majority of São Paulo's delegates voted to allow religious instruction in the public schools. Otherwise the political influence of the Church was restricted. Though theoretically national in scope, the Catholic Electoral League, established by Cardinal Sebastião Leme in 1932, had a limited impact in São Paulo. Although most PD and PRP leaders did acquiesce in the League's program, Leme's favorite political group in the mid-1930's, the Integralists, faced two well-organized and well-financed rivals.[139]

The archbishop of São Paulo, Duarte Leopoldo e Silva, thwarted the attempts to link the Church to Integralism through his conspicuous bairrismo. His support for the Constitutionalist revolt in São Paulo in 1932 was so blatant as to embarrass Cardinal Leme in Rio. The following year Dom Duarte refused to attend the inauguration of Vargas's military interventor, Valdomiro Lima.[140] The archbishop, an intimate friend of ex-governor Altino Arantes, a PRP leader and prominent lay Catholic, probably blunted any attempt by Leme to encourage a close association of the Church and the supernationalistic and authoritarian Ação Integralista Brasileira.[141] In any event, the Church seems to have had significantly less political power in São Paulo in the 1930's than it had in Minas and Pernambuco, especially in the latter during the Estado Novo.

Monarchism, even in the early Republic, was less of a force than organized Catholicism. It was sustained by a few members of the landed elite and their dependents, the most prominent of whom was Eduardo Prado, who set up *O Comércio de S. Paulo* as a monarchist paper in the capital in 1895. In November of that year a Monarchist Party was founded, only to be suppressed by Governor Campos Sales 11 months later. Yet the millenarian revolt at Canudos in 1896–97, and its misinterpretation, kept the fear of restorationist plots alive; in fact, a rather pitiful monarchist rebellion erupted in the interior of São Paulo in 1902 and was easily quashed.[142] By that time monarchism was a dead letter, though it remained an obsession with a few vigilant Historical Republicans.

There were no further attacks on the legitimacy of the liberal Republic until the 1920's and 1930's. Brazil's peculiar brand of fascism emerged with the appearance of the Integralist Party in 1932–33. Its founder and Duce was Plínio Salgado, a renegade from the PRP. Like the proto-nationalist Alberto Torres, to whom Salgado and many others of his generation looked for inspiration, the national AIB Chefe (his official title) had grown up in the Paraíba Valley, one of the first regions to be impoverished as coffee lands wore out. Salgado's nationalism had roots in the culture of São Paulo. This state was the center of Brazil's national bourgeoisie (in Hélio Jaguaribe's sense),[143] and São Paulo's bourgeoisie was responsive to both an intense regional pride and a new nationalism. Salgado, a self-educated journalist and novelist, was influenced by the nationalistic reviews *Revista do Brasil* and *Brazilia*, founded in São Paulo in 1916 and 1917, as well as by the Liga Nacionalista, founded in the same period. In the 1920's, Salgado became a member of the reformist wing of the PRP, significantly named National Action, and served as a PRP deputy in the legislature under Governor Júlio Prestes. He was also prominent in the nationalistic Verde Amarelo (Greengilt) literary group, which took its name from the national colors.[144]

At the other end of the spectrum were the anarchists and Communists, and São Paulo bid fair to outdistance the Federal District as a hotbed of radicalism. Both Santos and the state capital vied with Rio as centers of strike activity, and a Marxist group in Santos was the first in Brazil to observe May 1 as International Labor Day, in 1895.[145] The Partido Comunista Brasileiro, founded in 1922, was the nucleus of the 1935 rebellion. According to one student, however, the anarchists in São Paulo were "at least as important as the PCB until 1930 or 1931."[146] The bulk of São Paulo's working class before the First World War was probably born in Italy, Spain, and Portugal, where anarchist traditions were much stronger than Marxism.[147] Yet it is hard to say how much of anarchism and anarcho-syndicalism (the "updated" version for industrial society, and the most important variant in São Paulo) was brought over directly from Europe, since most immigrants were from the ideologically "retarded" rural areas. A good part of that movement was certainly imported, for the works of theorists and activists from southern Europe were frequently cited in São Paulo's anarchist press. The anarchists, probably more than the Communists and other Marxists, were hurt by the repeated deportation of their leaders (who were mostly foreign-born, like their constituents). The enabling legislation was sponsored by two Paulista congressmen—Adolfo Gordo, in two famous laws bearing his name, and Arnolfo Azevedo.[148]

Rio de Janeiro was the center of the tightly organized PCB, but for a time in 1931–32 São Paulo's capital was the seat of the party, prefiguring that city's dominance in later years. During a strike in May 1932, however, the "illegal" Paulista government effectively broke up the PCB leadership, and the party's headquarters was shifted back to Rio. Like the PC and the PRP, the PCB divided over the presidential elections in 1937, with the São Paulo branch dissenting from the position of the Rio group on tactics. In the words of a discouraged PCB activist, the party "practically ceased to exist in São Paulo" from 1937 to 1945.[149]

In the 1930's there was another, and perhaps even more important Marxist group operating in São Paulo—the Trotskyists. In 1934, by the estimate of the United States consul, they numbered some 2,000, compared with 1,500 Stalinists; after the 1937 split in the (Stalinist) PCB, the Trotskyist strength in the state may have increased.[150]

On the federal level, the Paulistas led the way in the effort to fight communism in the Vargas years, just as they had earlier led the movement in Congress to repress anarchism. Vicente Ráo, Getúlio's Minister of Justice, was one of the authors of the Law of National Security (1935) and the first official to implement it. His fellow Paulistas were instrumental in pushing the law through Congress.[151] In 1936, Ráo organized the federal government's Commission to Repress Communism.

Representation and Elections

For the coffee barons and their business allies, "adequate" regional representation in the central government was an issue that long antedated the fear of the working class. In the late Empire, São Paulo, which had nearly 10 percent of the national population in 1890, was seriously underrepresented, with only nine of 125 deputies in the Chamber, and four of 60 senators. Thanks to the strength of the PRP in the Republic's Constituent Assembly and the Provisional Government, the state was given its full share of deputies, 22 of 212. (Each state had three senators.) But the more populous states of Bahia and Minas Gerais did not fare as well: Minas had 22 percent of the population in 1890, but got only 17 percent (37) of the delegates; and Bahia, with 13 percent of the population, had the same number of deputies as São Paulo. Since there was no reapportionment during the Old Republic, São Paulo, with its rapidly expanding population, was again patently underrepresented in Congress by 1930. (Thus President Washington Luís may in part have been seeking "compensation" in refusing to observe the custom of alternating the presidency between Minas and São Paulo by insisting on his fellow Paulista Júlio Prestes as his successor; the relative weakness of São Paulo in Congress could be redressed by prolonging São Paulo's control of the presidency.) The state's share of deputies was increased under the 1934 Constitution, but it was still underrepresented. It had only 14 percent of the seats in Congress from 1934 to 1937, compared with a 17 percent share of the national population in 1940, the nearest federal census year. (Minas too was perhaps slightly underrepresented, with 17 percent of the population in 1940, including the disputed Serra dos Aimoré, and 15 percent of the deputies in the mid-1930's.) São Paulo's interests, however, were probably better served than most states' by the addition of 50 "class" deputies to the 250 who represented geographical constituencies, even though the "class" deputies were beholden to President Vargas. In particular, Roberto Simonsen was an effective spokesman in Congress for Paulista industrialists.

But São Paulo had another and continually growing source of power: its expanding share of the electorate in a political system where the President, until the 1930's, was chosen by direct popular vote. Population growth accounted only in part for the swelling number of voters. There was also the fact that the sons and daughters of immigrants were citizens, whereas their parents generally were not.[152] A third reason was São Paulo's rising rate of literacy, because only literates had the franchise.

As we saw in the preceding chapter, São Paulo's literacy rate was below the national average in 1890, partly owing to its large slave population in the closing years of the Empire. By 1920, however, it had the second-highest rate, after Rio Grande do Sul. The two states still ranked in that order in 1940, when both had a rate of slightly more than 50 percent in the five-and-over age group.[153]

Like São Paulo, Minas had only a middling literacy rate in the early years of the Republic. But the two states nevertheless led the other states in vote totals. In the first direct presidential contest in 1894, each supplied 9 percent of the vote. After 1906, Rio Grande do Sul also became a major vote producer, and the three states together sometimes accounted for half the national totals. After 1894, Minas drew ahead of São Paulo, to hold first place in all federal elections throughout the rest of the Old Republic, but by 1930 the two states were nearly even again (20 percent and 19 percent, respectively). In the next election, that for the Constituent Assembly in 1933, the Paulistas' vote total outnumbered the Mineiros' for the first time, 22 percent to 21 percent. In the 1934 congressional elections (the last simultaneous national contests until 1945), the states were even once more (20 percent of the national vote in each), with Rio Grande still in third place (11 percent).[154] From 1902 on, Minas commanded a high and roughly constant share of the total vote; but the shares of São Paulo and Rio Grande rose, increasing the tendency for three states to dominate the federal contests.

From 1889 through 1930, interparty competition was almost meaningless and usually nonexistent in São Paulo. This lack of competition corresponded to a low level of political mobilization, which for the establishment party made patronage and the distribution of public works easier to process. Though voting data do not tell us much about political "output," such records do provide important information on the changing levels of political participation, the occupational structure of the electorate, the locus of political power among the state's regions, and, to some extent, the significance of the urban vote.

If we take voter participation as a rough index of political mobilization, São Paulo made rapid advances from the Empire to the closing of the federal system in 1937. Some 31,000 valid ballots were cast in the 1892 gubernatorial race. This was already more than twice the size of the vote in the 1886 parliamentary elections; and the vote in the 1936 município council elections was 485,000, or 15.5 times the 1892 figure. Since the number of inhabitants rose 4.7 times between 1890 and 1934, voter participation grew—irregularly—three times faster than the population.[155]

Though no occupational breakdown of the São Paulo electorate was published after 1905, the data through that year show why coronelismo played such an important role in the electoral process. In 1886, 1893, and 1905, more than half the registered voters were engaged in agriculture. If we ignore the "unknown" categories, the proportion in commerce (the second-largest group) declined from 19 percent to 10 percent; there was no obvious trend among tradesmen and public employees, the third- and fourth-largest groups.[156]

When and how the power of the vote changed within the state as the population shifted depends on the definition of appropriate zones. I have chosen to correlate population and voting patterns on the basis of Camargo's 10 regions, rather than by electoral districts, since their boundaries were not constant.* Table 4.2 shows how the voting pattern changed between the 1892 gubernatorial race and the 1936 município council elections.

The 1892 voting pattern offers a clue to why the Rodrigues Alves group and other ex-Conservatives in the Paraíba Valley were sought after by the PRP at the outset of the Republic. But as we see, the Valley's importance dwindled. Over the whole period there was a greater change in its share

---

*The Republic reduced the Empire's nine parliamentary districts to seven for congressional elections, and then compressed these into four in 1905. Constituent Assembly delegates in 1933 and congressmen in 1934 were elected in the state at large. State senators and representatives also ran at large from 1891 until 1905, and then as candidates in 10 new districts that cut across the federal electoral zones.

TABLE 4.2
Distribution of the Vote in São Paulo by Zone, 1892 and 1936
(Percent)

Zone	Share of the vote			Difference in share of population, 1890–1934
	1892	1936	Difference	
Capital	8%	19%	11%	11%
Paraíba Valley	30	9	−21	−17
Central	18	16	−2	−10
Mogiana	17	15	−2	−2
Baixa Paulista	5	11	6	−2
Araraquarense	5	11	6	12
Alta Paulista	—	6	6	9
Alta Sorocabana	10	8	−2	2
Baixa Sorocabana	5	2	−3	−3
Southern Coast	3	4	1	1

SOURCE: Population for 1890, Brazil, Sexo, pp. 126–37; for 1934, Camargo, Crescimento da população, 2: table 22. Voting data for 1892, SP, Annaes: (Câmara), 1892, pp. 456–58; for 1936, OESP, April 4, 1936, p. 4.

NOTE: The vote shares for 1892 are based on 30,652 of the 31,120 votes cast; the other 468 were omitted because I could not identify the zone. The 1936 returns used here are incomplete, but are the last to appear in OESP and accounted for 99% of the final vote (see OESP, April 26, 1936, p. 19). Final official talleys seem never to have been published. Percentages do not total 100 in every case because of rounding.

of the vote (downward) than in any other region (in either direction). The Capital zone advanced the most, but the three "pioneer" zones together (Araraquarense, Alta Paulista, and Alta Sorocabana) gained almost as much.[157] The three new zones gained more in population than in voting strength (23 percent compared with 10 percent), and older and relatively declining zones lost less proportionally, or even gained slightly.

The results of the 1936 elections were mentioned earlier; but it bears repeating that the PC won a smashing victory that year. The party got a majority or a plurality in 172 of the 240 municípios reporting in mid-April 1936, compared with only 55 for the PRP. Local parties had a majority or a plurality in 13 municípios; the Integralists won none. The PRP did best in the Mogiana zone (15 councils), an outcome that indicates the persistent strength of the Arantes and Cunha Junqueira families, but even there the PC won the majority. Perrepistas led in nine municípios in both the Paraíba Valley zone and the Central zone. The Rodrigues Alves clan was still powerful in the Paraíba Valley, and the Central zone had been the initial base of PRP power. In no other region did the Republicans carry more than five municípios.

Another indication of the distribution of political power among the 10 zones would be the dues collected by the PRP when it enjoyed a monopoly of power, but unfortunately, this information was lost in the fire in the PRP headquarters in 1930; data for 1895, however, survive from another source. Those figures show the relative insignificance of the Capital zone, the importance of the Paraíba Valley, and above all, the importance of the west at the time: the Central, Mogiana, and Baixa Paulista zones. These three zones accounted for more than half the total dues, just as they accounted for the bulk of coffee output in that period.[158] In the early years of the Republic the PRP was increasingly a planters' party.

No reliable urban-rural breakdown of the vote is available for the years 1889–1937, but the two overwhelmingly urban municípios were São Paulo city and Santos (Campinas was not). Together, their share of the vote rose from 7 percent in 1892 to 20 percent in 1927. In 1936, however, they still provided the same share of the vote as in 1927. If we consider the Capital and Southern Coast totally urban zones—in the 1934 state census they were the only two with a majority of urban dwellers —and if we consider the others totally rural, the "urban" share of the vote by zone was 11 percent in 1892 and 23 percent in 1936.[159]

Twenty-three direct gubernatorial and presidential elections were held in the years between 1892 and 1930 (see Table 4.3), and these "contests" revealed the degree of single party dominance by the PRP. Unlike Minas Gerais and Pernambuco, São Paulo witnessed no seriously contested elections in any of these races. Indeed, there was no presidential race in which the PRP-backed candidate won less than 73 percent of the vote; and even in 1910, when the opposition could count on support at the federal level, Rui Barbosa garnered 77 percent. Control of the governorship was tighter still: only two of the 12 governors got a less-than-unanimous mandate; they got "only" 98 percent and 99 percent of the ballots cast. In both Pernambuco and Minas, by contrast, the governor's seat was contested in three races; and each state had one election in which the winner received less than 60 percent of the vote.[160]

The electoral data for the 1930's, a period of relatively "clean" contests, show the extent to which traditional liberal ideals and the parties that professed them were still dominant in São Paulo as late as the institution of the Estado Novo. Both the PRP and the PD-PC were "nineteenth-century" liberal parties by ideology, advocating individual liberties; limited state interference in the economy and the society (except for aid to the coffee industry, which both parties endorsed); a prominent

TABLE 4.3
Voting for Governor and President in São Paulo, 1892–1930

	Governor			President			
Year	PRP-backed candidate	Percent of vote won	Number voting	Year	PRP-backed candidate	Percent of vote won	Number voting
1892	Bernardino de Campos	100	31,155	1894	Prudente de Morais	100	28,655
1896	Campos Sales	100	44,017	1898	Campos Sales	95	53,164
1898	Fernando Prestes	100	40,311	1902	Rodrigues Alves	95	53,908
1900	Rodrigues Alves	100	46,345	1906	Afonso Pena	98	29,526
1902	Bernardino de Campos	100	42,077	1910	Rui Barbosa	77[a]	108,618
1904	Jorge Tibiriçá	100	50,022	1914	Wenceslau Braz	93	64,097
1908	Albuquerque Lins	100	64,728	1918	Rodrigues Alves	99	48,241
1912	Rodrigues Alves	98	95,966	1919	Epitácio Pessoa	73	55,250
1916	Altino Arantes	100	118,330	1922	Artur Bernardes	91	99,355
1920	Washington Luís	100	80,139	1926	Washington Luís	98[b]	125,124
1924	Carlos de Campos	100	96,926	1930	Júlio Prestes	89	365,600[c]
1927	Júlio Prestes	99	135,286				

SOURCE: For the state, SP, *Annaes* (Câmara), 1892–98, 1902–27; *OESP*, April 24, 1900, p. 1. Federal tallies are in Brazil, *Diário*, 1894–1906, 1914–30; and DGE, *Annuario estatistico*, 1908–12, 1: 66 (for 1910 election).

[a] Rui's share of the vote is based on unofficial returns. The *Diario do Congresso* did not publish the results for the state as a whole.

[b] This is a *minimal* figure for Washington Luís; no state-by-state breakdown of the winner's vote was published, and this figure is based on the assumption that all of the 2,110 votes for other candidates were cast in São Paulo.

[c] This total differs from the figure I used to compute São Paulo's 19% share of the national vote (367,439), which was not broken down by share for the winner in the *Diario do Congresso*.

role for foreign capital in the public and private sectors of the economy; territorial rather than functional (corporate) representation in Congress; implicitly, separation of Church and State; and, of course, a high degree of autonomy for members of the Federation. A related ideological feature of "mainstream" politics in São Paulo was the tension between regionalism and nationalism. Regionalism was regnant throughout the period under review, but by the 1930's it was losing ground to nationalism for several reasons. In the economic sphere markets and sources of supply for industrial products had expanded beyond state frontiers by the Depression years, and concurrently coffee growers were searching for new lands and government aid that São Paulo could not provide. At the ideological level, Paulista intellectuals, an important segment of the national bourgeoisie, were articulating an authentic nationalism that went far beyond the xenophobia of nativism. Nevertheless, the growing power of the state government probably helped define the "polity" in the minds of Paulistas as São Paulo alone (Força Pública, state judiciary and civil police, labor department, health and education agencies), at least until the 1930's. Both social and political mobilization followed the rhythms set by the state economy and government.

From 1889 to 1937, the PRP and its liberal rivals and successors in power, the PD and the PC, kept the loyalty of the vast majority of their constituents. In the late years of the Empire, the PRP leaders had cannily and consistently pursued two objectives amid a series of opportunistic shifts on other issues, namely, the decentralization of authority and support for immigration. Gaining new power for their state in 1889, agricultural, banking, commercial, and later industrial groups in the PRP showed a genius for cohesion, and exhibited a flexible oligarchic style, at least down to 1926, when the PD appeared. Like the PRP, the other two "traditional" parties based their dominance on steady economic growth and the continuous incorporation of new agrarian elements on the frontier, the political effect of which was to keep urban groups from having a significant and distinct voice in politics.

In the Great Depression, the traditional ruling strata turned the failure of agrarian-export policies (under a Paulista President) into an asset within São Paulo. Between 1930 and 1932, they mobilized new groups on the basis of regional cleavages. Their electoral success in that decade was achieved in the face of a rapid rise in political participation. In the presidential election of 1926, for example, some 125,000 Paulistas cast ballots. This was the largest number ever for any contest, local or federal, in the state. Yet that number tripled just 10 years later. So did the proportion of the population who participated, though the figure barely topped 7 percent—at a time when women and eighteen-year-olds were already casting ballots.[161] Thus in São Paulo, as in Minas Gerais, where the pattern might have been more predictable, the control of state politics by traditional ruling groups was not seriously threatened by internal challengers representing new social forces. The failure of São Paulo's traditional liberal parties in 1937 was at the federal level, part of which was underestimating the appeal of federal solutions to the problems of powerful constituents at home. These issues are considered in Chapter Six; in the following chapter I shall examine state politics from a different perspective, sketching a collective portrait of São Paulo's political elite.

1. Chácara Dona Veridiana, a Prado family retreat in the Capital Zone, 1903.

2. Colono house at state-sponsored Núcleo Campos Sales (Central Zone), 1908.

3. Coffee planters on an outing to the groves, 1908.

. Colono family tending grape vines at state-sponsored Núcleo Tibiriçá (Baixa Paulista Zone), 1908.

5. Stevedore loading coffee at Santos, ca. 1910.

6. The immigrant coffee king Francisco Schmidt, ca. 1915.

7. The six Republican deputies in São Paulo's Provincial Assembly in 1882. Standing, from left: Martinho (Martinico) Prado Júnior, Manuel Campos Sales, Gabriel Toledo Piza e Almeida. Seated, from left: Francisco Rangel Pestana, Prudente de Morais, Antônio Gomes Pinheiro Machado.

8. Prudente de Morais, Governor of São Paulo, 1889–90, President of the Republic, 1894–98.

9. Manuel Campos Sales, Governor of São Paulo, 1896–98, President of the Republic, 1898–1902.

10. Francisco Rodrigues Alves, Governor of São Paulo, 1900–1902, 1912–16, President of the Republic, 1902–6, 1918–19 (with pince-nez and goatee); Altino Arantes, Governor of São Paulo, 1916–20 (to the President's right, holding bowler hat); and Congressman Cincinato Braga (face partly hidden by Rodrigues Alves), ca. 1906. The man in the center is unidentified.

11. Washington Luís Pereira de Sousa, Governor of São Paulo, 1920–24, President of the Republic, 1926–30.

12. A rally of affluent Paulistas demanding the return of constitutional government in 1932. One banner quotes (in Latin) the motto of São Paulo city: "I am not led; I lead."

13. Interventor Armando Sales greeting the President of Argentina, General Agustín Justo, on his visit to São Paulo in 1933.

CHAPTER FIVE

The Political Elite

DESPITE THE MASSIVE changes in São Paulo's economy and population mix in the first half-century of the Republic, its political elite remained strikingly homogeneous. Its leaders, like those of Minas Gerais and Pernambuco, tended to come from a small circle of families, closely linked by blood and marriage; went to the same schools or the same sorts of schools; and were wont to adopt European cultural values. Shared values and experiences, similar career patterns, and common recruitment pools for the Brazilian elite at large were legacies of the Empire. In all three states, the traditional agrarian upper class during the Republic became more urban- and market-oriented without losing its rural foundations, and the same was true of the smaller political elite. I define this group as Wirth and Levine define theirs in the companion studies, namely, the holders of important positions in the government and in the leading political parties at both the state and the national level from 1889 through 1937; the São Paulo elite consisted of 263 persons.[1]

In this chapter I consider the São Paulo political elite from both quantitative and qualitative perspectives. The first part, largely quantitative, focuses on the elite as a whole, as well as some component subgroups, and examines the following sets of characteristics: participation in political events; leadership functions outside politics; foreign, interstate, and family linkages; education; and occupation. I also consider the generational and geographical composition of the elite. The chapter concludes with a series of case studies designed to illustrate the variety of careers of real (as opposed to composite) political actors. Quantitative and qualitative judgments about São Paulo's larger socioeconomic elite or upper class are, of course, not tested here, though the temptation is strong to regard the state's political elite as "the executive committee of the ruling class."

Composition of the Elite

One indication of the homogeneity of the state's political elite was the absence of anyone from the working class. Nor was there a labor leader of any sort (compared with two in Pernambuco). Only one man was an immigrant, and just 11 others (5 percent) were definitely identifiable as sons of immigrants (i.e. had at least one foreign-born parent). Of these, at least two were sons of parents wealthy enough to educate their off-spring abroad (Alfredo Ellis and José Levy Sobrinho). The immigrant, Miguel Costa (who came to Brazil as a child from Portugal, via Argentina), was perhaps the most radical figure among those who formed the elite. Vicente Ráo, the only identified son of lower-class immigrants, was probably the most reactionary.

An indirect indicator of the long-term penetration of the elite by immigrants is the presence of non-Portuguese names in the group (though this indicator obviously does not identify late arrivals among the Luso-Brazilians). By this measure, people of immigrant stock were relatively slow to join the elite. Only 22 persons had partly or wholly non-Portuguese surnames (less than 9 percent of the total). This compares with a 15 percent population share for non-Portuguese immigrants in 1920—a figure, moreover, that omits second-generation Paulistas of non-Portuguese descent.[2] Significantly, only four men had Italian or Italian-derived names, whereas nine had English names, despite the negligible representation of Anglo-Saxons in the population and the heavy immigration of Italians from the late nineteenth century onward. (But in Minas Gerais there were only four persons with non-Portuguese names in the state elite.)[3]

That immigrants and their children would emerge slowly in the political elite is perhaps to be expected. On the other hand, São Paulo's political elite in our period was not, on the whole, an "ancient" one, though it included a few persons from the so-called 400-year-old families. The Rodrigues Alves clan, which supplied the only twice-elected President of Brazil and the largest number of men of the same surname in this elite (six), was founded by a Portuguese settler who reached Brazil in 1832.

Another indication of the group's homogeneity is found in the amount and type of education they received. Fewer than 8 percent lacked university degrees, and most of the members were of the generation born before 1869, for whom higher education was slightly less important in attaining high political office. Over three-quarters of the total group held the traditional *bacharel* degrees of law or medicine, and 63 percent had received their higher education at the São Paulo Law School in the capital. (In all, 70 percent had law degrees.) Higher education of some sort was almost a sine qua non for the Paulista elite in the era under study.[4] As a result, the pool for elite recruitment was exceedingly small: even by 1940, only one of every 250 Paulistas held a university degree.[5]

The São Paulo Law School's importance as a source of political leaders cannot be overstated. Apart from its role inside the state, it supplied an impressive number of the top national officeholders under both the Empire and the Old Republic. More than half the imperial Ministers from 1871 to 1889 were educated there. Seven of Brazil's 12 Presidents in the Old Republic were graduates, as was one acting President; and another President took part of his training there.[6]

Still another sign of the homogeneity of the São Paulo elite was its interlocking nature: 43 percent of the group were related to at least one other member (through first cousin, directly or by marriage), and 20 percent were members of or related to the imperial elite.[7] Though few were related to other state elites, fully half the members of the São Paulo elite had at least one of the three types of family ties. Cross-tabulating this information by Camargo's 10 zones, we find the highest proportion of the three types of family connections (77 percent) in the group from the Central zone (around Campinas), rather than among those from the tradition-oriented Paraíba Valley (55 percent), as one might expect.[8]

Kinship ties were probably more common in the higher echelons. There were two cases in which fathers and sons served as governor (Fernando and Júlio Prestes, Bernardino and Carlos de Campos), and one case in which brothers-in-law held that post (Campos Sales and Cerqueira César). Moreover, one governor was the son-in-law of another (Cardoso Melo Neto and Francisco Rodrigues Alves), and still another was the son-in-law of a man who had been governor under the Empire (Tibiriçá and Antônio Queiroz Teles). Finally, Rodrigues Alves's brother Virgílio was a lieutenant governor. (In Minas Gerais, there were considerably fewer family ties among the governors: a pair of brothers-in-law were the only close relatives there.) Seventy-six percent of São Paulo's governors had at least one of the three types of family tie (to the state elite, to the imperial elite, or to another state elite), compared with only 47 percent for the non-governors.[9]

In another approach to elite networks, I have used a broader set of criteria for linkages, taking into account common membership on boards of directors of business firms as well as kinship. (The latter includes in-law relationships that are seldom noted in North American culture, but constituted important forms of solidarity in Brazil at the time.) This procedure, illustrated in an endnote,[10] yields a continuous network of 97 men. In other words, more than a third of the whole elite formed a single complex of business and kinship ties.

The group was almost uniformly male. There was only one woman in an elite post (Maria Teresa de Azevedo, a member of the executive committee of the PC), and her role was clearly peripheral.* The next-most-common characteristic—probably—was religious affiliation, but data are sparse and were not coded. The overwhelming majority of the elite were secularized Catholics, whose wives and children practiced religion, if they did not. There were, in addition, at least one Positivist, one atheist, and one practicing Catholic of presumed Jewish descent.[11] No Protestants were discovered in the Paulista elite, but then only a little more than 2 percent of the Paulistas were Protestant as late as 1940. Nor were there clerics—in contrast to the elites of Minas Gerais and Pernambuco, which had a handful between them.

The cultural and political traditions of São Paulo were highly secularized by the late nineteenth century, and by the indicators discussed in Chapter Three, the state did not display an intensely religious culture compared with other units of the Federation. Moreover, the Church was probably rather less influential in politics in São Paulo than in Minas and Pernambuco. Religion could not have figured heavily in politics, it would seem, if an avowed atheist, Jorge Tibiriçá, could twice be placed in the governor's seat, and if that selfsame atheist could then throw his support to a gubernatorial candidate who was the best-known Catholic activist in the elite, Altino Arantes.[12]

---

*She served but one year. Another Paulista, Carlota Pereira de Queiroz, a member of the federal Constituent Assembly of 1933 and Congress (1934–37), was "the first Brazilian woman to sit in a legislative body." Hilton, Who's Who, 6: 194.

Even more scarce than data on religion are data on race. At least two mulattoes (Francisco Glicério and Armando Prado) played important legislative roles, but probably few of the members of the elite would have voluntarily owned up to any black ancestors. Nor is there any appreciable information on Indian forebears, even though such a background was less "damaging" than African ancestry.

An examination of the political bases of the elite reveals an extraordinarily high degree of concentration. Fully 67 percent of those whose home bases could be identified ($n = 238$) operated out of the capital city. (This figure is increased by our decision to code all presidents of the state supreme court as based in the capital, but even if those men are eliminated, 64 percent of the remaining group—139 of 217 persons— were based in São Paulo city.[13]) A substantial number of the governors, however, came from the Central zone (28 percent, compared with 56 percent from the Capital zone).[14] The political homes of the men outside the Capital zone were scattered, with no more than 8 percent of the total group in any single zone. All the elite members in the Capital zone were in São Paulo city.

Table 5.1 treats a slightly smaller group, namely, those elite members for whom we have both birthplaces and political bases ($n = 229$). In the first column we see a confirmation of the expected preponderance of the first three zones; and in the second, the striking shift to the capital as a political base, as well as the relative strength of the old West (Central, Mogiana, and Baixa Paulista zones).

Like São Paulo's upper class in general, many members of the political elite had estates in the interior as well as homes in the capital. An astonishing 51 percent of the fazendeiros ($n = 89$) had their political base in the capital city. This compares with only 10 percent of the fazendeiros in Minas Gerais, possibly indicating that the elite there was less heavily engaged in commercial agriculture.[15] Many members of the São Paulo group had in fact lived in several places in the interior of the state, as they pursued legal, political, and bureaucratic careers or followed the coffee frontier as planters. Those who became chiefs of police or members of the state supreme court almost always had had several posts in the interior before coming to the capital. Aspiring politicians were expected to hold some position in their home município. When Castilho Cabral, son of a PRP coronel in the Alta Sorocabana, asked Governor Júlio Prestes

TABLE 5.1
Distribution of the São Paulo Elite by Zone, 1889–1937

Zone	Birthplace	Political base
Capital	57	154
Paraíba Valley	34	11
Central	57	17
Mogiana	14	14
Baixa Paulista	11	18
Araraquarense	4	3
Alta Paulista	0	2
Alta Sorocabana	5	3
Baixa Sorocabana	0	0
Southern Coast	7	7
Out-of-state	37	—
Foreign	3[a]	—
TOTAL	229	229

NOTE: Figures include only those for whom both the birthplace and the political base are known. Federal interventors, whose political base was the Federal District, are excluded.
[a] Two of the three foreign-born (Jorge Tibiriçá and Adalberto Queiroz Teles) were sons of wealthy Brazilians temporarily residing in France. There was only one naturalized immigrant in the elite (Miguel Costa).

for a job in the capital, Prestes replied: "No. You are going to do a stint in the *sertão*, just as I did." Six months was all the would-be politician could take of it, and by his own reckoning, this lost him the chance to be a state deputy.[16]

Most of the Paulista elite had multiple careers, a practice that also helped to weaken the urban-rural cleavage. In a state where, as noted, only one in 250 Paulistas held a university degree in 1940, the graduate was in great demand. The members of the Paulista political elite were thus by no means confined to politics. On the average, they had three occupations other than "politician" or "public man," a profession common to all by definition. In Minas Gerais and Pernambuco, by contrast, the average number of outside occupations was closer to two than three, perhaps pointing again to lesser involvement in the economy by those elites. In São Paulo, after lawyer (69 percent), the most common occupations were fazendeiro (38 percent), industrialist (28 percent), journalist (27 percent), and educator (21 percent).

Geographical movement was a predominant theme. Almost 70 percent of the elite had political bases outside their native municípios. This does not always reflect a movement from interior to capital; on the contrary, there were several instances of movement in the other direction. More important, of the total based in the interior ($n = 71$), 63 percent were not based in their native municípios.[17] Geographical mobility among the elite was in part a consequence of the coffee boom. In Ribeirão Preto, the coffee município par excellence around 1910, only 20 percent of the municipal councilmen from 1910 to 1928 had been born in the município, and only 32 percent had even been born in São Paulo state. (But in other respects, the council was found to be socially homogeneous in those years.)[18]

Many members of the elite also traveled abroad. Republican statesmen probably had more ties with Europe through travel and education than their imperial predecessors because of the growth of the export economy. Europe now of course meant France, Belgium, Britain, Switzerland, and Germany, and not Portugal, the cynosure of Brazilian students before 1830. Of 17 São Paulo elite members who studied abroad at the university level, only one went to Portugal, and he chose a nontraditional subject—agronomy.[19] Most foreign degrees were earned in engineering and medicine, and one of the most powerful members of the elite, Tibiriçá, earned two degrees in science.

The São Paulo elite had a more elaborate network of foreign ties and more extensive contacts with foreign cultures and the international economy than the elites of Minas and Pernambuco. The Paulistas had the highest rate of residence abroad (32 percent, compared with 20 percent for the Pernambucanos and only 9 percent for the Mineiros). They also led in two other significant types of foreign linkages: one in every 11 São Paulo elite members was an investor in or manager of a foreign-owned firm, and roughly the same proportion had been decorated by a foreign government—presumably for services rendered.

On the composite variable of all foreign ties, 48 percent of São Paulo's elite had at least one of the attributes, compared with 33 percent for Pernambuco and only 16 percent for Minas. For the composite variable of occupations associated with the agricultural export complex, the Paulistas scored 40 percent, against 26 percent for the Pernambucanos and 17 for the Mineiros.

Similarly, São Paulo's political elite was more extensively involved in the economy than the elites of Pernambuco and Minas, as indicated not only by the "export" variable, but also by the relatively high proportion of industrialists, bankers, and merchants among its elite members:

Occupation	São Paulo	Pernambuco	Minas Gerais
Industrialist	28%	13%	18%
Banker	18	9	15
Merchant	17	13	6

On the composite variable businessman, the São Paulo elite scored 41 percent, compared with 35 percent for Minas and only 24 percent for Pernambuco.[20] (São Paulo also had more than twice as many fazendeiros, proportionately, in its elite as Minas and Pernambuco, but the data for those states are probably weaker on this point.)

Members of the state elites often met each other in Congress, but many became acquainted through their professions and especially through their education. Out-of-state schooling at secondary and university levels was sometimes followed by professional and (noncongressional) political jobs out of state. Of the three elites, the Paulistas had the highest percentage of births and of secondary schooling outside the state (19 percent and 20 percent, respectively), but, of course, a far lower rate of out-of-state legal training than the Mineiros. Before Minas and other southern states got their own law academies into operation in the late 1890's, the São Paulo Law School offered the most important opportunity for interstate school contacts.

All three state elites exhibited low rates of family ties with the elites of other states, but the Paulistas had fewer than 1 percent, compared with 12 percent for the Pernambucanos. Though the São Paulo data may be weak on this point, this low score is interesting, given the within-state rate of 43 percent for family ties. Paulistas, even more than Mineiros, seemed to marry at home. Since the extended family was everywhere a fundamental form of group solidarity, this finding may help explain the Paulistas' insularity and strong sense of identification with their own state.

The Paulistas also preferred to work at home. Only 17 percent had held out-of-state jobs (in administrative, political, or private employment), compared with 22 percent of the Mineiros and a striking 44 percent of the Pernambucanos, whose own state offered few job opportunities. In addition, fewer than a third of the Paulistas were ever in Congress, compared with over half of the Mineiros and Pernambucanos, possibly because they were less interested in establishing professional or patronage-related contacts in Rio.[21] On the composite variable of all out-of-state ties, the Paulistas again were lowest (39 percent, compared with 65 percent of the Pernambucanos and 72 percent of the Mineiros).

Entry into the São Paulo elite was predictably easier in times of crisis or renovation. The average was 5.4 persons per year for 1889–1937, with the largest number entering in 1891 (23), 1934 (21), and 1932 (20). The changes in 1891 are partly explained by Brasiliense's reorganization of the PRP executive committee; likewise, the large number of entrants in 1934 was partly the result of the creation of the executive committee of the newly organized PC; the 1932 group entered the political elite in the tumultuous year of the Constitutionalist Revolution. In the years after the Vargas revolution, São Paulo had a considerably larger share of new elite members than Minas and Pernambuco (37 percent, 22 percent, and 15 percent respectively). By contrast, in the heyday of the *política dos governadores*, there was little change in the São Paulo elite. An average of only two new members joined the elite each year from 1899 through 1925.

The Three Generations

For the consideration of longer-term processes, the most interesting variable was generation. The generations defined for this study were (1) persons born in 1868 and earlier, who reached maturity before the fall of the Empire; (2) those born between 1869 and 1888, who came of age by the middle of the Old Republic; and (3) those born during the Republic (1889 and later). Forty-six percent of the elite fell into the first generation; 34 percent into the second, and 20 percent into the third—which of course had not reached its zenith by the terminal date of this study.

A generational breakdown reveals a progressive "provincialization," i.e., an increasing tendency for the members of the elite to be recruited within the state and to obtain their relevant political experience there. Twenty-two percent of the first-generation members were born outside São Paulo, but only 11 percent of the third. Likewise, a larger percentage of the first generation had out-of-state ties of some sort.[22] Students at the São Paulo Law School also came into contact with relatively fewer non-Paulistas in the third generation than in the first. The experience of the men who became governors of São Paulo indicates a similar trend from Empire to Republic. Whereas the 48 governors of São Paulo who served at least 90 days during the Empire had, on the average, governed two provinces, only one of the 21 governors and interventors with at least 90 days' tenure from 1889 to 1937 had directed another unit. And that one exception was Américo Brasiliense, who gained his out-of-state experience under the Empire.[23] These findings are consistent with those

TABLE 5.2
Generation by Select Variables
(Percent)

Variable	Generation 1	Generation 2	Generation 3
Base			
Capital	70%	71%	68%
Pioneer zones	1	3	14
Family ties	57	55	33
Foreign ties	43	64	37
Residence abroad	26	50	20
Occupation			
Banker	26	12	11
Magistrate	35	6	9
Engineer	4	19	11
Educator	15	21	39
Legislative			
experience	71	51	40
Reached elite			
before age 40	25	13	59

NOTE: Significance for the cross-tabulations of generation by variables: base, 0.0584; family ties, 0.0185; foreign ties, 0.0034; residence abroad, 0.0003; banker, 0.0125; magistrate, 0.0000; engineer, 0.0032; educator, 0.0041; legislative experience, 0.0007; under-40 entry into elite, 0.0000. Family and foreign ties are composite variables (items 67–69 and 16–28, respectively, in Appendix A).

of Roderick and Jean Barman. In their study of selected law-school classes, they discovered that an increasingly large share of the men who became imperial deputies and senators (the Empire's only elected national officials) represented their native provinces as the Empire grew older.[24]

Robert Shirley's analysis of the São Paulo judicial elite, defined as all the members of the state supreme court (Tribunal de Justiça), also confirms this trend. Under the Empire, for instance, the court—established in 1874 as the Tribunal de Relação—included only five native Paulistas, of 24 appointees. The proportion more than doubled under the First Republic.[25] From the Empire through the Vargas years (1930–45), the proportion of native Paulista justices continually rose, as did the share graduating from the São Paulo Law School.[26] That the provincialization of the state court continued under Vargas may reveal his willingness, after the 1932 revolt, to let Paulistas run São Paulo, though "new" men were often Rio-oriented.

As shown in Table 5.2, other important generational differences emerged. For one thing, the representation in the three "pioneer" zones (Araraquarense, Alta Paulista, and Alta Sorocabana) climbed from 1 percent to 14 percent across the three generations. For another thing, family ties became less common, suggesting the possibility of increasing social mobility.

Foreign ties, a composite variable, bulked largest in the second generation; and as we see, fully half the members of the generation had resided abroad. This parallels the experience of export-oriented Argentina: the generation of 1880—roughly corresponding to our first generation—studied at home, but their sons studied and traveled abroad.[27]

The cross-tabulation of generation by occupation yielded several statistically significant findings. Bankers and magistrates tended to be clustered in the first generation, engineers in the second, and educators in the third. (No statistically significant relationships by generation appeared for lawyers, doctors, industrialists, businessmen, or fazendeiros.) One might have expected engineers to have been the most important group in the third generation because of the more technocratic orientation of the post-1930 governments, but it was educators (i.e. professors at the law school and other professional schools) who appeared in larger numbers.[28] Lawyers nearly held their own: they supplied three-fourths of the personnel in the first generation and two-thirds in the other two.

The age at which members of the group first entered an elite office also shows up as an important generational difference. Twenty-five percent of the first generation reached the elite before age forty, in contrast to only 13 percent for the second; but in the third generation the figure rose to 59 percent.[29] Given the relative youth of the third generation, the decline in legislative experience, from 71 percent in the first generation to 40 percent in the third, is consistent with expectations.[30] For the group as a whole (ignoring generations), high office was achieved more slowly than in Minas Gerais or Pernambuco. The median age at which the Paulistas entered the elite was forty-five, three years older than in the other two states. (Surprisingly, the men who were named to head imperial ministries over the years 1822–89 were on an average a year younger than the average Paulista was when he got his first, usually state-level, elite post.[31]) Thirty-nine percent of the Pernambucanos and 42 percent of the Mineiros reached their first elite job before age forty, compared with only 27 percent of the Paulistas.

These interstate differences are an indication, perhaps, of a more bureaucratic political "style" in São Paulo. Its career police force, as we have seen, dated back to 1905–6, and its judiciary was probably the most professional in the country, at least after Washington Luís's 1921 reforms.

There are indications of greater bureaucratization in its political organization, too. The state's Republican Party had a full-time executive committee before its sister parties in Minas and Pernambuco—the PRP's was established in the 1870's—and it also had the first regular dues-collecting system.[32] Finally, in each of the three contested presidential elections of the Old Republic (1910, 1922, and 1930), the PRP had a smaller share of its members oppose the candidate it backed than did its counterparts in Pernambuco and Minas.[33] (The defection of 24 percent of the Pernambucano establishment in 1910, and 22 percent in 1930, indicates the low level of political discipline in that state and its consequent vulnerability to federal intervention.[34])

Before leaving the matter of age differences, let us look at one subgroup of the elite—the executive committee of the PRP. One of the party's problems, as we saw in Chapter Four, was its failure to transfer power to a younger generation. In the 41 years that the PRP monopolized power, 56 men served on the committee, and 51 were members of the first generation. Second-generation men began to appear on the committee in the middle of the 1920's, and by 1928 five of its 10 members were neither Historical Republicans nor adherents to the Republic. But by 1930, a majority were again either Historicals or former monarchists. In Minas Gerais, by contrast, more than 40 percent of the members of the establishment party's executive committee during the Old Republic were members of the second generation, showing that the PRM handled the turnover problem much more ably than the PRP.

In the state elite as a whole, São Paulo had a larger proportion of Historicals than either Minas or Pernambuco (more than double the share of the latter); it also led in the proportion of abolitionists.[35] As expected, a disproportionate share of the elite's Historicals came from the West of the late imperial era (the Central zone and its fringes). Both the Capital zone and the Paraíba Valley zone had smaller percentages of Historicals than their shares of the first-generation elite. Contrariwise, adherents were better represented in the Capital and the Paraíba Valley than in the Central zone:

Zone	Historicals	Adherents
Capital	59%	73%
Central	14	2
Paraíba Valley	4	12
Others	23	13

None of the other zones had even 10 percent in either category.[36]

As noted in Chapter Four, nine of the 11 governors of the first generation were Historicals and only two were adherents, and almost twice as
many Historicals as ex-monarchists sat on the PRP executive committee
from 1889 to 1930.[37] Though data are less complete for the PRP's years
in opposition (1931–37), it is clear that the overwhelming majority of
committee members in that period were "new" men, not those of the
first generation.[38] Even so, of the 64 PRP committee members from
1889 through 1936 for whom data are available, 70 percent fell into the
first generation, 28 percent into the second, and only 2 percent (i.e.,
one man) into the third.*

Other features distinguish the executive committees of the state's three
parties (PRP, PD, PC) from the elite members who did not hold top party
(as opposed to government) posts. First, the committeemen were much
more active in the economic sector than the non-committee members:
twice as many were involved in the export trade (56 percent against 27
percent), and a third more were businessmen (50 percent against 34 percent).[39] The PRP executive committee considered alone shows even
greater contrast—60 percent in business, compared with 34 percent for
the other committeemen.[40] Second, the committee members of the three
parties scored higher on the (composite) family tie variable than the nonmembers (59 percent against 42 percent).[41]

What differences separated the PRP committee members from their
rivals? Boris Fausto's revisionist thesis on the Democrats denies that they
were the "burguêses progressistas" of Paulo Nogueira Filho and charac-
terizes them as representing not industry, but agrarian interests, commerce and banking, and the more prestigious liberal professions.[42] Fausto's evidence consists of a close examination of the content of the original
PD manifesto and the careers of a few prominent members in 1926. I
have attempted a partial test of the thesis by comparing the biographies
of 28 PD executive committee members and their 26 PRP counterparts
during the lifetime of the PD (1926–34).† From the data presented in
Table 5.3, the Fausto thesis appears to be confirmed only in part. True

*Compare the percentages for the elite members who were not on the PRP executive
committee: first generation, 37%; second, 36%; and third, 27%. Significance: 0.0000.

†Though Fausto's group and mine are not the same, I do not believe that Vargas's
triumph in 1930 altered the social character of PD leadership by allowing new opportunists
to gain control of the organization. The PD remained an opposition party through most
of the period 1931–34, and a majority of executive committee members in 1931 had served
on the committee before the revolution (see Appendix B).

TABLE 5.3
Occupations of the Executive Committees of the Partido
Democrático and the Partido Republicano Paulista,
1926–1934
(Percent)

Occupation	PD (n = 28)	PRP (n = 26)
Professions		
Lawyer	81%	76%
Educator	39	16
Physician	12	4
Business and banking		
Industrialist	35	44
Merchant	19	20
Banker	8	36
Exporter	8	16
Fazendeiro	35	60

NOTE: The members of both groups had multiple careers, with an average of almost three occupations (excluding all posts held in the elite, party or otherwise).

enough, there were fewer industrialists among the PD's leaders than among the PRP's, but industry was still well represented. On the other hand, the PD had comparatively few bankers, fazendeiros, and exporters, and certainly far fewer than the PRP. That the Democratic leadership was heavily made up of upper-class professionals is confirmed. The PD's committee had more physicians, more educators, and even slightly more lawyers than the PRP's. The PD's leaders were more concentrated in the capital (77 percent, compared with 36 percent), just as they were concentrated in urban-based professions.

The PD's leaders may have been of higher social standing than the PRP's; more committee members belonged to leading social clubs (68 percent against 48 percent), and more belonged to the Sociedade Rural Brasileira (14 percent against 8 percent). The PD group was also better educated; all the men had been to college, whereas 16 percent of the PRP leaders had not. Yet these differences are marginal, and since we are dealing with small groups, evidence for the PD committee's higher social standing remains inconclusive.

An important feature that Fausto does not treat is the generational difference between the leaders of the two parties. The PRP group's median year of birth was 1875; the PD group's was 1890. Coming to maturity after 1910, the typical PD leader missed both the initial coffee boom and the first industrial surge, as well as the opportunity to invest in railroads; 4 percent of the PD leaders were directors of rail companies, against 20 percent of the PRP men. In part, perhaps, the PD had fewer railroad investors, bankers, fazendeiros, and exporters precisely because of the relative youth of its leaders. Yet all things considered, what the data show is how much alike the leaders of the two parties were.

Career Patterns of the Elite

To return to the whole São Paulo elite, the careers of its members tended, predictably, to reflect movement from state to federal positions of authority, as was the case for the elite of Minas Gerais; in both states the typical beginning positions were state cabinet posts and seats on the executive committees of state political parties. Patterns in Pernambuco are similar

TABLE 5.4

Office Groupings of State Elite by Sequence of Positions Held

(Adjusted frequencies in percentages)

Office group	First post	Second post	Third post	Fourth post	Fifth post	Sixth post	Seventh post	Eighth post	Ninth post
State									
S1	3%	3%	3%	13%	4%	7%	20%	20%	0%
S2	27	24	19	24	4	0	0	0	0
S3	15	5	10	8	9	13	0	0	0
S4	7	11	5	5	9	7	10	20	25
S5	7	2	2	0	0	0	0	0	0
S6	34	37	43	42	43	40	50	60	50
Federal									
F1	0	0	0	0	9	13	0	0	25
F2	2	8	5	3	0	13	0	0	0
F3	3	2	2	0	4	0	0	0	0
F4	1	5	10	5	17	7	10	0	0
F5	2	5	0	0	0	0	10	0	0
All state except S6	59	45	39	50	26	27	30	40	25
All federal	8	20	17	8	30	33	20	0	25
Absolute number in each group	263	120	58	38	23	15	10	5	4

S1. Governor.
S2. Secretaries.
S3. Other state executive posts (prefect, police chief, top administrator, bank president, lieutenant governor).
S4. State legislative posts (president of the senate, president of the chamber, majority leader).
S5. President, state court.
S6. Executive committees of the Republican parties and opposition parties.
F1. President of the Republic.
F2. Minister.
F3. Other federal executive posts (president of the Bank of Brazil, etc.).
F4. Congressional posts.
F5. Supreme court.

TABLE 5.5
Percent of State Elite with Tenure in More Than One Post

State	First post	Second post	Third post	Fourth post	Fifth post	Sixth post
São Paulo	100%	46%	22%	14%	9%	6%
Minas Gerais	100	42	21	11	6	3
Pernambuco	100	25	8	3	1	1

but less regular, perhaps reflecting the more anarchic political experience there, and the much greater importance of initiatives by the federal government in the political process.[43]

Seasoned Paulista politicians, as Table 5.4 shows, tended to return to positions of leadership in the state legislature. The Mineiros were much more likely to hold high congressional office as their fifth or sixth elite post, though the Paulistas show some tendency in that direction. In all three states the overwhelming majority of the presidents of the state supreme court obtained that position as their first elite post, and no one got it any later than the third, indicating that even in Pernambuco—perhaps because of the traditions of the Recife Law School—the court was set apart from the rest of the elite. In São Paulo, supreme court presidents rarely held a later post, except as justices of the federal supreme court.

Even though more men entered the Paulista elite as members of an executive committee of a political party than through any other single post, in São Paulo, more than in the other two states, the members of the elite were also increasingly inclined to take seats on the party executive committees as they gained in experience and prestige. This may indicate that such posts were more important in São Paulo than in the other two states. Finally, the São Paulo elite had a greater "survival" rate than the elites of Minas and Pernambuco (see Table 5.5). That fact supports the view that São Paulo had a more bureaucratized political system than those states, one that placed greater value on experience and seniority.

One feature the São Paulo elite shared with the elites in the other two states was an urban-cum-rural life-style; indeed, this was one of its most salient features. Moreover, its members were likely to have moved about a good bit. A man might have owned several physically separated fazendas over a lifetime; he might have attended several colégios (where he made lasting contacts with the sons of the upper classes), and, if a member of the first generation, he might even have attended both the São Paulo and the Recife Law School. (One could transfer after the completion of any academic year during the imperial era.) He owned a townhouse in the state capital, perhaps had a *sítio* nearby, and owned one or more fazendas in the interior. He might also have practiced law or represented the state government in several communities in the interior. His political base was the state capital, but he was probably born in the interior.

São Paulo city was of course the center of all political activity. During the First Republic, only when a Paulista was President did Rio figure as a principal center of power for the state elite. The governor was otherwise the leading personage in politics, and the PRP executive committee met in the state capital. Although the urban-rural or capital-interior dichotomy is probably nearly meaningless for the elite itself, there was nonetheless a sharp distinction between the bacharel-dominated elite oriented toward São Paulo city and the locally rooted coronéis. The bacharel was perhaps less at a loss in the countryside than the coronel was in the capital city, to judge by the satire *Madame Pommery*. Written in 1919, this novel relates how powerful coronéis, with plenty of cash to spend, were taken in by the citified ways of the girls of Au Paradis Retrouvé, a bordello where drinking champagne and lavish spending were de rigueur.[44] It is not surprising, after all, that the political elite and the coronéis were rather sharply divided, since the São Paulo elite was probably the most cosmopolitan of the three elites studied, and it was certainly the most fully integrated in the international economy.

Case Studies

Moving away from abstractions, let us consider several real and varied cases, because the variety of paths to prominence is just as important in understanding the São Paulo elite as a "typical" (and implicitly uniform) career pattern. In many ways, the model Paulista statesman of the era was Jorge Tibiriçá.[45] Aristocratic, immensely wealthy, and Europe-oriented, Tibiriçá was a modernizer both in business and in government. A member of the first generation, he was twice governor (1890–91; 1904–8), and held three other elite posts, including a total of 17 years on the executive committee of the PRP. Tibiriçá was born in Paris to a Brazilian father and a French mother in 1855; his father's string of sur-

names—Tibiriçá Piratininga de Almeida Prado—indicated his impeccable credentials as a member of the colonial aristocracy. (Revealingly,
where Jorge's father went to France for his schooling, his grandfather
had gone to Portugal.) João, the father, was a member of the founding
convention of the PRP in 1873 at Itu, which was also the site of the family
estate. The family property, located in the heart of the new coffee country, was larger than 5,000 hectares.

At home in the language of both parents, Jorge went on to learn German at a colégio in São Paulo and later in Switzerland. He graduated
from the school of agronomy at Hohenheim, Germany, and then took a
doctorate in chemistry at Zurich in 1879. Tibiriçá married as befitted his
station. His choice was his first cousin, the daughter of Antônio Queiroz
Teles, the Conde de Parnaíba, a founder of the Mogiana Railroad and
governor of the province in 1886–87. (Tibiriçá was also related through
his marriage to two other members of the elite.) Like his father, Jorge
Tibiriçá was a Historical Republican; he also believed in the gradual
emancipation of the slave, but was not an abolitionist. Before the end
of the imperial era, he was not only a prominent planter, but also a director of the Mogiana Railroad. He obtained several properties in the area
served by the Mogiana, and did not hesitate to sell the family estate at
Itu in 1891.

Appointed governor by Deodoro in 1890 but dismissed the following
year, Tibiriçá became a Florianista. As an insider in the reorganization
of the PRP after Brasiliense's ouster, he served as secretary of agriculture in 1892–95. It is no exaggeration to say that as governor between
1904 and 1908 he did more to shape São Paulo's future than any other
man. To repeat his achievements briefly: he instituted a professional
police force; brought in a French military mission to reform the Força
Pública; borrowed unprecedented sums abroad for public works projects;
set up the state Colonization Agency; authorized a French-financed agricultural credit bank and the introduction of Japanese immigrants (both
implemented by his successor); and, most significantly, instituted the
coffee valorization program.

Tibiriçá joined the PRP executive committee the year he retired as
governor, remaining on it until the 1924 reorganization of the party. In
his later years, he was also president of the state senate, and at the time
of his death in 1928, he was president of the Tribunal de Contas (the

state auditing agency). Educated in theoretical and applied science in an age of materialism, he remained an atheist all his life, but this fact was never effectively used against him in politics.

Another "aristocrat," though less prominent in his economic and political endeavors, was Arnolfo Azevedo, member of the PRP executive committee and president of the federal Chamber of Deputies, 1921–26.[46] Azevedo was a man of the first generation, but barely so; he was born in 1867. Through his parents, who were second cousins, he was related to the two leading families in the Paraíba Valley município of Lorena. Azevedo's father was an eleventh-hour baron (ennobled 1888), slave-owner, and boss of the local Conservative Party. After studying with private tutors, Arnolfo attended colégios in both the provincial and the imperial capital. At the São Paulo Law School, he was already a Republican before the end of the Empire (according to the biography written by his son). When, on his graduation in 1891 he married into the Gama Cochrane family of Santos, he forged a new political link: his father-in-law had been on the provincial executive committee of the Conservative Party in the last year of the Empire. Furthermore, Arnolfo was the grand-nephew of Pedro Vicente de Azevedo, last imperial governor of São Paulo, a member of the elite under study, and himself a relative of two other elite members.

Just out of law school, Arnolfo backed the PRP leaders against Deodoro's attempted coup d'état, and was soon rewarded with the leadership of the party in Lorena. He began as public prosecutor and quickly became a member of the municipal council, then prefect. Serving as a state deputy from 1895 to 1900, he obtained a public water supply for his home community. In a minor PRP squabble in 1899, Azevedo found himself at odds with the party's leaders; for the next few years, he withdrew from politics and devoted himself to improving his declining coffee estate by experimenting with new crops. By 1902, Azevedo's political dissidence was forgotten to the extent that he could again direct the local unit of the PRP. Under the patronage of the Paraíba Valley's powerful Rodrigues Alves family, Azevedo became a federal congressman in 1903. He remained in the Chamber of Deputies until 1926, associating his fortunes in later years with those of Washington Luís; he served as president of the Chamber from 1921 to 1926. Azevedo joined the PRP executive committee after the 1924 split (in which Washington Luís triumphed over the Rodrigues Alves family and others), and served as federal senator from

1927 to 1930. His political career was terminated by the Vargas revolution, and some of his assets were frozen by the new regime. This sober, honest, unexpansive, and humorless man, a product of a materialist age (like Tibiriçá), died in 1938, shortly after receiving his first communion.

Rodolfo Miranda, born in 1860 in Resende, Rio de Janeiro, had far more panache than Azevedo and conceivably had the most curious career in the PRP.[47] Miranda's maverick behavior from 1891 through 1914 shows how tolerant the PRP could be of a rich and talented man. During these years, he found himself in opposition to the ruling elements in the state party in four crises: he backed Deodoro's attempted coup and supported Governor Américo Brasiliense in 1891; he supported Francisco Glicério against Prudente in 1897 in the PRF crisis; he backed Campos Sales against the winning gubernatorial candidate, Albuquerque Lins, in 1907; and he broke with the state establishment over the presidential succession of 1910. Yet he remained a federal deputy from 1897 to 1909, and became Minister of Agriculture in 1909–10 (under President Nilo Peçanha). Siding with Hermes da Fonseca, the winning presidential candidate in 1910, he joined Pinheiro Machado in 1911 in toying with the idea of overthrowing the PRP on its home ground.[48] But Miranda seems also to have functioned as a conduit for Paulista interests in the Nilo and Hermes administrations, and in 1915 he found himself on the winning side in an internal division in the PRP. He served in the state senate from 1919 to 1928, and sat continuously on the PRP executive committee from 1917 to 1930. In 1933 he was instrumental in forming the Single Ticket coalition against Vargas's interventor.[49]

Sent by his father, the Barão de Bananal, to Paris to study at the Collège de France, Miranda attended an occasional lecture and was something of a playboy. In 1883, he moved to São Simão in the Mogiana zone, where he went "to plant coffee and preach the [coming of the] Republic."[50] He became a great landowner in the Alta Paulista region and founded the community that later became Marília. Rodolfo Miranda's assets, however, were by no means confined to real estate: he owned a textile factory in Piracicaba and had a commercial firm at Santos. He was also a banker, and his son Luís (also in the elite) followed in his footsteps. Miranda's two notable accomplishments in his brief term as Minister of Agriculture were the creation of the Indian Protection Service and the procurement of public works and other benefits for his home município, São Simão (including a federal agricultural school).

Miranda, Tibiriçá, and Azevedo were cultured and urbane, but the violence-prone "super-coronel" was not an unfamiliar figure in São Paulo. The most successful—some would say the most notorious—was Ataliba Leonel, boss of the Alta Sorocabana zone in the late years of the Old Republic.[51] From his photographs, Leonel looked the part—square-jawed, athletically built, with an air of authority. At a statewide level, his influence was greatest from the governorship of Washington Luís (1920–24) until the overthrow of the Old Republic.

Leonel was born in Itapetininga, in the Central zone, in 1875. From the beginning of the Republic, this município and the area southward were dominated by Fernando Prestes—lawyer, rancher, honorary general (for his prowess in the campaigns of 1893–95), banker, and director of the Mogiana Railroad. Prestes became the younger man's patron and served as a model for Leonel's own career.

Ataliba Leonel came from a family with roots in São Paulo dating back to the eighteenth century, and his father was an officer in the National Guard; yet Ataliba was apparently not related to any member of the political or imperial elite. He attended two colégios in the state capital, and graduated from the São Paulo Law School in 1895.

Leonel made his base at Piraju, on the edge of the rough-and-tumble Alta Sorocabana zone, where he was a fazendeiro as well as a lawyer. Four years out of law school, he became the boss of that município and began to extend his influence westward. After 1904, he usually held a seat in the state chamber or senate, though bringing in the vote in the Alta Sorocabana remained a major concern. Leonel was respected and feared, and his influence ultimately extended to the Mato Grosso border, almost 320 kilometers from Piraju.[52] In 1925, Leonel joined the PRP executive committee, to become, at the age of fifty, one of its youngest members.

Like Fernando Prestes, Ataliba Leonel was not only a political boss, but a military chieftain as well. In 1924, the two PRP leaders organized an "army" of their dependents to attack the military rebels of General Isidoro Dias Lopes, who were retreating westward from São Paulo city. The soldiers considered their antagonists jagunços (rude backlanders), but Leonel, like Prestes, gained the rank of honorary general in the army.[53] Leonel led his troops in 1930 against the Vargas forces moving on Itararé, and in the 1932 rebellion he organized the Brigade of the South, which ultimately swelled to 6,500 men. He lived in exile in Portugal following the armistice but returned to Brazil after an amnesty, to again set himself up as prefect of Piraju in 1934. He also returned to the PRP executive committee, but died the same year.

Silky and pensive, Armando de Sales Oliveira was a political leader whose style could not have contrasted more sharply with Leonel's.[54] As interventor and governor from 1933 to 1936, Sales was the most powerful figure in Paulista politics during the 1930's. But in the end he found himself trying to fend off the coup d'état that signaled the demise of his style of politics: Sales was one of those rare Brazilians whose background and period allowed him to combine a belief in traditional liberalism with an equally firm belief in technocracy.

Sales's father was an engineer and state senator, and his mother came from an important family of comissários in Santos. Armando was born in the capital in 1887 (near the end of the second generation) and received his secondary and higher education there. A serious and hardworking youth at the new Polytechnic School, he also found time for student politics. After his graduation, Sales spent several years in Europe, where he took some post-graduate engineering courses. On his return, he built several power plants in the interior of São Paulo and became a vice-president of the Mogiana Railroad before entering politics. He had been an officer of the reformist Liga Nacionalista, but his decision to pursue a full-time political career was probably more directly influenced by his marriage into the family of Júlio Mesquita, publisher of the state's most important newspaper, O Estado de S. Paulo. Like Arthur Sulzberger of the New York Times, Sales succeeded his father-in-law, directing O Estado from 1927. He belonged to all the leading clubs.[55] He was a militant in the PD; and in 1931, he founded the Institute for the Rational Organization of Labor (IDORT), a society that subscribed to an updated version of F. W. Taylor's scientific management as a solution to Brazil's economic depression.

Appointed interventor by Vargas in 1933 as a goodwill gesture toward the PD and São Paulo's constitutionalist aspirations, Armando Sales stood for oligarchic democracy and state autonomy. Among his achievements as interventor (and after 1934, elected governor) were the creation of the University of São Paulo; a reform of the state tax system; the initiation of social welfare programs; and the organization of the state-associated airline VASP. Sales resigned as governor in 1936 to launch a presidential campaign as the candidate of the PC (which he headed) and its national counterpart, the União Democrática Brasileira. In the final months before the institution of the Estado Novo, his defense of liberal values grew increasingly pathetic as he plaintively appealed to the army not to participate in a coup d'état. After November 10, he spent almost a year as a prisoner before being expelled from the country. Sales was allowed to return to Brazil shortly before the end of the Estado Novo, and helped found a new opposition party, the União Democrática Nacional; he died, however, before the Vargas dictatorship fell.

The preceding cases tend to show the importance of family and wealth. But the careers of two other members of the elite, Numa de Oliveira and Vicente Ráo, illustrate that upward mobility was not altogether denied to those of humble origins. Oliveira, "the more or less open representative of the Rothschilds," according to an American observer,[56] was a prominent banker and coffee planter who became secretary of finance in 1931. Born in 1870, Oliveira was a self-educated man who served in his youth as a stenographer in Portugal, in Rio de Janeiro, and finally in São Paulo during the governorship of Cerqueira César (1891–92). He was then invited to direct stenography operations in the state chamber of deputies. He furthermore became a client of Júlio de Mesquita, Cerqueira César's son-in-law. Oliveira's position in the chamber apparently provided excellent political and economic intelligence, as well as connections, and he was soon able to invest in coffee lands in the Ribeirão Preto area. He also became a comissário at Santos and a director (and later president) of the Banco do Comércio e Indústria, one of the state's most important private banks. Oliveira's modest beginnings did not block him socially. Far from it: he was a charter member of the Automóvel Clube, and was twice president of perhaps the most prestigious club of all, the Atlético. Oliveira's business acumen was outstanding, and he became almost as well known as a representative of the wealthiest coffee planters as he was a banker and agent of the Schroeder and Rothschild banks. The latter connections, however, were the source of a successful move to terminate his tenure as secretary of finance.

For Vicente Ráo, a member of the PD executive committee and Minister of Justice from 1934 to 1937, the route into the political elite was not business success but the law.[57] Ráo, the son of Italian immigrants, was a member of the third generation (born in the state capital in 1892), and was one of the few elite members not to have significant rural connections or investments. He first studied philosophy at the Catholic University of Louvain, then came back to São Paulo to take a law degree. Out of school, Ráo became a journalist, an investor in the construction industry, and, in 1927, a professor (catedrático) at the São Paulo Law School. Three years later, he was elected president of the Instituto de Advogados (state lawyers' association). Like Oliveira, Ráo moved up socially, as well as professionally, to be accepted in two important clubs, the Automóvel and the Comercial. In the year of the Vargas revolution, he briefly served as chief of police in the São Paulo Provisional Government. Along with other "Paulista patriots," he championed the state's cause in 1932, though from afar, since he undertook a diplomatic mission in Europe at the time. As Minister of Justice, he drew up the Security and State of War Laws, which helped set the stage for the 1937 coup. In the mid-1930's Ráo was a particular target for those who denounced the federal government's intermittent persecution of leftist politicians, intellectuals, and academicians. He had good connections with the Church (including close family connections: one of his brothers was a priest and one of his sisters a nun). Though he helped prepare the way for the Estado Novo, Ráo withdrew from political activity before its arrival. He enjoyed an important professional and political career after the Second World War, twice serving as Foreign Minister in the 1950's.

Yet impressive as Ráo's rise was, he was clearly an exceptional figure in the São Paulo political elite. Most of its members came from upper-middle- or upper-class backgrounds and were bound together by complex family, school, and business ties. Unfortunately, I was not able to obtain data on compadrio (ritual kinship), one of the basic forms of Brazilian family solidarity; such data would almost certainly reveal even more extensive intra-elite connections.[58] "This is nothing more than a government of compadres," charged federal Deputy Martinico Prado in 1891.[59] He was referring to the Deodoro administration, to be sure, but he might well have been speaking of the elite of his home state.

CHAPTER SIX

State and Nation: Political Dimensions

THE PAULISTA POLITICAL elite was sure of its birthright to run São Paulo. There were virtually no challenges to that assumption before 1930, since Democrats so closely resembled Republicans. Whether that elite made similar claims on the federal government is not so easily assessed. After 1930, and in some ways even earlier, Paulistas did not get what some of them considered their rightful due—what Raymundo Faoro has termed "hegemonic federalism." For instance, in 1932, the Partido Democrático offered as a partial solution to the imbalance of states, the conversion of some of the weaker and poorer ones into federal territories.*

The subject of this chapter is the state's "external" relations—mostly, with the central government, but also with other states and countries. Among other things, I shall consider São Paulo's role in the presidential system; its representation in the three branches of the federal government; the special role of Congress in dealing with economic issues of paramount concern to the Paulistas; and the unique dependency—and opportunity—that characterized São Paulo's relations with foreign investors.

To get what it wanted from the Union, I will contend, São Paulo did not have to "dominate" federal politics, if that meant supplying the Presi-

---

*Faoro, *Donos*, 2: 554; PD program in H. Silva, *1932 . . . A guerra paulista*, pp. 267–76, especially p. 267. The PD ultimately got its way in this matter, but not under the regime it wanted. Article eight of the Estado Novo Constitution declared that any state failing to meet its debt service obligations for three consecutive years would be converted into a federal territory until its finances were put in order.

dent and key cabinet officers. São Paulo's minimum political program during the years 1889–1937 consisted in dominating federal policies only in those areas where action at the state level was impossible or insufficient —namely, in monetary and exchange policy, in the guaranteeing of the state's foreign loans, in tax and immigration laws, and in the distribution of revenues between state and federal governments. Concerns shifted in the 1930's because of new markets for manufactures within Brazil and the long-term depression in coffee exports.

The Presidential System

The workings of the São Paulo economy are necessarily central to an analysis of the state's political relations, but the celebrated thesis of Celso Furtado, widely shared by others, that coffee planters (and by extension, São Paulo) controlled the federal government's economic and financial policies during the Old Republic fails to take into account that the executive had problems that often brought it into direct conflict with coffee groups.[1] To repay interest and principal on ever-more-burdensome foreign loans had policy implications in three areas: the need to improve the exchange rate, or at least to arrest its deterioration; the need to balance the budget and to stop the issuance of unbacked paper currency; and the need to secure a favorable balance of trade so as to acquire the requisite foreign exchange for servicing and repaying the loans. The first two requirements, of course, brought the federal government into conflict with coffee groups. Let us turn first, then, to a brief historical survey of the Paulista's relations with the presidency, noting where this conflict developed and how it was resolved.

São Paulo's role in federal politics falls into three phases—1889–1905, 1905–30, and 1930–37. The first, a period of Paulista dominance, commences with the birth of the Republic and ends shortly before the state relinquished the presidency. The second period begins with extensive borrowing abroad, the institution of chronically imbalanced state budgets, the introduction of valorization, and a diminished Paulista representation in high federal offices. This period is characterized by São Paulo's "control" of Brazil's foreign-exchange, monetary, and commodity-protection policies; it ends with the Great Depression and the overthrow of the Old Republic in 1930. The final phase coincides with São Paulo's opposition to federal leadership and its loss of control of exchange and coffee policies. This is a period of turmoil in state politics; it ends with the neutralization of São Paulo's political leaders and their acquiescence in the centralization of political authority.

The first phase began with the federal army rather than the PRP at stage center. But in general the PRP leaders were satisfied with the provisional government of Marshal Deodoro da Fonseca. São Paulo's irreducible demand for a federal republic was met; new business legislation was introduced, facilitating the formation of joint-stock companies; and the state got one of the four banks of issue (though only at Campos Sales's insistence, since Rui Barbosa had omitted São Paulo in his draft decree).[2] At the Constituent Assembly, the PRP's programs, with the support of Minas Gerais, fared well: the Paulistas won a near-autonomy for states in the federal system, undergirded by the export tax (which was sufficient as a revenue base for São Paulo alone); state control of public lands; and the "tacit naturalization" of immigrants.* In fact, the São Paulo position at the assembly even looked moderate next to the more radical version of federalism advocated by Júlio de Castilhos's disciplined delegation from Rio Grande do Sul.

Relations between Deodoro and Paulista leaders deteriorated with the resignation of the cabinet in January 1891, and became even worse in February, when Prudente de Morais insisted on opposing the Marshal for the presidency. Under the new constitutional system, the Paulistas had an advantage—for a time they virtually controlled the legislative branch of government. And of all the Presidents of Brazil in our period, only Deodoro faced a Congress with a majority that actively opposed him.[3]

As June Hahner has emphasized, after Deodoro's ouster, his successor, Floriano Peixoto, and the PRP developed a symbiotic relationship.[4] Among the things São Paulo had to offer was a military force that had doubled in strength between the fall of the Empire and the outbreak of civil war in 1893. In the same year, Francisco Glicério formed the Partido Republicano Federal, the instrument by which the Paulistas formalized and tightened their control over other congressional delegations. In the PRF's organizing meeting, neither Minas Gerais, nor Rio Grande do Sul was represented, a fact that heightened the Paulistas' influence.[5] The convention unanimously nominated Prudente de Morais for President for

---

*"Tacit naturalization" meant that all foreigners who did not register as nationals of other countries within six months of the ratification of the Constitution automatically became citizens of Brazil.

the term 1894-98. This was indeed a daring move, since a civil war was raging and military figures, not civilians, were the heroes of the hour.

Despite Prudente's health problems, resulting in a temporary withdrawal from the presidency, he managed to bring the government under civilian control. The Canudos rebellion made the army look impotent, and the President emerged a hero from a related attempt on his life; he then dealt firmly with those suspected of trying to overthrow him.[6] But however questionable Prudente's tactics may have been in bringing Congress under presidential control by breaking up the PRF, he did not impose a successor; Campos Sales's nomination took shape in the halls and cloakrooms of Congress, where a newly united Minas Gerais delegation was becoming the chief power.[7]

Manuel Campos Sales, as the father of the política dos governadores, formalized the system that was to last until 1930. In the eyes of a President whose central concern was bringing the foreign debt under control, the política was less the destruction of democracy than the orchestration of groups with votes to deliver.[8] In fact, the legitimacy of the political system did not suffer immediately from the arrangement because of the low level of political mobilization and the lack of coordination of the several opposition parties.

At any rate, the política's effectiveness depended on the new coherence of the congressional delegation of Minas Gerais, arising as it did out of Campos Sales's belief that he needed unqualified congressional support to carry out the provisions of the 1898 Funding Loan.[9] But in the end, his successful drive to improve the exchange rate angered planters as much as his budget-slashing policies angered the populace of Rio de Janeiro. Campos Sales's presidency provided the first and most striking illustration of the structural conflict between the financial interests of the federal government and those of the coffee groups, notwithstanding his previous career as planter and defender of coffee-related legislation.

The next President, Francisco Rodrigues Alves, was the third Paulista in succession, and had been handpicked by Campos Sales because of his hard-line position on finances. Rodrigues Alves had resigned from Floriano's cabinet in 1892 when the Iron Marshal refused to accept a Rothschild plan aimed at achieving financial stability. In the 1890's, Alves had earned a reputation for austerity budgeting, but as President-elect he planned to make the federal capital a sanitary and well-landscaped city, and this objective precluded other major outlays that would compete for the restricted monies left after the Funding Loan obligations were met. One of Rodrigues Alves's aims in the sanitation project was to attract more immigrants to Brazil,[10] and by extension to São Paulo, which under his governorship had already begun a significant sanitation program. In other respects, Rodrigues Alves remained a fiscal hard-liner, as Campos Sales had anticipated.

Clearly, São Paulo would sooner or later have to release its hold on the presidency, and the occasion arose during the presidential maneuvering of 1905, when the PRP was divided over the valorization issue. Bernardino de Campos, twice governor, former federal Minister and president of the Chamber, was the obvious Paulista candidate. But he hewed too closely to the austerity line traced out by Campos Sales. Bernardino, who had direct acquaintance with the federal government's problems as Prudente's Minister of Finance, was a *livre-cambista*, opposing the foreign-exchange controls so central to the planters' designs. He also believed that export taxes hindered economic growth, a position that plainly threatened the São Paulo government's fiscal base.[11] Furthermore, as governor, Bernardino had limited coffee planting in São Paulo by executive order in 1903, and the measure was quickly denounced by an assembly of planters (though the more far-sighted growers approved of it). Under these circumstances, Bernardino's candidacy was doomed in the face of the coffee crisis of 1905–6.

Still, the Paulistas found Afonso Pena, the Mineiro who succeeded Rodrigues Alves, pliant enough on the key issues of valorization and the Exchange Bank when his own congressional delegation threw their support behind those measures. Pena's selection as President initiated the second phase of São Paulo's role in federal politics, with the PRP releasing its control of the federal executive in order to guarantee support for the coffee industry. But Pena's willingness to assist coffee groups in São Paulo and Minas prevented him from meeting the fiscal standards set by his two immediate predecessors—a fact, to be sure, of little interest to pro-valorization groups in São Paulo, led by Governor Tibiriçá.

In the early soundings for the 1910 succession, the Paulistas were willing to go along with the President's favorite, the Mineiro David Campista, because Campista had been the leading congressional proponent of the Exchange Bank in 1906, and because they owed Pena a political debt for his endorsement of the £15,000,000 valorization loan of 1908.[12] Senator Pinheiro Machado of Rio Grande do Sul meanwhile worked with the anti-Pena faction in Minas (led by former Governor Bias Fortes) to block Campista. When Pinheiro came out for Marshal Hermes da Fonseca in May 1909, the Paulista congressional leaders stood by Campista because they thought that the army was divided, that the navy backed Campista, and that the treasury could be used on his behalf.[13] Though Pena died in June and the new President, Nilo Peçanha, decided to back Hermes, the PRP still refused to acquiesce. São Paulo had successfully "demilitarized" the Republic, and its three Presidents had earned a reputation for anti-militarism. True, the Paulistas had leaned heavily on the support of the increasingly powerful Pinheiro Machado for coffee and exchange legislation during 1906–8, but they probably felt less dependent on the Gaúcho senator when international coffee prices moved upward in 1909.[14]

To oppose the military candidate, the PRP turned to Rui Barbosa, the paladin of Brazilian liberalism who, in the words of the British ambassador, was "notorious abroad and renowned at home" for his loquacity at the Hague Peace Conference in 1907.[15] In Minas, the old Pena group also backed Rui. The Paulistas balked when Pinheiro brought his satellite groups into line behind Hermes, apparently with Nilo's approval, but also, Rui had maneuvered them into a position where they would suffer a serious loss of face if his running mate, São Paulo Governor Albuquerque Lins, withdrew from the race.[16]

In the campaign, both Rui and Albuquerque Lins attacked militarism and by implication, Hermes. But of course the issues were more complicated. There were echoes, for example, of the worldwide struggle for influence between Great Britain and Germany. The British, aware that Hermes had seen German field maneuvers as the guest of the Kaiser, feared Hermes as a Germanophile and militarist; the German ambassador privately hoped for his victory.[17] There is little evidence of direct pressure by either power, though financial groups in London were worried that Hermes would be a saber-rattler against Argentina.

As 1909 drew to an end, it was clear that Hermes would be the winner because of Pinheiro's allies in the army and the executive, as well as his followers in Congress, where the votes were counted. Why, then, did São Paulo persist in a campaign that constituted the first contested presidential race in the Republic, one Rui was sure to lose? For one thing, the Paulista leaders had put themselves on the line against Hermes when President Pena and the candidacy of Campista were still alive, and initially they had even expected Nilo to be neutral.[18] For another, there was a real concern that militarism might threaten Brazil's credit, a matter treated below.

Hermes da Fonseca's government brought in its train what the PRP had feared—an uncontrolled grab for power at the state level by military "redeemers," men so dedicated to taking control of the governor's mansion that they did not shrink from the use of artillery, if it came to that. São Paulo took a defensive position, holding onto its economic privileges, bolstering its military strength against attack, and attempting to wait out the term of a government that was discrediting both the military and Pinheiro Machado's Partido Republicano Conservador, the national "party" that legitimized Pinheiro's authority in Congress.

In 1913, Minas and São Paulo came together again to block Pinheiro as kingmaker. The result was the Pact of Ouro Fino, in which both states pledged their support to Wenceslau Braz, the Vice-President and former governor of Minas. In the end, Pinheiro yielded when he was offered the face-saving device of presenting Braz as the PRC candidate. After the inauguration, Cincinato Braga, São Paulo's financial expert in Congress, warned Braz that São Paulo could no longer tolerate Pinheiro's machinations in Congress and the executive branch.[19] This attitude, though not yet shared by all Paulista leaders, may have stiffened Wenceslau's resolve to resist the PRC. Pinheiro Machado's power waned as a succession of crises shook the various satellite states, while a united São Paulo stood firm behind the President. The PRP had escaped major schism under fire from Hermes, Pinheiro, and Rodolfo Miranda in the years 1909–14; and the 1915 split in São Paulo (see Chapter Four) came only after Pinheiro's assassination in September.

The election of the next President was a source of frustration for the PRP leaders, who felt that São Paulo should supply the chief executive at regular intervals. Elsewhere I have discussed the election of Rodrigues Alves, his death shortly after taking office, and the Mineiro-Paulista rivalry to supply his successor in early 1919. The governor of São Paulo, Altino Arantes, was the leading PRP candidate, but was rejected by Governor Borges de Medeiros of Rio Grande do Sul. Most slatemakers in Congress regarded both Altino and Governor Artur Bernardes, his rival in Minas, as too youthful for the presidency. Furthermore, some of the influential members of the PRP were not enthusiastic about Altino's candidacy, because of the difficult choices he had had to make during his governorship.[20] In the jargon of the era, during 1918 he had had to face the consequences of four *g's*—*guerra*, *gafanhotos*, *geada*, and *gripe* (war, a locust plague, a coffee-killing frost, and the Spanish flu). He may also have been hurt by the charge of a pro-German bias because of his business connections. The Paulistas and Mineiros finally agreed to accept Rio Grande do Sul's compromise candidate for chief executive, Epitácio Pessoa, of Paraíba, though they expected economic concessions in return.

It was in fact under Epitácio, Brazil's first and only civilian President from the Northeast in our period, that São Paulo made some of its greatest economic gains. In 1920, for example, Braga managed to tack on an amendment to a currency issue bill offered by Carlos de Campos, the Paulista majority leader in the Chamber, that authorized the issuance of 250,000 contos to banks for financing coffee exports. When the President balked, São Paulo, with the backing of Minas, forced him to give in.[21] The following year, the federal government assumed direct responsibility for valorization. Paulista politicians thus showed their ability to achieve major economic advantages even under a President more concerned with helping a competing regional interest—the drought-afflicted agriculture of the Northeast.

In this capsulized survey of the São Paulo establishment's relations with presidential administrations, we may note that the next President, Artur Bernardes, a politician born in Minas's coffee-growing Mata zone, provided the greatest surprises. Two considerations figured in Bernardes's famous reversal on coffee policy and near-break with São Paulo midway in his presidency: the imminence of the repayment of the Funding Loan and the need for increasing outlays on the armed forces to check the growing number of revolts. His decision to get the federal government out of valorization eased the way for his successor, Washington Luís, to do what Bernardes had not done—balance the budget. (In fact, he and his Paulista predecessors Campos Sales and Rodrigues Alves were the only three Presidents to accomplish this feat more or less consistently during their terms in office.) Admittedly, Washington Luís's Stabilization Bank did undervalue the currency, but one student has argued that his financial policies were designed not so much to help the coffee complex as to stabilize the exchange rate at a realistic level (an objective achieved until 1930), to curtail expenditures, and to begin paying off the Funding Loan (which was done on schedule in 1927).[22] Washington Luís's refusal to heed the coffee groups' demands for aid in 1930 shows once again how the presidency could change an incumbent's perspective on economic and financial problems, even a man who had built a career on planter support.

The world Depression not only brought about the ouster of Washington Luís's government and the abrogation of the Constitution, but also changed the political ground rules. São Paulo's strategy of relying on massive exports and foreign loans was no longer possible: loans were unobtainable, and the central government was able to increase its strength vis-à-vis São Paulo precisely because it had to assume a large share of the state's debt. The fall of the Old Republic ended the second phase of São Paulo's role in the Federation. During the final phase, 1930–37, the state no longer had "control" of Brazil's monetary, exchange, and lending policies. The period was characterized by a firm resistance to the Vargas regime until economic groups in São Paulo itself became convinced of the advantages of a strong central authority.

From the early months of the Vargas government, the dictator issued economic decrees that provided "compensation" for São Paulo's political setbacks. The Depression itself initially provided automatic benefits to coffee interests, since the exhaustion of the country's gold reserves led to a fall in the exchange rate. But the disaster of the Depression also revealed the stresses in the coffee complex. When Vargas's Provisional Government bought all existing coffee stocks in 1931, it was at a price so low as to benefit only those bankers who had recently financed coffee stocks; the Paulista Finance Minister, José Maria Whitaker, a banker, was accused of aiding his fellow bankers and abandoning the growers.[23]

Vargas's agent in São Paulo during 1932–33, Interventor Valdomiro Castilho de Lima, openly favored planters over financiers, who also formed part of the elite of the planter class. State export taxes were curtailed, and Valdomiro got Vargas to agree to a moratorium on plantation mortgages. This action, part of the Economic Readjustment, helped planters (who were now turning from coffee to cotton) and hurt lenders and exporters, as the considerable losses of the Wille company, discussed earlier, attest.[24]

Eventually, Getúlio's long tenure of office also had favorable consequences for São Paulo's industrialists. During the Old Republic, they had had little direct influence in forming the PRP's demands on the federal government. Benefits to industry largely derived from federal policies undertaken for other purposes—tariffs instituted to raise revenue, credit expansion, and the control of immigrant radicals. Exchange policies ceased to favor agriculture after 1930, but Vargas's refusal to go even further and favor capital goods imports in the exchange-rate schedules of 1932 and 1936 seems to show a lack of interest in industrialization before the advent of the Estado Novo.[25] As noted in Chapter Two, the federal government was equivocal in its attitude toward industrial development in the 1930's; no consistent policy outside the labor area was pursued. In the later Vargas years, however, the industrialists received a better hearing, a turnabout that was probably due to the declining power of coffee groups in the sustained depression in their overseas markets, to the association of industrial power with nationalism, embraced by Vargas during the Estado Novo years, and to the mutual desire of government and industry to retain social control (a trend that was evident even in the early 1930's).

Though Vargas offered paternalistic welfare policies to workers, the "two-thirds" law of December 1930 (by which two-thirds of the employees of every firm had to be Brazilian nationals) was backed by industrialists in São Paulo as a check to foreign-born agitators. Workers were also required to carry identity cards in the 1930's, and only officially recognized (and supervised) unions were permitted. At the local level, Vargas's first interventor in São Paulo, João Alberto, continued the policy of his constitutional predecessor in sending unemployed factory hands to the plantations. As many as 60,000 may have been dispatched to the countryside by mid-1931.[26] Over the next few years, Paulista manufacturers learned that they could profit from the growth of the new regime's paternalistic labor apparatus.[27]

Representation in the Federal Government

São Paulo, for all its economic importance, did not dominate the executive branch of the central government during the period under study. It was second to Minas Gerais in the number of years its representatives held cabinet posts during the Old Republic, a distant third behind Rio Grande do Sul and Minas in the early Vargas era (1930–37), and third overall in the entire period 1889–1937.[28] In the 11-year stretch between 1898 and 1909, the state did not supply a single cabinet Minister, though of course three Paulistas held the presidency during those years. Likewise, the state was unrepresented in the cabinet in 1914–18 (under Wenceslau Braz), and again in 1925–30.*

Nor did Paulistas predominate in the presidency of the Bank of Brazil, though they held office at critical periods, e.g., in the years 1921 and 1922, when the federal government took over valorization and the bank became the nation's sole bank of issue.[29]

In appointments to the Supreme Court, São Paulo received 11 of the 74 nominations in our period. Though this is a slightly higher number than would be indicated by São Paulo's average share of population, it is surprisingly low, considering that the state had one of the only two law schools in the country throughout the Empire, and that the school supplied so many Presidents. None of the first three Presidents from São Paulo named a Paulista to the Court; but Washington Luís, who had a high regard for the São Paulo judiciary he had reformed as governor, appointed three—more than any other chief executive.[30]

São Paulo probably had less influence in the Congress of the Old Republic than Minas Gerais, since the Mineiro deputies outnumbered the Paulistas five to three (37 to 22). The relative distribution was based on the results of the 1890 census. After the 1920 count, the Paulistas unsuccessfully pushed for reapportionment, and in the 1933 Constituent Assembly both states had the same number they had received in the Old Republic. During the brief life of the Constitution of 1934, São Paulo received 12 additional seats in the new Chamber. (Rio Grande do Sul registered the second-largest increase, three; Minas gained only one seat.) São Paulo's share of the total state representation (250 congressmen) now rose from 10 percent to 14 percent. But the gain was largely illusory, since 50 "professional" deputies representing corporate groups were added at the same time who typically followed the lead of President Vargas.[31]

The Mineiros held more positions of power in the Chamber than the Paulistas over the course of the Old Republic. The Paulistas, however, held sway to a large extent in the formative years: Prudente served as president of the Constituent Assembly; and Bernardino was president of the Chamber at the time of Deodoro's attempted coup (November

---

*But the 1925–30 period was another that overlapped with a Paulista presidency. The state's exclusion from the Braz government may be related to the PRP's interest in an alliance with the Partido Republicano Riograndense, a point that I shall take up in due course.

1891) and through the following months, when the PRP lent critical support to Floriano. Arnolfo Azevedo held the post during the turbulent years 1921–26. Paulistas likewise occupied the majority leader's position during the 1890's and 1920's. Glicério led his "20 brigades" (the state delegations) into the PRF in 1893 to nominate Prudente, but lost his power in the quarrel with the Paulista President in 1897. The Paulistas' control of the Chamber leader's post in the 1920's embraced the period of the federal government's assumption of valorization and Washington Luís's monetary reforms.

Of the various standing committees in the Chamber, the Paulistas were most interested in the Finance Committee (Orçamento until 1904, then Finanças), which combined the powers of a ways-and-means committee and an appropriations committee.[32] After 1915, São Paulo had two representatives on the committee, and after 1924, three (of 15). PRP representatives chaired this committee in 1899, 1900, and 1903–5, which is to say for most of the years that Campos Sales and Rodrigues Alves were in the presidency. The Mineiros then began a long stewardship, turning the post over to other states only four times in the next 21 years (São Paulo accounted for two of the four, in 1918 and 1919). According to John Wirth, however, the committee might as well have been chaired by São Paulo, since "for the most part Minas was the faithful executioner of its policies."[33] In 1927, the Mineiros relinquished the chairmanship to São Paulo again; the state kept the post for the whole of Washington Luís's term.

Paulistas were nearly always represented on the Justice Committee, the only other one on which they frequently had two members. They usually had at least one seat on the Public Works and Public Accounts (Contas) committees, and in the second half of the Old Republic, also served fairly consistently on the Agriculture and Credentials committees. (But São Paulo had considerably less influence in the Credentials Committee than Minas.) Except for the presidency of the Chamber, the Paulistas tended to shy away from the positions distributed by the Committee of the Chair, which were largely honorific.[34]

Still, positions of leadership were not awarded exclusively on the basis of the internal dynamics of the Chamber. A forceful President could also wield power in Congress. In 1930, for example, Washington Luís managed to remove the Mineiro and Gaúcho chairmen of two of the most important committees in Congress, Credentials and Public Works, and

Credentials passed into the hands of a Paulista. This meant that São Paulo had the chairmanship of four of the six standing committees in that year—Credentials, Finance, Accounts, and Agriculture.

In the Senate, after Pinheiro Machado's death in 1915, São Paulo indirectly controlled the vice-presidency (in effect, the position of majority leader, since the Vice-President of the Republic presided over the Senate). The man who succeeded Pinheiro in the job was a client of the PRP, Antônio Azeredo of Mato Grosso; he occupied the post without interruption until the Revolution of 1930.[35] As in the Chamber, São Paulo was especially interested in keeping a seat on the Finance Committee. Glicério usually represented São Paulo on the committee during his years in the Senate (1903–16) and was chairman several times.

São Paulo's influence in Congress, like that of Minas, was far greater than this brief account of committee assignments suggests. The PRP usually worked in tandem with the PRM to control other delegations (who feared the loss of office through the Credentials Committee's actions), and likewise had an important say in the outcome of the contested elections of governors.[36] Beyond that, the Paulistas had cash to spend, and even resorted to the out-and-out bribery of other politicians in Congress. The PRP also used its coffers to buy the good opinion of the press in the federal capital, as did the PRM. The Paulista party at various times subsidized *Correio da Manhã*, *O Paiz*, and *O Dia*.[37]

Congress and the Interests of São Paulo

To illustrate São Paulo's role in Congress, I have chosen the central issues for coffee groups—valorization and the Exchange Bank. These were the two most expensive economic programs during the Old Republic. Both were pressed on the government by the São Paulo delegation, and the two issues were seen by defenders and opponents as intimately related. They are significant, too, because they show the ability of Congress to outmaneuver the executive. The section on Congress ends with a brief consideration of two other issues of interest to São Paulo, interstate tariffs and the constitutional amendments of 1926.

In choosing to focus on these issues, I do not mean to imply that the São Paulo government or the state's representatives in Rio worked for the coffee complex alone. But it is certainly true that until 1930, at least, coffee legislation was at the heart of São Paulo's demands on the federal government. In Congress and elsewhere, the perennial Paulista theme—

almost a chant—was that coffee was a national asset, not just a regional one, and therefore deserved federal favors commensurate with its importance. Senator Alfredo Ellis, whose public utterances were anything but subtle, summed it up with his usual arrogance in the 1903 debates on coffee protection: "The wealth, since it is in São Paulo, is therefore in Brazil. . . . The coffee that São Paulo produces is a product of the nation. São Paulo belongs to the Federation, if I'm not mistaken!"[38]

In fact, the First Republic's exchange manipulation and foreign borrowing were usually geared to the demands of coffee interests. The chief restraint on domination by the coffee complex was not so much the countervailing power of other groups as the financial and fiscal obligations of the federal government itself. Valorization provided such a clear instance of special-interest legislation that Pierre Denis, the French geographer, observed in 1909 that the program "was undertaken to succor the large proprietor. Protectionism always entails this danger: its supporters think it is protecting a nation, but in reality it only protects a class."[39]

In part, the Paulista planters wanted price stability so that they could invest more rationally in a form of agriculture with an exceptionally long period between the clearing of the land and actual production. But the demand for stability was also related to the labor system on the western plateau: the *colonato* system, based largely on wage labor, meant that sudden decreases in the price of coffee could not be absorbed as they were in Rio State or Minas Gerais, where sharecropping prevailed. In the circumstances, it is not especially surprising that price-regulation schemes should originate in São Paulo.[40]

In addition to the theme of coffee as *the* national resource in the 1903–6 valorization debates, Ellis and other Paulistas chose to present the coffee fazendeiro as the hapless victim of foreign import cartels that dictated prices; as the victim of railroad monopolies (including Brazilian-owned ones); and even as the victim of grasping colonos on the estates.[41] In August 1903, most of the features of the subsequent valorization program were laid out in a bill presented by Cândido Rodrigues for the São Paulo delegation. But the measure ran into the opposition of President Rodrigues Alves because it put the chief burden of valorization on the federal government—one still mindful of its onerous Funding Loan obligations and committed to outlays on public works to modernize the federal capital. Moreover, powerful political figures in São Paulo opposed valorization, including Antônio Prado, who feared the monetary, fiscal, and exchange consequences of the program.[42] As it happened, however, Governor Tibiriçá controlled the congressional delegation.

Thwarted in this drive to thrust responsibility for coffee protection on the central government, the state then concluded the Taubaté Agreement in February 1906 with Minas and Rio State. But foreign bankers insisted on a federal guarantee for the tri-state loan. In Congress, São Paulo's spokesmen argued that if the loan was not obtained, overproduction would cause a crash in the international coffee market, spelling the ruin of the Brazilian coffee industry. The principal opposition to the guarantee came from Pernambuco, whose boss, Francisco de Assis Rosa e Silva, decried the regionalist favoritism of the bill in the Senate and marshaled 10 of Pernambuco's 17 votes against the federal guarantee in the Chamber. Yet the total vote was a massive victory for coffee—106 to 15. In the Senate, the result was 31 to 6, with all the nay votes cast by non-coffee states.[43]

In the end, São Paulo alone, not three states, bore the responsibility for valorization. But when financial arrangements had to be renegotiated two years later, the Paulistas put a new bill before Congress, again requesting a federal guarantee on a loan. Opponents pointed out that the amount involved was £15,000,000, and that the Funding Loan of 1898 had been for only £10,000,000! The Finance Committee of the Chamber, in recommending the bill, urged Congress to follow the example of Russia's defense of its wheat against German speculators by taking counter-monopolistic action.

João Pandiá Calógeras, breaking with the Mineiro delegation on the issue, presented the most incisive argument against valorization—that artificially high prices would cause supply to escalate beyond control. His prophecy was realized two decades later. Yet the bill sailed through the lower house 98 to 20, with Pernambuco again supplying the largest number of votes against the measure (eight). Only one vote each against the guarantee came from the coffee states of Rio and Minas (that of Calógeras); São Paulo's delegation voted for it unanimously.[44]

During the debate, Deputy José Carvalho of Rio Grande do Sul tried to obtain a similar guarantee for a hypothetical loan of £5,000,000 for support of exports other than coffee. Calógeras also offered an amendment to burn the valorization coffee, asserting that the federal guarantee obviated the need for stocks as collateral for the £15,000,000 loan. Neither amendment got beyond the Finance Committee.[45] In the Senate, the Finance Committee justified the bill in terms similar to those used by the U.S. Congress in underwriting the 1975 loan to New York City: valorization was the child of a regional interest, to be sure, but the failure to act would gravely damage the national economy. In the upper chamber's vote, the same handful of representatives from non-coffee states who had voted against valorization in 1906 opposed it in 1908.[46]

In 1917, São Paulo obtained a 110,000 conto loan from the federal government for valorization (foreign loans being unavailable during the war); and in 1921, Paulista statesmen temporarily got the Union to assume responsibility for valorization operations. The same arguments were used again and again in Congress: coffee was a national resource, weighing more heavily than ever in the export economy, and as such had to be protected for the welfare of the nation. When the issue of the protection of rubber arose in the congressional debates of 1915, São Paulo's specialist in economic and financial matters, Cincinato Braga, was quick to point out that Brazil no longer enjoyed a monopoly on rubber production, so that the valorization of rubber was an impossibility. Congressmen from non-coffee areas hardly needed reminding that after the collapse of rubber in 1913, coffee had become the sole pillar of the country's export economy, but Braga proceeded to lecture them on some other important facts of economic life, to wit: that São Paulo bought more from other states than it sold to them, and that the workers on its coffee plantations sent money home to other states. In addition, he indicated that if São Paulo should fail to export at good prices, both imports and (therefore) federal revenues would be crippled, as would the economies of other states.[47]

Braga had still other shots to fire in the 1915 debate. São Paulo had shown that valorization could work. The early loans were repaid on time; and thus the federal government was not mistaken in its confidence in the state. São Paulo's foreign loans would be backed by the state government's good credit record, plus gold receipts from the special coffee surtax (tied to valorization loans) and valorization coffee stocks.[48] Such arguments were used repeatedly to force currency issues, as well as to obtain coffee support.

The debate on the Exchange Bank began even before the congressional approval, in July 1906, of a federal guarantee for the Taubaté scheme, the tri-state valorization plan that was never put into effect. The Exchange Bank had not been part of the valorization plan proposed in 1903 by Alexandre Siciliano, the immigrant planter and industrialist usually credited with originating the price-support program. But it was included in the Taubaté Agreement, apparently at the suggestion of Nilo Peçanha, then governor of Rio State, though he may not have been the originator of the idea.[49] The bank was based on the simple observation that the infusion of £15,000,000 into the economy would cause the milréis to appreciate rapidly, adversely affecting exporters, who were paid in foreign currency. The proposal followed a long period (1901-4) in which low international prices, coupled with a rising exchange rate (promoted by Presidents Campos Sales and Rodrigues Alves), brought considerable losses to the coffee sector. The Exchange Bank proposal was thus readily embraced by coffee interests.

As Rosa e Silva noted with disapproval in the debate, the defenders of valorization put forth the Exchange Bank as the sine qua non for the success of that program.[50] The bill before Congress set up a special bank with a monopoly on the exchange of all the valorization gold entering the country, for which it would issue its own notes. These were always to be exchanged at a rate of 15 pence per milréis, though the free exchange rate stood at 17.5 pence in 1906. Obligations contracted at the old fixed official rate of 27 pence were still to be honored, however; thus debtors to foreign lenders would be hurt because of the external depreciation, and the most important of these were state and federal governments. The problem was a delicate one for Tibiriçá and the Paulista delegation, since President Rodrigues Alves had set himself "radically against" the bill.[51]

The São Paulo Senate sent a message to Congress in mid-1906 urging the passage of the bill, and it was duly approved by the Chamber Finance Committee. The floor manager of the bill was David Campista, Minas Gerais's most effective apologist for coffee and an advocate of agricultural protection in general. He argued that Argentina's experience with a similar bank since 1900 had had the effect of stabilizing the country's exchange rate and limiting speculation; he candidly conceded that the value of the milréis would rise if the bank was not created. Campista held that a stable rate was desirable, and that a decrease in the value of the rate of exchange could best be averted by orthodox means—increasing reserves in the gold-conversion fund (fundo de resgate) and decreasing the amount of unbacked paper currency.[52] As a defender of coffee, he conveniently neglected to mention that the lower exchange rate projected for the Exchange Bank would raise the profits of coffee interests (because, as noted in Chapter Two, their costs were calculated in milréis, but their profits were made in hard currencies).

Altino Arantes, making a debut in Congress that greatly impressed Tibiriçá, piled on more arguments. He bluntly asserted that though a high exchange rate might serve the interests of government, it certainly did not help the producers, whose interests should prevail. Noting that the "producing classes" (as he preferred to call the coffee complex) were the chief suppliers of treasury receipts—apparently referring to the fact that export receipts determined the capacity to import, and therefore the duties on which the federal government chiefly relied—he then claimed that low exchange rates encouraged exports. (No one noticed, apparently, that such an argument was invalid for a product on which Brazil had a near-monopoly, and for which the price-elasticity of demand was low.) Since a weak milréis also discouraged imports, Arantes said, low exchange rates were a form of protectionism without tariffs, which had the advantage of not provoking reprisals.[53]

Opponents of the bill argued that the Exchange Bank was a bald case of special-interest legislation; that inconvertible paper currency in circulation, already below par with gold, would depreciate further on the appearance of a huge gold-backed issue; and that the Exchange Bank would do much more to prevent rates from rising than from falling, since the free market trend was upward—a trend that would be even more pronounced after valorization sterling entered the country. It was also noted that Brazil's proposed Exchange Bank differed radically from Argentina's, because it did not cover all foreign exchange and did not result in an official currency devaluation. The Pernambucan congressman Afonso Costa argued further that sugar refiners could not modernize their equipment by purchases abroad because of the low value of the milréis. Deputy Antunes Maciel, a member of the minority from Rio Grande do Sul, sadly observed that the coffee-producing states could manipulate the exchange rate to their advantage through the large amount of foreign exchange they controlled, and he wondered aloud how other states were going to repay their foreign debts at the old official rate.[54]

The Chamber voted overwhelmingly in favor of the Exchange Bank, 118 to 17. Pernambuco provided nine of the negative votes, and the rest were scattered. The measure also passed overwhelmingly in the Senate, after scraping through five to four in the Finance Committee, where Pernambuco's Rosa e Silva was powerful. Legislative action was timed to ensure that Rodrigues Alves would no longer be President when the bill arrived at Catete, the presidential palace.[55] The Exchange Bank bill was signed into law by the new President, Afonso Pena, and his Finance Minister, David Campista, on December 6, 1906, three weeks after the inauguration. It called for the issue of up to 320,000 contos (the equivalent of £20,000,000 at the 15-pence rate).

In 1908, with no relief from the coffee crisis that had begun in the late 1890's, São Paulo made new valorization arrangements with a syndicate of foreign coffee importers. In the meantime, the Pena government had to take out a £4,000,000 loan with Rothschild to maintain the conversion rate. The Exchange Bank was thus able to prevent the rate from falling, but only at the cost of foreign borrowing. In 1909–10, Pena's successor, President Nilo Peçanha, attempted to raise the exchange rate and to withdraw some of the bank's reserves.

Congress engaged in a new debate during Peçanha's last months in office. The outgoing Minister of Finance, Leopoldo Bulhões, wanted to raise the rate for the Exchange Bank to 18 pence, but this measure was fiercely opposed by the São Paulo delegation. Paulista congressmen, for their part, wanted to double the ceiling on the bank's reserves—from £20,000,000 to £40,000,000 (thus doubling its currency-issuing powers) —and introduced a bill to that end. Galeão Carvalhal, a Paulista deputy on the Finance Committee, led the floor fight for the bill, supported by Cincinato Braga. The arguments of 1906 echoed through the Chamber again, but with a new twist: Braga now asserted that although São Paulo benefited from cheap exchange rates, the producers of rubber, sugar, cacao, and cotton needed even cheaper rates to be competitive in the international market. Braga received support on this point from delegates from Rio Grande do Norte and Pernambuco, though Costa repeated his plaint of four years earlier that sugar refiners were being denied the opportunity to buy machinery. Braga claimed that what São Paulo wanted was a stable rate rather than a low one, but the fiscal orthodoxy he recommended to that end was clearly unrealistic in a regime accustomed to unbacked paper issues (often urged on the government by São Paulo), a lack of gold reserves, and unbalanced budgets.

In the final Chamber version of the bill, a compromise rate was set at 16 pence, and the bank's total authorized deposits were set at £60,000,000

(£20,000,000 more than the Paulistas had originally proposed). The raised ceiling was opposed by Brazil's new President, Hermes da Fonseca, who was pledged to a rise in the exchange rate and believed that it could not be achieved at so high a figure. The bill nevertheless passed easily in the Senate, where Glicério was chairman of the Finance Committee. Hermes's spokesman in the upper house, Antônio Azeredo (later a client of São Paulo), saw that the promised rise in the exchange rate —it had already started to climb by late 1910—would be halted by the new legislation. But in the end, Hermes signed the bill.[56] This was an instance, reminiscent of the Exchange Bank maneuvers of 1906, in which the Paulista congressional delegation worked around a reluctant President to secure favorable economic legislation.

Another issue on which the Paulistas triumphed in Congress—interstate taxation—illustrates the limitations of federal authority in general. At the 1891 Constituent Assembly, the São Paulo delegates had successfully beaten back a constitutional provision allowing states to levy duties on foreign imports, but the Constitution was unclear on the matter of taxing "exports" and "imports" between states. In a series of decisions by the Supreme Court, that power had been denied the states, but this merely resulted in changes in the nomenclature of the taxes.[57] In 1900, Serzedelo Correia, a former military officer now representing Pará in Congress, introduced a bill requiring a ban on all interstate levies. The bill languished until 1903, when Arnolfo Azevedo and 11 other Paulista congressmen presented a substitute measure allowing a state to tax another's goods only in the retail trade, and then only at the same rate as it used in taxing local goods. Azevedo linked the issue of freedom of domestic commerce with the problem of São Paulo's economic crisis.* On the key vote in October 1903, the measure passed the Chamber by a margin of 85 to 25, with a minority of Mineiros casting the largest number of negative votes (five). Every Paulista, Gaúcho, and Pernambucano—representing states with major interests in the domestic market —voted affirmatively.[58]

The Azevedo bill became law on June 11, 1904, but it proved unen-

---

*On January 31, 1903, a congress of planters in São Paulo called for the elimination of interstate taxes in order to promote coffee sales to other states. Since such sales were relatively inconsequential, the appeal is perhaps an indication of how desperate the planters thought their position had become in that period of low international prices, temporarily exacerbated by "hard money" exchange policies that further reduced real receipts.

forceable. Minas Gerais, for example, abolished its "import" taxes at some sacrifice to its budget, but continued to give preferential treatment to some states in its "export" taxes. (A 1915 Minas statute on cattle exports set a rate of 6 percent for São Paulo, Bahia, and Espírito Santo, and 20 percent for the other states.) Many states continued to charge "import" duties under a variety of subterfuges. The government of São Paulo was hardly blameless in this respect, for it imposed a tax on the Minas coffee that passed through Santos on the way overseas. (The law, however, was voided by the Supreme Court in 1919). As late as 1924, the state applied a tax on all its own coffee exports out of Santos, including whatever was to be sold in Brazil.[59]

By the 1930's, taxes in restraint of interstate trade had become truly irksome to São Paulo, now a net exporter to the other members of the Federation. On this point, at least, the Paulistas and Vargas saw eye to eye. The 1934 Constitution limited the states to a 10 percent ad valorem tax on their exports to other states. In 1938, as dictator, Vargas issued Decree Law 379 requiring that all interstate taxes be phased out by the end of 1942. Some states, including Minas, resisted, but finally gave in to comply with a new law in 1943 ordering all such duties terminated by the beginning of 1944.[60] Thus, the Paulistas ultimately got their way on the matter of interstate taxation, but only under an authoritarian regime that itself met resistance and evasion on one of the hoariest problems to bedevil Brazilian federalism.

The final issue to be examined, constitutional revision, illustrates how the PRP's position altered in response to changing economic and political conditions. The revision of the federal Constitution became the pet project of President Artur Bernardes, who had taken an anti-revisionist position during his campaign in 1921–22. Probably concerned about external financial obligations, Bernardes submitted a program of constitutional amendments to Congress in May 1924, shortly after the completion of a British financial mission to Brazil. For a start, Bernardes wanted to broaden the conditions under which the President could intervene in the states; one proposal was to permit intervention if a state failed to service its funded debt for two successive years. He also wanted to give the President a partial veto on appropriations bills, so important in curtailing pork-barrel riders that drove up the deficit.[61] Other proposed changes included limiting the appellate powers of the Supreme Court, restricting the scope of habeas corpus, and allowing the executive branch to expel undesirable aliens at its pleasure.

São Paulo, one of the bastions of anti-revisionism in the early years of the Republic, had altered its stance by 1910, when it supported Rui Barbosa and his revisionist platform. Now, in 1924, the Paulista congressmen eagerly embraced Bernardes's program. There were several reasons for this 180-degree turn. First, the PRP leaders were well aware of the need to bring federal finances into line to meet the Funding Loan obligations that fell due in 1927; a related consideration was that a Paulista would have the presidency for the next four years (partly in exchange for supporting the constitutional amendments). Second, the growth of Paulista investments and markets beyond São Paulo's frontiers (especially in coffee production) made PRP leaders more amenable to a greater degree of central authority. And third, the disruptive revolts of the early and mid-1920's made a strengthening of the national government much more palatable to the "law-and-order" Paulistas. As for the risks of federal intervention, the state probably thought itself safe enough with a strengthened Força Pública (which grew from fewer than 9,000 men in 1924 to 14,000 in 1925).

The Bernardes program took two years to enact, and São Paulo's congressional delegation cooperated fully in that endeavor. In fact, Paulistas led the floor fight in both houses. The floor manager in the Chamber was Herculano de Freitas, a law professor and member of the Justice Committee. Legislative strategy began in a meeting in Freitas's home in Rio, and his committee's report faithfully reflected the ideas of Bernardes. (In 1926, Bernardes appointed Freitas to the Supreme Court.)

In the Senate, the floor manager was Adolfo Gordo, who, as the author of anti-anarchist legislation, was presumably enthusiastic about the provision to expel foreign-born agitators. Indeed, Bernardes had cited the 1924 uprising in São Paulo as his inspiration for that provision.[62] The minority members vociferously objected to undertaking revisions while constitutional guarantees were suspended in large areas of the country, but they controlled few votes, far short of what was needed to block the program.* Bernardes's reform package went through Congress without

---

*The Constitution required a two-thirds majority. The minority consisted almost entirely of men who held seats by virtue of the constitutional requirements for representation of the opposition.

major substantive change, and became part of the Constitution on Independence Day, September 7, 1926.

Public Works

In contrast to their intense interest in financial and fiscal policies, the Paulistas were little concerned with procuring federal public works for their state—certainly far less so than the leaders of other states. There were two reasons for this: the dense network and economic viability of São Paulo's privately owned railroads, and the state's ability to raise its own capital for public works, partly through foreign borrowing. Most railway lines in the state were privately built and operated, and they remained profitable into the 1930's. A few, like the Ituana and the Sorocabana, had to be subsidized, and in 1919 the federal government took over the Noroeste, a line principally located in Mato Grosso. But by 1930, when the era of railroad-building was virtually over, more than half of São Paulo's nearly 7,000 kilometers of track was still in private hands. The federal government owned only 12 percent and the state 34 percent. In Minas, by contrast, 70 percent of the track was federally owned, and two of the federal lines in São Paulo were actually feeders to Minas. Though São Paulo had the best statewide rail network, the federal government owned more track in seven other states.[63]

Fazendeiros in São Paulo complained about the freight rates of the private railways, but in fact the spread between private and public rates was only about 9 percent in 1930. Indeed, in that year, the federally owned Central do Brasil charged higher rates than the Companhia Paulista. Furthermore, São Paulo taxed rail freight (on both public and private lines) less than Minas, Rio, and the Federal District.[64] There was almost no demand for state or federal control of the private companies that were making a profit, though it is fair to note that some of São Paulo's most prominent political figures sat on their boards of directors.

The other major area of state claims on the federal treasury for public works was port improvements, and here the Paulistas asked nothing. They relied on domestic private capital in the form of the Companhia Docas de Santos. Yet São Paulo did obtain a tax break: in the Old Republic, Santos was exempted from the 2 percent duty designated to maintain federally owned or subsidized ports. This policy obviously aided the state's importers and exporters, as it did the manufacturers whose raw materials were transported by coastal freighter from other states.[65]

Overall, we may generalize that São Paulo was more concerned about the government's economic policies than its patronage powers, though such concern was not chiefly a claim on public works. The Paulistas wanted support in some form for valorization, and they wanted control of currency and exchange policies. Once federal commitments were made in these areas in 1905–6, the Paulistas less frequently claimed the highest posts in government. The valorization issue temporarily divided the Paulistas and allowed Pinheiro Machado of Rio Grande do Sul to vastly increase his influence in Congress by picking up Glicério's cudgel. Tibiriçá, then governor, personally favored the candidacy of Bernardino de Campos, but felt that in view of what São Paulo was asking from the federal government, the PRP should not seek to supply a President in 1906.[66] President Rodrigues Alves's death in 1919 at the outset of a four-year term frustrated the PRP's return to the presidency until 1926, and in general the Paulistas failed to bid effectively for the top posts in the executive and Congress in the years after 1906.

During the Constituent Assembly debates in 1890, a representative of Minas Gerais had argued that the spoils of the Republican victory (in terms of federal posts) had gone to São Paulo. In 1924, by contrast, we find one prominent Paulista charging that his state was suffering "deprivation" in federal jobs.[67] But this allegation was basically a reaction to the widespread notion that São Paulo was exploiting the nation's monetary and fiscal policy for its own ends; the fact is, the Paulistas did not make any great claims on the federal government in this respect, having jobs aplenty within their own borders. In the public sector, for example, São Paulo had 28,000 state employees in 1920, when Minas had fewer than 6,000. By contrast, Minas had 19,000 federal employees, and São Paulo 13,000.*

Relations with Other States

In general, São Paulo's relations with the other states depended on the extent of its economic influence over them. The exception was Minas Gerais, where a true partnership existed in the political sphere. That the two should collaborate in the matter of coffee policy is hardly surprising.

---

*Some 14,000 of Minas's federal employees were railroad workers, as were 13,000 of São Paulo's state employees. Hence railroads were not only important as public works, but also as a permanent source of government employment. For data, see Martins Filho, "Minas e São Paulo," pp. 124–29.

Paulista fazendeiros owned large properties in Minas, and Minas was Brazil's second-largest producer. But beyond this, the migration of Mineiro families into São Paulo in the eighteenth and nineteenth centuries provided links between the state elites. São Paulo Governor Bernardino de Campos, for example, was born in Minas.* Likewise, the Mineiros' enrollment in the São Paulo Law School in the nineteenth century strengthened bonds between the two states. Occasionally, matriculation led to new interstate family ties, as in the marriage of Afonso Arinos Melo Franco and Antonieta Prado, daughter of Antônio.

The *café com leite* alliance of Minas and São Paulo emerged in the first year of the twentieth century with the política dos governadores. But what held it together was the valorization program that greatly benefited the major economic group in both states. In the definitive federal valorization legislation of 1908, Minas's congressmen successfully promoted federal authorization of São Paulo's foreign loan, and the Mineiro government agreed to collect a surtax on the coffee it shipped abroad. São Paulo, on its part, was to extend protection through grade 9 for the poorer quality coffee of Minas and Rio State.[68]

Cooperation between São Paulo and Minas Gerais might have been less frequent had not temporary lapses in the liaison shown the fragility of Brazil's oligarchic democracy. As noted earlier, the follies of the Hermes years brought about the Paulista-Mineiro pact at Ouro Fino in 1913 to stop Pinheiro Machado from naming the next President. Failing to agree on Rodrigues Alves's successor in 1918, the leaders of Minas and São Paulo nevertheless contrived to dominate Epitácio's government by having São Paulo play the role of bully and Minas that of mediator. This scheme proved its worth in 1920, when the Paulista Carlos de Campos threatened to resign as majority leader of the Chamber if the President did not meet São Paulo's demand for a large issue of paper currency, and the Mineiro politicians persuaded Epitácio to yield.

São Paulo readily agreed to Bernardes's succession to the presidency in 1922. President Washington Luís's falling-out with the PRM in 1929 over his imposition of a Paulista successor has been widely recognized as one of the causes of the revolution of 1930. In part the revolution also grew out of the PRM's resentment of the President's action in forcing

---

*Two other São Paulo governors were born out-of-state—Albuquerque Lins in Alagoas, and Washington Luís in Rio de Janeiro. Scarcity of administrative personnel was in general a counterweight against Paulista bairrismo.

the Credentials Committee to award 14 of Minas's 37 seats to the pro-Prestes opposition: Minas was thereby treated as a "little state." After 1930, the alliance was never the same. Minas was drawn closer and closer to a government from which the Paulistas remained thoroughly alienated for several years.

The PRP's cooperation with the political establishment of Rio Grande do Sul was at best fitful. The Gaúchos isolated themselves from national politics during the first 15 years of the Republic, then emerged as a force to be reckoned with as Pinheiro Machado gained influence in the Senate. Pinheiro was a supporter of Paulista interests—he frequently pushed coffee legislation through the Senate[69]—and the two states developed closer economic ties with the completion of the São Paulo–Rio Grande railway line in 1910. But political cooperation was intermittent, and the governor of Rio Grande, Borges de Medeiros, remained cool to Rodrigues Alves's suggestion in 1916 that the two state machines join forces in national politics, presumably to the detriment of Minas Gerais.[70] Rio Grande's "natural" ally was the army,[71] but a Gaúcho-military front was effective only when Minas and São Paulo were divided. Riograndense influence in national politics began to decline in 1932, because the Constitutionalist Revolution, which temporarily united São Paulo, had the opposite effect in Rio Grande, rending both Gaúcho parties.

São Paulo and Rio Grande, like São Paulo and Minas, were linked by personal political ties. Pinheiro Machado's father had come from São Paulo to settle in Rio Grande, and in the early years of the Republic, the senator's brother Angelo represented São Paulo in the federal Chamber. Pinheiro also owned property in São Paulo. Rivadávia Correia, Hermes's Minister of Justice and sometime Gaúcho congressman, had served in the São Paulo legislature. Later, Vargas viewed Osvaldo Aranha as a link to São Paulo because of his relatives in Paulista society.

The last gasp for big state alliances came with the attempts of João Neves of Rio Grande to unite the state establishments of Rio Grande, São Paulo, and Minas just before the outbreak of the Paulista revolt.[72] But the situation in 1932 was not that of the Old Republic—not only because two of the three states had been participants in the 1930 revolution, but also because each state now had two parties sharing power rather than one.

São Paulo had few faithful satellites in a political sense, but rather tended to recruit and lose allies in Congress in competition with Minas and Rio Grande. However, as São Paulo's economy expanded into Mato Grosso and Paraná, those states became economic satellites, and to some degree, this affected their political behavior.

The expansion of the coffee frontier in Paraná and of cattle ranching in Mato Grosso—and above all, the penetration of the railroad into both —brought Paulista interests and Paulista political influence to those states. Júlio Mesquita Filho celebrated this development as "beneficent imperialism" and identified the railroad as its principal instrument.[73]

Until 1914, Mato Grosso was economically dependent on the Rio de la Plata (where a Buenos Aires firm had obtained a virtual monopoly on the state's yerba mate business). Once the two states were linked by the Noroeste railroad, however, the Paulistas were quick to move in.[74] One of the biggest investors was a former Paulista congressman, Artur Diedrichsen. The states were also linked by important elite-level ties. Campos Sales as President had allowed the Murtinho family to consolidate its power by violence in Mato Grosso in 1900, and São Paulo's Força Pública had been deployed for that purpose.[75] More important, in the longer term, was the Paulistas' relationship with Mato Grosso's Antônio Azeredo, the man who acted as São Paulo's catspaw in the Senate for 15 years. In the 1932 revolution, southern Mato Grosso, the most densely settled part of a state the size of Alaska, supported the Paulistas, and two years later the Liga Sul Mato Grosso petitioned the Vargas government to separate the south from the rest of the state.*

Paraná became a true economic satellite of São Paulo only in the 1930's, as coffee investment turned southward. As early as 1892, however, we hear a governor of Paraná warning his legislature of a Paulista takeover of the public lands. Speculators from São Paulo soon joined hands with local claim-jumpers in northern Paraná. Railroad development, as in Mato Grosso, was accompanied by Paulista investments in real estate. British investors arrived in the 1920's to form the Companhia Terras Norte do Paraná, a large land development company, but Paulistas bought them out in 1944.[76]

One important political figure in Paraná who had ties with São Paulo was Ubaldino Amaral de Fontoura, a Historical Republican who held a

---

*U.S. Consul Cameron to Ambassador Gibson, Jan. 20, 1934 (São Paulo Political Report no. 61), United States, Decimal File, 1930–39, 832.00/879, pp. 5–6. In May 1977, the federal government announced its intention to make the south into a new state, called Mato Grosso do Sul; this change took effect in January 1979.

variety of top-level posts in the 1890's. Fontoura had gone to law school in São Paulo and had practiced law at Sorocaba. Elected as a senator from Paraná, he had presided over the Committee of Twenty-one that framed the 1891 Constitution. Subsequently, he was named to the Supreme Court by Prudente, served as prefect of the Federal District, and became president of the Bank of Brazil.[77]

Foreign Dependence

São Paulo's political behavior was influenced in an important way by another set of relations—those between the political elite and foreign investors.[78] In considering this matter, let us briefly review some of the material in Chapter Two. Foreigners, as we saw, were deeply involved in the economy of São Paulo long before the turn of the century, especially in the export and railroad sectors. After the coffee crisis began in the mid-1890's, foreign firms no longer remained mere exporters, but began to move into the production and financing of coffee, as local capital markets collapsed. From 1895 to 1907, 87 percent of the coffee trade was in foreign hands.[79] Foreigners also had control of warehousing and buffer-stocking in Brazil until the late 1920's. Indeed, in one brief period, at the outset of the Great Depression, the foreign firm of Hard, Rand was given a monopoly of sales of Paulista coffee.[80]

Railroads were another leading area of foreign investment. Here the amazing thing was the Paulistas' success in sharing in the profits by organizing their own companies. But profits generally fell short of the earnings of the Inglesa, the railway that opened up the plateau to coffee growing and held a monopoly on the traffic through the funnel down to Santos. Moreover, this was only one of several foreign railroads in São Paulo. For a short time, in fact, the American entrepreneur Percival Farquhar, through his European financiers, got controlling interest in the Sorocabana, the São Paulo–Rio Grande, and even the Mogiana and Paulista lines.[81] And even when the Mogiana and Paulista companies were under Brazilian control, as they were through most of our period, they were dependent on foreign loans and technology.

Though Brazilians owned the bulk of the coffee lands, the holdings of foreigners (chiefly immigrants) accounted for a significant proportion of the value of those lands (34 percent in 1934). Moreover, on the eve of the First World War, the state's three largest operations were in the hands of foreign producers: the British-owned São Paulo Coffee Estates, which had acquired lands in 1897, the opening year of the depression, owned 2,300,000 trees in 1912; the Dumont Coffee Company, another British concern, owned 4,000,000; and the German immigrant Francisco Schmidt, soon to become a business partner of Theodor Wille, owned 7,900,000. European investors were also important in land-colonization companies, notably in the Mogiana zone (Wille and an English group) and in the Alta Sorocabana (a French firm). A circle of British investors based in Santos, as owners of Companhia Terras Norte do Paraná, controlled one-ninth of the territory of that state.[82]

The growth of foreign banking accompanied the rise of export firms. Most of the British, French, and German banks opened in São Paulo between the fall of the Empire and the First World War; in 1915, the Americans moved in to replace the European capital markets that were tied up during the war. These foreign banks not only made loans to private firms (e.g., to the industrialist Matarazzo), but also underwrote the state government's valorization program and purchase of the Sorocabana Railroad. During the 1920's, American lenders began to dominate the foreign credit market for Brazil, in part because of the greater aggressiveness of Wall Street bankers; and this was the case in São Paulo as well. The National City Bank, for example, had U.S. $10,000,000 in deposits in the state by 1930.[83] As time passed, the foreign banks lost much of their influence in Brazil, but of those that were still active in 1935, 45 percent were domiciled in São Paulo; and in 1936 they still accounted for a quarter of the total deposits in the state.[84]

Of the foreign firms with commercial operations in São Paulo, the two most powerful were Theodor Wille and the Brazilian Warrant Company, rivals for control of the international coffee trade. The Hamburg-based Wille company, whose founder had been a Prussian consul in São Paulo in the 1840's, was the agent for the international lenders in the early valorization loans, representing, among others, the German-born Hermann Sielcken, New York importer and chief organizer of the valorization syndicate. The Wille firm handled all of the first valorization coffee sales. Although Wille never went directly into banking, it did form an alliance, in 1926, with the London-based J. Henry Schroeder Company, whose namesake was one of the owners of the São Paulo Coffee Estates.[85]

By 1924, Wille owned "imposing estates" in the Ribeirão Preto area, including one of more than 30,000 hectares.[86] The firm went into cotton production in 1925, had a coffee-marketing arrangement with Matarazzo, and was engaged in international shipping and insurance. Because of its strong position in the exchange markets, enabling it to buy capital equipment at good prices, Wille was also able to move into the electric power industry, as well as manufacturing.[87]

Wille's chief rival, Brazilian Warrant, was an outgrowth of the London-based E. Johnston and Company, a dealer in Brazilian coffee since 1842. After 1909, Brazilian Warrant assumed direct control of its affiliates, the Companhia Paulista de Armazéns Gerais and the Companhia Registradora de Santos. These coffee warehousing concerns even obtained a guaranteed interest rate (6 percent) from the state on capital they invested in thei operations, to the disadvantage of Brazilian exporters and comissários. During the First World War, Brazilian Warrant made tremendous strides over Wille, which was hard hit by British blockade and blacklisting practices, and was forced to consign its coffee to the English firm. In 1918, in fact, the British government had some thought of squeezing Wille out of the coffee trade altogether.[88] But this came to naught, and once the war was over, Wille and Brazilian Warrant were again locked in competition. Both went into coffee warehousing in Minas Gerais in 1928. Brazilian Warrant's director, Edward Greene, also became a leading investor in the Companhia Terras Norte do Paraná, mentioned above.

The industrial West's domination of export-connected activities in underdeveloped countries is an old tale. But little attention has been given to the specific linkages between foreign interests and domestic politics in such circumstances. To exemplify the connections in São Paulo, we shall briefly examine the relations between Paulista politicians and Wille and Brazilian Warrant.

Wille's chief conduit was Artur Diedrichsen, born in Brazil, but a son of the director of the Santos branch of Wille in the late nineteenth century. The Diedrichsens were cousins of the firm's founder, and they had several other relatives highly placed in the European offices of Wille. Artur was not only the general manager of the Wille plantations and a one-time partner of Francisco Schmidt, but also a political leader in Ribeirão Preto at the outset of its days of glory as the world's coffee capital; he twice went to Congress. In 1900, he gave up politics to devote himself exclusively to business. With his command of both German and Portuguese and his political contacts, he was ideally situated to handle problems with state authorities for Wille.[89]

Diedrichsen was a land speculator and entrepreneur on the coffee frontier; and just as domestic politics and foreign investment were directly linked in his person, so also were European capital and frontier development. Among other things, he built the first modern road between São Paulo and Mato Grosso, established large-scale cattle ranching in Mato Grosso, and organized steamer service on the Paraná River.[90] Through Diedrichsen, the Wille firm became a business partner in the Central Eléctrica Rio Claro, along with five of the most important members of the Paulista political elite: Olavo Egídio Souza Aranha, Elói Chaves, José Martiniano Rodrigues Alves and his father, Virgílio Rodrigues Alves, and Cardoso Melo Neto, related to the Rodrigues Alveses by marriage. A Wille official was also a partner of the younger Rodrigues Alves and another elite member, Joaquim Martins de Siqueira, in a different firm in Santos. Elite member Luís Silveira, who represented São Paulo's economic interests at the Versailles Peace Conference, was still another Wille associate.[91]

The Wille company also had real estate dealings with Cerqueira César, and was linked through its partnership with Francisco Schmidt to Schmidt's son-in-law Alberto Whatley, a member of the elite of the 1930's. A representative of the Wille firm was a business partner of Antônio Prado, the Paulista who had, so far as I can ascertain, the largest number of intra-elite business and family linkages in my group.[92]

As a board member of the Brazilian Warrant Company, the enterprising Prado was also a partner of Edward Greene; and Prado's son Paulo (also a member of the political elite) was a director of Greene's Companhia Registradora. During the First World War, Antônio Prado pulled political strings for British businesses in exchange for having his concerns removed from the British backlist.[93] Such other Paulista notables as the industrialist Roberto Simonsen and Senator Alfredo Ellis had major business dealings with Brazilian Warrant.[94]

We may assume that many ties with foreign companies are not listed in the available biographical data, but I have found at least 23 members of the elite who were directors of, or legal counselors for, foreign-owned firms. Four of these men, like Cardoso Melo Neto, served as governor— Bernardino and Carlos de Campos, Altino Arantes, and Júlio Prestes. All four were connected with a German-owned textile firm. Another, José Carlos de Macedo Soares, was Minister of Justice and Foreign Minister in the 1930's (and served later, in 1945–47, as São Paulo's governor). When Macedo Soares was appointed to the Foreign Ministry in 1934, the British consul in São Paulo reported to his embassy that he "has undoubtedly a very strong liking for the British [since he is] a director of one of the important local insurance companies in which British interests are largely involved."[95] Apart from these open ties, with 41 percent of the elite of known occupation (n = 240) identified as merchants, industrialists, bankers, or comissários, it is safe to surmise that the indirect links between the political leaders and foreign businesses were considerable (e.g., through bank loans or sources of supply).

Public as well as private debt had its political consequences. By 1906, São Paulo, between its purchase of the Sorocabana Railway and its first valorization, had incurred more than half the total foreign debt of the 20 states (£9,200,000 of £17,700,000).[96] New loans were contracted, and though many were retired, the trend was upward: from 1892 to 1929, the state's foreign funded debt rose from £1,200,000 to £11,900,000, plus U.S. $43,000,000 and 10,700,000 Dutch florins. In 1937, São Paulo still accounted for about half the total foreign debt of the states.[97] Since valorization almost always entailed foreign financing, satisfying overseas creditors became a central preoccupation of Paulista statesmen after 1905.

The state and federal governments were both responsive to the claims of foreigner bondholders, but on the whole, the Paulistas were much less concerned about the problems of amortization than the federal authorities were. The central government was not only less subject to direct control by the coffee complex; it also had a much larger external debt than São Paulo, and was ultimately responsible to foreign creditors for any default by state governments. Just as important, most federal debts were more onerous than São Paulo's valorization loans because there was no simple mechanism for repayment corresponding to São Paulo's gold surtax on coffee exports. For this reason, the federal government tended to resist pressures to devalue the currency. Presidents and Finance Ministers who hailed from São Paulo usually took a different view of devaluation on assuming office.

Foreign credit operations sometimes affected political relations between the state and federal governments.* On at least one occasion, São Paulo's overseas debt played a role in the maneuvering to select a President. This

---

*Foreign borrowing had another consequence within São Paulo: it strengthened the executive against the legislature by making the governor less dependent on the assembly for appropriations. Foreign loans also increased the governor's power vis-à-vis the PRP executive committee, once the state began borrowing money on a large scale.

was the agreement referred to above, by which the PRP accepted President Pena's choice for the 1910 succession, David Campista, in exchange for a federal guarantee on São Paulo's £15,000,000 valorization loan. In general, however, foreign loans were a unique resource that helped free the São Paulo establishment from political obligations to the federal government. As late as the Constituent Assembly of 1933–34, the São Paulo delegation was still defending the right of the states to contract foreign loans without federal interference.[98]

State leaders, appreciating that a high degree of external dependency was inevitable, developed a unique "strategy"—perhaps only partly at a conscious level—to obtain a near-autonomy from the federal government by becoming heavily indebted abroad. (Minas Gerais and Rio Grande do Sul could have opted for similar policies, though they had lesser economic endowments against which to borrow. In any event, their debt policies were more cautious.) In the process of borrowing overseas, a more subtle form of dependence developed. Paulista leaders believed, along with their European creditors of the era, that irregular (nonconstitutional) governments produced upheavals, to the detriment of foreign creditors and investors.[99] In the minds of both, however, stability was a more basic concern than constitutionality. When it was impossible to support an unambiguously constitutional government (in Paulista municípios, in other states, and at the national level) because of rival claims to authority, Paulista politicians backed whoever offered the best prospects for stability. Instability in the governing process could lead to a loss of investor confidence abroad, in turn producing a fall in the value of Brazilian and Paulista bonds, the flight of foreign capital, and a drop in the exchange rate (favored by planters but not by officials concerned with fiscal problems). At the worst, the situation could lead to gunboat diplomacy —at the expense of the central government.

That the "worst" could happen was not beyond the realm of possibility. Campos Sales, who as President-elect traveled to London in 1898 to refinance Brazil's foreign debt personally, later wrote, with no apparent disapproval, that the directors of the House of Rothschild conjectured in his presence that "beyond the total loss of credit of the country, [the suspension of Brazil's international debt payments] could gravely affect national sovereignty itself, provoking claims that would perhaps end in foreign intervention."[100] In fact, Britain, Germany, and Italy blockaded the main port of Venezuela four years later to collect debts. In Brazil,

the federal government bowed to French diplomatic pressure in 1901
and covered a defaulted loan of Espírito Santo, then bowed to pressure
by Germany the following year to buy German equity in a bankrupt railroad in Minas Gerais.[101]

President Campos Sales had something of an obsession about the relation between domestic disorders and foreign credit. Before becoming
President he was concerned that monarchists and the rebels at Canudos
would adversely affect the nation's credit, and during his presidency even
a minor instance of military insubordination raised in his mind the specter
of a damaged credit rating.[102] But he was hardly alone in this. In 1891,
even before São Paulo had become so locked into its foreign obligations,
other Paulistas shared this concern. During the attempted coup d'état
of Deodoro, Cincinato Braga, then a deputy in the state legislature, argued that Rothschild would have nothing to do with an illegal government
(and in fact Rothschild did oppose the coup). "Foreign bankers have no
alternative," Braga declared in the State Assembly, "when they know that
once constitutional norms [legalidade] are violated, revolts break out;
given a revolutionary situation, the foreign creditor cannot foresee which
faction will win, and which will make good on the debt."[103] Two years
later, the PRF leader Francisco Glicério expressed a similar fear that
political instability would hurt Brazil's credit abroad.[104]

Another instance of the Paulistas' concern about "legality" and foreign
investors' attitudes can be found in São Paulo's role in Brazil's first contested presidential election in 1910. Brazilian newspapers and lawmakers
were sensitive to foreign bankers' opinions on the outcome of the election,[105] and the Paulistas' decision to stand by another slate may have
arisen in part from their fears about the reaction abroad to a Hermes
victory. Rumblings from across the seas could not have escaped their attention. The Economist of London, for instance, had reacted quickly to
the news of Hermes's selection as the "official" candidate: "Enormous
amounts of British capital have been placed in Brazil, and should Marshal
Hermes be elected we must be prepared for the worst. [His election]
would lead in all likelihood to revolution." Furthermore, it warned,
Hermes was "a strong partisan of war with Argentina" and could be expected to spend huge sums on an armaments program. The attitude of
The Economist and other British opinionmakers was apparently the cause
of a drop in the value of São Paulo state bonds on the London market.[106]

During the campaign, Rui Barbosa tried to laugh off suggestions that he had received 700 contos (about U.S. $217,000 in 1909) from the São Paulo government with the blessing of Theodor Wille. But he did flatly assert that the election of his opponent would be regarded abroad as evidence of militarism in government, and would adversely affect the nation's foreign credit.[107]

Two years later, when the wily Pinheiro Machado, now *éminence grise* of the Hermes administration, toyed with the notion of provoking a federal intervention in São Paulo, Governor-elect Rodrigues Alves issued a warning to the federal authorities: "Those who speak out against the autonomy of the states and rashly preach armed intervention as a normal means of settling local political disputes do not understand our financial situation; neither do they realize the influence that the threat of disorder exercises over public credit abroad."[108]

The concern was an enduring one. In a 1930 publication entitled "The Point of View of the PRP," a party spokesman wrote: "Foreign bankers are wary of doing business [in Brazil], and their reticence is natural. In 1922 we had a revolution; in 1924, another that lasted until 1926, and one in which the damage done to the property of foreigners living here was far from negligible. [Now] yet another revolution is announced for 1930. [We therefore live] in an unstable South American republic, where there are no guarantees for foreign capital, given the continual uprisings of the 'natives.'"[109]

The revolution of October 1930 was in fact a reaction to a general depression in the international economic system that no sector of the Brazilian elite had defended as conspicuously as the politicians of São Paulo. For many Brazilians, the collapse of the international economy was also the failure of São Paulo, whose political establishment would have continued to run Brazil if President-elect Júlio Prestes had been inaugurated in November. And it was perhaps consistent with Paulista political tradition that the most violent civil conflict in this century was São Paulo's "Constitutionalist" rebellion against the Vargas dictatorship in 1932.

In that conflict, the Paulista rebels' behavior was constrained by financial problems. One was that most of the currency in the state was in the hands of foreign banks. When the state government attempted to obtain a contribution to the war effort from three British banks, His Majesty's consul informed the state secretary of finance that such an effort would "undoubtedly be most detrimental to São Paulo's credit in the City."[110] The matter was dropped.

The power of foreign lenders and their connections with the Paulistas were perceived and denounced not only by the Left, but also by the Right. As early as 1927, in the novel *O Esperado*, the future Integralist Chefe, Plínio Salgado, had depicted a struggle between British and American lenders in São Paulo for control of loans to state and município governments. The Integralist Gustavo Barroso brought direct charges against foreign banks and their Paulista agents in the 1930's.[111]

In the late 1930's, foreign credit remained unavailable, but the possibility of foreign borrowing still had force as an illusion. As late as 1937, when private firms, state governments, and federal agencies were all turning to the Bank of Brazil for credit, Senator José de Alcântara Machado of São Paulo's Partido Constitucionalista argued against the continuation of Vargas's "state of war" because it was damaging to the country's credit abroad.[112]

In the period 1889–1937, at least, it seems clear that the political elite of São Paulo was unwilling to come to grips with such issues as the domestic financing of the state's economic programs. The daring experiment of valorization was underwritten by foreign investors, even though it was directed against the manipulation of coffee prices overseas; moreover, foreigners were allowed to consolidate their control of coffee marketing and financing within São Paulo. Alternative formulas that could have provided the impetus toward more autonomous economic growth, such as direct taxation and the consistent support of industry, were never seriously entertained. The locomotive pulling empty boxcars was fueled abroad. Major strides toward political and economic integration were achieved only when the international financial system was in crisis, and when Paulista economic interests were more fully oriented toward the rest of Brazil.

In the domestic context, the 1930's brought about a sharp reduction in the power of the state's establishment, but São Paulo was not so dependent on its position in Congress as Minas Gerais, and was in any case manifestly weaker in that body. São Paulo's political power rested primarily on its economic position, but it also rested on the internal unity of its elite, whose essential cohesion is indicated by the lack of contested gubernatorial races throughout the Old Republic. Even in the 1930's, the state's new dependency on the federal government to shoulder the debt burden was partly offset by the ability of the state government to repay its loans through export, and later, turnover taxes.[113] In the following chapter, we shall examine the relationship between São Paulo and the Union from a different perspective, considering several forms of organization building, and the relationship between such activities and national integration.

CHAPTER SEVEN

Toward Integration

DESPITE THE LONG-TERM tendencies toward centralization in twentieth-century Brazil, state loyalties, at least in critical areas like São Paulo, may account for the great symbolic significance of the federal system, which has remained the form of government in every Brazilian constitution since 1891, including that of the Estado Novo. If national integration may be provisionally defined as the intensification of linkages across state lines and the strengthening of loyalties to the nation-state rather than its component units, Paulista political leaders viewed the process in a unique way: their state formed the growth pole around which the nation should organize itself. Even in defeat, in 1930 and 1932, few Paulistas turned away from the nation as a focus of allegiance, though public assertions of the need for Paulista leadership grew more clamorous.

The relationship between part and whole was implicitly hegemonic for most of São Paulo's industrial, agricultural, and political leaders. When attempts at hegemony failed, Paulista pride could still be assuaged by appeals to the bandeirante heritage, a set of symbols that accommodated allegiances to São Paulo and the nation. In this chapter, I will consider the sorts of symbols and institutions that linked Paulistas to one another and to other Brazilians. I hope to show that if the symbols and institutions demanding loyalty to São Paulo sometimes conflicted with those associated with Brazil, at least as frequently they reinforced national allegiances; and that, in any case, both loyalties were dynamic and transcended those to family and locality.[1] The story is, on balance, one of successful integration, but one charged with ambiguity along the way.

In the formation of voluntary associations, as we shall see, most of the success was in developing allegiances and foci of activity at the state rather than at the national level.

We will concern ourselves here with what Johan Galtung calls "organizational" and "associational" integration, and accept as a given "territorial" integration, the third type he identifies, based on simple spatial proximity.[2] Organizational or "vertical" integration depends on a division of labor, and therefore on interdependent actors ranged in hierarchies of complementary and unequal units. Organizational integration is especially important in the process of production, but also shapes relations between levels of government. Since organizational integration in its bureaucratic mode is associated with social and economic development and increasing degrees of economic equality, whereas patron-client networks are associated with traditional and relatively rigid stratification systems, we would expect to find the former growing in a modern economy and the latter declining. True, in São Paulo, as in Brazil in general, some patron-client networks did disappear or lose significance in the years 1889–1937; yet others, often associated with the increasing authority of government—for example in the labor apparatus—arose, illustrating the fact that such systems are dynamic phenomena, not simply residues.[3]

Associational, or "horizontal," integration is based on voluntary communication arising from a similarity of status or values among persons or groups. It was the associational form of integration Ernst Haas had in mind when he defined integration as "the process whereby political actors in several distinct . . . settings are persuaded to shift their loyalties, expectations, and political activities toward a new center, whose institutions possess or demand jurisdiction over the pre-existing [units]." This change requires that the activities of key groups be "refocused on a new set of central symbols and institutions."[4]

São Paulo faced a unique problem in creating new loyalties—the assimilation of a large immigrant population. Our interest in this connection is not the cultural assimilation of immigrants (a subject that was discussed in Chapter Three), but rather the ways in which their loyalties shifted to, or were made to shift to, local, state, and national entities—governmental or otherwise. In some respects, these newcomers were more easily integrated into a culture beyond the locality than the caipiras, because of their initial dealings with the state and federal governments and their continual movement from plantation to plantation, or from countryside to city.

São Paulo had less of a problem in integrating its zones or subregions than Minas and Pernambuco. In São Paulo, the march of the coffee frontier, drawing on previously settled zones, tended to minimize subregional ties; and the integration of the zones was further assisted by an extensive railroad network (which also facilitated newspaper circulation), a considerable amount of interzonal investment, and the geographic circulation of economic and political elites. On top of all this, there was the growing influence of São Paulo city itself, especially in the economy and communications; by the 1930's, the state's 10 zones had essentially become a single region organized around the metropolis.

With these prefatory remarks, we may turn to a more specific consideration of the processes of integration in São Paulo. I shall first discuss the manipulation of the symbols of integration, and then present a case of organizational integration—the shifting relations between federal and state military forces. The remainder and the bulk of the chapter will be devoted to associational integration, exemplified in voluntary associations and their congresses.

Bandeirismo

At a symbolic level, a Eurocentric cosmopolitanism—most notable in the arts as late as the appearance in Brazil of futurism and Dada—yielded decisively in the post–World War I era to both nationalist and regionalist currents. In São Paulo, the literary journal *Klaxon* (1922–23) was the vehicle for a cosmopolitanism associated with the events of Modern Art Week. The review *Terra Roxa* (1926) had a nationalist orientation,[5] but the purple coffee-growing soil for which it was named implied that this nationalism was based on an identification of São Paulo with Brazil. Was this synechdoche, or was the part actually confused with the whole?

The parallel growth of a regionalist orientation, spurred by a scholarly and general interest in the bandeirante phenomenon, was heartily encouraged by the state government. In 1924, Afonso de Taunay began to publish his *História geral das bandeiras*, a project that ended only with the appearance of the eleventh volume in 1950. The 1920's also witnessed a reprinting of Taques de Almeida's *Nobiliarquia Paulistana*, an eighteenth-century genealogical work glorifying not only the bandeirantes, but also their descendants. Brazil's centenary year, 1922, saw the appearance of the *Anais do Museu Paulista* and the concerted effort of Governor Washington Luís to raise the public's awareness of São Paulo's past by subsidizing historical and commemorative projects. The Museu Paulista, after all, was located at the site where Prince Pedro had declared Brazilian independence in 1822.

It was bandeirismo, São Paulo's indefatigable search for adventure and opportunity in the colonial era, that offered a symbolic resolution to the problem of competing loyalties to state and nation. Bandeirismo was not racist—at least by the standards of the day. It glorified the Portuguese, the Spaniard, the Indian, the *mameluco* (half-breed), and even the Negro, all of whom were among the original bandeirantes,[6] and therefore implicitly justified the assimilation of new immigrants and migrants from other states. The lack of racism and acceptance (sometimes even celebration) of race-mixture also meshed with anti-racist theories originating elsewhere in Brazil in the 1930's, notably those of the Pernambucano Gilberto Freyre. Bandeirismo's overarching appeal in São Paulo, of course, grew out of an implicit belief in "hegemonic federalism"—in São Paulo as the leader of Brazil, as the engine pulling empty boxcars, as the node of progress in a field of backwardness. Thus regionalism and nationalism were compatible, and the acceptance of this viewpoint provided a needed boost to regional pride after the defeat of 1932. This compatibility was the thrust of books like Cassiano Ricardo's *Marcha para oeste*, the capstone of bandeirante literature, which appeared in 1940. It surveyed the history of the bandeirantes of the colonial era, and identified twentieth-century industrial leadership with bandeirismo.[7] At the time of publication, Ricardo was director of the State Press, and the book thus assumed a semiofficial status.

Military Federalism

Nowhere was bandeirante leadership more obvious than in the history of São Paulo's Força Pública. Its relations with the army perhaps best illustrate the changing power relations between the state and federal governments and will serve as our case study in organizational integration.

The relations between the Força Pública and the federal army often depended on the Paulista leaders' interpretation of their state's interests. São Paulo's troops made a critical contribution to Floriano's government in the civil war of 1893–95 by blocking Gumercindo Saraiva's march to

Rio; and in 1894, Governor Bernardino de Campos kept volunteer units ("Patriotic Battalions") mobilized until Prudente de Morais was inaugurated as President.[8] In 1897, São Paulo dispatched state police units to Canudos to defend the federal government; it was the only state south of Bahia to do so. Paulista troops traveled to Mato Grosso in 1900, probably with federal approval, to support the Murtinho faction in a local war. They were ordered to Rio in 1904 to help control rioting and stymie a putsch against Rodrigues Alves.[9] In the turbulent 1920's, São Paulo's troops helped the army quash tenente revolts in Mato Grosso, Rio Grande do Sul, Santa Catarina, Paraná, and Ceará.[10]

These activities were all designed to strengthen the federal government at times when Paulista statesmen wished to buttress federal policies; but the Força Pública was also used to offset central power. Indeed, the French military mission of 1906 may have been inspired in part by the state's wish to protect itself against federal interference in the valorization program.[11] During the tense years of the Hermes administration (1910–14), when state leaders feared that federal intervention might be instigated by Senators Rodolfo Miranda and Pinheiro Machado, they increased the Força's strength by 50 percent; they also resurrected the Patriotic Battalions of earlier years and organized new volunteer units throughout São Paulo. In 1917, during the anxious months between the rupture of diplomatic relations with Germany and Brazil's declaration of war, the state government, jealous of its autonomy, even refused to allow the Força Pública to become a reserve force for the army.[12]

Although loyalists in the army and the Força Pública were driven together by the uprising of 1924 (in which rebels from both organizations took part), the revolution of 1930 divided them again. Getúlio Vargas immediately saw the threat that the Força Pública posed to his government, and moved quickly—albeit not very effectively at first—to limit its power. Vargas nationalized the air wing and tried to hold down expenditures on state troops. Contraband arms, however, flowed into São Paulo in 1931–32.[13]

In general—and in part because of a comparable level of professionalization—São Paulo's Força Pública was subject to the same divisions as the army. Both institutions were split by tenentismo at an ideological level, and by the interruption in regular promotion procedures after 1930. In April 1931, state troops were temporarily divided by an attempted coup against the tenente government of João Alberto and Miguel Costa, as was the federal military establishment in São Paulo; but loyalist officers quelled the budding revolt, and Costa, a rebel in 1924, briefly became commander of the Força Pública.[14]

Significantly, Vargas, presumably fearing a reaction by autonomists in São Paulo, did not attempt to put the Força Pública under the command of an army officer in 1930. Furthermore, the Força got its first armored tanks in 1931.[15] Only in November 1932, after the defeat of the Constitutionalist Revolution, did a regular military officer assume command of São Paulo's state police. But by 1934 it was once again under the direction of a Força-trained officer, Arlindo de Oliveira. Though Oliveira had been a tenente rebel in 1924, he had fought on São Paulo's side in 1932. So had the man who replaced him three years later, an army officer named Milton de Almeida.[16] Getúlio Vargas did not in fact definitively remove the Força Pública as a threat to central authority until the early months of the Estado Novo, when his personal candidate, army Colonel Mário Xavier, became its commander.[17] (All the same, as we will see in Chapter Eight, the state lost significant ground to the Ministry of War in the 1930's in the amount of money devoted to security forces.)

Although Paulistas took pride in a professional state police force, few of them apparently aspired to officers' careers in the army. Consider, for example, their representation among the generals of division and brigade: 1 of 30 in 1895, 0 of 30 in 1930, and 0 of 40 in 1937. Moreover, not one of the 25 Ministers of War who served from 1889 through 1937 was a Paulista.[18] Of the few military figures in our political elite, all were imposed by Vargas after 1930, and all were replaced after Armando Sales became interventor in 1933. (Minas Gerais had no military officers in its political elite, but Minas was not subjected to federal intervention in 1930.) Since senior military officers stationed in the São Paulo military region were usually "outsiders," this situation perhaps posed an implicit obstacle to political integration.

High-ranking officers tended to come from Rio Grande do Sul, the Federal District, and Mato Grosso—many were born to officer-fathers stationed in those areas—or from the North and the Northeast, where there were few attractive professions other than soldiering. By contrast, the Paulistas had many other career opportunities, including those in the Força Pública. Besides, for the business-minded Paulistas, a military career was not the obvious route to success.

In establishing civilian rule in the early Republic, the Paulista Presidents contributed to the state's "anti-military" reputation. Campos Sales, as we saw in Chapter Six, was concerned about the negative aspect militarism would have on the exchange rate, and Paulista statesmen railed against militarism in the presidential contests of 1891 and 1910. But it seems obvious that being "anti-militarist" was a fairly safe stance as long as the state could rely on the Força Pública as a counterweight to the army. Few federal troops were stationed in São Paulo during the Old Republic, and even as late as 1965, the Força had more men under arms in São Paulo than the army.[19]

The state police force was also glorified at a symbolic level. Both of the only two books I discovered that deal with military heroes of São Paulo in this period—*Great Soldiers of São Paulo* and *The Paulista Military Spirit* —have to do with the Força Pública; both in fact were written by Força officers.[20] The Paulistas' strategy of relying on state troops to offset the power of the army differed sharply from the strategy adopted by the Mineiros. Like São Paulo, Minas supplied few high-ranking officers. But though its Força Pública was less powerful than São Paulo's by almost any gauge, Minas provided an indispensable support for federal policies in exchange for internal autonomy.[21]

On the state level, São Paulo's Força Pública contributed to organizational integration by helping to concentrate authority in the hands of the governor. Coupled with the reform of the state's criminal justice system, the militarization of the Força in 1906 weakened coronel authority, preventing the rise of "warlord" coronéis comparable to Franklin Lins or Horácio de Matos in Bahia.[22]

Associations and Congresses

Although voluntary associations were not absent from the military sphere, as the formation of Paulista Patriotic Battalions indicates, the bulk of these groups were "horizontal" organizations based on shared interests rather than on "vertical" hierarchies. The remainder of this chapter will treat voluntary associations of various sorts, on the premise that one of the key elements in political and social integration is the formation of these organizations ("associational" integration). If such groupings are not limited to a single locality, they imply their members' awareness of bonds of solidarity that transcend mere proximity. We shall consider the frequency, scope, and content of selected meetings and congresses.

The state experienced a virtual explosion of associational activity in the

twentieth century. This was due in part to the rising level of urbanization, but it was also an outgrowth of a worldwide revolution in transportation and communications. The number of international congresses,
whose growth was impressive even in the 1870's, later proliferated at a
geometric rate, to reach an average of well over 200 meetings a year by
1910–13.[23] The number of new international cultural, scholarly, and
scientific societies showed a similar trend.[24] National and international
fairs made their first appearance in the nineteenth century, and the imperial government of Brazil and its Republican successor took part in
many expositions. The central government also participated in international congresses on specific commodities—coffee and sugar (both in 1902)
and two on cotton after the First World War, the second of which Brazil
hosted in 1922. The federal government, with assistance from the states,
also organized two national expositions, in 1908 and 1922.

Voluntary associations likewise sprang up all over Brazil, and here
São Paulo was clearly in the vanguard. Of the 172 scientific, artistic, and
literary societies in the country in 1911, São Paulo accounted for 33,
almost twice as many as Pernambuco and the Federal District, the units
tied for second place. Most of these organizations had been founded in
the period after 1890.[25]

Organizations were formed in various ways, but there were three general patterns: emulation of an existing organization elsewhere (notably,
sports and social clubs); formation of branches of national or international
organizations (Scouting and the Sociedade Paulista de Agricultura); and
establishment of a group to offset another group in the economy (manufacturers against workers). These patterns were not mutually exclusive,
however. For example, the Sociedade Paulista de Agricultura, founded
in 1902, was established in part to offset the collusion of coffee importers
overseas.

The impetus to organization at the state level usually came from a national or Rio-based entity, but in some cases (e.g., Scouting) the direction
was reversed. A number of congresses on public issues in São Paulo and
elsewhere had eventual repercussions at the federal level or brought
about activity elsewhere in Brazil. In the area of education, for example,
São Paulo state officials hosted the First National Congress on Secondary
Education in 1911;[26] and the state government organized the First Brazilian Congress on Rural Education in 1937.

Early congresses in São Paulo tended to be associated with agricultural or religious activities. Coffee growers held a number of state meetings after the onset of the coffee crisis in the late 1890's. São Paulo city was the site of a Brazilian bishops' congress in 1890; this was followed by the first regular meeting of the bishops of southern Brazil (Archdiocese of Rio de Janeiro) in 1901. With the rise of a new generation about 1910, however, a succession of new cultural, professional, and "public interest" congresses took place: in 1909, the state hosted the First National Student Congress; in 1910, the First National Congress on Geography; in 1911, the First National Congress on Secondary Education; in 1914, the First National Congress on Brazilian History; and in 1917, the First National Congress on Highway Development.[27] Subsequent congresses of most of the new organizations tended to move from one state capital to another, and not to focus exclusively on Rio de Janeiro.

Generally, the congresses within the state were held in São Paulo city, with the important exception of agricultural congresses, which moved through the coffee zones. Campinas became a very distant competitor of the capital as a meeting place, after enjoying some popularity in the 1890's, when it had the advantage of being in the heart of the coffee country and was easily accessible from the capital by rail. Campinas hosted an agricultural convention in 1899 and then became the seat of a coffee growers' organization.

It bears repeating that in the economic sphere, the holding of congresses and the forming of associations were the products not only of a "demonstration effect" of groups already established in Rio or Europe, but also of economic crises. This fact seems clear in the history of agricultural associations (see below). And accordingly, the meetings of most producers' groups had a general theme: to get the state or federal government (or both) to intervene in the economy on their behalf. Both levels of government reacted by encouraging organization along corporate lines, beginning with a federal statute in 1903 that permitted the creation of agricultural syndicates with legal corporate status to defend fazendeiro interests. This law marked the beginning, in fact, of Brazil's extensive corporatist legislation on representative associations, and held out the possibility of effective access to governmental decision-makers.[28]

The coffee growers, of course, provide the most obvious case of an organized economic group's ability to use government for its own ends.[29] Despite the celebrated power of the fazendeiros, however, the history of the planters' associations frequently shows a welter of competing or allied organizations rather than a solid phalanx. The main source of cleavage was apparently between the planters whose sole or primary interest was agriculture and those with large investments elsewhere, notably in banking, exporting, commerce, or industry. There were also cleavages over valorization, the coffee export tax, and noncoffee agricultural production.[30]

There were few obvious conflicts between planters located in the several zones of the state, at least after the fall of the Empire, when the plaints of the planters in the agriculturally exhausted Paraíba Valley ceased. Since the agricultural organizations were headed by large planters who were quick to invest in new frontier lands, interzonal cleavage was probably less intense than in Minas, a state twice as large and one in which only two zones of seven (the Mata and the Sul) were major coffee producers. In São Paulo, a series of agricultural congresses between 1910 and 1915 covered five of the state's 10 zones. (Omitted were those where little coffee was grown—the Capital, Paraíba Valley, Baixa Sorocabana, and Southern Coast zones—and the Alta Paulista, where coffee had not yet come into large-scale production.)

In south-central Brazil, planters' attempts at organization for political action began at least as early as the 1870's, with the founding of the Clube de Lavoura in Rio in 1871, and an interprovincial agricultural congress in 1878, both of which were concerned with the prospects for agriculture in the face of impending abolition. But the drive toward permanent organization in São Paulo came several years later, with the coffee crisis of the 1890's. The 1896 decline in prices brought about a state agricultural congress the same year, as well as efforts by the São Paulo government to reach an accord with four other coffee-producing states to promote coffee consumption abroad. Rio State and Minas ultimately refused to approve the plan, and it failed, but the crisis had forced Paulista planters to look beyond their state's borders in seeking to resolve marketing problems.[31]

In 1897, the Sociedade Nacional de Agricultura was established in the Federal District, and two years later an SNA representative attended an agricultural congress at Campinas. Several dozen município-based planters' clubs sent representatives, including many of the most powerful fazendeiros in São Paulo. The president of the congress, José Duarte Rodrigues (also a leading banker), called for aid to agriculture in the form of mortgage banks modeled on the Prussian Central-Landschaft. Campinas was selected as the site of a permanent secretariat to coordinate activities.[32]

In 1901, the SNA held a national agricultural congress, an event that stimulated the formation of new groups in Bahia, Minas Gerais, and São Paulo.[33] In São Paulo, the continuing coffee crisis, exacerbated by an exchange-rate policy that further reduced the coffee groups' receipts, and a decline in the flow of immigrants were important fillips to more effective organization. The Sociedade Paulista de Agricultura was organized in the offices of the State Secretariat of Agriculture by some of São Paulo's most prestigious planters and comissários. Since the SPA's membership was limited to these two groups, the founding of the society may have been in part a reaction to the foreign export houses' control of the international coffee trade, as well as to price manipulation by overseas importers. In addition to demanding government credit and lower export taxes, SPA leaders called for the granting of small plots to immigrants, so that they would be available on a standby basis to large plantations when the workload was heavy.[34]

At the beginning of 1903, as noted earlier, Congress and President Rodrigues Alves reacted to a petition by the SNA and authorized the creation of agricultural syndicates. A new group in São Paulo quickly responded to the decree: the União dos Lavradores organized a planters' congress less than a month after the presidential action. The União not only wanted government aid; unlike the SPA, it also wished to revoke the state law of 1902 prohibiting the planting of trees on new estates until other states also agreed to ban such plantings.[35] This suggests that the União represented the less well-established fazendeiros, or at least those with greater investments in frontier lands. It faded away, however, perhaps from lack of support by leading planters, leaving the field to the SPA.

The SPA, meanwhile, had begun to press its policies on the state and national governments. It was to the SPA that Alexandre Siciliano presented his valorization plan, and the organization got virtual control of coffee policy under Governor Jorge Tibiriçá, who successfully promoted the Exchange Bank at the federal level. In 1904, Tibiriçá sent Augusto Ramos on a world tour to learn about competition in the coffee industry.*

* Several other Paulistas undertook agricultural missions on behalf of the state and federal governments in later years. F. Ferreira Ramos (Augusto's brother) went to Europe in 1906. Edmundo Navarro de Andrade, the founder and editor of *O Fazendeiro*, made two world tours to study agriculture, in 1913 and 1918. Antônio Padua Sales, as Minister of Agriculture, went to England to promote the sale of Brazilian cotton in 1919, and in the

In the meantime, the SPA sponsored coffee exhibits at national and international expositions.[36] In 1908, the SPA began to receive a state subsidy;
and in 1909, a planters' goal was realized at the federal level when the
Ministry of Agriculture, in limbo since the beginning of the Republic,
was reestablished. The first Minister was Cândido Rodrigues, a Paulista
coffee planter and SPA member. He was succeeded by another Paulista
coffee magnate, Rodolfo Miranda.

But another group of planters was emerging, apparently consisting of
those who had fewer direct ties with the export complex. A new series
of state agricultural congresses, with representatives of município-wide
associations, met at least 11 times in different towns in the interior between 1910 and 1915. One of the hotly debated issues at these meetings
was plantation labor relations, and these congresses probably helped
shape the State Labor Department (authorized in 1911), whose principal
responsibilities lay in agriculture. In 1913, at the seventh of these congresses, the representatives called for the importation of Brazilian workers for São Paulo's coffee fields, if foreign colonos were not available in
sufficient numbers. Governor João Pinheiro's agricultural credit cooperatives in Minas were discussed at the congresses of 1913 and 1914; but the
argument apparently prevailed that cooperatives were not worthwhile,
because the investments required for São Paulo's coffee industry were too
large and the credit structure too closely tied to the comissário houses.[37]

The organizers of the agricultural congresses set up a secretariat and
criticized the SPA for not sponsoring the events. The SPA finally took
up the challenge, hosting the seventh and later meetings (1913–15), and
granting a state subsidy. Meanwhile, in 1912, the Centro Agrícola Paulista was established by prominent SPA members and those who led the
congresses before SPA involvement.[38] The Paulista planters were again
united, at least on the surface.

In 1916, perhaps in an effort to accommodate non–coffee growers, the
SPA held a special congress on rice production, a crop of rising impor-
tance as the Allies' food requirements swelled, and as the city of São
Paulo experienced rapid industrialization and population growth. But this

---

same year Roberto Simonsen was a Brazilian delegate to the International Congress of
Cotton Industries in Paris. In 1937, the future Minister of Agriculture Teodureto Leite de
Almeida toured several Central and South American countries to study coffee production
for the São Paulo government.

was a one-shot affair, and the congress concluded that rice cultivation would be "truly remunerative" only when irrigation was employed (as it was in Rio Grande do Sul).[39]

The crisis in international trade caused by the First World War and the changing import requirements of the Allies gave rise to a new organization in 1919, the Sociedade Rural Brasiliera. Among its founders was Artur Diedrichsen of the Theodor Wille firm. The SRB also had two representatives of foreign meat-packing houses (*frigoríficos*) among its initial slate of officers, though most were blue-blooded planters.[40] Cattle ranching and meat packing were emphasized in the early years. The SRB explicitly looked to its English, French, and Argentine predecessors as models,[41] and the emphasis on ranching was probably not only to take advantage of the frigorífico business (booming because of Allied wartime and postwar demand), but also to appeal to owners of declining coffee plantations in search of new uses for their land.

The Liga Agrícola Brasileira, an association founded in 1921, was a group of a far different order from the SPA and the SRB. In 1920, local followers of the American political economist Henry George had persuaded Governor Washington Luís to bring a specialist on the rural land tax (imposto territorial) from Uruguay to São Paulo to help make the tax more effective.[42] In 1922, two LAB leaders called for a meaningful property tax to replace the export levy, and cited George on the virtues of the single (land) tax. One of these men noted that the substitution of the rural property tax for the export tax would tend to break up latifundia, whose owners would be forced to produce or sell.[43] (The speaker clearly assumed that the export tax fell most heavily on the planters, and that many latifundia were tracts held by speculators.) In short, the LAB tilted toward the "little" planter, who opposed speculators and magnates with fallow lands.

One of the state's great coffee barons, Carlos Leôncio Magalhães, attacked the Georgists through the SRB. Magalhães argued that it was the consumers of coffee who ultimately paid São Paulo's export taxes through higher prices.[44] Meanwhile, Governor Washington Luís abandoned the idea of making the imposto territorial a major source of revenue, perhaps because of his success in obtaining large new loans abroad in 1921.

After the great frost of 1918, many coffee planters began to plant cotton, and in 1922 the LAB took a leading role in seeking to expand cotton production in São Paulo. When members of the International Cotton Congress (meeting in Rio) came to São Paulo, they were received at the offices of the LAB, not at those of the SRB or the SPA.[45]

All three organizations were led by rich planters, and sometimes even by the same men—though apparently not simultaneously. Artur Diedrichsen was an officer of both the SRB and the SPA, and Gabriel Ribeiro dos Santos was (at different times) president of both the SRB and the LAB.[46] The three groups frequently cooperated, as in 1921, when all proclaimed their support for a bill before Congress for the permanent defense of coffee, or in 1923, when they jointly urged that fazendeiros be represented in the governance of the proposed state Coffee Institute.[47] The SRB emerged as the strongest of the three, and the Coffee Institute, when it came in 1924, was founded at its headquarters. (Note the reversal of roles from 1902, when the SPA was founded in the Secretariat of Agriculture.) In 1930, the American consul in São Paulo estimated that the SRB had about 1,500 members, the SPA about 400, and the LAB about 500 (but there was considerable overlapping of membership).[48]

I have not found any clear correlation between these agricultural associations and the political parties of the late 1920's. Of the three groups, the LAB was the least satisfied with official policies, and several of its leaders helped form the Partido Democrático—among them Cândido Rodrigues, the former Minister of Agriculture, and Otaviano Alves Lima, who had been a Georgist in the early 1920's. But Gabriel Ribeiro dos Santos, a onetime president of the LAB, was a perrepista who served as São Paulo's secretary of agriculture from 1924 to 1927. The man who was probably the most influential in shaping the agricultural policy of the Democrats was Cesário Coimbra, president of the SRB and twice president of the Coffee Institute in the early 1930's. After the merger of the three agricultural groups in 1931 in an enlarged SRB, the association was clearly identified with the Partido Democrático.

It was the LAB that convoked an inter-association meeting of fazendeiros in December 1929 to attack the state government's valorization policies and to demand government support for coffee prices and greater control of the Coffee Institute by planters. The LAB was then led by Afrodísio Sampaio Coelho, a graduate of Cornell University, son-in-law of Jorge Tibiriçá, and a member of the political elite of Chapter Five. Sampaio Coelho placed the whole blame for the disastrous state of the coffee industry on the state government. "Although called on very short notice," reported the American consul, the meeting "was attended by representatives of about one-third of the entire number of coffee trees in the state."[49] LAB leaders soon suggested a fusion of the three agricultural organizations, an achievement realized at the outset of 1931, in a reconstituted SRB.

Meanwhile, the state and central governments were trying to cope with the coffee disaster. In January 1931, Interventor João Alberto reorganized the Coffee Institute, allowing greater planter participation in its governance. The next month, Vargas and Finance Minister Whitaker announced that the Provisional Government would buy coffee stocks. In April, São Paulo officials called a meeting of representatives of six coffee-producing states to regulate production and sales, a broadening of São Paulo's effort in the late 1920's to coordinate the warehousing of stocks. In June, Vargas and Whitaker created the National Coffee Council (CNC), with a policy board composed of representatives of the coffee-producing states. At the international level, Brazil sought to deal with the crisis by persuading the governments of competing countries to limit planting. But the Second International Coffee Conference, which met in São Paulo in June 1931, was a failure because Colombia refused to cooperate. Soon thereafter, João Alberto reorganized the Coffee Institute again, giving five of the six places on the governing board to planters. But the SRB, now closely associated with the PD, which had broken with Vargas and João Alberto in March, cried fraud when the procedures to choose the Institute's new board were announced.

As the recently united SRB went over to the opposition after the planters had seen their demands met for virtual control of the Institute, another planter organization sprang up—the Comissão de Organização da Lavoura. Its leaders—including former LAB leader Sampaio Coelho—issued a manifesto in August 1931, following the dismissal of Interventor João Alberto, whose favor they had been courting. In this document, they denounced the prices at which the federal government, under Finance Minister Whitaker, a Paulista banker, had been buying coffee stocks,[50] and attacked bankers, dependence on foreign loans (especially onerous after the fall of the exchange rate), and the recently imposed federal gold surtax on coffee, used to service foreign loans. They also appealed for the "regimentation" of planters in São Paulo, for price supports, for the gradual elimination of the export tax, for the "decongestion" of cities (an appeal to keep workers in the countryside with better educational and health services), and for the elimination of protectionist tariff schedules that benefited "illegitimate industries" (i.e., manufacturing). The manifesto ended with a call to planters to "save the national economy."[51]

The Comissão became the Federação das Associações de Lavradores in November 1931, and shortly thereafter forced the resignation of São Paulo Finance Secretary Numa de Oliveira, because of his ties with foreign bankers; it also helped secure the resignations of Interventor Laudo Ferreira de Camargo and Finance Minister Whitaker.[52] But the SRB, linked with the PD and dominated by the old planter-exporter group, took a narrow majority of seats on the executive board of the Coffee Institute in the December 1931 elections. Cesário Coimbra, the SRB president and PD member, now became president of the Institute. Apparently the SRB won out over its rival in shaping policy for the new National Coffee Council at the end of 1931, though both groups were represented in the São Paulo delegation.[53]

The Comissão (or Federação) faction came back after the 1932 revolution, when São Paulo was again under military rule. Sampaio Coelho became president of the Coffee Institute in late 1932; in 1933, Luís Figueira Melo was named president, and Múcio Whitaker became president of the State Bank. All were signers of the Comissão's 1931 manifesto. Their program of aiding the planter against the banker and exporter reached its acme in the Economic Readjustment (announced in April 1933), a program that canceled a large share of the planters' debts. The Comissão group was the backbone of Interventor Valdomiro's Partido da Lavoura, which unsuccessfully contested the Constituent Assembly elections with the Single Ticket coalition in May 1933. In 1934, the new civilian and Paulista Interventor, Armando Sales Oliveira, again named Cesário Coimbra as director of the Coffee Institute. That agency, however, became increasingly irrelevant after the formation of the National Coffee Department (DNC) in February 1933 (before Sales came to office), because the central government set DNC policy.

Given the desperation of planters in the early 1930's, it is interesting how few were really organized in voluntary associations, despite the Comissão's appeal in 1931 for the "regimentation" of coffee growers. A decree by Interventor Valdomiro in February 1933 (10 days after the creation of the National Coffee Department) encouraged the creation of agricultural syndicates; and by August, according to the Coffee Institute, some 42,000 growers, each owning at least 1,000 trees, had joined up. One political implication seems to be an increase in the prestige of the (pro-Valdomiro) Comissão group, well organized at the local level. But a later investigation under Interventor Armando Sales revealed that this figure was simply the number of fazendeiros who had registered with the Institute, as required by law, to export coffee. In truth, fewer than 2,400 planters were affiliated with syndicates at the time, and this number was only slightly larger than the combined membership of the SRB, SPA, and LAB in 1930.[54]

Let us now turn to some other types of associations in the economy—those of the working class, and more specifically, of the urban working class, since Paulista planters in the Old Republic did not permit any form of labor organization among their colonos.[55] Unions were probably the voluntary associations that had the greatest integrative effect on São Paulo's immigrant population, since immigrants bulked so large in the urban labor force. Furthermore, we must also consider another form of collective activity—strikes. The reasons for the success or failure of labor organizations and their strikes are not far to seek. In a broad sense, the concentration of the labor force in urban areas was basic to successful organization (e.g., in the textile industry). Another key to success was a trade or activity linked to the export sector, because in these jobs the wages were relatively high, benefits were more likely to be on an impersonal cash basis, and the communications flow among the workers was reasonably good.

All these things helped bring about the organization of the stevedores of Santos and the state's railroad workers in the early years of the Republic.[56] Yet the most important thing in the case of these two groups (especially the stevedores) was their strategic leverage. The whole economy of São Paulo was endangered if the dock workers refused to load the freighters at Santos. Other factors in successful organization were the skill levels involved in a given activity and the relative inability of employers to resist strikes—both were important in the early gains of construction workers in Santos.[57] Another element in determining the success or failure of labor organizations was the counter-organization of employers—e.g., in textiles, where the formation of the Centro de Indústrias was a direct reponse to worker militancy. And finally, of course, an important factor was the attitude of government, especially at the state level.[58] The state government could alleviate bad working conditions, as it attempted to do (in theory) in the Sanitary Code regulations of 1911 and 1917. It could be a paternalistic mediator—through the State Department of Labor—or a repressor, as it was in 1906 and 1917, when the Força Pública was used against strikers.

The goals of most labor groups and strike efforts were not revolutionary or utopian, despite the visibility of anarchists in the labor press and in some leadership posts. The general strike of 1907 had as a major goal the achievement of the eight-hour workday, and many workers temporarily secured it.[59] The great wave of strikes in 1917–20 was provoked by falling real wages and food shortages, and had some effect in restoring a wage packet eroded by inflation.[60] Most workers, at least in the early years of the century, probably thought in terms of upward social mobility. An absolute majority at that time were immigrants, and the very fact that they undertook to cross the Atlantic testifies to their aspirations for a better life. In his novel *O estrangeiro*, Plínio Salgado has a worker declare of the 1917 strikes: "We won't go off the job. The wages aren't too good, and we work long hours, but tomorrow we can be the bosses. Our situation is only temporary." Such an attitude was probably widely shared.[61]

The level of effective association was the citywide or statewide trade union, though organization at higher levels was sustained for several years at a time. According to Azis Simão, there were only seven "primary," or trade union, associations in the period 1888–1900. But the number then jumped dramatically—to 55 in 1901–14, to 91 in 1915–19, and to 131 in 1930–40.[62] Strikes to some extent mirrored these trends; there were 25 in the first period, 91 in the second, and 116 in the third. But in the fourth period, 1930–40, there were only 91, no doubt because strikes were outlawed in 1935 by a state of siege, and remained illegal through the Estado Novo. In the 1888–1900 period, strikes by railroad and urban transport workers were most frequent. In the second, third, and fourth periods, strike activity was greatest among the textile workers, as one might expect of the most numerous and concentrated group in the state.[63]

Mutual-aid societies reflected a more conservative side of the labor movement. Twenty-one such societies had been formed by 1900; 29 were formed in 1901–14, 15 in 1915–29, and none after 1930, presumably because of the new role of the state in creating pension funds. The vast majority of mutual-aid societies were confined to the state capital, where access to banking institutions facilitated such activity. Anarchists opposed the societies; the Church supported the Catholic ones.[64]

On the statewide level, the Federação Operária was relatively early on the scene, formed in 1905 by four craft unions. Its representatives participated in a national Workers' Congress in Rio in 1906, a meeting that produced the Confederação Operária Brasileira in 1908. According to São Paulo's Federação Operária, the COB had 57,400 members in São Paulo in 1912, 15,000 in Rio Grande do Sul, and only 5,000 in Rio, where Mário Hermes, son of the President, had formed the government-manipulated Confederação Brasileira do Trabalho.[65]

The Federação Operária had a spotty existence. It ceased to function after 1913, but gained new life during the 1917 strike wave and managed to continue in existence until it was suppressed in Vargas's emergency of 1935.[66] Interstate activity was intermittent, though two more Workers' Congresses were held, in 1913 and 1920.[67] A series of new but short-lived state federations came along in the 1930's, among them the Communist-organized Federação Sindical Regional, which was suppressed along with the old Federação Operária in 1935. A Catholic workers' federation apparently survived into the Estado Novo era, but was less important than the government-backed Federação Operária dos Sindicatos da Indústria (from 1937).[68]

Both the Catholic Church and the federal government began to shift their positions on the labor question as early as the general strike of 1917, in which some 40,000 to 50,000 workers participated. The Church became less interested in mutual-aid societies and even attempted to create something approximating labor unions.[69] In the 1920 general strike, however, the new (Catholic) Centro Operário came out for the *classes conservadoras*, condemned the strike, and called for the repression of anarchism.[70] The federal government, on its part, gave benefits to a limited number of workers in the form of a workmen's compensation act in 1919 and a pension law in 1923; but repressive legislation also arrived in 1921 with statutes that facilitated the deportation of foreign-born labor leaders. All the relevant bills were introduced in Congress by Paulistas.[71]

The pension law was authored by Elói Chaves, a man who had considerable experience in labor matters. He was an industrialist and had been secretary of justice in São Paulo during the strikes of 1917, when he had deployed the Força Pública against workers. The Elói Chaves Law applied to the workers of the privately owned railroads; the idea for the law in fact originated with the São Paulo Railway Company, the "Inglesa."[72]

Participation in Chaves's pension program was obligatory; the worker, the employer, and the federal government all contributed, and the government was charged with regulating the use of the retirement funds. Backed by the Bernardes administration, the Elói Chaves Law was the first extension into the private sector of a program already in force for federal government employees. Its coverage was later broadened, to take in dock and maritime workers in 1926, public service workers in 1931, miners in 1932, bank and commercial employees in 1934, and industrial workers in 1938.[73]

By the 1930's, the principle that organized labor had a legitimate place in the economy—however modest and regulated—had been accepted. There were no general strikes in São Paulo in the 1930's, but a textile workers' strike involving some 30,000–40,000 people occurred in 1931. By the 1930's, Marxism was replacing anarchism among militants, as second-generation Brazilians moved into the labor force, to become the targets of Communist and Trotskyist recruiters. Meanwhile, the government's role expanded slowly but steadily. In 1939, the single government-sanctioned union (*sindicato único*) was required, and a minimum wage was set in 1940. (There was no comprehensive body of labor legislation, however, until 1943.) The Estado Novo kept the occupation-based union as the basic unit of organization, probably to keep interunion solidarity to a minimum. According to Azis Simão, a labor bureaucracy began to emerge in São Paulo about 1940.[74]

The geographical effectiveness of the new apparatus can be seen in the number of occupational identity cards issued. São Paulo passed the Federal District in this regard in 1938, and remained in first place through the Second World War.[75] Until 1939, the Ministry of Labor in Rio was content to enforce labor laws principally in the Federal District, just as the São Paulo Department of Labor concentrated on the capital city.[76] But the department nonetheless assumed statewide responsibility for enforcing federal regulations through a series of central government decrees from 1933 to 1940.[77]

Since the process by which labor was wedded to government in the 1930's involved the organizational form of integration, the relaxation of control might have led workers to reject the existing regime. Voluntary associations lost their significance as government moved in to control all labor activity, suppressing dissident unions and jailing workers who resisted the growing *apparat*. This was a general pattern in Latin America, best known in the cases of Mexico and Brazil. What was unique in Brazil between 1930 and 1945 was the decentralization of government mechanisms for the control of labor.

The voluntary associations of the Church in the labor field formed only a small part of its activities among laymen. As I pointed out in Chapter Three, São Paulo was not a conspicuously religious state. Nonetheless, the Church in São Paulo was a wealthy and dynamic institution with able leadership, and its voluntary organizations developed rapidly in the period under study.

Lay associations depended in large measure on the foundations laid by the hierarchy in the early years. An extraordinary congress of Brazilian bishops took place in São Paulo in 1890, in which the prelates protested against the separation of Church and State and the consequent leveling of Catholicism with "error," i.e., other religions.[78] Two years later, the diocese of São Paulo was raised to a Metropolitan See; simultaneously Brazil was divided into two great jurisdictions—the Archdioceses of Bahia and Rio de Janeiro.

In 1899, a Council of Latin American Bishops assembled in Rome and decided on triennial meetings of bishops in each archdiocese; the first for southern Brazil occurred in São Paulo in 1901.[79] Concurrently, the first congress of Catholic clergy and laymen assembled in the diocese of São Paulo.[80] In 1905, Bishop José Camargo Barros held a second diocesan congress, which resulted in the launching of a daily Catholic newspaper. Its purpose, significantly, was confined to covering the traditional pious activities; it did not attack the policies of the secularized state.[81] The bishop also established a lay Catholic Confederation to coordinate the activities of pious associations in the diocese.[82] This flurry of activity derived in large part from a new spirit of social engagement in Rome, but it may also have been influenced by the formation of the Liga Anticlerical in São Paulo, founded in 1903 by the Positivist and political elite member Luís Pereira Barreto and others.[83]

The central figure in the Paulista Church through most of our period was Bishop Camargo's successor, Duarte Leopoldo e Silva (archbishop, 1907–38),[84] the son of a Portuguese tailor who had immigrated to the Paraíba Valley. His elevation coincided with the creation of a new archbishopric in São Paulo, with six suffragan bishoprics, all but one within the state. Taking advantage of São Paulo's new wealth and responding to its growing population, Dom Duarte built scores of churches (quintu-

pling the number of parishes in his archbishopric while in office),[85] as well
as the capital's present cathedral, a seminary, and an archepiscopal palace.
Dom Duarte sought to invigorate Catholicism by organizing the faithful beyond the ranks of the traditional *bien-pensants*. He organized a
workers' group as early as 1907. In 1915, he convoked an archdiocesan
congress of the Catholic Confederation and also authorized a Eucharistic
Congress. He created lay organizations for the two sexes—the Legião de
São Pedro for men and the Liga das Senhoras Católicas. In 1928, he organized the first Congress of Catholic Youth, an event that was attended by
Governor Júlio Prestes and other state officials—and by 5,000 young people who claimed to speak for some 60,000 others.[86] The following year,
Dom Duarte organized the Congress for Devotion to Mary at Aparecida,
the shrine near his birthplace at Taubaté. In 1930, Nossa Senhora da
Conceição Aparecida was proclaimed the Patroness of Brazil. Eventually,
a national basilica was built at her shrine, an edifice that is the third
largest church in the world.[87]

An even more influential Paulista churchman was Cardinal Sebastião
Leme, the leading figure of Brazilian Catholicism in his day. Born in the
Mogiana zone, near Minas, Leme studied at the seminary in São Paulo
city and was a protégé and friend of Dom Duarte.[88] Leme had a broader
range of experience than Leopoldo e Silva, studying eight years at the
Colegio Pio Latino in Rome, and serving in both São Paulo and Pernambuco before becoming an auxiliary bishop in Rio in 1910. (Dom Duarte,
by contrast, spent his whole life in São Paulo, except for a year as a student in Rio and three years as bishop of Curitiba.)

Leme became the auxiliary archbishop of Rio de Janeiro in 1921, and
created a Catholic Confederation there in 1922; this was the prototype
of Brazilian Catholic Action, founded in 1935. Since Leme had worked
with the Catholic Confederation in São Paulo under Bishop Camargo
Barros (Leopoldo e Silva's predecessor), this seems to be an example of a
state or archdiocesan organization helping bring about a national counterpart.[89]

Cardinal Leme's organization of a nationwide Catholic Electoral League
in 1932 had a significant but limited impact in São Paulo, as noted in
Chapter Four. Although Archbishop Leopoldo e Silva was an ardent supporter of the ephemeral league, he was also an ardent bairrista and shared
little of Leme's enthusiasm for Integralism. (In announcing the com-
mencement of work on São Paulo's cathedral in 1913, Dom Duarte had

proclaimed: "Through a law decreed by fate, São Paulo must always march in the vanguard, and must fulfill a great social and political mission. Its hegemony, both civil and religious, can no longer be contested."[90] Later, he justified his support for the Constitutionalist Revolution of 1932 as defending "the dignity of the State [of São Paulo]" in a "campaign on behalf of religion and patriotism."[91])

Yet at a confessional (as opposed to a political) level, the archbishop's mobilization of Catholics in new parishes and organizations strengthened the national Church structure over which Cardinal Sebastião Leme presided in Rio. Church activity may also have helped assimilate immigrants —the majority of whom were Catholics—into regional and national cultures. In addition, for Dom Duarte and his generation of Paulistas, Aparecida perhaps played a symbolic role in the religious sphere analogous to bandeirismo in the sphere of historical myth: as the location of Aparecida, Brazil's national shrine after 1930, São Paulo was an epicenter of Brazilian religious life.

As elsewhere in Brazil, there was generational tension, if not conflict, in São Paulo over the Church's place in the structure of state and society. With an inevitable lag, Brazil experienced a partial recatholicization of its intellectual elite, influenced by the Catholic revival in France at the beginning of the century. Though the conflict of generations was not as sharp as in France (as indicated, for example, in Roger Martin du Gard's *Jean Barois*), it is hard to imagine an atheist like Tibiriçá (born in 1855) appearing in the third generation of the political elite (born after 1888), which gave rise to such notable Catholic lay activists as Ataliba Nogueira and Vicente Ráo. Altino Arantes, of the second generation (born 1876), was a transitional figure, imbued with "liberal" attitudes in his youth, according to a friend, but proudly associating with Archbishop Leopoldo e Silva from his first year as governor (1916) and later accepting Church honors.[92]

Members of the third generation were especially active in another group of voluntary associations, all of which revolved around the São Paulo Law School. One of these, however, dated from the first generation. This was a secret society of law students and alumni called the Burschenschaft, or Burcha, obviously derived from the German prototype. The Burcha certainly played a role—but a poorly understood one because of its clandestine nature—in the oligarchic politics of state and nation (since many law school graduates hailed from other states).[93] The

Burcha's membership overlapped that of a non-secret organization of law students, the XI de Agosto, organized in 1903 and named after the date of the founding of the law school in 1827. This group was dominated by elite families until 1926, when the institution of a secret ballot brought bourgeois students, rather than the scions of coffee barons, to power.[94] The Partido Democrático was formed in the same year, and several former XI de Agosto officers and Burcha members were among its founders.[95]

Student organizations mostly associated with the second and third generations clearly illustrate the role of international events in associational activity. An inter-American student congress took place in Montevideo in 1908, and was attended by four Brazilian delegates. Three were from São Paulo, representing the law school and the São Paulo Polytechnic (Armando Sales). The fourth was the future radical politician Maurício Lacerda, a law student in Rio.[96]

The following year, Paulista students hosted the First Brazilian Student Congress, with Sales and another of the Paulista delegates at Montevideo in leadership posts. The congress debated such issues as how to form closer relations among Brazilian university students; whether students and professors could be a force for political regeneration; and whether universities (as opposed to isolated professional schools) should be established in Brazil.[97] In the same year, Gofredo Silva Teles—a future member of the political elite—represented São Paulo at an international student congress in Paris; he was the officially designated representative of the state government.[98] A permanent national student association, however, would have to wait until 1938, when the União Nacional de Estudantes was formed in Rio. This organization was directly inspired by the Brussels-based Confédération Internationale des Etudiants, but its initial meeting was called the Second National Student Congress, in memory of the São Paulo events of 1909.[99]

A group in which law students, professors, and alumni were dominant was the Liga Nacionalista, the Paulista counterpart of the Liga de Defesa Nacional in Rio. Both were founded in 1917 at the instigation of the parnassian poet and nationalist Olavo Bilac. Though in many ways a youth movement, the Liga Nacionalista included a few dissidents from the 1901 split in the PRP. Later, there was a close association between the Liga and the Partido Democrático; many PD leaders had been members of the organization, and the party continued much of its program.[100]

The Liga Nacionalista was founded in a climate of nationalist fervor after Brazil broke relations with Germany (and during a wave of strikes in São Paulo).* Its leaders called for attacks on illiteracy, support for compulsory military service, the creation of military reserve units (*linhas de tiro*), and the institution of the secret ballot. During the founding ceremonies, the future law professor Valdemar Ferreira cited the experience of Argentina under the Sáenz Peña Electoral Law of 1912 requiring all male citizens to vote; the fact that the reformist Unión Cívica Radical won the Argentine presidency in 1916 was not lost on anti-PRP intellectuals.[101] The Liga Nacionalista was less interested in military preparedness than its Rio counterpart, and more interested in the diffusion of education and the assimilation of immigrants. But its members saw themselves as an elite, and foreign-born Brazilians were excluded from membership.[102]

President Bernardes suppressed the Liga Nacionalista in the aftermath of the military rebellion of 1924, because of the part its president, Vergueiro Steidel, and another prominent member, José Carlos Macedo Soares, had played in dealing with rebel troops to prevent the destruction of the capital. (Macedo Soares was acting in his capacity as president of the São Paulo Commercial Association.)[103]

Two other organizations had overlapping leadership with the Liga Nacionalista. One was the Brazilian Association of Scouting, which had an important place in the Liga program. Macedo Soares and Vergueiro Steidel sat on the association's Higher Council. The scouts, founded in São Paulo in 1914, had achieved an impressive growth in the course of a decade. By 1925, there were 100,000 members in São Paulo, as many as the combined total in all the rest of Brazil.[104] (As elsewhere in the country and the world, Scouting in São Paulo primarily involved urban middle- and upper-class youth.) The other group with Liga connections was the Instituto dos Advogados de São Paulo, founded a few months before the Liga Nacionalista, and linked to a national organization of lawyers. Francisco Morato—soon to be a law professor and later the leader of the PD —and Spencer Vampré, another law professor, were the Instituto's first president and secretary, respectively.[105] Both were charter members of the Liga.

---

*On the anniversary of the founding of the Republic in November 1917, President Braz sponsored a Congress of Brazilian Youth, held simultaneously in each of the 20 state capitals and the Federal District. Thus the federal government too sought to mobilize Brazil's youth against the Central Powers.

In the preceding pages we have surveyed different types of organizations to show a variety of forms of integration. In the sphere of associational integration, the successful voluntary organizations were largely those of the well-to-do. For them and their middle-class followers, loyalty to Brazil was compatible with a deep state pride, nurtured through frequent references to bandeirismo and other symbolic representations of São Paulo as the epicenter of Brazil. Part of the tension between state and national loyalties grew out of São Paulo's economic integration into the capitalist economy of the North Atlantic; and though this integration may have favored allegiance to the state and its established economic groups, such loyalties first flourished and then diminished during the crisis of the 1930's. Paulista planters in any case had sought ties with counterparts from other states even in the 1890's, and they later made valorization a national issue. Fazendeiros had distinct interests from those of bankers and exporters, many of whom were foreign-based. Planters tried to use the state to offset the power of foreign groups, though the picture is immensely complicated by the fact that some of the most successful planters were also bankers and exporters.

As for organizational integration, the state government played a role similar to and sometimes "in advance of" its federal counterpart—in the area of coercion, as well as in that of public services. Although this process probably brought about a new awareness of the state and the nation among the urban masses, such an observation in no way implies a subsequent diminution of social conflict, but only the possibility of new forms of cleavage.

In the first four decades of the century, government participation in the economy and society broadened from intervention in foreign markets on behalf of organized coffee groups to the assumption of new responsibilities for social welfare. Yet though the central government was assuming more powers by the 1930's, it nevertheless ceded responsibilities to the state of São Paulo—not only in matters affecting labor, but also in agricultural affairs. (State Secretariats of Agriculture received new powers from the Ministry of Agriculture in 1936.[106]) The State Labor Department and a public-aid agency were latter-day developments in a patrimonial federalism, beginning with a radical decentralization of revenues in 1891. This decentralization made possible a semiautonomous export policy, opened up a large number of public-employment posts at the state level, and permitted a modest welfarist role for the state by the 1930's.

Such power for the state was not necessarily dysfunctional in the process of national integration: financial "autonomy" and employment in the state government provided a means of satisfying a powerful regional elite and its middle-class dependents, groups that otherwise might have pursued with greater energy their demands for hegemony, or even separation.

CHAPTER EIGHT

Fiscal Federalism

São PAULO WAS A wealthy state, and that wealth was translated into a well-funded state treasury, even though taxes were regressive and benefits for the populace, especially before the 1930's, were modest. In this chapter I discuss São Paulo's tax system; its domestic and foreign borrowing, and debt servicing; its expenditures by sector; and the finances of its municípios. In the final section, I consider the distribution of revenues and expenditures among São Paulo, the other states, and the Union. Taken together, these data show that however much Paulista statesmen grumbled about the federal tax burden in their state, São Paulo had huge and growing resources at its disposal. It is even tempting to say that the distribution of monies and obligations between the state and the central government *was* fiscal federalism, considering São Paulo's huge share of the states' combined totals in both departments: more than a third of the income and expenditures after 1910, and more than half the foreign debt.

São Paulo's 1892 budget, the first under the new federal system, brought in three times the receipts of the previous years (in constant terms at 1912 values), and simultaneously rose from the equivalent of 4 percent to 17 percent of federal revenues.[1] As we see in Figure 2, in 1912 terms, revenues rose 37 percent in the decade 1900–1909, fell briefly in the war years, recovered in the 1920's, and then rose so steeply that the annual average receipts in 1930–37 were more than twice what they were in the 1920's. In the meantime, the state's revenues also rose in relation to the federal treasury's. Expenditures displayed a parallel trend, and like revenues, grew at a faster rate than the federal govern-

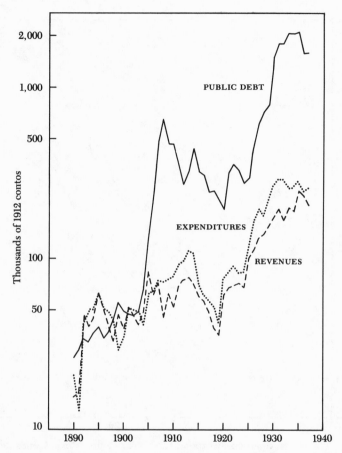

Fig. 2. Revenues, expenditures, and public debt of the state of São Paulo, 1890–1937, in thousands of 1912 contos. Compiled from Appendix C, series A-2, B-2, and D-2.

ment's. By 1930–37, they averaged 25 percent of federal outlays, more than double the percentage for 1900–1909.

Before the 1920's, São Paulo's general revenues, omitting the extra-budgetary coffee surtax, were typically more than twice as large as Minas Gerais's and five to six times Pernambuco's. (See Fig. 3.) The gap widened in both cases in the years 1930–37. São Paulo's share of total state revenues rose steadily from the decade 1897–1906 (29 percent) to the decade 1927–36 (38 percent). Expenditures followed a similar path, rising rapidly in the early 1890's, and then pushing upward in every subsequent

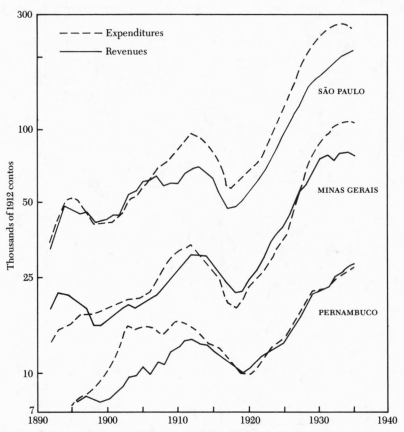

Fig. 3. General revenues and expenditures, São Paulo, Minas Gerais, and Pernambuco, 1892–1935. Five-year moving averages in thousands of 1912 contos. Compiled from Appendix C, series A-3 and B-3; data for Minas Gerais and Pernambuco are in the companion books.

decade through the 1930's, with the largest jump in the last decade (as was true also of Minas and Pernambuco). The peak year relative to federal expenditures was 1931, when São Paulo spent more than a third as much as the Union. Among the states, São Paulo's share of total state outlays rose from 29 percent in the decade 1897–1906 to 43 percent in 1927–36.[2]

But expenditures outpaced revenues. Deficits were incurred in 40 of the 48 years under study—and were incurred, moreover, without interruption from 1906. No other state had as many deficit years in our period.[3]

In constant terms, the deficit was greatest in the years 1930–37, when expenditures outran income by 33 percent. Part of the problem was bad planning. Though revenues exceeded projected income in 30 of 48 fiscal years, expenditures exceeded authorized amounts in 45, and by larger sums. In 1927, outlays were nearly double the authorized figure.

The difference in projected amounts and actual receipts and expenditures narrowed over the decades. In 1890–99, actual revenues exceeded anticipated income by 49 percent, and outlays exceeded the authorized amounts by 55 percent. This compares with a 7 percent shortfall in anticipated income and an 18 percent overdrawal on the expenditure side in 1930–37. Thus, whereas both sides of the ledger had been underestimated by half in the early Republic, by the 1930's the state government had brought its budget under greater control—at least in the narrow sense that its projections were closer to reality. Yet the absolute deficits in the 1930's (in constant terms) had never been larger.

The central government's budgets, like São Paulo's, tended to run in the red during the Empire and the Old Republic. One of Getúlio Vargas's first priorities in 1930 was to curtail federal expenditures. He was equally determined to reduce state expenditures. But the states heeded the federal government's example more than the dictator's decree. The Vargas administration consistently rolled up a deficit from 1930 through 1937. So did São Paulo, and at an average shortfall more than a third the size of the central government's. Thus São Paulo's behavior alone would justify attention to the states' role in the debate on whether an implicit countercyclical fiscal policy was in effect during the early Vargas years.[4]

The significance of São Paulo's role in the fiscal affairs of the Empire was slight. But in absolute terms São Paulo was unarguably the greatest fiscal beneficiary of the change of regime, as indicated by its rapid rise in revenues in 1892. The central government, by contrast, lost part of its revenue-extracting powers. By the Constitution of 1891, it surrendered to the states taxes on exports (usually its second-largest income producer under the Empire),[5] the transfer tax on property, the urban real estate tax (*décima urbana*), and licensing taxes (*indústrias e profissões*).

The imperial government had collected an annual average per inhabitant of 24$100 (in 1912 contos) in 1882–89; the new Republican government collected an annual average of only 18$400 from 1892, the first full year of the new fiscal system, through 1899.[6] Though the data are incomplete, as a whole the states (formerly provinces) and municípios surely gained.[7] In 1873–74, the provinces had only 18 percent of total government receipts, and the municípios, 4 percent. By 1910, the states generated 22 percent of the revenues, and the municípios, 19 percent. If we omit the Federal District from the município total, the states accounted for 23 percent, and the municípios 14 percent. Over the next three decades, the state share rose and the município share declined slightly.[8]

Another major change from Empire to Republic was state and municipal borrowing overseas, an activity that had been limited to three loans (by São Paulo, Bahia, and the city of Santos) at the end of the imperial regime. In most of Latin America, foreign borrowing by subunits of the central government was negligible or prohibited, as in Mexico after 1917. Argentina was the only country that could compete in this regard with Brazil. In the Depression year 1932, when foreign borrowing was no longer possible, the Argentine government owed 61 percent of the total consolidated foreign debt, compared with the Brazilian government's 56 percent. Of the remainder, the states owed 33 percent, and the municípios 11 percent.[9]

Taxes

Just as the Union depended on customs duties as its principal source of ordinary revenue, so São Paulo depended on its export taxes, almost all of which came from foreign coffee sales. However, the proportion of total revenues provided by these taxes fell steadily, dropping from 64 percent in the 1890's, to 26 percent in the 1920's, and to a mere 8 percent in 1933–35.* Though the coffee tax was still the largest single revenue earner in 1935, it disappeared from the books the next year, at least in theory. In Minas, by contrast, export taxes steadily provided about half the total state revenues from 1905 through 1932.[10]

There were two distinct sets of taxes on coffee. In addition to the export tax, the state began to impose a surtax in 1906 specifically for the servicing of valorization loans. Except for a brief period, the regular tax was an ad valorem duty, collected at the rate of 11 percent through 1904 and then at 9 percent until 1921. In that year, a fixed rate per kilogram was introduced, but this was replaced three years later with a variable

*No coffee tax data are available by zone, but the reader may infer the relative importance of the 10 zones' contributions from coffee output figures in Table 2.1, above.

rate based on the prices for the previous six months.[11] The surtax was collected in gold (French) francs.[12] Beginning in 1921, part of these funds was used to service non-coffee state debts, but the surtax was not transferred to general revenues until 1930.

During the 1930's, new arrangements were made to tax coffee exports in an increasingly complex set of duties divided between the state and federal governments. In December 1932, the state collected 9 percent ad valorem for general revenues, a five-franc surtax on each bag shipped abroad for the valorization loans, and two other hard-currency taxes for the debts of the state Coffee Institute and the National Coffee Council, which had just assumed part of São Paulo's external obligations.[13]

As noted in Chapter Two, there is considerable disagreement over who ultimately bore the burden of the coffee export tax, but I myself believe that, at least until the 1930's, most of the tax was passed on to the foreign consumer, because of coffee's price-inelasticity of demand, coupled with Brazil's dominant position in the world market.[14] This was apparently the rationale for piling on more taxes in the early 1930's, but the policy failed in the wake of a sustained glut, and was abandoned in 1937.

Reliance on export taxes had disadvantages. It made budgeting a matter of guesswork, because of sharp fluctuations in the international market, and many Paulistas believed such taxes hurt sales abroad, because the inelasticity of demand was partially offset by importer stockpiling and speculative buying. The effort to abolish the export tax won a powerful adherent in Bernardino de Campos as early as 1905, but his bold stance in favor of direct taxation contributed to his loss of the presidential nomination.[15]

São Paulo witnessed several tax reforms before the export tax was frontally attacked in the 1930's. Fifteen taxes were abolished or consolidated under other rubrics between 1892 and 1894. A new property transfer tax was introduced in 1891, to become the second-largest revenue producer until 1932. A series of fiscal measures to stimulate coffee sales became law in 1904. Specifically, excess coffee production caused the state to place a prohibitive tax on new coffee trees; to decrease the export tax on coffee to 9 percent; to exempt banks and comissários from taxes in certain dealings with planters; and to decrease railroad freight rates. Strangely enough, all but the first of these measures—which was poorly enforced and finally revoked in 1911—seem to have been designed to put more coffee on a market already burdened with excess supply. Apparently the aim—unrealistic in the face of the inelasticity of demand—was to expand sales in order to make up for declining profits, owing in part to the deflationary policies of the Campos Sales and Rodrigues Alves governments.[16]

In 1905, in an effort to decrease the state's dependence on coffee *and* to relieve the coffee sector, new taxes were levied on commerce and industry, on profits and lending. A rural property tax (imposto territorial) was also added.[17] But this tax amounted to only one-tenth of 1 percent of the property's assessed value per annum, and specifically excluded all coffee holdings, on the grounds that coffee was already heavily taxed at the port. At the time the law was passed, noncoffee lands were estimated at only a fifth of the value of coffee properties. Though the property-tax rate was later raised to 1 percent, the imposto territorial was not even the fourth-largest revenue producer until 1935.[18] The example of Rio Grande do Sul, where the taxation of rural property was a major source of income, showed that this was a feasible choice in the period under consideration, but the Paulista government opted against it, in part because São Paulo could rely so extensively on foreign borrowing for government projects.

The other new taxes in 1905 did modestly alleviate the state's fiscal dependence on coffee, as indicated by its declining contribution to the government's receipts. But in the decade 1910–19, coffee still provided an annual average of 42 percent of the state's total income. Governor Altino Arantes in 1917 renewed the call for tax reforms to make the state less dependent on the "anti-economic" coffee export tax, but he did so principally because of the disorganization of the international market caused by the war. Arantes placed his hopes in the rural land tax. Three years later, Governor-designate Washington Luís—in the same speech in which he termed the labor question a matter for the police—branded export taxes harmful to the economy and inequitable to coffee producers. He wanted to base state revenues more solidly on the property tax, and, assuming federal consent, on a state income tax.[19]

But further tax reform had to await the governorship of the Taylorite engineer and publisher Armando Sales (1933–36), who held office in a period in which reorganization of the tax base was no longer postponable. Export taxes were limited by the 1934 Federal Constitution to 10 percent ad valorem, though São Paulo was not charging that much. Now the state's coffee tax provided less than 10 percent of receipts, and budgetary deficits were huge. Part of the problem was the new absence of proceeds from foreign loans. One reason tax reform could be put off in earlier decades was precisely the substitution of loans for coffee revenues.

Armando Sales eliminated some taxes and combined others, reducing the total number from 22 to eight. The "basic tax" of the new system was to be the tax on "sales and consignments," a turnover tax of 1 percent on all transactions. Before coffee was sold abroad, it too was subject to the tax; but, as Sales proudly indicated, the sales-and-consignments duty spread the tax burden far beyond the depressed coffee sector. The turnover tax provided 24 percent of state revenues in its first year, 1936, and 30 percent the next year.

Armando Sales's reforms, coming after decades of feckless attempts at fiscal reorganization, did at last place revenues on a more solid foundation, and allowed the government to forecast its revenues better than in the years when coffee revenues were the chief item. In 1936 and 1937, the spread between projected and actual revenues averaged only 6 percent. Sales-and-consignments revenues grew rapidly with the advance of São Paulo's industrial economy, and by 1949 provided nearly three-fifths of the state's total revenues. (The shift to sales and consignments, to be sure, meant continued reliance on indirect taxation; according to one student, indirect taxes accounted for nearly three-quarters of the state's income in 1946.)[20]

The abolition of the coffee tax relieved a sector of the economy whose leaders continually doubted that the burden of coffee taxation was being passed on to the foreign consumer, or who thought that at best such duties restricted sales abroad and thereby aided competitors in other countries. Outside São Paulo, the export tax in the year of the Estado Novo coup was still the single-largest source of revenue for 15 states, including Minas Gerais. The other states relied on the sales-and-consignments tax, which for most probably still meant—as it did not in São Paulo —a disguised export tax.[21]

The frustrating problem of interstate taxes had been addressed as early as 1831, when an imperial law had abolished interprovincial import and export duties "under whatever name."[22] But we find such imposts being explicitly outlawed again in 1904, and yet again in 1932. The Estado Novo, it seems, finally got rid of them in 1944, 113 years after they were first made illegal. Or did it? Perhaps the issue was still a matter of definition, since in 1953 the São Paulo supreme court ruled that Armando Sales's sales-and-consignments tax could be applied to coffee even if "the seller has paid the tax in another unit of the Federation where the coffee was acquired."[23]

Debt

São Paulo's considerable revenues were not sufficient to pay for the programs the state undertook; and loans, domestic and foreign, were resorted to frequently. Coffee debts were always kept in a separate account, were largely financed abroad, and were, in theory, self-liquidating through the gold surtax. Over the years, this debt was subject to much greater fluctuations than either the ordinary state debt, consisting of noncoffee foreign and domestic funded obligations, or the domestic floating debt. The state's debt burden, for coffee and noncoffee uses alike, was massive by the 1930's.

São Paulo's foreign debt alone was disproportionately heavy relative to its economic position in the Union. From 1888 to 1930, the state contracted 25 foreign loans, for a nominal total of £68,752,500, U.S. $82,500,000, and Dutch florins 18,000,000, or roughly U.S. $424,000,000 in 1930 values (though many of these loans were fully repaid by that year). Even as early as 1906, São Paulo accounted for more than half the total foreign obligations of the states; by 1933, the figure had risen to 60 percent. The foreign debts of São Paulo and Minas were roughly equal until 1905, but by 1931 São Paulo's indebtedness was 12 times as heavy as Minas's and 14 times as heavy as Pernambuco's.[24]

Relative to the federal foreign debt, São Paulo's obligations abroad jumped from the equivalent of 4 percent in 1904 to 14 percent in 1906, and reached a peak of 33 percent in 1908, the year the valorization loans were resubscribed and almost wholly financed abroad; it rose to 33 percent again in 1930, and averaged 25 percent over the years 1930–37. Of the entire federal, state, and municipal foreign obligations in 1933, São Paulo and its subunits owed 21 percent, and the Union 60 percent.[25]

São Paulo's total debt (coffee and noncoffee, foreign and domestic, including the floating obligations) reached a level in 1908 (in constant contos) that was not surpassed until 1928. But the new high doubled by 1930 and peaked in 1935. By this time, much of the state's debt had been converted into domestic loans from the federal government, foreign

sources having dried up. This shift inevitably had its political consequences, since the federal government had to intercede with São Paulo's
creditors and to assume directly or indirectly the state's overseas financial
obligations. However, São Paulo's ability to help repay the debt through
taxation mitigated the new dependency.

São Paulo's creditors were forerunners of today's multinational corporations. Rothschild was probably the best known for its international
connections. But Schroeder, which lent most frequently to São Paulo,
had large operations in both London and New York by the end of the
First World War. On three occasions, Schroeder made part of a loan from
New York and part from London, each on identical terms. Many other
loans were partly financed by cooperating firms in Europe and New York.
Given these linkages, the state's opportunities to take advantage of competition between banks in the world's financial capitals were limited.

São Paulo's foreign loans were used for five general purposes: to underwrite public works, chiefly railroads; to consolidate previous debts; to
fund mortgage loans by the State Bank to coffee planters; to subsidize
immigration; and to carry out the valorization program. Among the states,
the last two uses were unique to São Paulo. Its first foreign loan (in 1888)
was also the only one used to promote immigration. Thenceforth through
the end of the Republic, subsidies were completely financed from general state revenues or provided by the federal government.

The huge coffee debt was of a different order from the ordinary sort
of state obligation. First incurred with the start of valorization in 1906,
it was triple the amount of the regular state debt by 1908. With the reorganization of the valorization system in that year, foreign financing
became the primary, and in most years until the 1930's, the exclusive
source of funding.

The 1908 reorganization of the then-stuttering valorization program
saw an increase in the export tax from three francs to five, an infusion
of £15,000,000 in foreign money, and a federal guarantee of a loan five
times the size of any other foreign loan to a Brazilian state from 1900 to
1910.[26] São Paulo completely retired this debt by 1915, a fact that was
hailed as a proof that the risks of valorization were acceptable.

The next major valorization operation was carried out with federal funding in 1917–20, when, because of the war, foreign loans were unobtainable. The third valorization loan (1921–24), though again financed abroad,

was primarily a federal project, which helped remove the financial onus from São Paulo; in fact, the state transferred 15,000 contos to the federal government to assist in valorization operations.*

A new coffee debt burden came with the organization of the State Bank and the Coffee Institute in 1926, after President Bernardes had taken the federal government out of the coffee business. Both institutions received large foreign loans in the late 1920's, and the State Bank held the majority of shares in the Coffee Institute. Thus the coffee debt, virtually liquidated in 1921, was renewed in 1926, and rose to 86 percent of an ever-growing "ordinary" state debt in 1930.

Was the coffee price-support program expensive to administer? Coffee support—a measure of the annual current costs of operating the program, as distinct from the loans involved—was certainly modest. Only in 1908 did the support program seem out of control, with current costs rising to the equivalent of 119 percent of all other state expenditures. Until the 1930's, coffee support was usually negative, i.e., it turned a profit for the state. This was the case, at least, in 11 of the first 15 years of valorization (the data on the 1920's are lacking). The state kept borrowing, however, to maintain its continually expanding coffee stocks. The foreign coffee debt almost doubled between 1929 and 1930, and the total coffee debt tripled.

In February 1931, Vargas announced that the central government had to assume control of the foreign debts of the states, and throughout the decade, schemes were introduced for São Paulo and the federal government to share the state's foreign obligations, which could no longer be met because of the collapse of foreign trade in general and coffee sales in particular. By 1932, as noted earlier, agencies of both the federal and the state government were simultaneously levying taxes on coffee exports to pay off the Paulistas' foreign coffee debt.

São Paulo's last foreign debt of our period, the Coffee Realization Loan, was contracted in April 1930, for a nominal amount of almost U.S. $98,000,000 (subscribed in dollars and pounds). This was a desperate effort to salvage valorization, one that also seems in hindsight a dangerous gamble for the bankers involved. The loan was arranged by J. Henry Schroeder, and it is easy to speculate that the loan was authorized in part

*The state took advantage of its relief from the direct burden of valorization in 1921 to consolidate most of its internal floating obligations by shifting its debt abroad: in current contos, its noncoffee foreign debt more than tripled that year.

because of the Schroeder family's investment in São Paulo coffee plantations.[27] The security was a coffee stockpile of 16,500,000 bags and a three-shilling export tax; the effective rate of interest was between 9 percent and 10 percent.

The nation's debt structure, however, followed the path of the economy in an inexorable crash. Interest and sinking fund payments went into default on most state and federal loans in Brazil between June 1931 and December 1932. Indeed, the junta that ruled in the brief interim between Washington Luís and Getúlio Vargas ordered a partial default on the federal debt. The Coffee Realization Loan went into default on its sinking fund in April 1933.[28]

This situation was hardly unique to Brazil. There were only three Latin American countries that did not default on their foreign loans in the 1930's.[29] One was Argentina, which was tightly linked to British imperial trade policies under the Roca-Runciman pact. The other two were Haiti and the Dominican Republic, both of which had continued under formal United States fiscal supervision after the departure of the Marines.

Brazil's solution was simply to defer payment on the bulk of its foreign debts. A federal decree of March 2, 1932, written by Finance Minister Aranha, divided Brazil's loans into seven grades. The more famous "Aranha Plan," a decree of February 5, 1934, added one more category, but basically kept to the same scheme of establishing priorities for the payment of interest and the repayment of principal. In both plans, the first grade was reserved for Brazil's three federal Funding Loans (1898, 1914, and 1931), and the second exclusively for São Paulo's Coffee Realization Loan. The first grade called for loan repayments and full interest as scheduled; in the case of the São Paulo loan, interest was to be paid on schedule, but the repayment of the principal was to be stretched out. In the 1932 plan, no state loans other than those of São Paulo were assigned a priority higher than grade four. In the 1934 scheme, São Paulo was the only state to have loans in the first five grades (of which only the first two repaid any principal); grade six, in which only a small fraction of interest was to be paid, was reserved for the rest of the São Paulo loans, plus those of Rio Grande do Sul and Minas Gerais. Grade seven, paying even less interest, covered the obligations of São Paulo city and Santos, and those of the important cities in Rio Grande do Sul and Minas; the Federal District; and various states and their capital cities, including Pernambuco. Grade eight, the lowest category, paid no interest and no principal until further notice, and included state and municipal obligations in an arc extending from Espírito Santo to Amazonas.[30]

All told, São Paulo and its agencies and subunits accounted for 21 percent of the total interest and principal owed from 1934 to 1938 by municipalities, states, and the Union, and for 66 percent of the non-federal debt. Under the Aranha Plan, the state was to defer payment over a four-year period of 978,366 contos at 1933 values (U.S. $77,900,000) on the contracted principal and interest; this was twice as much as the state's income in 1934.[31]

Foreign investment and coffee sales remained low in the mid-1930's, and Vargas chafed under the exchange restrictions on the export sales that paid the foreign debt. On the day of the Estado Novo coup, November 10, 1937, he announced his intention of suspending foreign loan payments; some remittances continued, however, until 1938. Two years later, the government once again began making payments—but in minuscule amounts. The problem was finally resolved in 1943 with the Souza Costa Plan.

Unlike the Aranha Plan, which simply postponed the paying-off of loans, this scheme was designed to reduce the total amount due. Investors in dollars and sterling issues had two options. By one option, the bonds would be maintained at their face value, but the accumulated interest payments would be drastically reduced. The other option, chosen by most bondholders, involved a reduction in the face value of all bonds, with a uniform interest rate of 3.75 percent. In both cases, a grading system was retained—in the first instance a grading of interest rates, in the second, a grading of face value. São Paulo's obligations were classified more or less as in the Aranha Plan, with the 1930 Coffee Realization Loan receiving the same treatment as the best federal bonds. At the bottom of the scale were the bonds of the state of Ceará, which were to be redeemed at a mere 12 percent of their face value.[32]

The Souza Costa Plan, by one observer's estimate, reduced Brazil's combined foreign debt in 1943 from U.S. $837,000,000 ($168,000,000 of which was owed by São Paulo and its agencies and municípios) to $521,000,000. According to the same writer, São Paulo was now able to write off $51,000,000 of its debt.[33] Thus one of the prices São Paulo had to pay for greater federal attention to its foreign obligations was a smaller reduction in its overseas debt than Brazil's federal, state, and municipal governments received as a whole. On the other hand, São Paulo was in a better position to pay than the other states, with its expanding industrial economy and with the comeback of the international coffee market during the war.

In any event, São Paulo got off at less than the contractual cost of its debts. Before the defaults of the 1930's, however, the state had paid high effective interest rates, and foreign borrowing had allowed the Paulista politicians to postpone tax reform until the loan market dried up. More important, the early loans had placed valorization coffee under foreign control, and the particular arrangements of valorization over the years strengthened the ties between foreign export houses and foreign lenders (e.g., between Schroeder and Wille in joint ventures initiated between 1906 and 1926). These ties, in turn, reinforced the coffee sector's claims on government favors. Almost half the total foreign debt by 1930 was contracted for the direct support of coffee valorization (not to mention the 1926 loan to finance coffee-estate mortgages), rather than for purposes of economic development. The direct costs of valorization were huge, though the program indirectly helped accumulate capital that was in part shifted to industry. In any case, the collapse of the program in the 1930's meant that in the succeeding decades, most of the debt burden was passed on to the dynamic industrial sector, the only sector where sufficient taxes could be raised to pay off the debts of the Old Republic.

São Paulo's interest rates were probably as favorable as any obtained elsewhere in Latin America. Governor Campos Sales lamented in 1897 that the state could not get new loans at a better rate than the near-bankrupt federal government, even though its existing obligations were quoted above par. But following Campos Sales's rise to the presidency and his implementation of orthodox fiscal and financial policies, Brazil had a good record as a debtor nation and enjoyed relatively low interest rates (at least on its British bonds) until 1932.[34]

São Paulo's early loans, mostly subscribed in London, usually bore a 5–6 percent (nominal) rate of interest; this compares with a 7–8 percent rate after the First World War. The earlier (and usually British) loans were typically discounted at a higher rate than the later (frequently American) loans. A 1904 loan at 5 percent paid out only 88 percent of the nominal capital; a 1925 loan at 8 percent paid 97 percent. To these calculations must be added carrying charges and other discounts, in part because bankers resold the issues to the public. In 1899, President Campos Sales complained to Rodrigues Alves that Schroeder was charging an effective

rate (after discounts) of 10.5 percent on a loan to São Paulo, and then selling the issue to a syndicate that resold it to the public. Brokerage charges
brought the total cost to São Paulo up to 13.5 percent.[35] But this rate
was in a period in which Brazil had not yet "proved" its credit-worthiness
in London. By the 1920's, a loan typically bore an effective rate of 9 percent to 10 percent, somewhat higher than the typical rate on earlier loans.
Nonetheless, São Paulo and the other states borrowed heavily at these
rates. Indeed, Latin America as a whole doubled its foreign debt in that
prosperous decade.[36]

The security on São Paulo's loans was of two sorts—commodities (valorization coffee) and future receipts of the government. Specific taxes, including those on coffee, were earmarked to repay specific loans, just as
the federal government had to earmark customs duties to repay Rothschild for the 1898 Funding Loan. By 1929, 11 percent of the state revenues, excluding the coffee surtax, was pledged for debt payment.[37]

The following remarks apply to the noncoffee debt, which was paid out
of the regular budget. (The valorization debt was "self-supporting" because of the extra-budgetary gold surtax.) As a share of budgetary outlays, São Paulo's debt servicing—excluding amortization—hit peaks of
28 percent in 1923 and 26 percent in 1931.[38]

The average decennial outlay remained constant at 22 percent over the
1920's and 1930's. Of the three states under study, São Paulo was clearly
in the deepest water. On average, Pernambuco spent 20 percent of its
budget on debt service in the 1920's and 19 percent in the 1930's, and
Minas averaged only 9 percent in 1920–29 and 15 percent in 1930–37.
Yet as a proportion of the outstanding noncoffee debt, servicing decreased
every decade for São Paulo, from 9.0 percent in the 1890's to 7.9 percent
in the 1920's, and to 5.0 percent in 1930–37, when default was the rule.
São Paulo's total (current) servicing on the noncoffee debt was 1,228,000
contos in 1930–37. If we assume the same proportion of servicing to debt
(5.0 percent) for the coffee debt, São Paulo's total interest payments from
1930 through 1937 were some 1,878,000 contos—six times the amount
Minas paid in this period and 20 times what Pernambuco paid.

In the 1930's, the export taxes tied to servicing the foreign debt were
shifted from hard currencies to milréis, probably reflecting Brazil's recognition of its inability to pass such duties on to the foreign consumer. In
November 1937, just after the coup, Vargas's government reduced the
export tax from 45$000 a bag to 12$000, following the failure of an inter-

national coffee marketing agreement, and probably with a view to obtaining political support from the coffee sector.[39] As noted earlier, on November 10, Vargas announced his intention to end loan payments because of the lack of foreign exchange formerly earned by coffee.

Sectoral Accounts

Debt servicing was only one cause of an expanding state budget. As we have seen, spending—excluding the coffee account—made its largest advances both absolutely (in 1912 terms) and relative to federal spending in the 1930's. In that decade, São Paulo's noncoffee outlays alone were more than twice as large as Minas's and eight times the size of Pernambuco's.

Table 8.1 shows selected sectoral expenditures as a percent of the actual state budget in our period (omitting, as before, the self-financed coffee account, which was not part of the regular budget). As a share of total expenditures, public works hit a peak in the 1890's, as did public health, immigration, and the police, and education bulged in the middle decades. The repayment of the noncoffee debt consumed nearly a quarter of the budget in the 1920's and 1930's, more than doubling its share in the 1890's. (The figure clearly would have been much higher in the 1930's had there been no defaults.) Railroad expenditures—part of which were recoverable in the charges for services—were greatest in the 1920's and 1930's, when the state assumed direct operation of the Sorocabana.

Of all the state's various undertakings, the Paulistas were probably

TABLE 8.1

Select Sectoral Expenditures in São Paulo:
Percent of Actual Budget, by Decade, 1890–1937

(Thousand current contos)

Period	Debt service	Education	State troops and police	Public works	Immigration	Public health	Railroads
1890–99	10	9	19	23	8	20	—
1900–1909	14	14	16	11	4	11	7
1910–19	18	18	15	10	3	10	3
1920–29	22	12	10	12	3	9	19
1930–37	22	12	10	8	—	7	16

SOURCE: SP, Relatorios (Fazenda), 1894–1929, and Contas (Fazenda), 1930–37.
NOTE: All outlays are not listed, and the expenditures on waterworks and sewers are included in both the public health and the public works columns.

most proud of their support of public education. Using figures for the census year 1920, one propagandist for São Paulo noted that though the state had only 15 percent of the nation's population, it supplied 25 percent of the country's students and 39 percent of the money spent on education.[40]

Per-capita figures reveal, as the table does not, the huge increase in the amounts expended over the decades. Education is one of the most striking examples. By 1937, the state was spending the equivalent of 4.8 1912 milréis per inhabitant for its school system, an increase of 400 percent over the amount spent in 1892. What makes the 1937 figure all the more stunning is that the number of Paulistas had meanwhile increased by almost 6,000,000.

Reliable per-capita figures for Minas Gerais are lacking because of inflated population counts before 1940, but where São Paulo had spent only 20 percent more on education (in absolute terms) than Minas in the 1890's, it spent two or three times as much after 1910, though it probably had a smaller population than Minas until the late 1930's. Pernambuco, for which reasonably good yearly population estimates do exist, was far behind São Paulo in educational outlays from the start. São Paulo spent three times as much per capita as Pernambuco in 1894, a spread that grew to six to one by 1937.*

In public health, as in education, São Paulo was a pioneer, and thanks to its large outlays in that field in the 1890's, it was able to keep its mortality rates low at relatively modest cost in subsequent decades, though rising standards of living, including improvements in diet and housing, probably played an important role as well. In 1894, São Paulo spent three and a half times as much on health as it spent on education—and 66 times

---

*Although São Paulo was in most ways a leader in Brazilian education, it levied one tax in this sphere that appears to have been designed to hinder the social mobility that education might otherwise have stimulated. This was the tuition fee (taxa de matrícula) on secondary and higher education, which brought in a negligible amount of revenue but served as a social barrier. In 1920, students in public high schools paid 120 milréis a year, and those at the university level, 300. Egas, Impostos, p. 108. In the same year, factory workers outside the capital made less than 150 milréis a month, and domestic servants, only 47. Cardim, Ensaio de analyses, p. 28. Clearly, the tuition charges must have kept most lower-class children out of even the public secondary schools, not to mention university-level institutions.

São Paulo's outlays for higher education were usually 1–2 percent of total outlays. Though absolute expenditures more than doubled from 1934 to 1935, as Armando Sales began to organize the University of São Paulo, higher education still accounted for only 2 percent of the budget in 1935–37.

as much per capita as Pernambuco. By 1937, the educational budget was one and a half times the size of the public health budget, but even then, the state was outspending Pernambuco by almost five to one for each inhabitant.

São Paulo was the only state to spend significant sums on immigration, and its leaders induced the federal government to do the same between 1889 and 1896, and again after 1906, when the coffee glut appeared to be ending. Like outlays on public health, expenditures on immigration peaked in the 1890's; they fell in every subsequent decade, despite a brief rise in the mid-1920's. Governor Prestes proudly declared that the immigration subsidy could be eliminated after 1927; outlays did not quite disappear, but they were relatively small, and some of the funds in the 1930's were employed to attract migrants from other states.[41] Though immigration was a comparatively small item in the São Paulo budget, the state spent nearly twice as much on immigration in the 1890's as Pernambuco spent on its largest sectoral expenditure, public works.[42]

I have calculated railroad expenditures separately from public works, but inconsistencies and incomplete information make it impossible to determine the net annual costs of the state's rail system. The percentages I discuss here are based on outlays exclusive of capital expenditures, which were not considered part of the regular budget. Until 1905, current expenditures composed less than 1 percent of the state's total outlays. The figure then jumped to 18 percent, reflecting the operating costs of the Sorocabana (but not the purchase price, which was funded by the state's extra-budgetary capital account). Costs fell again in 1907–19, while the Sorocabana was under lease to a private company, then skyrocketed in 1920—to 25 percent of outlays—when the state reassumed direct control of what had become São Paulo's longest line. State expenditures on railroads remained at high levels thereafter, principally to maintain the Sorocabana, and to a lesser extent to build an extension of it from Mayrink to Santos (beginning in 1929) to break the British-owned São Paulo Railway's monopoly on the export route.[43]

Railroads, essential to the coffee complex, constituted a privileged sector of industry, which otherwise had little financial help from the state, even in the 1920's and 1930's. An electro-metallurgical concern got a subsidy in 1929 amounting to 0.4 percent of state outlays; and Viação Aérea de São Paulo (VASP), the São Paulo–based airline modeled on VARIG, got the same share of the 1936 and 1937 budgets. More important, loans were not made available to industry through the State Bank that had so lavishly financed export agriculture. Thus industry, and especially manufacturing, was almost completely neglected in the federal unit with the largest industrial plant. And this in a state that not only underwrote immigration, agricultural extension services, and railroads for the coffee sector, but so heavily borrowed for the direct support of coffee that its accumulated coffee debt by 1930 was more than two and a half times the amount of its total expenditures for that year.

Among the few things the state did for industry was to exempt frigoríficos from export taxes for up to 10 years, and one suspects this had something to do with the fact that the only meat-packing plant in the state at the time the concession was made (1915) was owned by the coffee planters Antônio Prado and Alexandre Siciliano.[44] Rio Grande do Sul and Minas Gerais provided similar tax incentives to frigoríficos during the First World War, a period when Brazil could profitably export meat products.

Niggardly with industry, the state was generous with its military forces. Yet these expenditures fell every decade as a share of the total budget, to level off at 10 percent in the 1920's and 1930's. All the same, in absolute terms, São Paulo spent almost three times as much on its troops and police as Minas in the 1930's, and six times as much as Pernambuco. Such spending reflected the Paulista political elite's wariness of the federal government "externally" and fear of the urban working class internally.

These figures exclude "wartime" military expenses in 1894, 1924, and 1932. If we were to add in the 137,000 contos expended during the turmoil of 1932, for example, we would find that the state spent a whopping 29 percent of its budget on troops and police that year, and the 1930–37 average would rise to 12 percent. Moreover, if we compare the outlays of the whole Secretariat of Security in the year before the Constitutionalist Revolution with those of its federal counterpart, the Ministry of War, we find a single state spending 21 percent as much on its forces as a central government with continent-wide responsibilities. The proportion fell to 15 percent in 1935 and to 12 percent in 1937, as Vargas and Góes Monteiro expanded military spending in preparation for the coup d'état.[45]

One interesting change in this category over the years was the gradual rise, beginning in the 1920's, of the police budget at the expense of the Força Pública's. The trend was accelerated in the following decade, so that by 1936 the police were getting more money than the Força. The long-term reason for this shift was apparently the rise of militant workers' groups and the increase in urban crime as the capital city grew. A short-term reason in the 1930's was probably the state government's eagerness to evade Vargas's stringent limitations on state military expenditures. Federal authorities, for example, found that São Paulo's authorized budget for 1932 met the limitations on military outlays established in the Code of Interventors, and meanwhile declared that the military budgets of seven other states, including Minas Gerais, did not.[46] After the Estado Novo coup, Vargas was wholly agreeable to the perpetuation of the trend so as to contain the threat of the Força Pública, with the result that by 1940 the state troops had to make do with nearly a quarter less money than the police.

Municipal Finances

Providing police protection was one of several areas where responsibility was shared by the state and local governments. São Paulo's municípios not surprisingly enjoyed a relative wealth denied the municípios of other states, accounting for 35–40 percent of all the local government revenues and expenditures (excluding the Federal District) between 1907 and 1936.[47] Typically, the combined municipal revenues in the state came to about a fourth of the state revenues, and outlays to a fifth, though there was wide variation because of large loan receipts in certain years.[48] Since the capital grew faster than· the state as a whole and could count on urban sources of income, município wealth was increasingly concentrated there. The city's shares of these revenues and expenditures grew from 29 percent and 26 percent, respectively, in 1896, to 56 percent and 62 percent in 1938.[49]

For the rural municípios, coffee tree taxes provided only modest resources. In 1911, for example, the licensing tax on industries and professions was the chief source of income for the municípios (apart from loans), rather than the one duty they were allowed to levy on coffee, a tax on the number of trees in production.[50] Coffee-derived revenue was low even in Ribeirão Preto, the world's coffee capital in the middle of the Old Republic. According to one student, "the coffee tree tax produced a modest 11% of município income [in Ribeirão Preto] in 1910 and a paltry 1.8% in 1930."[51] Tax evasion may be one of the explanations for this low collection rate. Using Warren Dean's figures in *Rio Claro*, which compare município tax records with plantation records, we find that tax declarations were made on only 71 percent of the coffee produced on the

Santa Gertrudes estate between 1896 and 1905.[52] (It was presumably harder to evade state export taxes collected at the sole part, Santos.)

Intermunicípio taxes—like interstate taxes—were a vexing problem in the early years of the Republic. All município taxes on trade between local units were specifically outlawed in December 1907, but seven months later, planters in several parts of the state were reportedly still complaining about such duties, suggesting that some illegal taxes were being levied on coffee in transit.[53]

The combined expenditures of the municípios in 1911 reveal the significance of borrowing in their budgets, with debt payments at 25 percent of the total, the largest single item. (Their second-largest outlay was on public works.) The richer municípios probably borrowed more; Ribeirão Preto was already earmarking 36 percent of its authorized outlays for debt repayment in 1910, and 39 percent by 1930.[54] As a whole, the municípios faced a disastrous debt situation by the 1930's. In 1931, this item (foreign and domestic loans, including amortization) cost them 67,600 contos, or 48 percent of current revenues. The capital's obligations alone amounted to 31,800 contos, or 62 percent of its income.[55] Under the circumstances, the city's default on its foreign debts in 1931 was inevitable.

Although the legislature had to approve all foreign loans by municípios, the state government, unlike its counterparts in Minas and Rio Grande, did not intervene in international capital markets on their behalf. Nonetheless, Santos and São Paulo city accounted for 37 percent of Brazil's total município foreign debt in 1931.[56] That year the state tightened its control of local finances with the creation of the Department of Municipal Administration, a reform soon adopted by other states and recommended to all units of the Federation in the 1934 Constitution.[57]

State and Nation

Until the 1930's, at least, few Paulista statesmen complained about municipal financing, but the opposite was true of federal fiscal operations. Federal and state finances in São Paulo were intimately related because of the large share of revenues the Union collected there. At the Constituent Assembly in 1891, São Paulo's delegation had served the fiscal interests of the Union in opposing the double taxation of imports by the states, in a relatively close vote, 110 to 92. The upshot of the assembly's deliberations was to make São Paulo the only state whose revenues virtually freed it from the need to petition the federal government for public works and federal patronage.

In the 1890's, São Paulo contributed 13 percent of federal receipts, more than any unit except the Federal District, which contributed an enormous 52 percent between 1890 and 1899. The Federal District was still ahead of São Paulo from 1928 to 1937, but the state now produced 30 percent, compared with the District's 45 percent.[58] Though import duties were the central government's principal source of income, they fell to a low of 46 percent in 1918, owing to the disruption of trade in the war years, at which time the country depended on the federal consumer tax for almost a third of its revenues (up from 13 percent in 1912).[59] Import duties declined again in the early 1930's, then rose in 1936 and 1937, when they represented about 50 percent of the federal revenues collected in São Paulo. By 1940, however, the consumer tax on *produtos industrializados* passed import duties in both São Paulo and Brazil as a whole, and remained more important after the Second World War. Comparing federal receipts in São Paulo to state revenues, we find that the Union took an increasingly large bite, and that by the 1930's, the federal receipts in São Paulo were greater than the state receipts because of the growth of traditional revenues (customs and the federal consumer tax) and the newer income tax.[60]

The Paulista political leaders repeatedly registered two sorts of complaints about the federal taxes collected in their state: first, that other units of the Federation, especially Minas Gerais, did not pay enough; and second, that the federal government spent too little in São Paulo compared with what it took out. Let us examine each complaint in turn.

At the Constituent Assembly of 1933–34, São Paulo's delegates charged that their state paid a far higher ratio of federal to state taxes than the other two leading states, Minas and Rio Grande—5:3 compared with 1:4, in the case of Minas.[61] This was an invidious comparison, however, for Minas was a landlocked state, and nearly half the federal government's import duties were collected at Santos in the 1930's.[62] Looking at Pernambuco, with its important port, for example, we find the federal receipts collected there were greater than those collected in Minas Gerais every year from 1925 until 1941, when Minas pulled ahead.[63]

All the same, the Paulistas did have grounds for complaint, at least as far as Minas was concerned. For example, we find, from retrospective federal data, that in absolute terms São Paulo contributed five times as much to the federal coffers as Minas in 1925–30, and between seven and eight times as much in 1931–37. In relative terms, the Paulistas also come out second best, by my calculations, for the first years in which per-capita income data are available (1939–40). At that time, they outpaid the Mineiros—not counting the import tax and discounting income differences—at a per-capita ratio of 2.9:1.[64] Furthermore, even if we accept the argument that part of Minas's federal consumer taxes were really paid out-of-state, because a number of goods in the period under study (including textiles) were taxed at the factories, we still find the Mineiros with a decided advantage. Let us assume, for this purpose, that their consumer taxes were understated by a full 100 percent in 1939, and that São Paulo's taxes were overstated by the same amount. Shifting a sum equal to Minas's recorded consumer tax payments from São Paulo's column to that of Minas, we learn that the result is still not equality, but just a narrowing of the gap between the states; São Paulo was still paying more, by a ratio of 1.9:1, again discounting income differences.[65] In short, by any measure, there is little doubt that Minas was getting off lightly, at least by the late 1930's, when relevant data are first available. São Paulo's greater tax burden in part reflects the fact that the collection of consumer taxes (like income taxes) is facilitated by urbanization.[66]

As for the Paulistas' second complaint, on the simple basis of statistics, that too seems justified. In fact, the Paulistas had denounced the "exploitation" of São Paulo even under the Empire; in 1886–87, in fact the ratio of imperial receipts to expenditures in São Paulo had been 6.7:1. But the Republic went still further, progressively increasing the gap—to 7.1:1 in the 1890's, 7.2:1 in 1928–37, and 8.7:1 in 1937. The ratio for Minas in 1937, by contrast, was 1.6:1, and Pernambuco's was 3:1.[67]

But São Paulo's situation was unique only in degree. The federal government took more out of most states than it returned to them. In 1937, for instance, only four states—Mato Grosso, Piauí, Maranhão, and Goiás—experienced a net gain from federal treasury operations. (Since their combined surplus of federal expenditures over receipts was less than one five-hundredth of the surplus of federal expenditures over revenues in the Federal District,[68] São Paulo, it appears, was only the leading contributor in a redistribution scheme that subsidized the territorial unit with the highest per-capita income.)

Moreover, the federal government obviously did a lot more for São Paulo than its direct expenditures in the state would indicate—viz., underwriting valorization in various ways, maintaining pro-coffee exchange policies (until 1931), assuming São Paulo's foreign debts, and granting loans from the Bank of Brazil. The first three items having been dealt with in this and previous chapters, let us turn to the fourth (where for lack of earlier data, we must confine ourselves to the 1930's). For a start, we note that from 1932 to 1933 São Paulo's debt to the Bank of Brazil fell from 358,000 contos to 217,000 because of the federal government's assumption of some of the Coffee Realization debt—in exchange for the dubious security of stockpiled coffee.[69] Data on the bank's state-by-state loans (which are available only for 1933 and after)[70] reveal a clear favoritism toward São Paulo: by 1937 São Paulo accounted for 41 percent of the bank's total outstanding private loans, and for more than half the cumulative total of loans outstanding to state governments.[71] The largest single item in the São Paulo government's debt to the bank that year was a 200,000-conto loan for the redemption of state bonds issued during the 1932 revolution against Vargas. In October 1937, the outstanding Bank of Brazil loans to the federal government for coffee defense amounted to more than half the federal total for all purposes.[72] In addition, the famous Economic Readjustment, initiated in April 1933, canceled half the mortgage loans on coffee estates and limited interest rates on plantation mortgages.* The Readjustment was a federal scheme to issue bonds to the planters' domestic creditors, and therefore to transfer losses in the coffee sector to the Brazilian public at large. Vargas made a point of "not humiliating" São Paulo at the end of the struggle in 1932,[73] and however bitter the peace settlement was for proud regionalists, it was certainly sweetened by economic concessions exchanged for the surrender. The Readjustment and the Bank of Brazil loans were for planters, however, not industrialists. The bank was authorized to make industrial loans in 1937 through the Carteira de Crédito Agrícola e Industrial, but, as noted in Chapter Two, loans to industry remained insignificant until 1941. At any rate, the outlays of the federal government in the Economic Readjustment, in the assumption of valorization debts and other São Paulo obligations, and in the Bank of Brazil's loans to the state call into question Martin Katzman's judgment that "the center [São Paulo] has been fiscally exploited by the periphery" before and after Brazil began to industrialize.[74]

*As with other matters affecting coffee, São Paulo was the principal but not the exclusive beneficiary, yet 54 percent of the Readjustment payments from 1934 to 1945 went to São Paulo. The Economic Readjustment was viewed by Vargas as a way to offset the exchange policies that affected planters adversely. See Venâncio Filho, *A intervenção do estado*, pp. 114–15; and Villela and Suzigan, *Política do governo*, pp. 200–201.

Vargas brought governmental intervention in the economy to new
levels of involvement. Federal responsibility for coffee protection became
permanent in 1931, and other agricultural products were also subsidized
in the 1930's, e.g., sugar, yerba mate, and wheat. The 1930's also saw the
rapid expansion of government services, however paternalistic, to non-
propertied groups—as indicated by the creation of the ministries of
Education and Labor.

On the other hand, state government intervention not only paralleled
but often preceded federal activity. Though the central government assumed primary responsibility for coffee protection after 1931, São Paulo
assisted in this endeavor into the 1940's. In November 1932, a state mortgage bank, modeled after one in Argentina, was established to aid owners
of small farms.[75] Furthermore, the Secretariat of Agriculture directly
promoted the expansion of cotton production in the 1930's by developing
and distributing long-staple cotton seeds, and the Commodities Exchange
(Bolsa de Mercadorias) helped create domestic markets for cotton. The
state also built fruitpacking houses and subsidized the transportation and
storage of fruit, while encouraging the planting of orange trees on old
coffee estates.[76]

The state likewise broadened its responsibilities in the social sphere—
for example, by creating a Secretariat of Education in 1930 and a Department of Urban Labor in 1931.* Yet São Paulo's spending schemes were
far more "progressive" than its revenue-raising methods. Relative to the
value of exports from Santos, general revenues were smaller in the 1920's
than for the period 1892–99. To be sure, general revenues rose relatively
in the 1930's because of the coffee crisis. But it was only at this point that
the growth of revenues ceased to reflect the general growth of the export
economy, even though the state's reliance on the coffee export tax had
diminished earlier. In addition, Armando Sales's new tax system in 1934
was based on indirect and regressive taxation. Nor did the state government's "extractive" powers increase in constant (1912) per-capita terms
over the decades. After a dramatic initial jump in the years 1890–92,
when São Paulo's per-capita revenues almost tripled, stagnation set in,
and the per-capita figures were virtually the same in the late 1930's as
in 1892.[77]

* In 1933 this department was merged with the Department of Rural Labor, established
in 1912.

TABLE 8.2

State Income as Percent of Federal Income, 1901–1945

Period	All states	São Paulo	São Paulo income as percent of state total
1901–10	38.2%	11.2%	29.4%
1911–20	47.1	14.9	31.8
1921–30	52.0	18.8	36.1
1931–37	57.9	21.7	37.6
1938–45	55.7	22.6	42.3

SOURCE: SP, *Relatório* (Fazenda), 1949, p. 72; IBGE, *Anuário estatístico*, 1939/1940, pp. 1409–10, 1412–14; IBGE, *Brasil em números*, p. 140.

Nevertheless, São Paulo's revenues were huge by Brazilian standards, and one of the most interesting and seldom appreciated facts in the context of intergovernmental relations is an apparent countertrend against centralization in fiscal matters. Using as a baseline the average decennial figures for 1901–10—comprehensive state data are not available from the outset of the Republic—we can see, in Table 8.2, that combined state revenues rose relative to federal revenues in 1911–20 and again in 1921–30; rose still more in the first Vargas phase; and remained above the 1921–30 level under the Estado Novo. São Paulo not only accounted for a considerable part of this trend, but even improved its position relative to the central government during the Estado Novo years.[78]

As noted in Chapter Six, São Paulo's leaders in the years 1889–1937 tried to control federal financial and fiscal activity in areas where state action was impossible or inadequate—monetary and exchange policies, foreign loan guarantees, legislation on tariffs and immigration, and diplomatic representation relevant to financial and economic affairs. Paulista statesmen did not expect the public works and patronage concessions (entailing reciprocal obligations) that were central to the Mineiros' strategy. São Paulo alone had the option of intervening in the economy at its own initiative, and for limited periods it could point the way toward new governmental responsibilities. But state and national economic and fiscal affairs were so interdependent that São Paulo could not have pursued a long-term strategy of isolation from federal politics, as Rio Grande did from 1894 to 1906. By the 1930's, four factors were at work that augmented central authority or diminished Paulista resistance to it: the expansion of Paulista markets and sources of supply within Brazil; the growing military power of the federal government; the problem of coffee marketing; and the state's inability to cope with its foreign debt on its own.

In our period, the sphere of governmental activity expanded markedly at both the state and the federal level. Yet government aid to manufacturing was conspicuously lacking at both levels before the Estado Novo. One reason the Paulista industrialists failed to get Vargas's ear before the 1937 coup was that they had failed to wrest the state government apparatus away from groups interested in agriculture and welfare—but not industry. Industrialists seemed to settle for rather little: strict government regulation of the labor force.

Despite the broadly expanded role of government by the end of the period, the oft-noted centralization trend must be qualified, especially with reference to the state of São Paulo. First of all, we should note the obvious: namely, that however fiscal "centralization" is defined, it must entail a relative shift of revenues and expenditures toward the central government. Yet São Paulo in fact increased its share of total revenues and expenditures in every decade from the beginning of the Republic to the Estado Novo and beyond. In constant terms, the state's 1940 income was 16 times higher than its 1890 income. (In 1973, the state's income and expenditures were more than a third as large as the Union's.[79])

The concentration of political power in Rio de Janeiro during the 1930's, it may be concluded, was a much more clear-cut process than the concentration of administrative power. Compared with the United States, Brazil's federal fiscal system seems to have been fairly well centralized after a year of the Estado Novo: in 1938, where the United States government received only 40 percent of all the revenues collected at the federal, state, and local levels, and made only 46 percent of the expenditures, the Brazilian government collected 56 percent and spent 60 percent. But compared more broadly with other nations of the hemisphere, Brazil had a relatively decentralized government. In 1940, for example, the Canadian government collected 61 percent of all taxes, compared with Brazil's 58 percent.[80] The ratio of state to central government revenues in Brazil under the allegedly centralized Estado Novo was also more than three times the ratio then prevailing in the Federal Republic of Mexico.[81] Perhaps Brazil's most distinctive contribution to corporatist practice in the 1930's, after all, was its partly decentralized administration, in contrast to the unequivocally centralized regimes in Italy and eastern Europe.

Conclusion

TO RETURN TO a theme of the Introduction: What is the value of the regional approach to the problems of politics and economics in Brazil during the era in question? More bluntly, does the regional approach make sense?

In the nineteenth century, the English sometimes referred to Brazil as "the Brazils," whereas Argentina was simply "the Argentine." In the twentieth century, the novelist Erico Veríssimo referred to the Brazil of 1945 as an archipelago, and as late as the Goulart years (1961–64), individual states carried on something very close to their own foreign relations with the United States.[1]

From the historian's point of view, one could argue for the regional approach on the simple grounds that political life in this period was formally defined by relatively decentralized governmental structures, and the demands of regional economic groups were articulated by political parties whose "jurisdictions" coincided with state boundaries. But a more convincing argument, perhaps, is that the actors in the period *thought* that regionalism was important, made decisions based on that conviction, and sometimes marshaled the populace behind them. The fact that there was a decreasing degree of experience outside the state of São Paulo across the three generations of our political elite may have made the Paulista leaders even more bairrista in the 1930's than earlier. In 1932, on the eve of the outbreak of São Paulo's Constitutionalist Revolution, Maurício Cardoso, Getúlio's Minister of Justice and fellow Gaúcho, wrote the dictator that the Union was "an abstraction" and states "the concrete reality"—a point of view that persists among at least some sectors of São Paulo's caipira population, as Robert Shirley shows in his study of Cunha in the 1960's. At the elite level, even during the Estado Novo we hear the Paulista industrialist and economic nationalist Roberto Simonsen arguing that "in the final analysis, the national interest is the algebraic sum of regional interests."[2]

At a symbolic level, the continuing importance of federalism—and by implication of regionalism, the form of politics that provided the largest constituency for a federal regime—is shown by the fact that the centralized Estado Novo was formally predicated on a Federal Constitution, as all successive regimes have been. Finally, the regional approach adopted here may in part be "justified" by the fact that it includes an examination of national integration, to determine in what degree the regional frame of reference was transcended in this period.

A related issue: Is the relative emphasis on the political elite and the larger social and economic elite a useful way to tap the regional dimension of the Brazilian polity and economy? Other groups have not been ignored, but the elites have purposely received more attention. I believe this emphasis is justified by the class structure and degree of urbanization of the era, and the consequent nature of politics (i.e., the comparatively low level of political mobilization). The concentration of power, both political and economic, in a small segment of society, even in relatively developed São Paulo, is striking. Furthermore, there was little intersectoral conflict, owing to coffee's central position in capital accumulation, and the community of interests between agriculture and commerce—and to some degree between agriculture and industry. Family ties and cross-sectoral investments also helped to keep the peace, as did the partial shift to cotton among planters by the 1930's.

It was the economic elite that linked the frontier society to the urban society and ultimately to the North Atlantic market, by continually investing in new frontier lands. Its members moved easily from countryside to city and back. There was no "rural oligarchy": Jorge Tibiriçá was no less a fazendeiro for having been born in Paris.

The political elite and probably the wider economic elite were homogeneous groups and were closely interlocked in intricate networks of business interests and family relationships. Moreover, they were the vital link to another major element in the Paulista story, foreign investors. More than three times the proportion of São Paulo's political elite was directly associated with foreign firms than were those of Pernambuco and Minas Gerais; in absolute numbers, the Paulista elite had four times as many members with such associations as the other two groups.

Across the Atlantic, a web of economic relationships also bound powerful men together. Two directors of the Brazilian Warrant Company were also directors of the Bank of England, and one of these, Charles Johnston, was a vice-president of the London and Brazilian Bank. (In fact, it was banker Johnston who toasted Campos Sales on his arrival in London to negotiate the Funding Loan of 1898.)[3] By the 1920's, Brazilian Warrant had constructed a vertically integrated network of coffee production and distribution. In the federal valorization of 1921 the company played the same role as Theodor Wille had in the original agreement—to supervise the valorized coffee. Moreover, a Brazilian Warrant officer in Britain was a director of the São Paulo Railway (the Inglesa), which held the monopoly on traffic down the escarpment until 1937.[4] The Wille and Brazilian Warrant operations were successful in part because they offered something to the local economic elite, "cutting in" men like Antônio Prado.

To a significant degree, the economic and political elites even shared an upper-class European culture with their overseas patrons. Young men from families owning coffee export firms—Alves Lima and Monteiro Barros, for example—studied in Europe, partly to master the coffee trade.[5] Many others from wealthy families went to Europe or the United States for professional training, and of the three political elites, twice as many Paulistas had studied abroad as Pernambucanos or Mineiros.

The economic elite and its political representatives developed an ideology identifying their interests with São Paulo's, and São Paulo's interests with Brazil's: thus the compatibility of regionalism and nationalism (or one form of it), and the ambivalence not only in the elite's allegiances, but to some extent in those of the whole of the politically aware population of São Paulo. In addition, because the economic and political leaders of the state were not fascinated by the bright lights of Rio de Janeiro, as the elites of other states were, one element that helped erode regionalism elsewhere was lacking in São Paulo.

The state's political parties were probably more bureaucratized and better disciplined than analogous groups elsewhere, with the possible exceptions of Minas Gerais and Rio Grande do Sul. Early PRP demands on the central government focused on liberty of action for São Paulo, and part of this freedom was the right to borrow abroad. Paulista statesmen were aware of the relationship between foreign debt and their relative autonomy in the national political arena. But the collapse of the borrowing strategy in the 1930's effected a new dependency of the state on the central government, as the latter became São Paulo's chief creditor and mediator with foreign lenders.

In the Old Republic, the PRP failed to transfer power to a new generation, even to the *second* generation in the scheme employed here, a fact that was probably significant in the organization of the Partido Democrático. Nevertheless, the events of the 1930's, and especially the war of 1932, brought new life to the "liberal" PRP and PD, enabling them to polarize the population of São Paulo on the basis of traditional regional cleavages. Yet São Paulo's economy had burst through the chrysalis of state autonomy, and the state political elite could not cope with the problems of industrialists, or even of fazendeiros, who saw that solutions to economic crises had to come at the federal level. In a sense, and perhaps unwittingly, Vargas had let the Paulista elite try to cope, by allowing their state's revenues and expenditures to grow so rapidly in the 1930's.

The Paulistas' strong identification with their state poses yet another question: Did Paulista regionalism at some point become a "colonialism"? The relationship between colonialism and regionalism seems to be one of degree, that is, they fall on a continuum, and the concept of "internal colonialism" is an attempt to relate the two. Contiguity of territory seems to be a poor sole criterion for distinguishing regionalism from colonialism, yet its importance cannot be dismissed. For example, is Madeira's continued allegiance to Portugal a regional or a colonial issue? For the island-group's inhabitants—or at least its bourgeois leaders—the relationship between islands and mainland is interpreted more and more frequently as a colonial rather than a regional problem.[6] This is a case free of the ethnic or racial tensions associated with most colonial situations, but the perspective is also clearly shifting in French Canada, where there is territorial contiguity, to be sure, but also ethnic cleavage, based partly on income differences between the English- and French-speaking populations. When the "colonial" interpretation triumphs, separatism becomes an almost automatic policy prescription.

Regional income differentials in Brazil have been severe. In the 1950's, according to the economist J. G. Williamson, Brazil had the greatest regional disparity of income distribution among the 26 countries he studied. A later study, based on the economic census of 1970, reported even greater disparities than Williamson had found between the Southeast (including São Paulo) and the Northeast.[7] Yet contiguity of territory, extensive race mixture and interregional migration, and a common language and culture have made separatism less of a danger to Brazil than to some countries where the regional income inequalities are not nearly so pronounced.

However we define São Paulo's role in present-day Brazil, it had probably not yet passed into a "metropolitan" relationship with the rest of the country at the end of our period. According to the economist Wilson Cano, before 1930, at least, São Paulo did not appropriate significant amounts of capital from "peripheral" regions: coffee increased the capacity to import, and the state's production of foodstuffs expanded rapidly enough (as Cano carefully demonstrates) to prevent capital from being used up on agricultural "imports" for a growing and wealthier population.[8] Clearly, São Paulo's first "hinterland" to exploit was the area incorporated by its own westward-moving frontier. But before the era was over, Paulista investors were pushing into Paraná, Mato Grosso, and Minas Gerais.

Of course, São Paulo exploited dependent or peripheral regions in indirect ways. For one thing, it used the federal government until 1931 to obtain the exchange rates its coffee and commercial interests demanded, a practice that hurt other regions (or so their representatives in Congress believed) by making the exchange rate higher than it would have been for the less internationally competitive sugar and cotton exports of the Northeast. For another, the coffee complex maneuvered the federal government into subsidizing immigration and into underwriting (or directly assuming) loans for valorization. And finally, São Paulo got the lion's share of the Bank of Brazil's state loans, at least in the 1930's, when data are first available.

On the other hand, São Paulo's political leaders were not especially interested in federal patronage and public works projects, areas where the Mineiros profited handsomely in their dealings with the patrimonial federal state, and the Pernambucanos took what they could get.

It seems clear that São Paulo's role as an expanding "center" or "metropolis" within Brazil was inextricably bound up with its role as "periphery" or "satellite" in an international economic system directed from the North Atlantic. With respect to its relationships within that system, one program—valorization—and the foreign borrowing that made it possible placed São Paulo's economic and political elites far above the *comprador* class, i.e., mere domestic agents of foreign enterprise.[9] True, valorization led to greater foreign dependency, which in turn affected the political behavior of Paulista statesmen, but it also had decided advantages, putting Brazilian producers in a position to offset an importer's monopoly, to increase their share of coffee profits, and even, after 1926, to keep excess coffee stocks out of the hands of foreign importers and speculators. Moreover, Cano has argued—with more exclusive emphasis than Warren Dean—that the growth of manufacturing in São Paulo was dependent on capital generated in the coffee sector.[10] If, in addition, we accept as fact a direct relationship between valorization and the growth of the coffee industry, valorization appears in an even more favorable light over the short and middle terms. The disaster, when it came, was brought about by valorization's excesses, not by the principles on which it was based.

The relative success of valorization was facilitated by the fact that no single bank, or group of banks from a single country, had a stranglehold on São Paulo's foreign credit to the degree that Rothschild monopolized the purchase of the federal government's bonds.[11] Similarly, no single firm monopolized the export business or foreign markets: Brazilian Warrant and Theodor Wille, among others, were rivals, with mutually hostile governments behind them.

Yet the relationships involved in economic dependency are complex. This study suggests that foreign investment was less important in banking in the 1920's and 1930's than in earlier decades, but it also suggests, albeit more tentatively, that foreign investment was more important in manufacturing than is currently acknowledged. At all events, forward and backward linkages in production, as well as "spread" effects, were limited by the vertical integration of foreign firms in coffee growing, processing, marketing, financing, insurance, shipping, and overseas distribution.

Those who directed São Paulo's economy would have seen things in an altogether different light, of course. For the men who owned factories in Brás or coffee groves in Ribeirão Preto, Brazil was entering the community of prosperous and civilized nations, led by São Paulo. The state's economic leaders saw the international order as an interdependent system, a point of view directly deducible from the theory of comparative advantage in international trade. If, in the 1930's, São Paulo's captains of industry attacked the notion that Brazil should remain content with its status as a producer of tropical goods, their perspective was still one of interdependency. Even Mihaïl Manoïlesco, the archpriest of protectionism whose works Roberto Simonsen and other Paulista industrialists cited to legitimate their program, had argued that protectionism was necessary for industrialization, and that the diffusion of industry would lead to greater international exchange.[12]

Industrialists, like the leaders of the coffee complex, clamored for more federal aid and authority in the 1930's, just as planters half a century earlier had demanded radical decentralization. What, we might ask, is the relationship between Brazil's economic development and governmental centralization? Perhaps the question is better put, how do levels of government interact as the processes of economic development, urbanization, and social differentiation and mobilization intensify? The state and federal governments in Brazil during the years 1889–1937 were largely the instruments of one economic class. Organizations of planters and industrialists consistently called for state and federal assistance in an age of laissez-faire. Yet by the 1930's, the Brazilian state was no longer merely a "joint stock company of the ruling class." It had become instead what Francisco Weffort has dubbed an Estado de Compromisso, because of the relative balance of new urban groups and fazendeiros,[13] a concept perhaps inspired by Engels' view that it was the precarious political balance between the bourgeoisie and the nobility that allowed the absolutist regime in Europe to maneuver as an independent actor.

The Brazilian government began occasionally acting "independently" of coffee interests as early as 1898, because of the need to meet the requirements of the Rothschild Funding Loan. It was thereafter always more concerned about the repayment of loans than the state government was, for two reasons: first, because it had no "automatic" repayment device comparable to São Paulo's coffee surtax for its foreign obligations; and second, because it was ultimately responsible for all debts incurred by the constituent units of the Federation.

Meanwhile, São Paulo's government accompanied, and often led, the central government in more extensive commitments to intervention in economy and society, in many areas other than the justly famous valorization experiment of 1906 and its successors. Granted, São Paulo was exceptional, but so were the other two leading states, Minas Gerais and Rio Grande do Sul, whose governments also adumbrated federal responsibilities in social and economic matters at least until 1930.

But it is in the fiscal sphere, above all, where São Paulo was (and remains) uniquely a state within a state. The Estado Novo did not centralize the fiscal system. The dictatorship in a sense fulfilled the program of the earliest opponents of (and rebels against) the Constitution of 1891, Gaspar Silveira Martins' Federalist Party, which demanded "administrative decentralization with political centralization." Indeed, São Paulo's share of revenues as a percentage of federal revenues grew even larger in 1938–45.

Admittedly, one cannot deny the dramatic shift toward federal assumption of responsibility in the 1920's and 1930's. And yet this very trend was ultimately ambiguous, from the viewpoint of São Paulo's economic elite. Coffee growers in São Paulo had wanted a federal solution to the problems of overproduction since the valorization debates of 1903.[14] By the mid-1930's, they at last had it. The Paulistas' ambivalence toward the authority of the central government had always conditioned their behavior; when Getúlio Vargas resolved the issue for them in 1937, his coup silenced a generation of liberal oligarchs who, in their hour of defeat, could still congratulate themselves on shaping a regional society that could only be envied by their counterparts in Minas Gerais, and remained undreamt of by those in Pernambuco.

Appendixes

A Note on Elites

THE POLITICAL ELITE examined in Chapter 5 is a group defined as holders of important positions in state parties and governments, plus the state's representatives in important federal posts, during the years from the birth of the Republic to the Estado Novo. Thus, statistically speaking, the elite is a population rather than a sample. Since some persons held office for as little as one day, a 90-day minimum tenure was required for inclusion during the period November 15, 1889, to November 10, 1937. All persons are included who could be identified by name and dates of tenure, whether or not any other information was discovered. In fact, however, virtually complete biographies were obtained for more than 90 percent of the elites of the three states—Minas Gerais, Pernambuco, and São Paulo.

The authors agreed on the inclusion of 17 to 18 state government posts and 17 at the federal level. In the states the list consisted of the governor and his important elected and appointed assistants in the executive, and top-ranking legislative and judicial figures. Federal posts were defined analogously, but were included only when held by representatives of the state under study.

Specifically, state elite members consisted of the governor; the lieutenant governor; the secretaries of justice, finance, agriculture, transportation, education and health, security, and the governorship; the state chief of police; the president of the state bank; the prefect of the state capital; leading administrators peculiar to each state (viz., presidents of the Coffee Institutes in São Paulo and Minas; director of the state press in Minas; director of the port authority and inspector of municípios in Pernambuco); the presidents of the state chamber and senate; the majority leader in the chamber; and the president of the state supreme court.

Federal officials included the president of the Republic; the vice-president; the ministers of justice, finance, agriculture, transportation, education, labor, and foreign affairs; the president of the Bank of Brazil; the prefect of the Federal District; the president of the National Coffee Department; the president of the federal chamber of deputies; the vice-president of the

senate;* the majority leader of the chamber; the leader of the state delegation in the chamber; and members of the federal supreme court.

Thus the elites were defined uniformly except for the "leading [state]
administrators" specified above. To have eliminated such key positions as
the presidencies of the Coffee Institutes in São Paulo and Minas because
the post did not exist in Pernambuco seemed unduly procrustean, since the
central purpose of the definition of elites was to obtain comparable *wholes*
from each state. The size of the elite populations ranged from 214 in Minas
Gerais, to 263 in São Paulo, to 276 in Pernambuco.

Three nongovernmental positions are also included in the elites—the
executive committee of the Republican Party (the "establishment" party in
the Old Republic), and those of the most important non-Republican party
before 1930, and from 1931 to 1937. (The roles of the Republicans and
their opponents were reversed after 1930, or new establishment parties
brought in many leaders of pre-1930 opposition groups.) It seemed essential to include this nongovernmental sector of the elite because of its
leading role in the larger political process. Separate computer runs of party
executive committee members against nonmembers tended to confirm our
qualitative judgment on this point: committee members held more elite-
defining positions than nonmembers, and they were more prominent in the
economy and society. Thus, in the manner of Frank Bonilla's definition of
the Venezuelan political elite, in *The Failure of Elites* (Cambridge, Mass.,
1970), p. 16, party executive committees were included to better approximate the effective power structure.

The elite was defined to exclude military and naval officials, since these
groups were members of virtually self-regulating corporations and had
tenuous ties with the three state machines. In the cases of the ministries of
war and navy, in only one administration (Pessoa, 1919–22) were civilians
appointed to the posts; they were excluded from our elites, though officers
holding the specified "civilian" posts were not. Regional military commanders, with the possible exception of those in Rio Grande do Sul, had no
enduring ties with state political machines, and these career officers were
rotated around the country. Commanders of the state military police forces
were subordinated to the civilian political leadership, and in none of the
three states did they play significant roles in political decision-making.

In each case our institutional definition omitted a few individuals who
might have been included had the elite been defined on a "reputational"
basis. Yet the exclusion of two or three persons in a group of 753 seemed
an acceptable sacrifice to maintain a cohesive definition across the states:
those left out would have changed the profile of the group only a percentage point, and many data were too "soft" to justify claims of precision
at a fraction of a point.

Approximately 100 variables were recorded on the elite's characteristics.
They were grouped under the headings of political ideology, roles in major
political events at both national and state levels, social and cultural activities, foreign ties, interstate ties, age, education, occupation, *municípios*

* The vice-president of the Republic was ipso facto president of the senate.

and zones of political activity, and family ties. (For coding schemes, the reader may obtain code books from the authors.) Biographical data were strongest on educational and official positions held; they were weakest on economic assets.

Though the computer program was designed to show progression through the elite posts during the period studied, it does not cover whole career patterns, and thus we have not produced a political recruitment study analogous to Frederick W. Frey's *The Turkish Political Elite* (Cambridge, Mass., 1965). Frey's elite is much more simply defined than ours; it includes all members of the Turkish National Assembly serving between 1920 and 1957, i.e. occupants of one post rather than 37 (p. 7).

Data were obtained from a variety of sources: official obituaries in state gazettes, obituaries and centenary-of-birth notices in newspaper morgues, almanacs, membership lists of voluntary associations, biographies, interviews of elite members and their descendents, questionnaires to these groups, professional school graduation lists, publications of political parties, biographical dictionaries and encyclopedias, and commemorative albums.

An initial problem was to construct lists of officeholders and dates of tenure, since in the majority of cases none existed. For the executive committees of the Republican Parties in Minas and São Paulo, it was discovered that elections for state and national offices would always bring forth an "electoral bulletin" signed by the current members of the respective committee. Historical reconstruction of the committees therefore began with a search for the dates of elections in the annual reports of the secretary of justice. This was followed by an examination of the *Correio Paulistano* and the *Minas Gerais* on the day preceding the contests to discover the signers of the bulletins. (A similar procedure was used in Pernambuco, but with less success, because of the lower degrees of party cohesion in that state.) The compilation of lists of officeholders and dates of tenure should provide basic chronologies for the historian of institutions, and a complete listing for the state is found in Appendix B.

Conventions Used in Classifying Elite Characteristics

1. Members of the elite had to be Brazilian nationals.
2. If a member held the same post more than once, he was coded for each separate tenure of that office.
3. In the absence of data for a given characteristic in cases where data were virtually complete, it was assumed the elite member lacked the attribute, and the item was coded negatively. Only in those cases where the overwhelming majority of data were missing was "missing data" coded.
4. The "not applicable" code was entered whenever a member was too young to have participated in a given event, had already died, or had withdrawn from political activity.
5. All events and experiences that were coded positively occurred during the stated chronological limits, except those specifically referring to pre-1889 events and items pertaining to education, foreign parentage, and residence abroad, all of which included pre-1889 experience as well.
6. If a member represented a state in a federal post other than the one

for which he was coded, that portion of his career outside the state under study was not coded. (E.g. Rivadávia Correia in his youth was a member of the São Paulo elite, but later represented Rio Grande do Sul as a federal minister.)

7. Multiple professions were coded, viz., all those professions and occupations ascertainable in the 1889–1937 period. Specific conventions: an exporter was also classified as a merchant; a comissário was not classified as a banker, since the latter term implies a director of a larger operation (though there was considerable overlap); newspaper publishers, building contractors, and railroad builders were all coded as industrialists, and all magistrates were also classified as lawyers.

8. All state supreme court justices were coded as having their political base in the appropriate state capital. Since most were professional magistrates, they were so classified because they had no home constituency and depended on directives from the state government to which they were attached.

9. Presidents of the Bank of Brazil included only that group who held office between 1906 and 1937. The bank was completely reorganized in 1906 with a more fully national mission. Before the reorganization it had no agencies outside the Federal District, and by 1927 there were 70.

The Brazilian Elite—Political Offices Held

STATE
Secretary of Justice, or General Secretary
Secretary of Finance
Secretary of Agriculture
Secretary of Education and Health (Interior)
Secretary of Transportation (*Viação*)
Secretary of Security (*Segurança*)
Secretary of Governorship or Interventorship
Governor or Interventor
Lieutenant Governor
Prefect, State Capital
Police Chief of State
Top State Administrator (SP [São Paulo] def.: pres., Coffee Institute. MG [Minas Gerais] def.: director, State Press, and pres., Mineiro Coffee Institute. PE [Pernambuco] def.: dir., Port Authority and Inspector General of municipalities)
President, State-owned bank
President, State Senate
President, State Chamber, or President, Constituent Assembly
Majority Leader, State Chamber
President, State Supreme Court
Leader of largest non-PR party or coalition, through 1930 (SP def.: member, executive committee, Partido Democrático. [MG: not applicable.] PE def.: member, Martins Jr. and José Mariano factions; member, pre-1910 anti–Rosa e Silva group; member, anti-Dantas group, 1911–18; member, Partido Democrático, 1920's)

Leader of largest non-PR party or coalition, 1931–37 (SP def.: member, executive committee, PD [1931–34]; member, executive committee, Partido Constitucionalista, 1934–37. MG def.: member, executive committee, Partido Progressista. PE def.: member, dissident Partido Social Democrático bloc [anti-Lima Cavalcanti faction])

Member, executive committee, Partido Republicano (MG def.: PR, 1889–90; Partido Republicano Constitucional, 1893–97, defined as leaders signing voting slates; Partido Republicano Mineiro, 1897–1937)

FEDERAL

Minister of Justice
Minister of Finance
Minister of Agriculture
Minister of Foreign Affairs
Minister of Education
Minister of Labor
Minister of Transportation
President of the Republic
Vice-President of the Republic
Prefect, Federal District
President, Conselho Nacional do Café, or its successor, Departamento Nacional do Café
President, Bank of Brazil (1906–37)
Vice-President, Federal Senate
President, Chamber of Deputies, or President, Constituent Assembly
Majority Leader, Chamber of Deputies
Leader, state delegation (*bancada*), Chamber of Deputies
Minister, Supreme Court (*Supremo Tribunal Federal*)

The six-page table that follows shows variables and values for Pernambuco, Minas Gerais, and São Paulo

Variables and Values in the Three Elite Studies
(Adjusted frequencies in percentages)

Categories and variables	Pernambuco		Minas Gerais		São Paulo		Composite	
	Value	Number	Value	Number	Value	Number	Value	Number
POLITICAL EVENTS								
1a. Monarchist who adhered to the Republic by public affirmation, Nov. 15, 1889–Dec. 31, 1891	73.8%	80	48.2%	83	49.5%	105	56.3%	268
1b. Monarchist who adhered to the Republic, 1892–1900	3.8	80	2.4	83	0	105	1.9	268
1c. Historical Republican: a self-proclaimed Republican before abolition (May 13, 1888)	21.3	80	41.0	83	49.5	105	38.4	268
1d. Eleventh-hour Republican: publicly declared self a Republican between May 13, 1888, and Nov. 14, 1889	1.3	80	8.4	83	1.0	105	3.4	268
2. Abolitionist before Jan. 1, 1887, calling for complete termination of slavery within one decade or less	16.8	95	8.6	116	19.8	111	14.9	322
3. Deodoro backer: supported Deodoro's attempted coup between Nov. 3 and 24, 1891	5.2	97	5.9	118	12.3	122	8.0	337
4. Break on valorization: break with the state establishment's position at any time	0	114	0	131	1.0	206	0.4	451
5. Break with state establishment's position over presidential succession in 1909–10	23.7	135	10.7	149	7.9	164	13.6	448
6. Break with state establishment's position over presidential succession in 1921–22	6.8	117	4.6	151	0.6	178	3.6	446
7. Break with state establishment's position over presidential succession in 1929–30	22.1	113	5.9	136	3.2	125	9.9	374
8. Tenente: Tenente or political associate of tenentes after Oct. 24, 1930	18.9	111	2.9	138	5.8	171	8.3	420
NONPOLITICAL LEADERSHIP								
9. Magistrate: Juiz de direito or higher	25.9	205	16.8	214	19.4	242	20.6	661
10. Cultural leader: member, state academy of letters, or national academy of letters	8.2	196	4.7	214	5.8	241	6.1	651
11. Labor leader: officer, labor union (local), or higher unit or organization	1.0	196	0	214	0	243	0.3	653

Item	%	N	%	N	%	N	%	N
12. Social club member: any one or more of the following: SP def.: Sociedade Hípica, Clube Comercial, Jockey Clube, Clube Atlético Paulista, Automóvel Clube. MG def.: Automóvel Clube, Jockey Clube. PE def.: Clube Internacional, Jockey Clube Sport, Centro Pernambucano do Rio	15.3	196	11.2	214	27.4	241	18.4	651
13. Agricultural society officer: SP def.: Sociedade Rural Brasileira, or any of its constituent entities before consolidation—Centro Agrícola, Sociedade Paulista da Agricultura, Liga Agrícola Brasileira, or Associação de Lavradores de Café. MG def.: Sociedade Mineira de Agricultura. PE def.: Sociedade Auxiliadora de Agricultura de Pernambuco	6.6	196	1.9	214	6.7	239	5.1	649
14. Officer, state Commercial Association	4.1	196	0.5	214	3.7	242	2.8	652
15. Officer, Ordem dos Advogados or Instituto dos Advogados	0.5	196	5.1	214	4.1	242	3.4	652
FOREIGN TIES								
16. Lawyer for foreign company operating in Brazil. Def. of foreign: at least 51 percent of stock owned by foreign nationals	4.3	187	2.3	213	0.8	240	2.3	640
17. Importer: manager or director of, or investor in, importing firm	1.1	188	0	214	2.9	239	1.4	641
18. Exporter, manager or director of, or investor in, exporting firm	7.4	189	0.5	214	6.7	239	4.8	642
19. Manager or director of, or investor in, foreign firm operating in Brazil; foreign defined under 16	2.7	188	2.4	211	9.2	239	5.0	638
20. At least one foreign-born parent	4.3	188	2.8	213	4.6	239	3.9	640
21. Foreign-born wife	1.1	188	0	214	2.1	238	1.1	640
22. At least one year of foreign study at any level	6.9	189	5.1	214	13.4	239	8.7	642
23. Residence abroad for at least six months	20.3	187	7.5	214	31.9	238	20.3	639
24. Consul for foreign government	2.1	188	0	214	0.4	239	0.8	641
25. Decorated by foreign government	1.6	188	0.9	214	8.8	239	4.1	641

NOTE: This is not a list of all variables tested; in some cases data were too incomplete to be recorded here. Values omit cases where no data were found and those for which the item was not applicable. Number refers to the number of valid cases from which the percentages were derived.

Variables and Values in the Three Elite Studies (Continued)

Categories and variables	Pernambuco		Minas Gerais		São Paulo		Composite	
	Value	Number	Value	Number	Value	Number	Value	Number
26. Procurer of immigrants: director or manager of, or investor in, private or government immigration-promoting enterprise	0.5%	188	0.9%	214	4.2%	239	2.0%	641
27. Naturalized Brazilian	1.1	188	0.5	214	0.4	239	0.6	641
28. Foreign title: holder of foreign or papal title of nobility	2.1	188	0.5	214	0.8	239	1.1	641
INTERSTATE TIES								
29. Political or administrative officeholder in another state: *Juiz de direito*, state deputy or federal deputy, or above (i.e. the defining positions—17 to 18 state posts and 17 federal ones)	6.9	195	6.1	214	7.1	238	9.7	647
30. Professional career in another state, then returns: minimum time, one year	12.9	194	3.3	214	7.1	240	7.6	648
31. Professional career in Federal District	17.5	194	14.5	214	1.3	240	10.5	648
32. Professional career in Federal District, then returns	7.2	194	2.3	214	5.8	240	5.1	648
33. Employee in any official interstate agency: e.g. an interstate coffee convention	4.6	195	0.5	214	0.4	239	1.7	648
34. Out-of-state birth	14.5	193	13.1	214	18.6	236	15.6	643
35. Political or administrative officeholder in another province or in the Município Neutro before Nov. 15, 1889: Def. officeholder is *Juiz de direito*, provincial deputy, general deputy, or above (i.e. imperial equivalents of posts cited in 29)	21.2	193	4.2	214	12.5	112	12.3	519
36. Colégio in another state or Federal District: minimum time, one academic year	8.3	193	13.6	211	19.7	234	14.3	638
EDUCATION								
37. Law degree, in state	71.8	196	14.1	213	62.5	240	49.8	649
38. Law degree, other state or Federal District	3.6	193	42.3	213	5.0	241	16.8	647
39. Law degree split: at least one year at law school in a state (or Federal District) other than the one where he graduated	1.6	193	5.1	214	2.9	242	3.2	649

	%	N	%	N	%	N	%	N
40. Medical degree, in state	0.5	193	0	213	0.4	241	0.3	647
41. Medical degree, other state or Federal District	7.3	193	10.4	212	5.0	240	7.4	645
42. Medical degree, split: analogous to 39	0	193	0.9	214	0.4	242	0.3	649
43. Engineering degree, in state	3.1	193	8.4	214	4.5	242	5.4	649
44. Engineering degree, other state or Federal District	2.6	193	2.3	213	2.1	242	2.3	648
45. Military degree: graduation from Agulhas Negras, Escola Militar in Rio, Colégio Militar in Pôrto Alegre, or its imperial equivalent in Ceará	4.1	193	0.9	214	2.1	241	2.3	648
46. Pharmacy degree	0.5	193	3.7	214	1.2	242	1.8	649
47. Other university degree	4.1	193	0.9	214	10.4	241	5.4	648
48. Secondary school graduate, but no higher degree	4.7	193	7.1	210	5.8	241	5.9	644
49. Up to secondary school, but no diploma	1.0	193	1.9	209	1.7	241	1.6	643
OCCUPATION								
50. Lawyer	55.1	214	67.9	212	69.3	241	64.3	667
51. Physician	7.1	197	12.1	214	7.1	241	8.7	652
52. Journalist	35.0	197	23.8	214	26.6	241	28.2	652
53. *Fazendeiro*: owner of estate producing agricultural or pastoral goods primarily for cash sale	18.8	197	16.7	210	37.7	239	25.1	646
54. Merchant	13.3	196	5.6	213	16.6	241	12.0	650
55. Industrialist: owner of, or investor in, manufacturing or processing operation (e.g. *usineiro*)	12.6	199	17.8	214	27.8	241	19.9	654
56. Banker: manager, director, or legal counsel of, or investor in, bank	9.1	198	15.0	214	18.3	241	14.4	653
57. Educator: secondary- or university-level teacher	27.3	199	32.2	213	21.2	241	26.6	653
58. Engineer	9.4	202	12.7	213	9.9	242	10.7	657
59. Cleric	2.5	198	0.5	214	0	253	0.9	665
60. Military officer	4.6	197	0.5	214	2.5	242	2.5	653
61. Magistrate: *Juiz de direito* or above	19.8	197	17.3	214	19.1	241	18.7	652
62. Rural land dealer	1.0	197	0	214	2.9	241	1.4	652
63. *Comissário*: Short-term lender to *fazendeiros*	0	197	0	214	3.8	240	1.4	651
64. Manager, director, or legal counsel of, or investor in, railroad company operating in Brazil	0	197	5.6	214	9.5	241	5.4	652
65. Mine owner or investor in mining	1.0	197	3.3	213	0	241	1.4	651
66. Other profession or occupation	2.0	197	6.5	214	4.6	241	4.4	652

Variables and Values in the Three Elite Studies (Continued)

Categories and variables	Pernambuco Value	Number	Minas Gerais Value	Number	São Paulo Value	Number	Composite Value	Number
FAMILY TIES								
67. Related to at least one other member of same state elite, through first cousin—consanguineal or affinitive	34.3%	198	46.3%	177	42.5%	240	41.0%	615
68. Member of, or related to, imperial elite, through first cousin, con. or aff., or direct descendant through grandson. Def. of imperial elite: senators, or title-holders of *barão* or above	27.4	197	16.2	185	19.7	239	21.1	621
69. Related to at least one member of any other analogously defined state elite (not just those of PE, SP, or MG), through first cousin—con. or aff.	12.0	192	4.3	185	0.8	241	5.3	618
70. In federal congress: served at least once (appointed or elected) for 90 days or more, in chamber or senate	55.7	192	51.2	209	31.7	252	45.0	653
71. In state legislature: served at least once (appointed or elected) for 90 days or more, in chamber or senate	30.9	194	47.4	209	48.6	255	43.0	658
OTHER VARIABLES: COMPOSITES OR ITEMS DERIVED FROM "POLITICAL OFFICES HELD"								
Historical Republican: composite of 1c–1d	22.5	80	49.4	83	50.5	105	41.8	268
Adherent to the Republic: composite of 1a–1b	77.6	80	50.6	83	49.5	105	58.2	268
Age at first elite-defining position:								
Minimum	19	186	23	181	25	230	—	597
Maximum	78	186	80	181	85	230	—	597
Mean	43.0	186	43.3	181	46.0	230	44.2	597
Median	42.3	186	41.9	181	45.1	230	43.3	597
Age at first elite-defining position, grouped in 10-year intervals:								
29 or less	16.7	186	5.0	181	3.5	230	8.0	597
30–39	22.0	186	36.5	181	23.9	230	27.1	597
40–49	29.6	186	32.0	181	39.6	230	34.2	597
50–59	18.3	186	20.4	181	21.3	230	20.1	597
60 or over	13.4	186	6.1	181	11.7	230	10.6	597

Political generation:

First: born before 1869	50.8	193	50.3	181	46.1	230	48.8	604
Second: born between 1869 and 1888	29.5	193	31.5	181	33.9	230	31.8	604
Third: born in 1889 or later	19.7	193	18.2	181	20.0	230	19.4	604
Held first office after 1930 Revolution	14.9	268	21.5	214	37.3	263	24.7	745
Out-of-state job: composite of 29–33	43.6	195	22.4	214	16.8	238	26.7	647
Out-of-state link (education, experience, family tie): composite of 29–34, 36, 38–39, 41–42, 44–45, 69	64.9	185	72.1	183	39.3	229	57.3	597
Foreign tie: composite of 16–28	33.3	186	15.7	210	48.1	237	33.0	633
Bacharel: composite of 37–42	81.3	194	73.8	210	76.2	239	76.9	641
Lacking university degree: composite of 48–49	5.7	193	9.2	206	7.5	241	7.5	640
Businessman: composite of 54–56, 63–65	24.4	197	34.9	212	41.3	240	34.1	649
Member of agricultural export complex: composite of 13, 18, 53, 63	26.2	187	17.1	210	40.3	233	28.4	630
Relative of Republican or imperial elite: composite of 67–69	45.3	192	52.9	170	49.6	236	49.2	598
Member of PR executive committee	14.9	276	32.2	214	28.5	263	24.6	753
Opposition leader: composite of all members of non-PR executive committees	10.5	276	8.4	214	20.5	263	13.4	753
Party leader: composite of all members of PR and non-PR executive committees	25.4	276	38.8	214	48.3	263	37.2	753
Governor	6.2	276	7.9	214	8.0	263	7.3	753
Legislative experience: composite of 70–71	65.6	276	68.4	209	57.1	252	63.2	737

INTRA-STATE VARIABLES: SÃO PAULO POLITICAL EVENTS

Emancipationist: Supported phased abolition within 5 years, between Jan. 1, 1887 and May 13, 1888	7.3	109
Break with PRP majority, 1897	6.7	120
Break with PRP majority, 1901	17.0	135
Break with PRP majority, 1907	13.8	145
Break with PRP majority, 1915	6.9	173
Break with PRP majority, 1924	6.9	174
Member, Liga Nacionalista	13.8	203
Município of major political activity different from município of birth	68.9	235

287

Tenure in Elite Posts

Governor or Interventor

Junta: Prudente de Morais Barros, Francisco Rangel Pestana, and Joaquim Sousa	[Nov. 16, 1889–Dec. 14, 1889]
Prudente de Morais Barros	Dec. 14, 1889–Oct. 18, 1890
Jorge Tibiriçá	Oct. 18, 1890–March 7, 1891
Américo Brasiliense [de Almeida e Melo]	March 7, 1891–Dec. 15, 1891
Sérgio Tertuliano Castelo Branco	[Dec. 15, 1891]
José Alves de Cerqueira César (interim)	Dec. 15, 1891–Aug. 23, 1892
Bernardino de Campos	Aug. 23, 1892–May 1, 1896
Manuel Ferraz de Campos Sales	May 1, 1896–Nov. 10, 1898
Fernando Prestes de Albuquerque	Nov. 10, 1898–May 1, 1900
Francisco de Paula Rodrigues Alves	May 1, 1900–July 3, 1902
Bernardino de Campos	July 3, 1902–May 1, 1904
Jorge Tibiriçá	May 1, 1904–May 1, 1908
Manuel Joaquim de Albuquerque Lins	May 1, 1908–May 1, 1912
Francisco de Paula Rodrigues Alves	May 1, 1912–May 1, 1916
Altino Arantes Marques	May 1, 1916–May 1, 1920
Washington Luís Pereira de Sousa	May 1, 1920–May 1, 1924
Carlos de Campos	May 1, 1924–April 27, 1927
[Antônio] Dino da Costa Bueno	[April 27, 1927–July 14, 1927]
Júlio Prestes de Albuquerque ·	July 14, 1927–March 26, 1930
Heitor Teixeira Penteado	March 26, 1930–Oct. 24, 1930
Hastínfilo de Moura (I)	[Oct. 24, 1930–Oct. 28, 1930]
José Maria Whitaker (I)	[Oct. 30, 1930–Nov. 6, 1930]
Plínio Barreto (I)	[Nov. 6, 1930–Nov. 25, 1930]
João Alberto Lins de Barros (I)	Nov. 25, 1930–July 24, 1931
Laudo Ferreira de Camargo (I)	July 25, 1931–Nov. 13, 1931

NOTE: Brackets indicate a period served of less than 90 days, too brief a time to be counted in the elite study.

Manuel Rabelo (I)	Nov. 13, 1931–March 7, 1932
Pedro de Toledo (I)	March 7, 1932–Oct. 2, 1932
Herculano de Carvalho e Silva (I)	[Oct. 2, 1932–Oct. 6, 1932]
Valdomiro Castilho de Lima (I)	Oct. 6, 1932–July 27, 1933
Manuel de Cerqueira Daltro Filho (I)	[July 27, 1933–Aug. 21, 1933]
Armando de Sales Oliveira (I)	Aug. 21, 1933–April 11, 1935
(constitutional governor)	April 11, 1935–Dec. 29, 1936
Henrique Smith Bayma	[Dec. 29, 1936–Jan. 5, 1937]
José Joaquim Cardoso Melo Neto	Jan. 5, 1937–April 25, 1938

Lieutenant Governor (office abolished
after 1930)

José Alves de Cerqueira César	June 13, 1891–1896
(interim governor in 1891–92)	
Francisco de Assis Peixoto Gomide	May 1, 1896–May 1, 1900
Domingos Correia de Morais	May 1, 1900–May 1, 1904
João Batista de Melo Oliveira	May 1, 1904–May 1, 1908
Fernando Prestes de Albuquerque	May 1, 1908–May 1, 1912
Carlos Augusto Pereira Guimarães	May 1, 1912–May 1, 1916
[Antônio] Cândido Rodrigues	May 1, 1916–May 1, 1920
Virgílio Rodrigues Alves	May 1, 1920–Sep. 21, 1922
Fernando Prestes de Albuquerque	Jan. 1924–July 14, 1927
Heitor Teixeira Penteado	July 14, 1927–March 26, 1930

General Secretary *

Antônio Mercado	Oct. 18?, 1890–March 7, 1891

Secretary of Justice

Manuel Pessoa de Siqueira Campos	Feb. 1892–July 31?, 1893
João Alvares de Rubião Júnior	July 31, 1893–Feb. 27, 1895
Teodoro Dias de Carvalho Júnior	[Feb. 27, 1895–May 1895]
João Batista de Melo Peixoto	May 1895–May 1, 1896
Carlos de Campos	May 1, 1896–April 27, 1897
José Joaquim Cardoso de Almeida	[April 27, 1897–June 15, 1897]
José Getúlio Monteiro	June 15, 1897–Nov. 10, 1898
José Pereira de Queiroz	Nov. 10, 1898–May 1, 1900
Bento Pereira Bueno (post combined	May 1, 1900–July 13, 1902
with Secy of Interior, 1902–5)	
José Cardoso de Almeida	[Feb. 1, 1906–March 13, 1906]
Washington Luís Pereira de Sousa	March 13, 1906–May 1, 1912
Rafael de Abreu Sampaio Vidal	May 1, 1912–Oct. 11, 1913
Elói de Miranda Chaves	Oct. 11, 1913–Dec. 14, 1918
[Uladislau] Herculano de Freitas	Dec. 14, 1918–May 1, 1920
Francisco Cardoso Ribeiro	May 1, 1920–May 1, 1924
Bento Pereira Bueno	May 1, 1924–July 14, 1927
Antônio Carlos de Sales Júnior	July 14, 1927–March 28, 1930
Mário Bastos Cruz	March 28, 1930–Oct. 24, 1930
Plínio Barreto	[Oct. 25, 1930–Dec. 5, 1930]
Florivaldo de Vasconcelos Linhares	Dec. 5, 1930–July 24, 1931
Abraão Ribeiro	July 25, 1931–Nov. 13, 1931

*I found no regular secretarial appointments until the governorship of Cerqueira César, Dec. 1891–Aug. 1892. It will be noted that secretaries occasionally directed two agencies simultaneously.

Florivaldo de Vasconcelos Linhares   Nov. 13, 1931–March 15, 1932
Manuel Carlos de Figueiredo Ferraz   [March 15, 1932–May 27, 1932]
Valdemar Ferreira   May 27, 1932–Oct. 6, 1932
Carlos Vilalva   Oct. 6, 1932–Aug. 21, 1933
Mário Mazagão   Aug. 21, 1933–Dec. 15, 1933
Valdomiro Silveira   Dec. 15, 1933–Sept. 20, 1934
Cristiano Altenfelder Silva   Sept. 21, 1934–April 2, 1935
Márcio Pereira Munhoz   [April 2, 1935–April 22, 1935]
Sílvio Portugal   April 22, 1935–Nov. 10, 1937

Secretary of the Interior (called Secy
of Education and Health after 1930)

Vicente de Carvalho   Feb. 26, 1892–Aug. 9, 1892
João Alvares Rubião Júnior   Aug. 25, 1892–Feb. 3, 1893
Cesário Mota   Feb. 3, 1893–1894
Alfredo Pujol   1894–May 1, 1896
[Antônio] Dino da Costa Bueno   May 1, 1896–Dec. 1897
João Batista de Melo Peixoto   Dec. 1897–May 1, 1900
Bento Pereira Bueno   May 1, 1900–May 1, 1904
José Cardoso de Almeida   May 1, 1904–Jan. 30, 1906
Gustavo de Oliveira Godói   Feb. 1, 1906–May 1, 1908
Carlos Pereira Guimarães   May 1, 1908–May 1, 1912
Altino Arantes Marques   May 1, 1912–May 1, 1916
Oscar Rodrigues Alves   May 1, 1916–May 1, 1920
Alárico Silveira   May 1, 1920–May 1, 1924
José Manuel Lobo   May 1, 1924–April 27, 1927
João Galeão Carvalhal Filho   [April 27, 1927–July 14, 1927]
Fábio de Sá Barreto   July 14, 1927–Oct. 24, 1930
José Carlos de Macedo Soares   [Oct. 24, 1930–Nov. 25, 1930]
Artur Neiva   [Dec. 5, 1930–Feb. 12, 1931]
Teodoro Augusto Ramos   Feb. 12?, 1931–July 21, 1931
Antônio de Almeida Prado   July 25, 1931–Nov. 13, 1931
Florivaldo de Vasconcelos Linhares   Nov. 13, 1931–March 7, 1932
Francisco de Sales Gomes Júnior   [March 7, 1932–May 27, 1932]
José Rodrigues Alves Sobrinho   May 27, 1932–Oct. 6, 1932
Augusto Meireles Reis Filho   Oct. 6, 1932–Aug. 21, 1933
Valdomiro Silveira   Aug. 21, 1933–April 11, 1935
Márcio Pereira Munhoz   [April 11, 1935–April 22?, 1935]
Cantídio de Moura Campos   April 22, 1935–Nov. 10, 1937

Secretary of Finance

Martim Francisco Ribeiro de Andrada   March? 1891–Feb. 26, 1892
Manuel Pessoa de Siqueira Campos   Feb. 26, 1892–Aug. 23, 1892
João Alvares Rubião Júnior   Aug. 23, 1892–April 15, 1896
Paulo de Sousa Queiroz   May 1, 1896–May 1, 1897
Firmiano de Morais Pinto   May 1, 1897–Sept. 1897
João Batista de Melo Peixoto   Sept. 1897–May 1, 1900
Francisco de Toledo Malta   May 1, 1900–July 13?, 1902
Firmiano de Morais Pinto   July 13, 1902–Aug. 12, 1903
João Batista de Melo Peixoto   Aug. 12, 1903–May 1, 1904
Manuel Joaquim de Albuquerque Lins   May 1, 1904–Oct. 31, 1907
Olavo Egídio de Sousa Aranha   Oct. 31, 1907–Aug. 6, 1909
Carlos Pereira Guimarães   Aug. 6, 1909–Nov. 6?, 1909
Olavo Egídio de Sousa Aranha   Nov. 6, 1909–May 1, 1912
Joaquim Manuel Martins de Siqueira   May 1, 1912–Oct. 11, 1913

Rafael de Abreu Sampaio Vidal	Oct. 11, 1913–Jan. 13, 1915
José Cardoso de Almeida	Jan. 13, 1915–1918
João Galeão Carvalhal	1918–May 1, 1920
Alvaro Gomes da Rocha Azevedo	May 1, 1920–May 1, 1924
Mário Tavares	May 1, 1924–July 14, 1927
Mário Rolim Teles	July 14, 1927–Oct. 11, 1929
Antônio Carlos de Sales Júnior	Oct. 11, 1929–Oct. 24, 1930
José Maria Whitaker	[Oct. 25, 1930–Nov. 3, 1930]
Erasmo Teixeira Assunção	[Nov. 6, 1930–Dec. 5, 1930]
Marcos de Sousa Dantas	Dec. 5, 1930–July 25, 1931
Numa de Oliveira	July 25, 1931–Nov. 13, 1931
Marcos de Sousa Dantas	[Nov. 13, 1931–Nov. 26, 1931]
José da Silva Gordo	Nov. 26, 1931–May 27, 1932
Paulo de Morais Barros	May 27, 1932–Oct. 6, 1932
Artur Viveiros Costa	Oct. 6, 1932–1933
José Caetano Mascarenhas	1933–Aug. 21, 1933
Francisco Alves dos Santos	Aug. 21, 1933–Jan. 1, 1935
Francisco Machado de Campos	Jan. 21, 1935–April 22, 1935
Clóvis de Paula Ribeiro	April 22, 1935–Nov. 10, 1937

Secretary of Agriculture

Alfredo Maia	Feb. 26, 1892–Dec. 12, 1892
Jorge Tibiriçá	Dec. 12, 1892–June 26, 1895
Teodoro Dias de Carvalho Júnior	June 29, 1895–May 1, 1896
Alvaro da Costa Carvalho	May 1, 1896–July 2, 1897
Firmiano de Morais Pinto	July 2, 1897–April 28, 1898
Antônio Francisco de Paula Sousa	April 28, 1898–Nov. 10, 1898
Alfredo Guedes	Nov. 10, 1898–May 1, 1900
[Antônio] Cândido Rodrigues	May 1, 1900–July 2, 1902
João Batista de Melo Peixoto	July 13, 1902–Aug. 12, 1903
Luís de Toledo Piza e Almeida	Aug. 12, 1903–May 1, 1904
Carlos José Botelho	May 1, 1904–May 1, 1908
[Antônio] Cândido Rodrigues	May 1, 1908–Aug. 6, 1909
Olavo Egídio de Sousa Aranha	Aug. 6, 1909–Nov. 7, 1909
Antônio de Pádua Sales	Nov. 7, 1909–May 1, 1912
Paulo de Morais Barros	May 1, 1912–April 14, 1913
Altino Arantes Marques	April 14, 1913–July 30, 1913
Paulo de Morais Barros	July 30, 1913–Nov. 9, 1915
Elói de Miranda Chaves	[Nov. 9, 1915–Nov. 17, 1915]
José Cardoso de Almeida	Nov. 17, 1915–May 1, 1916
Cândido Nogueira da Mota	May 1, 1916–May 1, 1920
Heitor Teixeira Penteado	May 1, 1920–May 1, 1924
Gabriel Ribeiro dos Santos	May 1, 1924–July 14, 1927
Fernando Costa	July 14, 1927–Oct. 24, 1930
Henrique de Sousa Queiroz	[Oct. 25, 1930–Dec. 5, 1930]
Edmundo Navarro de Andrade	Dec. 5, 1930–July 25, 1931
Adalberto Queiroz Teles	July 25, 1931–Nov. 13, 1931
Marcos de Sousa Dantas	[Nov. 13, 1931–Nov. 26, 1931]
Antônio Manuel Alves de Lima	Nov. 26, 1931–March 16, 1932
Teodureto de Camargo	[March 16, 1932–May 27, 1932]
Francisco da Cunha Junqueira	May 27, 1932–Oct. 6, 1932
Eugênio Lefevre	Oct. 12, 1932–Aug. 21, 1933
Adalberto Bueno Neto	Aug. 21, 1933–April 22, 1935
Luís de Toledo Piza Sobrinho	April 22, 1935–Nov. 9, 1936
Valentim Gentil	Nov. 9, 1936–Nov. 10, 1937

Secretary of Security, 1930 (combined
with Secy of Justice, 1931–35)

Miguel Costa	Dec. 5, 1930–July 24, 1931
Artur Leite de Barros Jr.	April 22, 1935–Nov. 10, 1937

Secretary of Transport and Public Works,
1927–

José Oliveira de Barros	Sept. 16, 1927–Oct. 24, 1930
Francisco Pais Leme Monlevade	[Oct. 25, 1930–Dec. 5, 1930]
Alberto de Oliveira Coutinho	Dec. 5, 1930–July 25, 1931
Francisco Emídio da Fonseca Teles	July 25, 1931–Nov. 13, 1931
Luís Anhaia Melo	Nov. 13, 1931–March 7, 1932
João de Mendonça Lima	[March 7, 1932–May 27, 1932]
Francisco Emídio da Fonseca Teles	May 27, 1932–Oct. 6, 1932
Luís Silveira	Oct. 6, 1932–May 30, 1933
Dilermando de Assis	[May 30, 1933–July 27, 1933]
Teófilo Oswald Pereira de Sousa	[July 27, 1933–Aug. 21, 1933]
Francisco Machado de Campos	Aug. 21, 1933–April 22, 1935
Ranulfo Pinheiro Lima	April 22, 1935–Nov. 10, 1937

Secretary of the Governor's Office

Ataliba Nogueira	Oct. 6, 1932–June 5, 1933
José Ulisses Luna	[June 5, 1933–July 27?, 1933]
Márcio Pereira Munhoz	Aug. 21, 1933–May 10?, 1935
Carlos de Morais Barros	[May 10?, 1935–June?, 1935]
Cassiano Ricardo [Leite]	June? 1935–1937?

Mayor of São Paulo City

Vicente Ferreira da Silva	[Dec.? 1889–Jan. 12?, 1890]
Clementino de Sousa e Castro	Jan. 12, 1890–Dec. 17, 1891
Carlos Augusto Ferreira Garcia	Dec. 17, 1891–1892
Pedro Vicente de Azevedo	1892–95
Antônio Proost Rodovalho	1896–99
Antônio [da Silva] Prado	1899–1910
Raymundo Duprat	1911–14
Washington Luís Pereira de Sousa	1914–19
Firmiano de Morais Pinto	1920–26
José Pires do Rio	1926–Oct. 24, 1930
José Joaquim Cardoso de Melo Neto	[Oct. 24?, 1930–Dec. 1930]
Luís de Anhaia Melo	Dec. 1930–July 25?, 1931
Francisco Machado de Campos	July 25?, 1931–Nov. 13?, 1931
Luís de Anhaia Melo	[Nov. 13?, 1931–Dec. 1931]
Henrique Jorge Guedes	Dec. 1931–May 27?, 1932
Gofredo T. da Silva Teles	May 27?, 1932–Oct. 6?, 1932
Teodoro Ramos	Dec. 1932–May 1933
Osvaldo Costa	[May 1933–July 27, 1933]
Antônio Carlos de Assunção	Aug. 1933–Sept. 1934
Fábio da Silva Prado	Sept. 1934–April 1938

Police Chief

Bernardino de Campos	Nov. 16, 1889–Oct. 14, 1890
Paulo de Sousa Queiroz	Oct. 14, 1890–March 7, 1891
Pedro Augusto Carneiro Lessa	[March 7, 1891–June 2, 1891]
Virgílio Siqueira Cardoso	June 2, 1891–Nov. 23, 1891

Raimundo Cavalcanti de Albuquerque	[Nov. 23, 1891–Dec. 15, 1891]
Lúcio A. Martins	[Dec. 15, 1891–Dec. 19, 1891]
Manuel Pessoa Siqueira Campos	[Dec. 19, 1891–Jan. 26, 1892]
Teodoro Dias de Carvalho Júnior	Jan. 26, 1892–Nov. 26, 1895
Bento Pereira Bueno	Nov. 26, 1895–May 26, 1896
José Xavier de Toledo	May 26, 1896–March 4, 1897
Francisco Martiniano da Costa Carvalho	May 31, 1897–Nov. 10, 1898
Antônio Cândido de Almeida e Silva	Nov. 10, 1898–May 1, 1900
Pedro de Oliveira Ribeiro	May 1, 1900–Jan. 1, 1902
Joaquim José Saraiva Júnior	[Jan. 1, 1902–Jan. 6, 1902]
José Cardoso de Almeida	Jan. 6, 1902–March 31, 1903
Luís Toledo Piza e Almeida	March 31, 1903–Aug. 11, 1903
Antônio de Godói Moreira e Costa	Aug. 11, 1903–April 20, 1905
Augusto Meireles Reis	April 20, 1905–July 6, 1906
Artur Pinheiro Prado (replaced by Secy of Justice, Sept. 1906–Jan. 1925)	[July 6, 1906–Sept. 17, 1906]
Roberto Moreira	Jan. 12, 1925–July 14, 1927
Mário Bastos Cruz (replaced by Secy of Justice, March–Dec. 1930, then by Secy of Security till July 30, 1931).	July 14, 1927–March 17, 1930
Eurico Sodré	[July 30, 1931–Aug. 13, 1931]
Osvaldo Cordeiro de Farias	Aug. 13, 1931–May 5, 1932
Antônio Bráulio de Mendonça Filho	[May 6, 1932–May 28, 1932]
Tirso Queirolo Martins de Sousa	May 28, 1932–Sept. 27, 1932
Durval Vilalva	[Sept. 28, 1932]
Brasílio Taborda	[Sept. 29, 1932–Oct. 3, 1932]
Edgard Pereira Armond	[Oct. 3, 1932–Oct. 6, 1932]
Osvaldo Cordeiro de Farias	[Oct. 7, 1932–Nov. 10, 1932]
José de Sousa Carvalho	[Nov. 10, 1932–Nov. 11, 1932]
Danton Coelho	[Nov. 11, 1932–Dec. 22, 1932]
José de Sousa Carvalho	[Dec. 22, 1932–Dec. 28, 1932]
Bento Borges da Fonseca	Dec. 28, 1932–May 20, 1933
Viriato Carneiro Lopes	[May 20, 1933–May 22, 1933]
Olímpio Falconieri da Cunha	[May 22, 1933–July 22, 1933]
Júlio Limeira da Silva	[July 22, 1933–Aug. 21, 1933]
Durval Vilalva	[Aug. 21, 1933–Aug. 22, 1933]
Mário Guimarães	Aug. 22, 1933–March 22, 1934
Vicente de Paula Vicente de Azevedo	March 22, 1934–Aug. 10, 1934
Artur Leite de Barros Júnior	[Aug. 11, 1934–Aug. 16, 1934]
Cristiano Altenfelder Silva (replaced by Secy of Security through rest of the period)	Aug. 16, 1934–Dec. 30, 1934

President, State-Associated Banks

(a) Banco de Crédito Hipotecário e Agrícola	
Ferdinand Pierre*	June 14, 1909–April 30, 1924
Altino Arantes Marques	April 30, 1924–Nov. 4, 1926
(b) Banco do Estado de São Paulo	
Altino Arantes Marques	Nov. 4, 1926–Nov. 12, 1930
José Joaquim Cardoso Melo Neto	Nov. 12, 1930–1931?

*Ferdinand Pierre was not a Brazilian citizen, and therefore did not qualify for the political elite as defined in Appendix A. This bank was essentially a French enterprise, controlled from Paris.

Antônio de Queiroz Teles	1931?–Dec. 14, 1931
José Martiniano Rodrigues Alves	Dec. 14, 1931–April 18, 1933
Múcio Whitaker	April 18, 1933–Aug. 30, 1933
Eliseu Teixeira Camargo	Aug. 30, 1933–Sept. 4, 1934
Antônio Carlos de Assunção	Sept. 4, 1934–June 3, 1938

President, São Paulo Coffee Institute, 1924 –
(post automatically held by Secy of
Finance through 1930)

Antônio Manuel Alves de Lima	Jan. 7, 1931–1931?
Cesário Coimbra	1931?–32?
Luís Américo de Freitas	May 1932–Sept. 1932
Afrodísio Sampaio Coelho	Sept.? 1932–Dec. 1932
Luís Vicente Figueira de Melo	1933?–34?
Cesário Coimbra	July 7, 1934–Nov. 10?, 1937

President, State Senate

Luís Pereira Barreto	Aug. 1891–Nov. 1891
Ezequiel de Paula Ramos	April 1892–June 1894
José Alves Guimarães Júnior	July 1894–July 1895
Francisco de Assis Peixoto Gomide	Aug. 1895–April 1896
Ezequiel de Paula Ramos	May 1896–March 1898?
José Alves de Cerqueira César	April 1898–April 1901
Francisco de Assis Peixoto Gomide	Sept. 1901–April 1905
Manuel Antônio Duarte de Azevedo	April 1906–July 1912
João Alvares Rubião Júnior	Nov. 1912–Aug. 1915
Jorge Tibiriçá	Nov. 1915–July 1924?
[Antônio] Dino da Costa Bueno (no senate in the legislature of 1935–37)	Aug. 1924–Oct. 24, 1930

President, State Chamber of Deputies

Augusto César de Miranda Azevedo	1891–92
Antônio Francisco Paula Sousa	1892
Luís de Toledo Piza e Almeida	1892–99
Carlos Augusto Pereira Guimarães	1899–1901
Antônio de Pádua Sales	1901–3
João Alvares Rubião Júnior	1903–6
Carlos de Campos	1907–15
Antônio Alvares Lobo	1915–26
Artur de Aguiar Whitaker (no legislature hereafter until 1935)	1927–Oct. 24, 1930
Laerte Teixeira de Assunção	1935
Henrique Smith Bayma	1936–37

Majority Leader, State Chamber of Deputies

Aureliano Oliveira Coutinho	July?–Dec.? 1891
Júlio de Mesquita	1892?
Alvaro da Costa Carvalho	1893?
Rivadávia Correia	1894?
José Manuel Azevedo Marques	1898–1900?
[Uladislau] Herculano de Freitas	1900?–3?
João Alvares Rubião Júnior	1903?–6?

Júlio de Mesquita	1907?–12?
Antônio Martins Fontes Júnior	1913?
Washington Luís Pereira de Sousa	1914?
João Sampaio	1915?
Antônio Martins Fontes Júnior	1915?
Mário Tavares	1916?–21?
Júlio Prestes de Albuquerque	1921–24
Armando [da Silva] Prado	1928?–30
Henrique Smith Bayma	1935
Ernesto Morais Leme	1936–Nov. 10, 1937

President, State Supreme Court

Carlos Augusto de Sousa Lima	1891–97
Frederico Dabney de Avelar Brotero	1897?–1900
José Xavier de Toledo	1900–1901
Ignácio José de Oliveira Arruda	1901
Pedro Oliveira Ribeiro	1902
Canuto José Saraiva	1903–5?
Augusto de Couto Delgado	1905
José Xavier de Toledo	1906–18
Francisco da Silva Saldanha	1918–21
Firmino Antônio da Silva Whitaker	1921–23
Benedito Filadelfo de Castro	1924?–25
João Batista Pinto de Toledo	1926
Urbano Marcondes de Moura	1927
Luís Aires de Almeida Freitas	1928
Eliseu Guilherme Cristiano	Dec. 1928–1929
Manuel Policarpo Moreira de Azevedo Júnior	1929–31
Manuel da Costa Manso	1932–33
Francisco de Paula e Silva	1933–34
Sílvio Portugal	1934–35
Afonso José de Carvalho	1935–36
Júlio César de Faria	1936–May 1937
Aquiles de Oliveira Ribeiro	1937–38

Executive Committee, Partido Republicano Paulista, 1889–1930

Manuel Ferraz de Campos Sales	1889; 1893–95
Adolfo da Silva Gordo*	1889–90; 1907–11; 1913–15
Manuel Lopes de Oliveira*	1889–90
Francisco Glicério Cerqueira Leite	1889; 1892–97; 1904–9; 1912–16
Domingos Correia de Morais*	1889–90; 1899
Vitorino Gonçalves Carmilo*	1890; 1892
Luís Pereira Barreto*	1891
Antônio Ulhoa Cintra, Barão de Jaguara*	1891
José da Costa Machado e Sousa*	1891
Joaquim Lopes Chaves*	1891
Rodrigo Lobato Marcondes Machado*	1891
Joaquim Celidônio Gomes dos Reis*	1891
Martinho [da Silva] Prado Júnior*	1891
Brasílio Rodrigues dos Santos*	1891

*Victim of the purge of 1891 or the counterpurge of 1892.

Francisco Antônio de Sousa Queiroz*	1891
Elias Antônio Pacheco Chaves*	1891
Antônio Carlos Arruda Botelho,	1891
Conde do Pinhal*	
João Carlos Leite Penteado*	1891
Prudente de Morais Barros	1892–93
Bernardino de Campos	1892; 1896; 1899–1900; 1907–14
Cesário Mota	1892
Júlio de Mesquita	1892–94; 1896
Francisco de Paula Rodrigues Alves	1892–94; 1899; 1917
José Alves Guimarães Júnior	1893–94; 1901
Alfredo Ellis	1893–94
José Alves Cerqueira César	1895; 1898; 1900
João Alvares Rubião Júnior	1896–97; 1899–1900; 1902–15
João Batista de Melo Oliveira	1896–97; 1899–1900; 1903
Manuel Pessoa de Siqueira Campos	1897; 1904–10
José Paulino Nogueira	1897
Luís de Toledo Piza e Almeida	1898
Antônio Carlos Ferraz Sales	1898; 1900
Ricardo Soares Batista	1898
Carlos Pereira Guimarães	1898
Alfredo Guedes	1898; 1901
Frederico de Abranches	1901–03
Antônio de Pádua Sales	1901–2; 1907–9; 1916–18; 1923–30
Antônio de Lacerda Franco	1901–6; 1914–27
Francisco de Assis Peixoto Gomide	1903
Fernando Prestes de Albuquerque	1903–6; 1914–22
Cesário da Silva Bastos	1907–15
Jorge Tibiriçá	1908–24
[Antônio] Dino da Costa Bueno	1908–9; 1919–30
Manuel Joaquim Albuquerque Lins	1914–25
Virgílio Rodrigues Alves	1916–19
Carlos de Campos	1916–24
Rodolfo Miranda	1917–30
Olavo Egídio de Sousa Aranha	1917–23; 1925
Altino Arantes Marques	1920–23; 1925; 1927–30
Arnolfo Azevedo	1925–30
Ataliba Leonel	1925–30
[Uladislau] Herculano de Freitas	1925
Washington Luís Pereira de Sousa	1925
Sílvio de Campos	1928–30
Manuel Pedro Vilaboim	1928–30
Artur de Aguiar Whitaker	1928–30

Executive Committee, PRP in Opposition, 1931–36 †

Alberto Whatley	1933–36
Antônio Carlos de Sales Júnior	1933–34

*Victim of the purge of 1891 or the counterpurge of 1892.

† On this committee, as on the two that follow, data were lacking for certain years (1935 here and for the PC; 1928 for the PD). I have assumed continuous service where the man had a seat on the committee the year before and the year after. No data are available on the PRP committee in 1931–32, when the party was outlawed; and none have been coded for 1937, when the party split.

Antônio Martins Fontes Júnior	1933
Francisco de Assis Vieira	1933
Heitor Teixeira Penteado	1933; 1936
João Sampaio	1933–34
José Alcântara Machado	1933
Oscar Rodrigues Alves	1933–34
Leônidas Vieira	1933
Fernando Prestes de Albuquerque*	1934
Altino Arantes Marques*	1934
Ataliba Leonel*	1934
Sílvio de Campos*	1934
Manuel Pedro Vilaboim*	1934–36
Elói Chaves	1934
Francisco Cunha Junqueira	1934–36
José Levy Sobrinho	1934
Luís Américo de Freitas	1934
Mário Tavares	1934–36
Rafael de Abreu Sampaio Vidal	1934
César Vergueiro	1936
Raul Rocha Medeiros	1936
Luís Rodolfo Miranda	1936
Eduardo Rodrigues Alves	1936

*Executive Committee, Partido De-
mocrático, 1926–34*

Antônio da Silva Prado	1926–27
Francisco Morato	1926; 1930–31; 1933–34
Luís Queiroz Aranha	1926–27; 1930
Luís Barbosa Gama Cerqueira	1926–27; 1930; 1934
José Adriano Marrey Júnior	1926–27; 1930–31
José Joaquim Cardoso Melo Neto	1926–30; 1932–34
Valdemar Ferreira	1926–30
Paulo de Morais Barros	1926; 1930–31; 1933–34
Paulo Nogueira Filho	1926–30
Antônio Cajado de Lemos	1926
Prudente de Morais Neto	1926–31
Henrique de Sousa Queiroz	1928–30; 1934
Joaquim Sampaio Vidal	1929–31; 1933–34
Manfredo Antônio da Costa	1930; 1932
Joaquim Celidônio Gomes dos Reis Filho	1931–32; 1934
Elias Machado de Almeida	1931–32
Antônio Carlos Abreu Sodré	1931–32; 1934
José Pinto Antunes	1932
Miguel Capalbo	1932–34
Antônio Prudente de Morais	1932–34
Nicolau Morais Barros	1932
Aureliano Leite	1933
Francisco Mesquita	1933
Cesário Coimbra	1933
Carlos Morais Andrade	1934
Vicente Ráo	1934
José Ferreira da Rocha Filho	1934
Henrique Smith Bayma	1934

*Served before 1931.

Executive Committee, Partido Constitucionalista, 1934–37

Valdemar Ferreira*	1934–37
Joaquim Celidônio Gomes dos Reis Filho*	1934
Cesário Coimbra*	1934
Oscar Stevenson	1934; 1937
Luís Toledo Piza Sobrinho	1934
Francisco de Assis Vieira†	1934
Sílvio de Andrade Coutinho	1934; 1937
Carlos de Sousa Nazaré	1934
Maria Teresa Nogueira de Azevedo	1934
Luís Sérgio Brito Bastos	1934
Bento Abreu Sampaio Vidal	1934; 1937
Vicente de Paula Vicente de Azevedo	1934
Laerte Teixeira de Assunção	1934
Benedito Montenegro	1934
Alárico Caiuby	1934
Domício Pacheco e Silva	1934
Fábio da Silva Prado	1934
José Joaquim Cardoso Melo Neto*	1936
Antônio Carlos Abreu Sodré*	1936–37
Henrique Smith Bayma*	1936–37
José Alcântara Machado†	1936
Ernesto de Morais Leme	1936
Gastão Vidigal	1936
Valdomiro Silveira	1936
Paulo de Morais Barros*	1937
Paulo Nogueira Filho*	1937
Elias Machado de Almeida*	1937
Armando de Sales Oliveira	1937
Carolino Mota e Silva	1937
Marcos Mélega	1937
Adalberto Bueno Neto	1937
Oscar Pirajá Martins	1937
Plínio de Queiroz	1937
Aristides Macedo Filho	1937
Celso Torquato Junqueira	1937

FEDERAL POSTS

President

Prudente de Morais Barros	Nov. 15, 1894–Nov. 15, 1898
Manuel Ferraz de Campos Sales	Nov. 15, 1898–Nov. 15, 1902
Francisco de Paula Rodrigues Alves	Nov. 15, 1902–Nov. 15, 1906; Nov. 15, 1918–Jan. 18, 1919
Washington Luís Pereira de Sousa	Nov. 15, 1926–Oct. 24, 1930

Minister of Justice

Manuel Ferraz de Campos Sales	Nov. 15, 1889–Jan. 22, 1891
[Uladislau] Herculano de Freitas	Aug. 11, 1913–Nov. 15, 1914

*Served on PD executive committee.
†Served on PRP executive committee.

| Vicente Ráo | July 24, 1934–Jan. 6, 1937 |
| José Carlos de Macedo Soares | June 3, 1937–Nov. 8, 1937 |

Minister of Finance

Francisco de Paula Rodrigues Alves	Nov. 23, 1891–Aug. 30, 1892; Nov. 15, 1894–Nov. 20, 1896
Bernardino de Campos	Nov. 20, 1896–Nov. 15, 1898
Rafael de Abreu Sampaio Vidal	Nov. 15, 1922–Jan. 1925
José Maria Whitaker	Nov. 4, 1930–Dec. 1931

Minister of Agriculture

Francisco Glicério Cerqueira Leite	Jan. 31, 1890–Jan. 22, 1891
[Antônio] Cândido Rodrigues	June 21, 1909–Nov. 26, 1909
Rodolfo Miranda	Nov. 29, 1909–Nov. 15, 1910
Pedro de Toledo	Nov. 15, 1910–May 24, 1912
Antônio de Pádua Sales	Dec. 12, 1918–June 27, 1919
José Pires do Rio	July 26, 1922–Nov. 15, 1922
Paulo de Morais Barros (simultaneously Min. of Transport and Public Works)	[Oct. 25, 1930–Nov. 3, 1930]

Minister of Transport and Public Works

Antônio Francisco de Paula Sousa	April 22, 1893–Sept. 8, 1893
Pedro de Toledo	[Jan. 27, 1912–Feb. 2, 1912]
José Pires do Rio	July 28, 1919–Nov. 15, 1922
Paulo de Morais Barros (simultaneously Min. of Agriculture)	[Oct. 25, 1930–Nov. 4, 1930]

Minister of Foreign Affairs

Antônio Francisco de Paula Sousa	Dec. 17, 1892–April 22, 1893
José Manuel de Azevedo Marques	July 28, 1919–Nov. 15, 1922
José Carlos de Macedo Soares	July 26, 1934–Jan. 1937

President, Bank of Brazil, 1906–37

José Cardoso de Almeida	Aug. 1919–Nov. 12, 1919
José Maria Whitaker	Dec. 20, 1920–Dec. 22, 1922
Cincinato Braga	Feb. 21, 1923–Jan. 2, 1925
José da Silva Gordo	June 3, 1929–Sept. 1929
Marcos de Sousa Dantas	[July 23, 1934–July 27, 1934]

President, National Coffee Council or National Department of Coffee

Paulo [da Silva] Prado	June 16, 1931–1932
Marcos de Sousa Dantas	1932
Luís Toledo Piza Sobrinho	Nov. 5, 1936–May 4, 1937
Fernando Costa	May 4, 1937–Nov. 13, 1937

Mayor of the Federal District

| Joaquim Xavier da Silveira Júnior | Oct. 1901–Sept. 1902 |
| Antônio [da Silva] Prado Júnior | Nov. 16, 1926–Oct. 24, 1930 |

Justice of Supreme Court

| Joaquim de Toledo Piza e Almeida | April 1, 1891–April 22, 1908 |
| Bernardino Ferreira da Silva | Oct. 10, 1894–Oct. 24, 1905 |

Américo Brasiliense [de Almeida e Melo]	Nov. 24, 1894–March 25, 1896
Canuto José Saraiva	May 1908–May 25, 1919
João Mendes de Almeida Jr.	Jan. 1917–Oct. 24, 1922
[Uladislau] Herculano de Freitas	Jan. 1926–May 14, 1926
Francisco Cardoso Ribeiro	May 25, 1927–May 16, 1932
Firmino Antônio da Silva Whitaker	June 6, 1927–March 5, 1934
Rodrigo Otávio Landgaard Menezes	Feb. 8, 1929–Feb. 7, 1934
Laudo Ferreira de Camargo	June 9, 1932–1951
Manuel da Costa Manso	Aug. 25, 1933–May 3, 1939

Vice-President of Senate

Prudente de Morais Barros	June 18, 1891–May 1894

President, Constituent Assembly

Prudente de Morais Barros	Nov. 21, 1890–Feb. 24, 1891

President, Chamber of Deputies

Bernardino de Campos	Oct. 31, 1891–Aug. 18, 1892
Arnolfo Azevedo	May 16, 1921–March 30, 1927

Majority Leader, Chamber of Deputies

Francisco Glicério Cerqueira Leite	April 1892–May 1897
[Antônio] Dino da Costa Bueno	1901
Fernando Prestes de Albuquerque	[May 1905–June 1905]
Carlos de Campos	Dec. 1919–May 1921
Júlio Prestes de Albuquerque	1926?–May 1927
Manuel Vilaboim	May 1928–Jan. 1930
José Cardoso de Almeida	Jan. 1930–Oct. 24, 1930

Leader, State Delegation, Chamber of Deputies

Francisco Glicério Cerqueira Leite	April 1892–May 1897
[Antônio] Dino da Costa Bueno	1900–1902?
[Antônio] Cândido Rodrigues	1903–5?
Fernando Prestes de Albuquerque	[May 1905–June 1905]
José Galeão Carvalhal	1910–15?
Alvaro da Costa Carvalho	1916?–18?
Carlos de Campos	1919–23?
[Uladislau] Herculano de Freitas	1924–25
Júlio Prestes de Albuquerque	1926?–May 1927
Manuel Vilaboim	May 1927?–Jan. 1930
José Cardoso de Almeida	Jan. 1930–Oct. 24, 1930
José de Alcântara Machado	1933–35
José Joaquim Cardoso Melo Neto	1935–Jan. 1937

Select Budgetary Data, 1879/80-1940

A WORD ON THE conventions and materials used in the table that follows. Blank cells indicate missing data. Most sectoral expenditures are missing for 1892 and 1893, because no itemized *secretaria* accounts were printed for these years. All figures are from the annual *relatórios* (1880–1929) or *contas* (1930–40) of the São Paulo Secretaria da Fazenda, unless otherwise noted. A dash indicates less than 0.5%, or less than 100 contos. Secretaria accounts do not disaggregate some overhead items (e.g., almoxarifado, general depository), and these are not included in affected sectoral series. (Notes on the methods used to construct various series and source information appear at the end of the table.)

I am grateful to Michael Conniff for helping to prepare these series.

Year	Revenues (thousands of current contos) A-1	Expenditures (thousands of current contos) B-1	Revenues (thousands of 1912 contos) A-2	Expenditures (thousands of 1912 contos) B-2	Revenues, 5-yr. moving averages of A-2 A-3	Expenditures, 5-yr. moving averages of B-2 B-3
1880	3.8	3.1	8.0	6.5		
1885	4.4	4.3	8.5	8.3		
1889	7.0	9.3	17.0	22.6		
1890	6.9	9.3	15.5	20.9		
1891	9.2	7.2	16.2	12.7	32.6	32.9
1892	38.1	34.0	46.9	41.8	32.5	35.1
1893	34.5	43.3	39.7	49.9	42.0	43.4
1894	37.3	42.1	44.4	50.1	48.8	51.0
1895	50.2	49.7	63.1	62.5	47.4	52.3
1896	50.8	51.6	49.8	50.6	46.2	51.0
1897	48.6	58.7	40.2	48.5	46.4	46.8
1898	42.3	54.8	33.3	43.1	41.7	41.0
1899	57.3	36.7	45.8	29.4	42.0	41.2
1900	42.6	36.3	39.4	33.6	43.1	41.4
1901	45.7	45.7	51.3	51.3	44.6	42.5
1902	37.6	40.9	45.7	49.8	45.0	44.7
1903	34.1	40.7	40.6	48.5	54.1	50.7
1904	42.6	35.9	48.0	40.4	55.9	53.1
1905	67.3	50.4	84.7	63.4	61.3	58.1
1906	59.0	61.6	60.8	63.5	62.2	62.8
1907	66.4	68.6	72.2	74.6	65.3	69.9
1908	42.7	68.0	45.4	72.3	58.8	73.1
1909	56.7	67.8	63.4	75.8	60.4	78.5
1910	43.3	65.8	52.2	79.4	61.1	82.9
1911	63.9	83.9	69.0	90.6	67.6	90.5
1912	75.6	96.6	75.6	96.6	69.1	97.0
1913	76.0	107.7	77.6	110.0	70.7	95.3
1914	65.7	100.2	71.1	108.4	68.3	89.8
1915	79.3	93.7	60.1	71.0	63.0	82.1
1916	79.2	87.4	57.0	62.9	55.2	70.7
1917	82.6	97.8	49.2	58.2	48.2	57.4
1918	77.6	106.2	38.8	53.1	48.3	58.7
1919	94.2	110.9	35.7	42.0	50.5	62.8
1920	175.7	223.4	60.8	77.3	54.5	69.3
1921	160.6	198.0	67.8	83.5	61.0	75.1
1922	157.0	204.9	69.5	90.7	67.5	83.4
1923	202.7	233.1	71.1	81.8	76.1	91.8
1924	227.0	278.7	68.4	83.9	85.1	107.9
1925	353.3	406.7	103.6	119.3	97.5	128.4
1926	352.6	511.2	113.0	163.8	111.2	147.8
1927	404.6	594.8	131.4	193.1	128.7	175.0
1928	408.4	523.8	139.4	178.8	142.4	203.3
1929	438.5	618.4	156.0	220.1	158.9	229.3
1930	418.0	634.0	172.0	260.9	166.5	248.6
1931	457.7	687.4	195.6	293.8	178.5	264.4
1932	398.9	680.6	169.7	289.6	185.2	272.8
1933	463.6	600.8	199.0	257.8	200.4	276.9
1934	475.9	657.0	189.6	261.7	207.5	267.3
1935	657.1	745.6	248.0	281.4	214.3	260.6
1936	703.6	747.4	231.4	245.9		
1937	665.2	837.7	203.4	256.2		
1940	878.2	1,108.2	255.3	322.1		

Budget surplus (thousands of current contos) A-2 − B-2	Revenues as percent of federal revenues A-4	Expenditures as percent of federal expenditures B-4	Price index, 1912 = 100 C-1	One conto in U.S. dollars C-2	Public debt (thousands of current contos) D-1	Public debt (thousands of 1912 contos) D-2
1.5	3%	2%	47.5		2.0	4.2
0.2	4	3	51.8		7.4	14.3
−5.6	4	5	41.2		9.9	24.0
−5.4	4	4	44.4		11.7	26.4
3.5	4	3	56.7		16.3	28.7
5.1	17	12	81.3	244.4	27.6	33.9
−10.2	13	14	86.8	230.3	28.2	32.5
−5.7	14	11	84.0	207.0	31.3	37.3
0.6	16	14	79.5	198.5	31.5	39.6
−0.8	15	14	102	177.6	34.6	33.9
−8.3	16	15	121	143.9	44.8	37.0
−9.8	13	8	127	136.4	55.8	43.9
16.4	18	12	125	146.1	69.7	55.8
5.8	14	8	108	186.2	53.0	49.1
0.0	15	14	89.0	223.0	42.0	47.2
−4.1	11	14	82.2	234.9	38.3	46.6
−7.9	8	11	83.9	239.9	41.4	49.3
7.6	10	8	88.8	251.8	58.7	66.1
21.2	17	13	79.5	309.6	104.1	130.9
−2.7	14	15	97.0	317.5	103.3	106.5
−2.4	12	13	92.0	301.3	151.4	164.6
−26.9	10	13	94.0	301.8	148.5	158.0
−12.4	13	13	89.5	303.5	152.4	170.3
−27.2	8	11	82.9	302.7	167.1	201.6
−21.6	11	12	92.6	321.0	169.6	183.2
−21.0	12	12	100	331.8	168.9	168.9
−32.4	12	14	97.9	321.3	178.1	181.9
−37.3	15	13	92.4	318.0	186.9	202.3
−10.9	20	14	132	292.7	208.6	158.0
−5.9	17	13	139	230.6	219.7	158.1
−9.0	15	12	168	247.5	207.4	123.5
−14.3	13	12	200	245.7	303.8	151.9
−6.3	15	12	264	267.4	407.7	154.4
−47.7	19	18	289	225.1	513.7	177.8
−15.7	18	17	237	131.2	721.6	304.5
−21.2	16	14	226	129.5	786.5	348.0
−10.7	16	15	285	102.3	942.4	330.7
−15.5	14	17	332	109.4	914.9	275.6
−15.7	20	23	341	122.0	1,018.2	298.6
−50.8	21	27	312	144.4	1,070.5	343.1
−61.7	20	29	308	118.4	1,321.3	429.0
−39.4	18	22	293	119.7	1,571.7	536.4
−64.1	20	26	281	111.1	1,671.1	594.7
−88.9	25	25	243	107.1	1,948.8	802.0
−98.2	26	34	234	70.3	2,636.6	1,126.8
−119.9	23	24	235	71.2	2,705.5	1,151.3
−58.8	22	25	233	79.6	3,049.6	1,308.8
−72.1	19	22	251	84.3	3,241.3	1,291.4
−33.4	24	26	265	82.9	3,522.0	1,329.1
−14.5	22	23	304	85.7	3,580.3	1,177.7
−56.2	19	20	327	86.4	3,948.6	1,207.5
−66.8	19	21	344	60.6	3,882.6	1,128.7

Year	Public foreign debt (thousands of current contos) D-3	Coffee debt (thousands of current contos) D-4	Foreign coffee debt (thousands of current contos) D-5	Combined public-coffee debt (thousands of 1912 contos) D-6	Combined foreign debt as percent of federal foreign debt D-7
1880	0	0	0	4.2	0%
1885	0	0	0	14.3	0
1889	7.1	0	0	24.0	3
1890	8.3	0	0	26.4	3
1891	12.3	0	0	28.7	3
1892	23.9	0	0	33.9	4
1893	24.7	0	0	32.5	4
1894	27.8	0	0	37.3	4
1895	28.0	0	0	39.6	3
1896	30.1	0	0	33.9	3
1897	35.0	0	0	37.0	3
1898	36.8	0	0	43.9	3
1899	66.5	0	0	55.8	5
1900	50.1	0	0	49.1	5
1901	40.1	0	0	47.2	4
1902	36.6	0	0	46.6	3
1903	34.0	0	0	49.3	3
1904	51.2	0	0	66.1	4
1905	95.1	0	0	130.9	8
1906	91.6	121.3	59.3	231.5	14
1907	127.7	294.7	94.6	484.9	19
1908	125.6	463.4	288.4	651.0	33
1909	123.0	271.0	271.0	473.1	31
1910	112.4	221.6	221.6	468.9	26
1911	110.3	155.2	155.2	350.8	19
1912	107.1	105.0	105.0	273.9	15
1913	103.9	143.9	143.9	328.9	16
1914	110.4	219.1	219.1	439.4	18
1915	127.4	217.1	217.1	322.5	16
1916	130.9	207.8	207.8	307.6	15
1917	118.8	208.8	148.6	247.7	13
1918	111.7	195.1	60.4	249.5	8
1919	101.1	171.2	19.2	219.3	8
1920	96.3	49.2	13.4	194.8	4
1921	341.4	16.3	16.3	311.4	9
1922	382.8	10.3	10.3	352.6	8
1923	504.3	1.6	1.6	331.2	9
1924	459.1	—	—	275.6	9
1925	559.5	—	—	298.6	15
1926	592.8	333.2	333.2	449.9	17
1927	699.4	558.7	558.7	610.4	21
1928	934.7	554.3	554.3	725.6	25
1929	938.6	536.5	536.5	785.6	25
1930	1,052.4	1,677.9	1,001.7	1,492.5	33
1931	1,323.2	1,598.9	1,124.5	1,810.0	27
1932	1,091.4	1,561.3	950.1	1,815.7	27
1933	1,227.0	1,794.2	1,076.2	2,078.9	27
1934	1,211.5	1,922.2	1,059.4	2,057.2	24
1935	1,212.2	2,034.3	1,059.7	2,096.7	24
1936	1,165.3	1,198.9	821.0	1,572.1	22
1937	1,161.9	1,204.6	819.7	1,575.9	17
1940	179.4	1,161.5	580.3	1,466.3	

Debt service (thousands of current contos) DS-1	Debt service as percent of expenditure DS-2	Coffee support (thousands of current contos) J-1	Immigration subsidy (thousands of current contos) K-1	Railroad expenditures (thousands of current contos) M-1	Education (thousands of current contos) E-1	Education, per-capita expenditures (milréis) E-2
0.2	6%	0	0	0.3	0.4	
		0	0			
		0	—			
0.7	8	0	2.9		1.1	0.8
0.7	10	0	0.9		1.2	0.8
		0			1.6	1.0
		0			2.9	1.8
5.1	12	0	1.2	0.2	3.2	1.9
2.3	5	0	7.2	—	4.1	2.2
2.8	5	0	4.6	0.1	4.8	2.6
		0			5.5	2.8
5.4	10	0	2.7	0.1	5.6	2.7
5.6	15	0	1.4	0.2	5.6	2.6
4.9	13	0	0.8	—	5.6	2.5
5.0	11	0	4.0	0.6	6.1	2.6
4.1	10	0	1.8	0.3	6.7	2.7
5.1	13	0	0.2	0.4	6.7	2.6
5.4	15	0	0.6	—	6.2	2.4
7.1	14	0	3.0	8.9	6.5	2.4
7.3	12	5.0	2.4	12.3	7.3	2.6
10.0	15	−7.3	1.6	11.7	7.9	2.7
10.4	15	80.9	1.7	8.2	8.5	2.8
16.3	24	−27.6	2.4	6.8	9.2	2.9
12.7	19	2.0	3.0	2.0	10.2	3.2
12.2	15	−18.3	3.4	3.0	12.7	3.8
15.0	16	−23.8	4.0	2.7	16.2	4.7
18.4	17	−21.7	5.3	4.0	19.0	5.3
16.4	16	11.0	2.5	3.3	18.0	4.8
18.9	20	−72.5	0.6	4.9	17.3	4.5
16.5	19	−4.0	1.0	1.9	18.5	4.6
19.0	19	−0.7	2.8	2.1	18.8	4.5
20.0	19	−43.4	1.5	2.5	19.3	4.5
17.2	16	−4.5	0.9	2.3	20.2	4.6
35.3	16	−23.9	2.3	56.2	25.9	5.6
46.5	23		7.0	36.0	28.6	6.0
54.9	27		5.2	35.2	29.0	6.0
66.2	28		8.4	43.3	29.6	6.0
66.5	24		16.6	46.8	36.7	7.2
78.1	19	0	14.5	10.6	45.2	8.7
87.6	17	0	15.4	136.6	52.0	9.7
143.9	24	0	12.0	125.0	54.3	9.9
115.0	22	0	2.5	119.1	60.1	10.7
137.9	22	0	1.8	147.4	68.8	12.0
159.8	25	113.3	0.5	109.0	77.0	13.1
180.9	26	44.0	0	116.0	76.2	12.6
89.6	13	253.9	0.1	88.7	75.4	12.2
131.7	19	7.5	1.3	102.4	81.6	12.9
124.0	19	−177.7	0	99.2	81.9	12.6
166.6	22	2.3	2.6	129.0	97.5	14.7
186.7	25	522.3	11.1		99.9	14.7
188.8	23	6.3	13.1		108.7	15.6
228.5	21	−15.5	3.2		136.9	19.0

Year	Public works (thousands of current contos) I-1	Public health (thousands of current contos) P-1	Public health, per-capita expenditures (milréis) P-2	Força pública (thousands of current contos) FP-1	Police (thousands of current contos) PO-1	Força and police as percent of expenditures PO-2
1880	0.2	0	0	0.9	0	29%
1885	0	0	0		0	
1889	0				0	
1890	0.5			1.6	0	17
1891	0.5			2.2	—	31
1892						
1893						
1894	13.4	11.1	6.6	6.5	0.6	17
1895	15.1	13.1	7.2	6.6	0.7	15
1896	17.8	16.3	8.7	6.3	0.6	13
1897						
1898	14.3	13.6	6.6	8.2	0.7	16
1899	3.9	2.9	1.3	6.9	0.6	20
1900	3.8	3.2	1.4	7.1	0.7	21
1901	6.3	5.8	2.5	7.6	0.7	18
1902	5.7	4.7	1.9	7.5	0.7	20
1903	4.1	4.2	1.7	7.2	0.7	19
1904	4.2	3.1	1.2	6.6	0.7	20
1905	3.9	3.7	1.4	6.7	0.6	14
1906	8.3	8.0	2.8	7.0	0.8	13
1907	10.5	10.6	3.6	7.6	0.7	12
1908	7.6	5.2	1.7	7.8	0.8	13
1909	4.5	7.8	2.5	7.8	0.8	13
1910	6.4	6.6	2.0	8.4	0.8	14
1911	14.4	8.4	2.5	9.4	0.9	12
1912	13.0	10.9	3.1	10.9	1.5	13
1913	12.2	11.9	3.3	12.2	1.8	13
1914	12.6	13.5	3.6	14.1	2.1	16
1915	10.3	11.4	3.0	12.5	1.6	15
1916	5.8	7.0	1.8	12.2	1.6	16
1917	6.6	7.0	1.7	15.3	1.8	17
1918	6.6	10.7	2.5	15.8	1.8	17
1919	8.3	11.8	2.7	18.9	2.0	19
1920	12.1	12.5	2.7	18.0	4.6	10
1921	15.6	13.2	2.8	19.9	3.7	12
1922	16.6	9.1	1.9	18.7	3.9	11
1923	21.2	12.0	2.4	21.7	4.2	11
1924	28.4	13.4	2.6	22.0	4.8	10
1925	30.8	22.8	4.4	33.0	7.2	10
1926	77.4	63.3	11.8	40.6	9.9	10
1927	181.1	117.9	21.5	42.9	11.3	9
1928	87.1	48.1	8.6	34.3	16.4	10
1929	82.7	65.4	11.4	37.8	18.3	9
1930	98.3	51.0	8.7	41.6	21.1	10
1931	28.6	33.4	5.5	34.1	18.7	8
1932	23.2	37.0	6.0	39.9	21.6	9
1933	25.5	40.7	6.4	32.3	25.3	10
1934	54.9	48.0	7.4	34.3	25.7	9
1935	63.5	57.0	8.6	37.5	32.5	9
1936	63.0	66.8	9.8	36.7	44.9	11
1937	67.7	72.2	10.4	41.3	52.5	11
1940	40.4	90.6	12.6	50.0	62.0	10

Notes to Table Column Heads

A-1, B-1. Revenues, Expenditures. For authorized budgets—which, except for the years 1931–33, always projected revenues to be at least as large as expenditures—see São Paulo, *Colleção das leis*, 1888–1936. Data for 1884–85, 1888–89, and 1897 are taken from São Paulo, Repartição de Estatistica, *Annuario estatistico de São Paulo (Brasil): 1910*, (São Paulo, 1912), v. 2, p. 132. Until 1892, the state's fiscal year ended on June 30; thereafter different periods were used, but all roughly corresponded to the calendar year. Fiscal year 1890 is the period July 1, 1889–June 30, 1890, etc. The figures for the transition period July–December 1891 have been excluded to preserve annual comparability.

A-1. Actual revenues, excluding credit transactions, intergovernment transfers, and specially earmarked revenues for coffee transactions. After 1930, state budgets treated the surtax on coffee exports as ordinary revenue, since the contractual limitations on its use had expired, and I have done likewise. For 1936 and later years, revenues exclude extra-budgetary items, because this category was redefined to include credit operations.

B-1. Actual expenditures, excluding credit operations. During the 1920's, this item included significant extra-budgetary items, outside the appropriations for the *secretarias*. After 1930, B-1 also included the disbursal of the coffee surtax. Coffee valorization costs and debt amortization are not included, except as noted under DS-1, below. I have excluded the purchase price of the Sorocabana Railroad (61,500 contos, 1905) because it was a capital expenditure funded by a special credit operation, as well as the expropriations of the Campos do Jordão Railroad (3,100 contos, 1916), the São Paulo Northern Railroad (15,700 contos, 1920), and the City of Santos Improvement Company (7,100 contos, 1920). I have included the recission of the Sorocabana contract (1920), however; this was a cost, not an investment, since the state already owned the line. The column includes extra-budgetary expenditures from 1928 through 1935; before and after those years it includes only special credits of extra-budgetary expenditures.

A-4, B-4. Revenues and expenditures as percentages of federal government revenues and expenditures. Federal government data from Instituto Brasileiro de Geografia e Estatística (IBGE), *Anuário estatístico do Brasil.* Ano V—1939/1940 (Rio, n.d.), p. 1409.

C-1. Price index, 1879/1880–1940. This index is a splice of a foodstuffs price index through 1929 and a general cost-of-living index from 1921 to 1939. Both were constructed for the city of Rio de Janeiro, for an upper-middle-class family. The price index is based on the prices of nine food staples, using a weight derived for the year 1919 (E. Lobo et al. "Evolução dos preços e do padrão de vida no Rio de Janeiro, 1820–1930—resultados preliminares," *Revista Brasileira de Economia*, 25, no. 4 [1971]: 235–65.) The cost-of-living index was developed by the IBGE, based on prices of food, clothing, rents, personal services, and general household goods; it is available in the *Anuário estatístico*, 1939/1940, p. 1384. The cost-of-living index is clearly superior for our purposes, but it only covers the years 1912–39. The two have been spliced during the 1920's, a period when they behaved similarly. In 1921 the price index was given a weight of .9 and the IBGE index .1; in 1922 the former was weighted .8 and the latter .2; in 1929 the former was weighted .1 and the latter .9. The index number for 1940 is derived from the food-price index in Annibal Villanova Villela and Wilson Suzigan, *Política do governo e crescimento da economia brasileira, 1889–1945* (Rio, 1973), p. 425.

C-2. Value of the Brazilian conto in U.S. dollars, 1892–1940. For the period 1892–1918, the figures are from the *Retrospecto commercial do Jornal do Commercio*, calculated from the mean of the highest and lowest quotation for the U.S. dollar in Rio. From 1919 on, I use New York rates, as cited in U.S. Department of Commerce, *Statistical Abstract of the United States*, various years.

D-1. Public debt. Internal bonded indebtedness, external loans, and the floating debt, consisting of domestic short-term obligations. The foreign debt was recalculated as described in the next paragraph, and added to the internal and floating debts. All loans specifically contracted for coffee valorization have been excluded. These appear as a separate item, Coffee debt, D-4. Note that (1) corrected figures for 1900 appear in the 1901 budget; (2) the floating debt was not reported for 1901–3; and (3) the data include special issues in 1917 and *créditos de diversos* for 1918 and later years.

D-3. Foreign public debt. The foreign debt (excluding coffee loans) was in pounds sterling until 1921, when loans were subscribed for the first time in U.S. dollars and Dutch florins. The state reckoned its foreign loans in milréis, but the official figures for the decades before 1930 had to be abandoned, because all such loans were calculated at their original exchange rate until amortized. Early loans were contracted at the exchange rate of 27 pence per milréis and were quoted at the same rate until the 1920's, when the milréis was only about a quarter of that value. To construct a more meaningful series, I have converted each year's indebtedness to contos at the annual average exchange rate. Until 1921, the procedure was simple: the foreign debt in pounds sterling was converted to contos based on the exchange rates in *Anuário estatístico*, 1939/1940, p. 1354. See note to C-2 for the source on the dollar rate; the florin conversion (to pounds sterling and then to milréis) is based on Netherlands, Centraal Bureau voor de Statistiek, *Statistisch Zakboek*, 1931 (n.p., n.d.), p. 114.

The difference between the debt thus calculated and the book value given in the *relatórios* was about 60% in the 1920's, clearly justifying the additional effort. For 1930 and after, I was able to use the official data, since the fiscal authorities began to figure in a "cost-of-foreign-exchange" factor that brings the debt total to almost exactly the value it would have had at current exchange rates.

D-4. Coffee debt. This debt is not included in the public debt column, D-1. The bulk of the coffee debt was contracted abroad. In 1906–8, however, the state contracted domestic loans, and in 1917–18 the federal government lent the state 110,000 contos. More intergovernment transactions followed in the 1930's.

D-5. Foreign coffee debt. This separates out from the coffee debt all the relevant obligations of the state and two dependent agencies, the State Bank and the Coffee Institute. For the years 1906–29, the value of the debt was recalculated in milréis, in the manner described under D-3. In the 1930's, the debt was adequately accounted for in the *relatórios* of the Secretaria da Fazenda. Supplementary information has been taken from Valentim F. Bouças, *Finanças do Brasil*, v. 3 (part 1) (Rio, 1934), *passim*.

D-7. Combined foreign debt as a percentage of federal foreign debt. Federal debt from *Anuário estatístico*, 1939/1940, p. 1424. The following sectoral expenditures include special credit appropriations and items in extraordinary and extra-budgetary outlays, and are consequently not limited to amounts disbursed by relevant secretariats. In any given year, not all expenditures on public works, for example, are found under the outlays of the secretariat of public works.

DS-1. Debt service. Interest, commissions, and exchange-rate losses, exclusive of those on the coffee debt. This item usually appears in the Secretaria da Fazenda accounts, but sometimes appears in the "credit operations" section of the general balance sheet. A small share of exchange losses was used for amortization, but these were not disaggregated, and so could not be factored out. For 1921–24, the surtax in French francs, originally for coffee operations, was applied in part to servicing the regular debt; beginning in 1925, the surtax was used exclusively to service the 1921 (non-coffee) loan.

J-1. Coffee support. This series was difficult to construct. Operations were extra-budgetary, and included income, outlays, and debt servicing. In no two years were coffee-support operations figured in the same way. Net income is reported in negative entries, and includes the surtax. For 1921–24, the multipurpose use of the surtax makes calculation impossible, and the coffee debt was liquidated in 1924. No valorization costs were listed in the *relatórios* for 1925–29, when the surtax was used against the non-coffee loan of 1921. Because of inconsistent accounting and possible attempts to hide true costs, the figures must be used with caution.

K-1. Immigration subsidy. This item is slightly overstated for a few years when "colonization" is not disaggregated from immigration costs. From 1932 on, it includes a small subsidy for migrants from other states.

M-1. Railroad expenditures. These are the costs of operating the several state railroads and tramways, but not the costs of their acquisition, a capital outlay. Data are not available from 1936 on, because the budgets do not disaggregate expenditures on railroads and highways, and the latter was a growing item.

E-1. Education. The sum of expenditures on education at all levels, including outlays for school construction. Apart from a few items listed by the secretariats of Agricultura and Fazenda, these are outlays made by the Secretaria do Interior. Expenditures on education are slightly understated, because depository expenses (*almoxarifado*) for Interior are not disaggregated. Outlays for 1892, 1893, and 1897 are from São Paulo, Departamento Estadual de Estatística (DEE), *São Paulo: 1889-1939* (n.p., [1940]), p. 9.

E-2. Education, per capita expenditures. Based on population data in DEE, *São Paulo*, p. 7; and IBGE, *Contribuições para o estudo da demografia do Brasil*, 2d ed. (Rio, 1970), p. 24.

I-1. Public works. Includes social overhead capital (excluding railroads, figured separately), but not public office buildings and monuments. Since this item does include sewage systems and water mains, there is a slight overlap with P-1, Public health expenditures. Relevant items were found under Fazenda, Agricultura, Viação, and for 1927-29, extrabudgetary expenditures. The amounts spent on highways in 1936, 1937, and 1940 are not disaggregated in the sources and are slightly understated.

P-1. Public health. Covers expenditures on public hygiene and prophylaxis, health-related research, waterworks and sewage works, asylums, and hospitals. Data for 1936, 1937, and 1940 are estimates, because the expenditures on hygiene, waterworks, and sewage are not disaggregated from public works. The figures given are 32% above the amount for remaining items, reflecting the average share of total public health outlays in 1933-35 for the missing items. Relevant items were found under the outlays of several *secretarias*. (See also I-1, Public works.)

P-2. Public health, per-capita expenditures. Population data from the sources listed for E-2, above.

FP-1, PO-1. Força Pública, Police. These items show the regular operating costs of the state's military and nonmilitary units. They omit special emergency appropriations for military operations in 1894 (3,600 contos), 1924 (4,500 contos), and 1932 (136,800 contos).

Notes

Complete authors' names, titles, and publication data for works cited in short form in the Notes are given in the Bibliography, pp. 355–77. The following abbreviations are used in the Notes:

ABM	Arquivo Borges de Medeiros
AP	Arquivo da Presidência
DEE	São Paulo, Departamento Estadual de Estatística
DGE	Brazil, Directoria Geral de Estatística
IBGE	Brazil, Instituto Brasileiro de Geografia e Estatística
INE	Brazil, Instituto Nacional de Estatística
OESP	O Estado de S. Paulo
SP	São Paulo state entries

Chapter One

1. Gardner, p. 83. Brazil's first national census, dated 1872, was actually carried out in São Paulo in 1874; I have chosen to use the official date, because it appears in all retrospective series and in the companion volumes by Levine and Wirth.

2. Jornal do Brasil, Aug. 7, 1973, p. 6.

3. IBGE, Anuário, 1969, p. 38.

4. Ab' Sáber, p. 19. For a dated but still useful bibliography on the immense geographical literature on São Paulo, see Brazil, Manual bibliográfico.

5. Monbeig, Pionniers, p. 62 (on climate); Little, p. 176 (on wood as fuel).

6. P. E. James, p. 777.

7. United Nations, Coffee, p. 15. Monbeig estimates that only 2% of São Paulo's land is terra roxa, but most students accept the 7% estimate. Pionniers, p. 66.

8. The distinction between demographic and pioneer frontiers is found in Souza Martins, "Frente pioneira," especially pp. 35, 37. Katzman provides a general discussion of the Brazilian frontier in Cities and Frontiers, pp. 10–30. For an example of frontier land title issues and the nature of local justice, see Cobra,

pp. 101, 114, 167, 196, 236. Compare the similar processes and violence in Brazil's frontier regions today, e.g., the violence and intimidation at Rio Maria, Pará, described in *Folha de S. Paulo*, Jan. 8, 1977, p. 5.

9. Alves Motta Sobrinho, p. 119.

10. Prado Júnior, *Colonial Background*, p. 68. Compare Singer's observation (p. 23) that in the colonial era, São Paulo was "principally the commercial entrepôt between the subsistence economy of the interior and the international economy."

11. See the hydrographic map in Aroldo Azevedo, *Brasil*, 1: 541.

12. Davidson.

13. The Portuguese title is *Marcha para oeste (A influência da "bandeira" na formação social e política do Brasil)*.

14. P. E. James, p. 780.

15. To range a bit further afield, it might be said that the historian Afonso de Taunay provided the same cloak of ancient tradition for São Paulo as his contemporary Herbert Bolton did for California. (Admittedly, Bolton had a harder task.) See Taunay's 11-volume study, *História geral das bandeiras paulistas*.

16. Saint-Hilaire, p. 117.

17. Schorer Petrone, pp. 110, 113, 223–24; Singer, p. 26.

18. On the cotton industry in the nineteenth century, see Canabrava.

19. The Paulista railroad, for one, "built behind and not ahead of demand." Mattoon, p. 100.

20. Nogueira de Matos, p. 381; IBGE, *Anuário*, 1939/1940, pp. 235–36.

21. Villela and Suzigan, p. 82; P. E. James, p. 788. James's statement on the density of rail lines refers to the 1960's, but the rail network was virtually completed in the period under study.

22. IBGE, *Anuário*, 1939/1940, pp. 273–75.

23. Monbeig, *Pionniers*, p. 122.

24. Araújo Filho, p. 72; Brazil, *Anuário estatístico do café*, p. 207.

25. Araújo Filho, pp. 72, 74, 90.

26. Viotti da Costa, *Da senzala*, p. 207.

27. *Ibid.*, p. 203–4; Eisenberg and Hall, p. 10.

28. Conrad, *Destruction*, p. 123. See also Slenes for the best discussion of slave population in the late Empire. On p. 76 the author argues that Brazil's slave population was overstated for 1885, and that, therefore, there was no precipitate decline between 1885 and 1887, the year of the last slave count.

29. On the immigrants as "cause," see Beiguelman, pp. 52–53. For a contrary emphasis, see Conrad, *Destruction*, p. 258. A recent general discussion containing new data is Holloway, "Immigration."

30. Hall, "Emigrazione," p. 139.

31. Quoted in *Correio Paulistano*, Sept. 10, 1892, p. 1. Note that colono means a landless rural worker in São Paulo, but a homestead farmer in Rio Grande do Sul.

32. For a discussion of this early experiment with wage labor, see Dean, *Rio Claro*, chap. 4, especially p. 104.

33. On the profitability of slavery in São Paulo in the 1870's and 1880's, see Hall, "Origins," pp. 23–24, 88; and Slenes, chap. 4. Viotti da Costa compares costs from Hamburg to Brazil and to the United States. *Da senzala*, p. 77.

34. Derived from data in T. L. Smith, pp. 122–23.

35. Holloway, "Migration," p. 149.

36. Camargo, 1: 132, 151; for a comparison of immigration to Brazil, the United States, and Argentina, see pp. 150–53. The rate of emigration from São Paulo and Argentina is discussed in chap. 3, below.

37. Ibid., pp. 151, 228; D. Graham, "Migração," p. 30.

38. Correio Paulistano, July 2, 1890, p. 2. Glicério's decree was dated June 28.

39. Republican leaders in the 1888 session of the Provincial Assembly opposed the introduction of Chinese coolies, but four years later Alfredo Ellis, well known for his low opinion of blacks, supported Chinese immigration in Congress. Deputados Republicanos, p. ii; Brazil, Annaes, 1892 (Câmara), 5: 203–5. For a discussion of the Chinese immigration issue, see Conrad, "Planter Class."

40. On this point Paulista planters were in agreement with estate owners elsewhere in the country, according to a survey of the national directorate of the Sociedade Nacional de Agricultura in 1926. Levine, "Some Views," p. 374.

41. The figures in the following discussion are derived from data in Holloway, "Migration," pp. 185–86. (The figures include spontaneous, as well as subsidized immigration.) Holloway includes 314,000 Brazilians in his total number of immigrants (2,537,000); I have excluded them in calculating the percentages of each foreign group.

42. Of the 1,372,000 persons entering Santos between 1908 and 1941, 64% were registered as members of families. Among the national groups, the Japanese had the highest percentage entering in families (95%); at the other end of the scale were the Syrians (51%) and the Portuguese (50%). Knowlton, p. 81.

43. D. Graham, "Internal and Foreign Migration," p. 39.

44. Gov. Júlio Prestes, "Mensagem," July 14, 1929, in SP, Annaes, 1929 (Câmara), 1: 44–45.

45. Carone, República Nova, p. 10.

46. Camargo, 1: 146. A sophisticated set of estimates of São Paulo's net gains through in-migration between 1920 and 1940 is found in D. Graham, "Internal and Foreign Migration," pp. 56, 60. Using alternate statistical techniques, Graham arrives at 433,000 and 356,000 persons; but these figures should not be confused with Camargo's net resident population in 1940.

47. IBGE, Recenseamento, 1940. Série regional, 17(1): 1. The census category for mulattoes changed over the years. They were called mestiços in 1890 and pardos in 1940. (It should be noted that racial data in Brazilian censuses are subject to a wide margin of error.)

48. F. Fernandes, Negro, pp. 62, 65. Fernandes criticizes but does not deny the validity of the tendency these data represent.

49. Ibid., pp. 76, 82, 83, 109, 117.

50. Ibid., pp. 207–21. None of the associations, however, survived into the 1940's. The Frente Negra Brasileira was banned as a political organization with Getúlio Vargas's imposition of the Estado Novo in 1937.

51. Mendes de Almeida, map 17.

52. Lage de Andrade, pp. 159–80, 186, 228 (slaughter of Indians and clashes at railhead); Lévi-Strauss, p. 51 (spreading smallpox among Indians); J. Ribeiro, Chronologia paulista, 2(1): 216 (poisoning); Cobra, pp. 143–45 (poisoning, slaughter of Indian women and children, Capuchin mission).

53. OESP, Dec. 25, 1976, p. 9.

54. Deffontaines, p. 173.

55. Baer and Villela, p. 229 (on data problems); Fishlow, "Origens," p. 25;

Simão, p. 45. Another problem is that the 1919 economic census used a much more restrictive definition of the industrial labor force than the 1920 demographic census.

56. Dean, *Rio Claro*, p. 12. See also Marcílio, pp. 160-62.

57. The 1904-5 census gives the number of properties by size categories, but not the value in each category.

58. For Prado Júnior, 100 alqueires (1 alqueire = 2.42 hectares) is a large property; and Milliet classifies all holdings between 100 and 500 alqueires as large properties, calling anything larger latifundia. Both cited in Camargo, 1: 190. Camargo warns that in São Paulo "a property of 100 alqueires can be a small, medium-sized, or large property," depending on the zone in which it is located. Referring to the Baixa Paulista zone in 1940, he calls properties of 100 alqueires and above large holdings (*Ibid.*, pp. 189, 200). Similarly, Shirley considers 100 alqueires the dividing line between "moderate" and "major" landowners in Cunha, in the Paraíba Valley. *End*, p. 193.

59. Denis, p. 200.

60. IBGE, *Recenseamento*, 1940. *Série nacional*, 2: 74, 92. Because the owners who had both urban and rural properties are not broken down in the census, I have included them with the owners who had only rural properties. Of course, in neither case was the person necessarily a rural resident.

61. McCreery and Bynum, p. 56; Prado Júnior, "Distribuição," p. 699.

62. Beiguelman, p. 80.

63. *Ibid.*, p. 81, referring to Botelho's address to the Sociedade Paulista de Agricultura in 1902.

64. Holloway, "Migration," p. 365.

65. *Ibid.*, p. 415; SP, *Estatística agrícola, 1934-35*, p. 21. Unfortunately, it is not clear in the 1934-35 data whether corporate holdings are included in the census.

66. SP, *Estatística agrícola, 1939-40*, p. 431. Data collected in 1940-41.

67. F. Fernandes, *Integração*, 1: 11; Graham and Buarque, p. 58; Simão, p. 32.

68. Canabrava, p. 288; Simão, p. 69; Maram, p. 52.

69. Penteado, p. 129.

70. Simão, p. 81.

71. Bresser Pereira, pp. 92-93. 83% of the respondents were the founders of the firms studied, and the rest were the chief developers of their respective firms. See also Dean, *Industrialization*, chap. 4.

72. Eisenberg and Hall, p. 22. On the same page Hall points out that vast numbers of immigrants had the good fortune to arrive at the outset of industrialization.

73. "Nearly all Brazilian [industrial] entrepreneurs came from the planter elite. By 1930 there was not a single manufacturer of native-born lower- or middle-class origins, and only a very few appeared thereafter." Dean, *Industrialization*, p. 46.

74. Hutchinson et al., pp. 10-11, 217-19, 225.

75. Nancy Stepan, pp. 66, 137; Blount, pp. 52, 151-52, 196.

76. *Correio Paulistano*, March 13, 1892, p. 1, cited in Blount, p. 53. Compare Nancy Stepan, p. 138.

77. Blount, pp. 74, 127, 141, 166-67.

78. Nancy Stepan, p. 140.

79. Blount, p. 117.
80. DGE, *Recenseamento, 1920*, 5 (3ª parte): 140–41, 144–50, 186–93.
81. Marcus, p. 153; Morse, p. 180; Blount, pp. 120–21, 125–26, 134–35, 156.
82. Blount, p. 170.
83. Monbeig, "Problemas"; Deffontaines, p. 53; Gonçalves de Oliveira.
84. Deffontaines, p. 51.
85. E.g., Deffontaines, Camargo, Milliet. After 1940 highways rather than railroads were most closely associated with rapid growth, and Gauthier's regionalization scheme for the state is based on road grids.
86. Camargo, 1: 192. By the late 1960's the capital had extended its economic network so deeply into the other regions that agrarian communities like Cunha, near the border with Rio State, which had been isolated and remote as late as the 1940's, were being satellized into provisioning bases for a metropolitan area then numbering 7,000,000–8,000,000 people. Shirley, *End*, p. 253 and *passim*.

87. Rocha Nogueira, p. 169.   88. Singer, p. 47.
89. Simão, pp. 43–44.   90. Souza Keller, p. 212.
91. Camargo, 1: 124, 133.
92. Computed from data in *ibid.*, 2: table 22; and IBGE, *Recenseamento*, 1940, 17(1): 56–60. My calculations omit the small number of persons of undeclared race.
93. Camargo, 2: table 11.
94. *Ibid.*, 1: 86.
95. *Ibid.*, pp. 195, 211.
96. *Ibid.*, p. 134 (on immigrants); IBGE, *Recenseamento*, 1940, 17(1): 59–60 (on the black and mulatto population).
97. Godoy, *Projecto*. On the Campanha revolt, see Wirth, *Minas Gerais*, p. 101.
98. See Stein, *Vassouras*.
99. Monteiro Lobato, *Cidades*, p. 6. (The sketches herein were first published as a collection in 1919.)
100. Camargo, 2: tables 58, 59.
101. *Ibid.*, 1: 142.
102. *Ibid.*, 2: table 22.
103. Milliet, p. 30 (on industry); Camargo, 1: 194 (on size of properties); Prado Júnior, "Distribuição," pp. 696–97 (on núcleos coloniais).
104. Camargo, 1: 89, 126, 131, 197; 2: table 22; IBGE, *Recenseamento*, 1940, 17(1): 56–60.
105. Martinez Corrêa, "História," p. 155.
106. Maeyama, p. 37.
107. Camargo, 1: 71, 91, 199, 201.
108. *Ibid.*, pp. 103, 131, 214, 245, 247, 248; 3: table 125.
109. Alceu Barroso, p. 92. For other references to grileiros in the Alta Sorocabana, see Cobra, p. 121; and SP, *Annaes da Assembléa*, 2: 228.

110. Cobra, p. 137.   111. Camargo, 1: 93, 143; 2: table 22.
112. Deffontaines, p. 170.   113. Camargo, 1: 95.
114. *Ibid.*, pp. 128, 142, 144, 247.
115. *Ibid.*, pp. 98, 113; Santos Abreu, *Formação*, p. 118 (on cotton).
116. Camargo, 1: 98; 2: table 41.

117. *Ibid.*, 1: 47.

118. *Ibid.*, pp. 75, 100−101, 141−43; 2: table 21. The Portuguese by 1940 were also the largest group of foreigners in the Capital zone. *Ibid.*, 2: table 52.

119. SP, *Quadro demonstrativo*, pp. 248−49.

120. Villela and Suzigan, p. 296. Note that this differs from Camargo's definition of urban.

121. M. Silva, "Tentativa," pp. 301−2.

122. Nor were there any in three other zones in 1920, namely, the Paraíba Valley, Baixa Paulista, and Baixa Sorocabana. Data from *ibid.*, p. 311.

Chapter Two

1. Estimates for 1920 computed from data in Lyra, pp. 44−45. Lyra's data are from the federal census, which unfortunately made no attempt to measure services as a contributor to national product. Data for 1939 from *Conjuntura econômica*, 24, no. 6: 95. By 1939 the Federal District had passed both Rio Grande do Sul and Minas Gerais in output.

2. SP, *Annaes* (Senado), appendix, p. 7.

3. Mouralis, p. 19.

4. Brazil, *Brasil actual*, pp. 126−27; Brazil, *Quarto centenário*, p. 187.

5. Villela and Suzigan, pp. 73, 74. But the terms of trade might have fallen further without government action to support coffee. International coffee prices rose again in the 1940's, and the terms of trade improved. *Ibid.*, p. 220.

6. Dean, *Industrialization*, pp. 8−10.

7. Villela and Suzigan, p. 334.

8. Between 1883 and 1913 the volume of the world's tropical trade grew at 3.6% a year; though the figure then declined, such trade still grew at an average annual rate of 2.2% between 1913 and 1955. Lewis, *Aspects*, p. 8.

9. McGreevey, p. 196; McCreery and Bynum, p. 56.

10. In a general sense, Lewis asserts that large agricultural units were not required for the efficient production of tropical crops: "Except in sugar and tea, large-scale production was political rather than economic in origin." *Tropical Development*, p. 24. In the matter of coffee, however, the terrain may have helped produce a pattern of smaller estates in Colombia and Minas. On financial institutions and opportunities for investment outside of real estate for large landowners as determinants of land-tenure patterns, see Katzman, "Brazilian Frontier," especially pp. 278, 284.

11. United Nations, *Coffee*, p. 11.

12. Ramos, pp. 200−201; McCreery, p. 64.

13. Taunay, *Pequena história*, p. 397. Taunay notes a nominal price rise by a factor of 100, which I have deflated by the price index in Appendix C. See also Guastini, *Café*, p. 45.

14. Viotti da Costa, *Da senzala*, p. 216.

15. Dean, *Rio Claro*, p. 142.

16. *Ibid.*, p. 140 (citing Robert Conrad), 151, 220n (citing Michael Hall); Slenes, pp. 75−76, 352−53.

17. Foerster wrote in 1919 (p. 284) that "had immigrants not come, the [abolitionist] movement could hardly have made its astonishing headway." For a recent statement, see Holloway, "Immigration," especially p. 176.

18. Hall in Eisenberg and Hall, p. 12; Holloway, "Condições," p. 153. Holloway's estimate that the number of coffee fieldworkers rose from 77,000 in 1887 to 403,000 in 1913 excludes the Paraíba Valley.

19. Brazil, *Questionarios sobre . . . São Paulo*, p. 360, and *Questionarios sobre . . . Rio Grande do Norte*, pp. 20–21.

20. Ramos, p. 201 (for early 1920's); F. Gonçalves, p. 25 (data on plantations for the 1880's refer to Campinas); McCreery, p. 73 (on the late 1920's, excluding capital outlay); Hall, "Origins," pp. 157–59 (on the early 20th century); Cano, p. 65 (Araraquarense zone); Alfredo Ellis, speech in Chamber, Sept. 27, 1902, in Brazil, *Politica*, 1: 81.

21. Cano, p. 21; McCreery, p. 73. Railroads were not the only element in the modernization of coffee-growing in the 19th century. On the mechanization of agriculture, see Viotti da Costa, *Da senzala*, pp. 177–88.

22. McCreery, p. 42 (3% charges at port, 12% on short-term credit in 1929). On the persistence of the 12% rate, see Laërne, p. 213; Alfredo Ellis, speech in Senate, Jan. 14, 1915, in Brazil, *Politica*, 2: 421; and Ramos, p. 483. In 1875 sugar planters in Pernambuco paid up to 6% monthly on short-term loans. Eisenberg, p. 63.

23. Laërne, pp. 212, 213; Ramos, p. 483.

24. Delgado de Carvalho, p. 173.

25. For the 9% interest rate, see advertisement by the Brazilian Warrant Co. in *OESP*, Jan. 2, 1910, p. 11.

26. Edward Johnston and Co., pp. 22, 24–26.

27. On the damage to the comissários' business, see Delgado de Carvalho, p. 174.

28. U.S. Consul Rosenheim to Secretary of State Day, July 27, 1898, in U.S. Dept. of State, dispatches from consuls in Santos, microcopy T-351, v. 5, roll 5; Lalière, pp. 346–47; Associação Commercial de Santos, pp. 35–36.

29. Lopes, p. 67; Zimmermann, p. 145.

30. For discussions of the politics of exchange rates, see Villela and Suzigan, pp. 35–36, 41–42, 46, 49–51, 53; and Carone, *República Velha (Instituições)*, pp. 96–99.

31. Clemenceau, p. 251.

32. Delfim Netto, pp. 53–59, 133; UK Ambassador Seeds to Foreign Secretary Henderson, "Annual Report, 1930," FO 371/15067 3749, p. 35.

33. Peláez and Suzigan, p. 175.

34. Delfim Netto, pp. 53–55.

35. Rodrigues, p. 19; Cândido Rodrigues, speech in Chamber, Aug. 28, 1903, in Brazil, *Politica*, 2: 132. See another plan, involving the destruction of excess coffee, in *OESP*, Jan. 30, 1903, p. 2. Compare the Pernambucano sugar producers' attempts to restrict supply from 1895 to 1909. Eisenberg, pp. 26–27.

36. In technical terms, "The economic prerequisite for unilateral intervention [in an export market] is that the nation's share of the world market for a commodity exceeds the price elasticity of demand for that commodity." For the full argument, see Krasner, "Manipulating International Commodity Markets," p. 494. See also Holloway, *Brazilian Coffee*. Together, the Krasner and Holloway studies offer the best introduction to the complexities of early valorization programs.

37. Krasner, p. 495.

38. Galeão Carvalhal, speech in Chamber, Sept. 23, 1903, in Brazil, *Política*, 1: 158; João Pandiá Calógeras, speech in Chamber, Nov. 18, 1908, in *ibid.*, 2: 20; UK Ambassador Haggard to Foreign Secretary Grey, "Brazil: Annual Report, 1909," FO 371/201 3822, p. 35; UK Ambassador Tilley to Foreign Secretary Curzon, "Brazil: Annual Report, 1921," FO 371/7190, p. 2.

39. Denis, p. 250.

40. And partly with American capital. Krasner, p. 508. On the "coffee trust," see Sensabaugh. On the chief figure in the trust and the organizing genius of the 1908 loan, Hermann Sielcken, see the portrait in Ukers, pp. 448–51, 458–60.

41. Santos, *Política*, p. 425. A later student of the federal debt concurs in Santos's judgment. Bouças, *História*, p. 219.

42. Wileman, p. 432.

43. Denis, p. 259.

44. Krasner, p. 500.

45. Pedro de Toledo, *Discursos*, p. 239, speech in State Chamber, Dec. 14, 1908, and UK Ambassador Seeds to Foreign Secretary Simon, "Brazil: Annual Report, 1931," FO 371/15810 3791, p. 2 (planters to pay); Ramos, p. 503 (exporters to pay); Sociedade Paulista, *Estatutos*, p. 9 (to minimize export taxes on high-grade coffee). Finance Minister Aranha in 1932 was convinced that consumers absorbed the export tax. Aranha to Borges de Medeiros, Rio [1932], Arquivo Aranha (copy). The economist Albert Fishlow has recently demonstrated theoretically that the export tax of the 1930's was largely passed on to the foreign importer and consumer. "Origens," p. 28.

46. Krasner, p. 499.

47. *Ibid.*, p. 505.

48. Toledo, speech in State Chamber, Oct. 15, 1907, in Toledo, *Discursos*, p. 105. Since the number of new trees coming into production did in fact begin to level off in 1907, the year of Toledo's speech, the 1902 law may have been enforced to some degree. (Information courtesy of Thomas H. Holloway.)

49. UK Ambassador Steel to Foreign Secretary Henderson, "Brazil: Annual Report, 1929," FO 371/14207 3746, p. 24.

50. UK Ambassador Seeds to Foreign Secretary Henderson, "Brazil: Annual Report, 1930," FO 371/15067 3749, p. 35; UK Ambassador Steel to Foreign Secretary Henderson, "Brazil: Annual Report, 1929," FO 371/14207 3746, p. 25.

51. Lalière, pp. 346–47; Zimmermann, pp. 122, 136, 148.

52. Lloyd et al., p. 632; Zimmermann, p. 122, 150, 157; Edward Johnston and Co., p. 32; Uebele, p. 111. On shipping, see also Richard Graham, *Britain*, p. 88; and Joslin, p. 160.

53. Lord Churston to S. Guiness, Dec. 11, 1916, FO 371/2640 4111, p. 3.

54. Peláez, "Análise," p. 110. This situation had been foreseen by the British Embassy in 1931: "For a period of ten years Brazil will be assuming the whole burden of destroying an enormous accumulation [of coffee] while other producing countries will reap the benefit; at the end of the ten-year period, therefore, Brazil will find her share in the world coffee supply materially and permanently reduced." UK Ambassador Seeds to Foreign Secretary Henderson, "Brazil: Annual Report, 1930," FO 371/15067 3749, p. 36.

55. Villela and Suzigan, pp. 67, 235; Peláez, "Análise," p. 66; Delfim Netto, p. 328.

56. Dean, *Industrialization*, p. 43.
57. Delfim Netto thought so. *O problema do café*, p. 141.
58. This is Furtado's "socialization of losses" thesis (pp. 205–6). The argument was anticipated by Santos in 1930. *Política*, p. 425.
59. Venâncio Filho, pp. 114–15; Villela and Suzigan, pp. 200–201; Nunes, "História," p. 36. As with other matters affecting coffee, of course, São Paulo was the primary but not the exclusive beneficiary.
60. Peláez, "Análise," p. 192; Peláez, "Balança," p. 47; Stein, *Brazilian Cotton Manufacture*, p. 196.
61. Wirth, *Politics*, pp. 19–20; Villela and Suzigan, pp. 189, 205; Suzigan, pp. 104–5.
62. Brandão Sobrinho, pp. 100, 102; IBGE, *Anuário estatístico*, 1939/1940, pp. 201–2. Though Pernambuco still produced slightly more sugar than São Paulo by weight in 1937, São Paulo then produced 17% of the national output, more than double its 8% share in 1910.
63. International Coffee Organization, p. 62. Values are expressed in 1962 dollars.
64. Data from Brazil, *Anuário estatístico do café*, p. 208.
65. Data from SP, *Relatorio* (Comissão Central), p. 123; SP, *Annuario estatístico*, 1921, 2: 263, 288–91; *Meio século*, unpaginated; Dean, *Industrialization*, p. 193. Note Dean's correction of A. G. Frank's erroneous assertion that São Paulo has had a net import balance in its coastwise trade since 1930. Dean, review of *Capitalism and Underdevelopment*, p. 455.
66. Cano, p. 263.
67. Wirth, *Minas Gerais*, pp. 46, 62.
68. See Dean's list of importers who became industrialists. *Industrialization*, pp. 26–28.
69. *Ibid.*, p. 141.
70. Baer, Geiger, et al., p. 20 (using data from the 1970 industrial census).
71. Baer, "Brazilian Boom," p. 12.
72. Cano, p. 228; IBGE, *Recenseamento*, 1940. *Série nacional*, 3: 184–85. The 1907 census had numerous defects and omitted many firms in São Paulo and elsewhere. For a critique, see Dean, *Industrialization*, pp. 93–94. But Dean does not suggest that São Paulo was more underrepresented than other units of the Federation.
73. *Conjuntura Econômica*, 24, no. 6: 95.
74. E.g., see Ricardo, 2: 246.
75. Suzigan, p. 102.
76. Dean, *Industrialization*, p. 9.
77. Simonsen, writing in the 1930's, seems to be the only student of São Paulo's industrialization who considers climate a significant factor (p. 36).
78. Dean, *Industrialization*, p. 8.
79. *Ibid.*, p. 39.
80. *Ibid.*, pp. 41, 46–47.
81. *Ibid.*, p. 44 (on government support of railroads). The limits of state aid may be inferred from Dean's own statement that "the Paulista entrepreneurs [in manufacturing] operated in an environment of almost perfect laissez-faire" (p. 64).
82. *Ibid.*, p. 37; Mattoon, p. 230.

83. Souza Martins, *Empresário*, p. 36; Stein, *Brazilian Cotton Manufacture*, p. 25 (on the Brazilian cotton industry in general in the 19th century). Compare David Landes's famous thesis on the "family firm" as a limitation on economic growth in France and the subsequent debate, reviewed in Zeldin, 1: 63–76.

84. Dean, *Industrialization*, p. 61; Souza Martins, *Empresário*, p. 43.

85. Souza Martins, *Empresário*, pp. 34–35, 76; Dean, *Industrialization*, p. 63.

86. Zimmermann, pp. 135–36; Cano, p. 171; Paiva Abreu, "Missão Niemeyer," p. 24n.

87. Data from Suzigan, p. 104.

88. Dean, *Industrialization*, p. 46. The categories lower- and middle-class and the term origins are undefined, and are therefore rather vague.

89. *Ibid.*, p. 87.

90. Vilella and Suzigan, p. 71.

91. *Ibid.*, p. 85. See also Baer, *Industrialization*, p. 21.

92. Structuralists include Furtado, Silber, and Cano; the neo-orthodox group, Peláez, Suzigan, and Villela; North Americans, Dean, Stein, Baer, Fishlow, and Leff. There is also a recent Marxist interpretation—Silva's *Expansão cafeeira*—but Silva's terms tend to be vague, and the empirical base is virtually limited to well-known published sources. Frank's *marxisant* view (he does not consider himself a Marxist) lacks a firm empirical base and, as Dean has shown, is wrong on an important change in São Paulo's trade balance (see note 65, above). The classical Marxist overview for industrialization at the national level is Prado Júnior, *História*.

93. For a review of the first assertions by Simonsen (1939) and Prado Júnior (1945) that World War I stimulated the industrialization of São Paulo, see Dean, *Industrialization*, p. 88. For the more recent debate, see Furtado, pp. 211–15; Baer, *Industrialization*, p. 15; Dean, *Industrialization*, pp. 83–104; and Peláez and Suzigan, pp. 195–221. Earlier, Stein emphasized that half the capital equipment of the cotton industry in 1945 had been installed before 1915, and that the industry had therefore not been born during World War I. *Brazilian Cotton Manufacture*, p. 103. See also Leff, "Long-term," pp. 474–76.

94. Peláez and Suzigan, pp. 186, 195–221; Peláez, *História da industrialização*, p. 213.

95. Cano, pp. 67, 147, and *passim*. Cano follows Fishlow on the investment in industry after World War I, and Silva on the growth of new industrial firms and employment from 1915 to 1919. See Fishlow, "Origens," p. 19; and S. Silva, *Expansão*, pp. 101–2.

96. Though women's wages were sometimes higher in São Paulo than in other units of the Federation, women received less than men, and their large numbers in São Paulo industry lowered the overall wage bill. Cano, pp. 122–23, 262.

97. Cano, p. 44. Earlier, Furtado had advanced a similar view without the data (p. 78).

98. Baer and Villela, p. 224.

99. Baer, *Industrialization*, p. 21.

100. Baer and Villela, p. 226; Villela and Suzigan, p. 87.

101. Villela and Suzigan, pp. 366–67; Suzigan, p. 107. Not surprisingly, given wartime shortages, especially in fuel supplies, the rate of growth of industrial output was lower from 1939 to 1945 than from 1933 to 1939. Suzigan, p. 107.

102. Fishlow, "Origens," p. 28; Silber, pp. 39–40.

103. Silber, pp. 47, 54; Fishlow, "Origens," p. 28; Versiani, p. 184. The policy of purchasing coffee also kept the terms of trade from falling lower than they did. Silber, p. 61.

104. Silber, pp. 54, 56, 61, 63. Furtado, originator of the thesis of "unconscious Keynesianism," also hypothesized that coffee planters in the 1930's transferred a significant proportion of their assets to manufacturing. But Peláez offers convincing evidence that most turned to cotton. See his "Análise," p. 192, and "Balança," p. 47. For the pre-1930 years more research is needed on the specific mechanisms, especially in banking, by which capital in coffee was transferred to industry, a process hypothesized by Cano (p. 118).

105. Luz, Luta, pp. 118, 161–63, and passim; Dean, Industrialization, p. 72; Baer and Villela, p. 221; Villela and Suzigan, p. 78.

106. Villela and Suzigan, p. 359. For a contemporary statement of the São Paulo textile industrialists' position, see Centro dos Industriaes.

107. Leme, pp. 360–61.

108. Pupo Nogueira, Em torno, especially pp. 29, 91–112, 136–38.

109. According to Dean, the 1931 tariff in the end resulted in less protection for industry than before. Industrialization, p. 196. But Paiva Abreu asserts that Dean has misread the evidence, and says that in any event the multiple exchange-rate system protected many Brazilian producers from foreign competition in the early 1930's. "Missão Niemeyer," p. 22. In Stanley Hilton's view, Vargas was heavily committed to industrialization in the years 1930–37, but I remain unconvinced; in any case, industrial recovery in the early 1930's was not necessarily closely connected with government policy. For Hilton's argument, see his "Vargas," pp. 756ff. On the damage to São Paulo's manufacturing growing out of Vargas's 1935 reciprocal trade treaty with the United States, see L. Silva, "No limiar," p. 180.

110. Villela and Suzigan, p. 235.

111. Stein, Brazilian Cotton Manufacture, p. 106. Fishlow argues that the availability of short-term domestic credit in the 1890's was "probably" more important than tariff protection in stimulating industrial development. "Origens," p. 16; "Algumas observações," p. 149. On the 1930's, see Silber, p. 56.

112. Villela and Suzigan, p. 79.

113. Pupo Nogueira, "Super-produção textil."

114. Dean, Industrialization, pp. 174, 238.

115. Calculated from data in SP, São Paulo, p. 29, and deflated by the index in Appendix C.

116. IBGE, Anuário, 1939/40, p. 1356, DEE, Boletim, Dec. 1938, pp. 112, 114.

117. U.S. Consul Goforth, report of Sept. 30, 1926, in United States, Decimal File, 1910–1929 832.516/117 (M-519, reel 31).

118. Souza Martins, Empresário, p. 30.

119. Osvaldo Aranha to Getúlio Vargas, n.p., [1931], AP, pasta 2, lata 4: "Interventor: São Paulo."

120. Villela and Suzigan, pp. 79, 216.

121. Laërne, pp. 222–24.

122. Egas, Galeria, 2: 159.

123. Goforth, cited in note 117, above.

124. DGE, *Annuario*, 2: 172.

125. Brazil, *Questionarios sobre* . . . *São Paulo*, pp. 359–60, and *Questionarios* . . . *sobre* . . . *Rio Grande do Norte*, pp. 20–21.

126. Nunes, "História," p. 18.

127. *Ibid.*, pp. 23, 32–33.

128. The two largest private Brazilian banks were the Banco Comercial do Estado do São Paulo in third place, and the Banco do Comércio e Indústria in fourth. The largest foreign bank was the Bank of London and South America, in fifth place. DEE, *Boletim*, Dec., 1938, pp. 112, 114.

129. British Chamber, *São Paulo*, p. 65 (figures exclude banks located outside the state capital); Dean, *Industrialization*, p. 36. On a similar trend in the 1920's at the national level, see Topik, p. 155.

130. Data from DEE, *Boletim*, Dec. 1938, pp. 112, 114. But some foreign-controlled firms may have adopted Brazilian registration. See note 150.

131. [Purport], Oct. 12, 1932, FO 371/15806 3795.

132. Oliveira to J. Henry Schroeder & Co., São Paulo, Sept. 9, 1932, FO 371/15808; U.K. Consul General Abbott [to Foreign Secretary?], Dec. 15, 1930, FO 371/15059 3746, p. 18.

133. DEE, *Boletim*, Aug. 1940, anexo, p. 173.

134. Mattoon, p. 135.

135. Lefevre, p. 448 (gives receipts and expenditures for 1895, 1905, 1915, 1929, and 1930).

136. See details in Mattoon, p. 149.

137. Rippy, p. 154 (source of quotation); Richard Graham, *Britain*, p. 66.

138. U.K. Ambassador Haggard to Foreign Secretary Grey, June 3, 1909, FO 371/201 3822, p. 2.

139. Mattoon, pp. 227, 239.

140. U.K. Ambassador Seeds to Foreign Secretary Simon, March 18, 1935, FO 371/18651 3885, p. 2; DEE, *São Paulo*, pp. 31–32.

141. Monbeig, *Pionniers*, p. 178; Little, p. 83.

142. For a comparison of roads and trucks in Minas Gerais and São Paulo in the 1920's, see Wirth, *Minas Gerais*, Table 2.5, p. 61.

143. IBGE, *Anuário*, 1939/1940, pp. 273–75; Gordon Smith, p. 130. According to Smith (p. 130), in the same year (1939) 95% of the nation's roads were of unimproved dirt.

144. Gordon Smith, p. 221; IBGE, *Anuário*, 1939/1940, p. 282. São Paulo had 19,000 automobiles and 24,000 trucks.

145. Villela and Suzigan, pp. 385–86.

146. Araújo Filho, pp. 72, 74, 91–92, 170.

147. Villela and Suzigan, pp. 385, 388.

148. *Ibid.*, p. 409.

149. IBGE, *Anuário*, 1939/1940, pp. 311–16.

150. E.g., for recent years, see the list of export houses in Lopes, pp. 67–68. Many of these firms are described as Brazilian- or partly Brazilian-owned. Where the mixed firm is a subsidiary of a foreign company, as in the cases of Wille, Anderson-Clayton, and E. Johnston, control is probably retained abroad. On varying intensities of satellization, see Frank, pp. 143–218.

Chapter Three

1. Prado, *Retrato*, pp. 45–88. The bandeirante Fernando Dias Pais (1608–81) probably comes closest in character to Conrad's protagonist.

2. *In memoriam*, pp. 248, 256. Historians now think that the Bueno "crowning" never occurred. See Ellis Júnior, *Lenda*.

3. Brazil, *Annaes* (Congresso), 3: 301; Mesquita Filho, p. 238.

4. A. Salles, *Patria paulista*, p. 255 and *passim*; Godoy, *Provincia*, p. 66.

5. Laërne, p. 308.

6. Osório, p. 143; Coaracy, pp. 41–42, 160.

7. Souza Martins, "Frente pioneira," pp. 35, 37.

8. See the principal laws in Castro Mascarenhas; and SP, *Collecção das leis*, 1921, pp. 167–68.

9. SP, *Collecção das leis*, 1921, p. 168; Alceu Barroso, p. 74.

10. Holloway, "Migration," pp. 314–15, 333–34.

11. Barroso, a state official, estimated that the state government lost 10,000 contos a year in unpaid land taxes in the Alta Sorocabana zone in 1936. "A civilização rural," p. 74.

12. *Ibid.*, p. 94; Lage de Andrade, p. 128; Tavares de Almeida, p. 195; Schmidt, pp. 374–75.

13. According to the agronomist Eugene Davenport, Luís de Queiroz, a prominent fazendeiro in Piracicaba in the 1890's, made a trip to Paraná, "where he secured some thousands of acres of land by the simple device of inducing government clerks to have it 'registered' in his name" (p. 54).

14. Rocha Nogueira, p. 203.

15. Shirley, *End*, p. 117.

16. Hernâni Donato, *Chão bruto*, in Silva Bruno, *Planalto*, pp. 304–5.

17. *Ibid.*, pp. 308, 311.

18. Cândido, *Parceiros*, pp. 155–56.

19. *Ibid.*, p. 163.

20. Monteiro Lobato, *Onda verde*, p. 16.

21. Mário de Andrade, "Casa em que entra bugre," in Silva Bruno, *Planalto*, p. 245.

22. Menotti del Picchia, *Dente de ouro*, in *ibid.*, pp. 197, 201, 207.

23. Monbeig, *Pionniers*, p. 122; Soares Júnior, 2: 370–71; Little, pp. 48, 99.

24. On the frequent marriages of merchants into fazendeiro families in Araraquara, see Martinez Corrêa, "História," pp. 161–62.

25. Dean, *Rio Claro*, p. 44; Maeyama, p. 37.

26. Bassanezi, p. 255 (see note 37); Dean, *Rio Claro*, p. 152; Holloway, "Migration," p. 94; Maeyama, p. 35.

27. Holloway, "Migration," p. 232; Hutter, p. 82; Carlo Castaldi, "O ajustamento do imigrante," in Hutchinson et al., p. 289.

28. Denis, p. 197.

29. Davenport, pp. 44–46.

30. Dean, *Rio Claro*, pp. 173–74.

31. Little, pp. 109–10, 117 (on Magalhães); SNA survey cited in Lowrie, p. 32.

32. The strike in question was in Ribeirão Preto in April and May, 1913. Hall, "Origins," pp. 176–77. Gifun appears to confirm the infrequency of rural strikes. He mentions those of 1905 and 1913, and implies that others took place in

Ribeirão Preto, but gives no details (pp. 175–80). Compare Carone's list of strikes in Brazil during the Old Republic, almost all of them totally urban in nature. *República Velha (Instituições)*, pp. 215–36.

33. F. Gonçalves, p. 18; Foerster, p. 294; Hall, "Origins," pp. 125, 132, 150 (source of quotation).

34. Hall, "Origins," p. 165.

35. Denis, p. 215.

36. Imre Ferenczi, cited in Thistlethwaite, p. 38. Presumably "exit" would be a more accurate term than the author's "repatriation," since migrants did not always return to their country of origin.

37. Bassanezi, p. 255 (on the Fazenda Santa Gertrudes) in Rio Claro; Denis, p. 206. The average (as opposed to the median) length of residence on the Santa Gertrudes estate was 7.6 years for colonos, and 3.1 for camaradas. Bassanezi, p. 255.

38. Denis, p. 200; Little, p. 113; Foerster, p. 296, 298; McCreery and Bynum, p. 26. Dean found the immigrant population of Rio Claro highly male-skewed between 1876 and 1908, but this situation seems exceptional, given planter ideology, the economic usefulness of children on which the ideology was partly based, and immigration figures into Santos (on which, see Chap. 1, note 42). *Rio Claro*, p. 61.

39. Foerster, p. 296; Viotti da Costa, *Da senzala*, p. 225; Laërne, pp. 359–60; Little, pp. 113, 115, 125.

40. Holloway, "Migration," p. 87; Little, p. 115.

41. Holloway, "Migration," pp. 87, 102; Rocha Nogueira, pp. 123–24; Dean, *Rio Claro*, p. 192.

42. Hall, "Origins," p. 145, 180–81 (citing Camargo's data).

43. To convert Holloway's figure of 250,000 to first-generation landowners, we must take into account that one-third of the whole number might have been Brazilian-born, since two-thirds of São Paulo's immigrant stream from 1882 to 1934 had arrived before World War I, a full generation before the 1934 census. If we assume that an equal number (83,000) had been landowners but had died before the census, we again arrive at 250,000, which may now be compared to the total number of immigrants for 1882–1934, i.e., 2,321,000 persons. Following Hall ("Origins," pp. 165–66) that "the overwhelming majority" of Italian immigrants went into agriculture, we may plausibly assume that a minority—say, of 321,000—initially chose to live in the cities. This reasoning yields 2,000,000 rural-bound people who presumably wanted to be landowners, for a "success" rate of 12.5%. Holloway, also speculating, arrives at a higher rate. However, his hypothetical pool of potential landowners seems significantly underestimated by his elimination of women as likely candidates, since the 1940 census showed that 45% of rural property owners in São Paulo were women. See Holloway, "Migration," pp. 168, 426–36; IBGE, *Recenseamento*, 1940. *Série nacional*, 2: 92.

44. Dean, *Rio Claro*, pp. 174, 188.

45. *Ibid.*, p. 190.

46. Little, pp. 178, 181.

47. Uebele, p. 60; Walker, pp. 87, 101–3; Lloyd et al., p. 632; Jardim, p. 211.

48. Monbeig, *Pionniers*, p. 145; British Chamber, *Personalidades*, p. 428; Sampaio Vidal, p. 43. See also Bartolotti, pp. 187–88.

49. Davenport, pp. 18, 23, 30.

50. *Ibid.*, p. 21. Moreira Alves (to his amazement) encountered the same practice of excluding women from the dinner table in Paracatu, Minas Gerais, in 1964 (p. 40).

51. Pierson, *Cruz das Almas* (a pseudonym for Araçariguama), pp. vi, 24, 131, 135, 216. The ancient tradition of *mutirão* (cooperative labor) had died in Araçariguama (p. 70), but it survived in Cândido's Bofete. There too, however, the culture was in crisis, as the capital city drew the community into its commercial orbit. A rising rate of economic failure and normlessness was the result. *Parceiros*, pp. 134–35, 156–57.

52. Cobra, pp. 220, 255, 258.

53. Walker, pp. 43, 45; Gifun, pp. 117–18.

54. Maeyama, pp. 38, 39.

55. Juergen Langenbuch, summarized in Morse, pp. 335–36. (Morse also describes other periodizations.)

56. Leite, *História*, p. 127; Greenfield, pp. 7, 11, 19; Martinez Corrêa, *Rebelião*, p. 104.

57. Greenfield, pp. 27–28, 32, 34. The original Viaduto do Chá was made of steel, but was later replaced by the concrete structure now in use.

58. Leite, *História*, p. 122; Greenfield, pp. 42, 48, 268–93 *passim*; Singer, p. 39.

59. Greenfield, pp. 44–45, 313; Singer, p. 39; Schompré, p. 217.

60. Greenfield, p. 25. Apparently these are undeflated figures.

61. *Ibid.*, p. 311.

62. *Ibid.*, p. 312.

63. F. Fernandes, *Integração*, 1: 9; Graham and Buarque, p. 58.

64. Greenfield, especially p. 323.

65. *Ibid.*, pp. 9, 10. Carone, *Estado Novo*, p. 109.

66. Singer, p. 36; Levi, p. 104; Clemenceau, p. 259.

67. *Correio Paulistano*, Oct. 29, 1874; Leite, *História*, p. 124; Knowlton, p. 252.

68. Silone, p. 210; Salgado, *Extrangeiro*, p. 120.

69. Some old families were related to Mineiro clans, since Paulistas had helped populate Minas during the 18th-century gold rush, and many Mineiro families moved back into São Paulo during the 19th century. There was an important connection in Minas's *zona da mata*, where such Paulista names as Monteiro de Barros, Junqueira, Leite Ribeiro, Cerqueira Leite, Gama Cerqueira, and Arantes appeared. Rebelo Horta, pp. 70, 73, 81–83.

70. Lampedusa, pp. 209–10; J. Silveira, p. 18.

71. Pierson, pp. 127; Berlinck, pp. 131, 136–37.

72. In the late 19th century, scions of the Paula Souza, Vergueiro, Souza Queiroz, and Souza Barros families studied in Germany and Switzerland; those of the Tibiriçá, Prado, and Lacerda families in France; and those of the Toledo Piza, Paula Leite, Alves de Lima, Lacerda Franco, and Pacheco e Silva families in the United States. Pacheco e Silva, p. 22. For engineering studies, Cornell was preferred, apparently because of the efforts of two American engineers and sometime Cornell professors employed by the Cia. Paulista. In 1874 there were 18 Paulistas studying at Cornell. Mattoon, p. 212n.

73. E.g., the Prado Chaves export firm, which originally handled coffee exports

of the related families of Prado, Chaves, Monteiro de Barros, Conceição, and Portela. Levi, p. 263.

74. J. Silveira, pp. 16–19, 24.
75. Saes, p. 30.
76. Morse's phrase (p. 380), summarizing Mário de Andrade. (See Andrade, *O movimento modernista*, especially pp. 30, 34.)
77. J. Silveira, pp. 35–45. 78. Mouralis, pp. 3, 7–9.
79. Lévi-Strauss, pp. 101–7. 80. Hutchinson et al., pp. 12–13.
81. Carlo Castaldi, in *ibid.*, pp. 306, 310, 311.
82. J. Silveira, p. 28.
83. Lévi-Strauss, p. 101.
84. Amado, p. 254.
85. Dean, *Industrialization*, pp. 151–52; Maram, p. 152.
86. Cardim, pp. 24–25, 28–29.
87. Davis and Davis, pp. 248–50, 252. The dollar equivalent of 320 milréis was calculated at the free (rather than the official) rate of exchange in this study. The authors suggest their report has a favorable bias, since information was hardest to obtain on the poorest workers (p. 253).
88. Maram, p. 154; Simão, pp. 70–73; Penteado, pp. 120–22, 125.
89. Maram, 28–29, 33, 41, 166, 176, 192, 196.
90. See Dean's discussion in *Industrialization*, pp. 159–60.
91. Fausto, *Trabalho*, p. 58; Simão, p. 79.
92. Penteado, p. 22; Robert Levine, personal communication.
93. Carlo Castaldi, in Hutchinson et al., p. 349; Penteado, pp. 57, 60, 230, 232; Cândido, *Parceiros*, p. 106.
94. Juó Bananére was the pseudonym of Alexandre Ribeiro Marcondes Machado, author of "La divina increnca" (The Big Screw-up) and other doggerel poems in Italo-Portuguese.
95. Brazil, *Imperio do Brazil*, pp. 330, 334–35, foldout after p. 336; Brazil, *Brasil actual*, p. 154.
96. Thorman, *Completo almanak*, p. 183; Brazil, *Sinopse*, p. 124; *Annuario administrativo*, p. 4282; IBGE, *Anuário estatístico*, 1939/1940, pp. 350–51.
97. One new periodical was founded in São Paulo in 1870–79; eight in 1880–89; 27 in 1890–99; 82 in 1900–09; 115 in 1910–19. Brazil, *Estatística da imprensa*, p. 123.
98. *Ibid.*, pp. vii, ix.
99. *Annuario administrativo*, p. 4290; Brazil, *Estatística da imprensa*, p. 135. Rio Grande do Sul, with 26, had the second-largest number of dailies in 1929; Minas followed with 15, and Pernambuco had 14.
100. Goulart, p. 345; Sousa, p. 65; British Embassy, "Annual Report 1935," FO 371/19767 3903, p. 37.
101. Brazil, *Estatística da imprensa*, p. xi.
102. See SP, *São Paulo*, last unpaginated map at end of text for airlines data.
103. British Embassy, "Annual Report 1935," FO 371/19767 3903, p. 37.
104. IBGE, *Anuário*, 1939/1940, p. 1404.
105. Penteado, pp. 189, 191, 195.
106. *OESP*, Jan. 3, 1915, p. 13.
107. Martinez Corrêa, "História," p. 325; IBGE, *Anuário*, 1939/1940, pp. 1122–23.

108. In 1950, São Paulo passed Rio Grande, to lead the nation in literacy (59%). DGE, *Recenseamento*, 1920, 4: x–xi; IBGE, *VI Recenseamento*, p. 257.

109. Based on data in Brazil, *Relatorio e trabalhos*, p. 27, and unpaginated table on population and instruction, 1872; and U.S., *Historical Statistics*, pp. 7, 207. P. 27 of the *Relatorio* gives one pupil in Brazil for 56 inhabitants, but the table indicates one pupil in primary and secondary schools for every 68 inhabitants. If we assume that university students were excluded in the first calculation, and, that at a maximum, they were as numerous as secondary students, the ratio would only rise to one to 63.

110. SP, *Relatorio* (Commissão Central), pp. 116–17; O'Neil, "Search," p. 15.

111. SP, *Estatística escolar*, pp. xxi–xxii; Lefevre, p. 243; SP, *São Paulo*, p. 7.

112. Marcus, especially pp. 122, 125–26, 150–52; Motta, *Cesário Motta*, pp. 93–97.

113. O'Neil, "Search," pp. 15, 17, 19.

114. *Ibid.*, p. 71.

115. *Ibid.*, pp. 92–98, 103, 108, 109. See educational budget data and price deflator series (in which 1912 = 100) in Appendix C.

116. SP, *Estatística escolar*, p. xxi; O'Neil, "Search," pp. 109, 129. Sampaio Dória resigned in May 1921, discouraged by the government's neglect of the 3rd and 4th years of schooling. O'Neil, "Search," pp. 118, 120.

117. O'Neil, pp. 103–4, 106, 126–27.

118. *Ibid.*, pp. 129–30.

119. Denis, p. 177; Mauro, 2: 78. The percentage of school-age children enrolled only reached 22% in 1929; in these figures, however, the range for the school-age population is seven to twenty-three years, which gives a downward bias to the achievement.

120. Nagle, p. 273; O'Neil, "Search," p. 142; Levine, *Pernambuco*, pp. 70–71.

121. O'Neil, "Search," pp. 226, 261.

122. *Ibid.*, p. 340; O'Neil, "Educational Innovation," p. 62.

123. I follow Fernando de Azevedo's definition of a "modern" university (p. 514n): one in which there exists a faculty of arts and sciences, rather than a simple combining of existing professional schools. See also O'Neil, "Educational Innovation," p. 60.

124. O'Neil, "Educational Innovation," pp. 62, 64.

125. The Estado Novo, however, put a damper on social research. *Ibid.*, pp. 63–66.

126. *Ibid.*, pp. 56–58.

127. For Everett Hagen's thesis on Antioquia and the subsequent debate, see his *On the Theory of Social Change*, pp. 353–84; Safford; McGreevey, pp. 190–94; and López Toro. On Monterrey, Nuevo León, see Strassmann, especially pp. 166, 177.

128. Prado, *Retrato*, p. 64; G. Barroso, *Sinagoga*, pp. 9, 22, 23, 54, 65, 142.

129. Piza, pp. 145–63.

130. DGE, *Annuario*, 1: 252, and 3: 192; and IBGE, *Recenseamento*, 1940. *Série nacional*, 2: 1, 142.

Among other religions, the Positivist cult was minuscule. In 1910 only 151 persons in the entire country professed Comte's Religion of Humanity. DGE, *Annuario*, 3: 230. Positivism's influence may have been out of proportion to its numbers, but even in its secular mode, its adherents were not prominent among

Paulista politicians after the consolidation of the Republic in 1891 (see Chap. 4). Luís Pereira Barreto, coffee planter, physician, and member of the São Paulo political elite at the beginning of the Republic, was the first to diffuse Comtian Positivism in Brazil through his book *As Tres Philosophias* (1874–76) cited in Lins, p. 84. To some Paulistas, however, Positivism may have seemed as bizarre as the burlesque that appears in Machado de Assis's *Memórias póstumas de Brás Cubas* (1880). On Positivism in São Paulo, see Lins, pp. 138–74.

131. Trindade, p. 94.

132. W. Martins, *Modernist Idea*, p. 15; Cavalheiro, p. 276. On the background of Modernism, see Silva Brito. An excellent documentary collection is Batista et al.

133. See, for example, Bardi, pp. 27–28.

134. Marson, p. 1037; W. Martins, *Modernist Idea*, pp. 62–63; Lara, "Klaxon," p. 30.

135. See note 21, above.

136. See the third chapters in the companion studies by Levine and Wirth.

137. Cândido, *Literatura*, p. 141.

138. Bandeira, quoted in Dassin, p. 67.

Chapter Four

1. Tavares Bastos, especially pp. 286, 292.

2. Marcus, pp. 28, 92, 94.

3. Oliveira Torres, p. 356. The other two provinces were Rio Grande do Sul and Rio de Janeiro, both of which had significant Republican movements.

4. Marc, 2: 178. On underrepresentation, see Viotti da Costa, "Proclamação," pp. 191–93; and the section on "Representation and Elections," below.

5. Tavares Bastos, p. 355; *A Provincia de S. Paulo*, March 3, 1889, p. 1.

6. On separatism, see the contemporary literature: A. Salles, *Patria paulista*; Laffitte Junior; Ribeiro de Andrada, p. 485; C. Martins, *Necessidades* (implicitly separatist). See also Campos Salles, pp. 39, 273; Boehrer, pp. 111, 236; and Almeida. The creation of new provinces was likewise a widely discussed theme in Minas and São Paulo in the closing years of the Empire.

7. Boehrer, p. 265; Mennucci, p. 161. Boehrer says that Gama remained a Republican, but his biographer, Mennucci, clearly implies he left the PRP.

8. Boehrer, p. 268.

9. Santos, *Republicanos*, p. 225.

10. *Deputados republicanos*, p. ii. On the Republicans' consistent support of immigration, see Bresciani, 1: 231.

11. Boehrer, pp. 80–81.

12. *Ibid.*, pp. 84, 86, 97–99; Debes, p. 100.

13. Laërne, p. 70.   14. Boehrer, pp. 87–89.

15. *Ibid.*, pp. 86–87.   16. *Ibid.*, p. 96.

17. *Ibid.*, pp. 107–8. Andrade Botelho, the Republican from Minas, also lost his seat.

18. Debes, p. 139; Campos Salles, p. 41.

19. Calculations based on data in Boehrer, p. 117, and IBGE, *Anuário estatístico*, 1971, p. 41.

20. Almeida, p. 40; Assis Cintra, *Bernardino de Campos*, pp. 47–48.

21. Assis Cintra, "Nos alicerces."

22. Costa Nogueira, p. 391.
23. Godoy, *Projecto*, pp. 5, 98, 170; Beiguelman, p. 61.
24. Toplin (p. 211) names six municípios that experienced revolts, all in the West. On the politics of abolition in São Paulo, see also Conrad, *Destruction*, Chap. 16; Luz; "Administração"; Hall, "Origins"; Holloway, "Immigration"; Viotti da Costa, *Da senzala*; and Beiguelman.

25. Toplin, p. 219.
26. Braudel, 2: 1243.
27. Luz, pp. 96, 98.
28. Eisenberg and Hall, p. 12.
29. Oliveira Carvalho, p. 97.
30. Boehrer, p. 114.
31. *Correio Paulistano*, April 13, 1887; Oliveira Carvalho, pp. 114, 117, 125; *A Provincia de S. Paulo*, June 20, 1889; *Diario Popular*, Aug. 21, 1889, p. 3.
32. *O Federalista*, Sept. 29, 1889, p. 2.
33. Santos, *Republicanos*, p. 277; Oliveira Carvalho, p. 111.
34. *Deputados republicanos*, p. 289.
35. Campos Salles, p. 43–44; Assis Cintra, "O P. R. P."
36. Barão de Lucena to Américo Brasiliense, Rio, March 1891, in Brasiliense, "Correspondência," p. 217.
37. Wirth, *Minas Gerais*, pp. 99–101.
38. In late November Floriano pretended to favor Brasiliense's continued tenure. But he removed a battalion from São Paulo against Brasiliense's request a week before he was overthrown, and ordered the military commander in São Paulo city to remain neutral in the disorders of December 14. Antônio Souza Campos to Brasiliense, Rio, Nov. 29, 1891, Min. of War João Simão Oliveira to Brasiliense, Rio, Dec. 8, 1891, and Gen. Carlos Machado Bitencourt to Brasiliense, São Paulo, Dec. 14, 1891, in Brasiliense, "Correspondência," pp. 241–42. On the violence that culminated in Brasiliense's downfall, see Oliveira Mello.
39. Brasiliense was a positivist of sorts, but Comtism seems to have had relatively little influence in the state government after his ouster. Luís Pereira Barreto, another positivist, fell from the PRP executive committee with Brasiliense in 1891. The positivist Alberto Sales served briefly in Congress. Gabriel Toledo Piza, who represented Brazil for many years as ambassador to France, was a positivist, but he played little or no role in the affairs of the state. See Lins, *História do positivismo*, pp. 45–92, 138–74, especially pp. 147, 152–53, 155, 160.
40. Assis Cintra, "Dissolução."
41. Compare the purge of the state supreme court that accompanied the executive committee purge. Shirley, "Judicial System," p. 39.
42. Arquivo *OESP*, pasta 5,050.
43. Ellis Júnior, *Parlamentar*, p. 368.
44. Adolfo da Silva Gordo was the brother-in-law of Antônio Carlos Ferraz Sales, who was the father-in-law of Paulo Morais Barros, who in turn was the nephew of Prudente de Morais. Cerqueira César was the father-in-law of Júlio de Mesquita.
45. Carone, *República Velha (Evolução)*, 186. Partido Republicano, *Scisão 1901*, pp. 105, 341. An additional irritant was a new state constitution in 1901 with a four-year term for the governor, imposed on the legislature by Gov. Rodrigues Alves. *Ibid.*, pp. 41–42.
46. *OESP*, Nov. 6, 1901, pp. 1–2.
47. See Prudente de Morais to Júlio de Mesquita, Piracicaba, SP, June 29, 1901, Arquivo Prudente de Morais.

48. Arquivo *OESP*, pastas 2,965 and 22,750; Thorman, *Almanak*, 1897, pp. 342–43; *Almanak-Laemmert*, p. 376; *Annuario commercial*, p. 419.

49. *OESP*, Sept. 25, 1907, p. 5. Earlier, however, Campos Sales had tentatively approved of the Taubaté convention. Melo Franco, 2: 460.

A more remote "ideological" consideration may have been the fact that Albuquerque Lins was an ex-monarchist, but the precedent of a former monarchist in the governor's mansion had been set by Rodrigues Alves in 1900–1902.

50. Martinez Corrêa, "História," pp. 333–38; Cobra, p. 191; Jardim, p. 206.

51. For details on the infighting, see Guastini, *Politica*. On common business interests, see Subiroff, pp. 13, 24 (Arantes and Rodrigues Alves family), 35–36, 119 (J. M. Rodrigues Alves, Olavo Egídio Sousa Aranha, Alvaro de Carvalho); and Schompré, p. 159 (J. M. Rodrigues Alves and Sampaio Vidal). But Arantes also had business ties with Carlos de Campos, the victor in the gubernatorial contest. Subiroff, p. 13.

52. Carone notes that this power derived less from the executive committee than the regional bosses. But the bosses either sat on the committee or designated trusted associates to represent them there. Carone and Arantes Junqueira, p. 138.

53. Two chefes of the Old Republic, Ataliba Leonel and Fernando Prestes de Albuquerque, virtually monopolized public works in southwestern São Paulo for their home municípios of Piraju and Itapetininga, respectively. Santos Abreu, *Formação*, p. 301.

54. Carone and Arantes Junqueira, pp. 144–46, 147, 149–50, 158, 159–61 (May 1, 1892, Feb. 25, 1893, Oct. 13, 1893, Feb. 4, 1896, April 16, 1896). These documents were not destroyed with the PRP archive because they were the personal property of Gov. Altino Arantes.

55. Partido Republicano, *Scisão*, p. 249.

56. The annual salary of 4:800 in 1895 was slightly less than that of a lieutenant colonel in the Força Pública; thus it was a full-time if modest salary. Carone and Arantes Junqueira, p. 156; Heloísa Fernandes, pp. 238–39.

57. Tarrow, especially pp. 68–69, 74.

58. Carone and Arantes Junqueira, pp. 149–50, 159–61.

59. E.g., Augusto Azevedo, *Factos*, pp. 16, 44–45, 47–49.

60. Carone and Arantes Junqueira, pp. 193–97 (Nov. 22, 1913).

61. *Ibid.*, pp. 199, 206 (June 5, 1916, June [should be July] 12, 1920); *Correio Paulistano*, Dec. 7, 1922, p. 3.

62. Walker, p. 109; A. Ribeiro, *Falsa democracia*, p. 59; Santos Abreu, *Formação*, pp. 211–12.

63. Melo Franco, 2: 774; Guastini, *Café*, p. 27; A. Ribeiro, *Falsa democracia*, p. 61; Guastini, *Politica*, pp. 205–7. On the power of the governor over the executive committee in the mid-1920's, see also Macedo Soares, p. 11.

64. For data, see Appendix C.

65. For further details on participation by generation, see Chap. 5.

66. Though established shortly before Washington Luís's unopposed election as President, the PD was not founded for the purpose of affecting the outcome of that race; nor did it run a candidate in the 1927 gubernatorial contest. On the background of the party, see Carone, *República Velha (Instituições)*, pp. 313–14; *(Evolução)*, p. 399; Nogueira Filho, Part I; and Fausto, *Revolução*, pp. 32–38.

67. See text of PD manifesto in Nogueira Filho, Part 1: 641–42.

68. See Fausto, "Revolução," p. 263; *Revolução*, pp. 32–38; and the critique of Fausto's thesis on the PD in Chap. 5.

69. Unfortunately, the figures on PRP dues have not survived except for the year 1895 (23:120$000). Comparing that amount on a deflated basis (1912 = 100) to the PD dues in 1930 (55:206$000) yields a figure of 29:082 for the PRP and 22:719 for the PD. On the PRP dues, see Carone and Arantes Junqueira, pp. 151–56; on the PD dues, see Arquivo do Partido Democrático, Livro 24: Livro de contribuições, no. 1, *passim*. For the price index, see Appendix C. (Note that the PD was an opposition party till the end of Nov. 1930.)

70. Love, *Rio Grande do Sul*, p. 212.

71. On the national Legião Revolucionária, see Flynn.

72. Carvalho e Silva, p. 15; Klinger, 7: 401.

73. U.S. Consul Cameron to Chargé Thurston, "São Paulo Political Report no. 48," July 30, 1932, United States, Decimal File 1930–39, 832.00/810, p. 33.

74. There are 600 such items in Leite's 1962 bibliography, "Causas"; and more memoirs have subsequently appeared, including Nogueira Filho's four-volume *A guerra cívica*. There is a good short account by the journalist Glauco Carneiro, "A Revolução Constitucionalista," but no major scholarly study has yet appeared on this important subject.

75. UK Consul General Abbott to Foreign Secretary Simon, Oct. 12, 1932, FO 371/15809, p. 10.

76. There is some disagreement on how much São Paulo's working class backed the revolutionary movement. See K. F. J. Edwards, "Extract . . . 15th August 1932," FO 371/15808, p. 10 (estimating partial support). A *Plateia*, with a working-class readership, supported the revolt (e.g., see issue of July 12, 1932, p. 1); opposing radical papers were suppressed, but the anarchist A *Plebe* subsequently condemned the revolt. See Arquivo Leuenroth, issue of Jan. 7, 1933, pp. 2, 3. On the popularity of the constitutionalist cause in the interior, see Walker, p. 149; and Santos Abreu, *Formação*, p. 266.

77. A British diplomat thought that morale was still higher in the Paulista forces than among the federal troops as late as the first week of September. UK Ambassador Keeling to Foreign Secretary Simon, Sept. 5, 1932, FO 371/15809, p. 2.

78. U.S. Ambassador Morgan to Secretary of State Stimson, Nov. 21, 1930, United States Decimal File 1930–39, 832.00/694, pp. 5–6; U.S. Military Attaché Sackville, "Federal Active Operations," no. 1055, Nov. 18, 1932, *ibid.*, 832.00/444. Sackville's estimate of killed and wounded is only for federal troops, and I have used this same number for São Paulo's losses.

79. U.S. Military Attaché Sackville, "Tenth Week of São Paulo Revolt," no. 1035, Sept. 15, 1932, *ibid.*, 832.00/410.

80. Paula, p. 206; Guastini, *Café*, p. 79. See the discussion of the Federação das Associações de Lavradores in Chap. 7.

81. U.S. Consul Cameron to Ambassador Gibson, "São Paulo Political Report, no. 58," Aug. 17, 1933, United States, Decimal File 1930–39, 832.00/861, p. 2.

82. UK Consul General Abbott to Chargé, Aug. 27, 1934, FO 371/17486 3884, p. 2.

83. Data from *OESP*, Jan. 11, 1935, p. 4.

84. For the PC manifesto, see *OESP*, Feb. 28, 1934, p. 4. In 1934 even the Socialist Party found it convenient to include an appeal to bairrismo in its motto: "For a strong São Paulo in a united Brazil."

85. The returns in detail are found in *OESP*, April 4, 1936, p. 4.

86. U.S. Chargé Scotten to Secretary of State Hull, July 1, 1937, United States, Decimal File 1930–39, 832.00/1040, pp. 2–3.

87. U.S. Consul Foster to Ambassador Caffery, Oct. 2, 1937, in *ibid.*, 832.00/1057, p. 3.

88. Basbaum, pp. 164–65, 173.

89. UK Ambassador Gurney to Foreign Secretary Eden, Jan. 7, 1937, FO 371/20603 3910, p. 2.

90. U.S. Chargé Scotten to Secretary of State Hull, Oct. 20, 1937, United States, Decimal File 1930–39, 832.00/1064, pp. 5–6, and Dec. 23, 1937, 832.00/1155, p. 3.

91. *Ibid.*, Oct. 20, 1937, 832.00/1064, pp. 5–6.

92. *Ibid.*, April 29, 1938, 832.00/1193, p. 2.

93. UK Ambassador Gurney to Foreign Secretary Halifax, May 10, 1938, FO 371/21422 3984, p. 1.

94. Dean, *Industrialization*, pp. 191–212, *passim*; Clovis de Oliveira; Federação das Indústrias do Estado de São Paulo, Circular 823, May 17, 1937. Dean sees the industrialists' change of attitude as correct (regarding their self-interest), given that Vargas changed his priorities from agriculture to industry in this period.

95. See Love, "Political Participation," pp. 7ff.

96. See, for example, Marcus.

97. And even later, though it competed with the federal government in the 1930's.

98. His efforts to attract large numbers of immigrants from northern Europe were not successful, though they probably had political value at the time.

99. From 1907 to 1919 the Sorocabana Railroad was leased to a private company.

100. A high-ranking judge in 1921 received 28:800$000 (almost £1,000). Shirley, "Judicial System," pp. 49–52.

101. At the beginning of his term as governor, Washington Luís also reorganized the state's debt, facilitating the establishment of the State Bank under Carlos de Campos, his successor. Washington Luís's school reforms took away a form of "patronage" from local notables, but (as noted in Chap. 3), Campos turned the control of schools back to local authorities.

102. Heloísa Fernandes, pp. 157–59; Dallari, *Pequeno exército*, p. 44.

103. Soares Júnior, 1: 39.

104. Heloísa Fernandes, pp. 241, 245; Brazil, *Almanak*, pp. 935–36 (contains salaries for 1910 and 1927); Brazil, *Relatorio* (Ministério da Guerra), p. 71; SP, *Collecção das leis*, 1909, tomo 19: 12–13; SP, *ibid.*, 1926, tomo 36: 42–43.

105. Almost 26% of the enlisted men and 10% of the officers were foreign born in 1911. Heloísa Fernandes, pp. 171–72.

106. Clemenceau, p. 247.

107. Andrade and Câmara, pp. 32–33; SP, *Collecção das leis*, 1931–37. All figures are the Força's authorized strengths.

108. Data from Appendix C.

109. Heloísa Fernandes, p. 162.

110. Yet there seems to have been a woeful lack of professionalization in the field operations and intelligence work among the rebels and loyalists in both the army and the Força Pública. One military observer went so far as to call one battle in 1924 a caricature, since there was virtually no contact between the two groups. Though the rebels left the capital on the night of July 27–28 fully armed and traveling by train, the loyalist troops only learned of the fact from civilians. Noronha, pp. 107–41, especially pp. 136, 138. The best general account of the revolt of 1924 in São Paulo is Martinez Corrêa, *Rebelião*.

111. Information on Galinha's career from Figueiredo. Most of the book is based on interviews with persons who remembered Galinha in the late 1940's, but the author also used the lieutenant's official dossier.

112. *Correio Paulistano*, Jan. 10, 1900, p. 2.

113. Heloísa Fernandes, p. 149; Vieira and Silva, pp. 201–5, 219–20.

114. Cobra, p. 122.

115. See Dean, "Latifundia."

116. Inferred from Cobra, p. 226.

117. For an example, see Santos Abreu, *Formação*, pp. 87, 90.

118. See *Manifesto das camaras municipaes de S. Paulo reunidos em congresso* (São Paulo, 1896). Washington Luís, who was a municipalista in his early career, took on the state government in a constitutional dispute as intendant (i.e., prefect) of Batatais. Washington Luís to Rui Barbosa, Batatais, July 8, 1898, Arquivo Rui Barbosa.

119. *Correio Paulistano*, Jan. 10, 1900, p. 2.

120. Nunes Leal's *Coronelismo enxada e voto* is the classic work on the subject. Pang's "The Politics of Coronelismo in Brazil" is the best case study of a single state (Bahia). For additional bibliography, see Love, "Political Participation," pp. 10–11; for a comparative treatment, see Kern.

121. Santos Abreu, *Formação*, especially pp. 210–11; Castilho Cabral, p. 3.

122. Walker, Chap. 4, especially p. 80; see also Jardim, pp. 199–215.

123. Santos Abreu, *Formação*, p. 219.

124. In the early years of the Republic, Col. Cunha Junqueira in Ribeirão Preto controlled the juiz de direito. Jardim, p. 201. Leonel successfully pressured the juiz de direito to recognize his favorites in Presidente Prudente in the município elections of 1922. Santos Abreu, *Formação*, p. 213.

125. Cobra, p. 147; Monbeig, *Pionniers*, p. 125.

126. *OESP*, Dec. 28, 1928, p. 6, Dec. 30, p. 3; Dep. Cyrillo Jr. in *Correio Paulistano*, Dec. 28, 1928, pp. 3, 4.

127. See Conniff, pp. 42–75.

128. The PRP's responsibility in blocking justice in the Carvalho crime is indicated by the lawyers the executive committee sent to defend him, including former governor Cerqueira César. The *juiz de direito* resigned rather than preside over the trial. Martinez Corrêa, "História social," pp. 248–51.

129. See, for example, Santos Abreu, *Formação*, p. 217, and Nogueira Filho, *Partido*, 1: 320–23 (cheating on totals); Cobra, p. 231 (voting illiterates); Arthur Paes to PD directorate, [Ipiranga?], Nov. 10, 1928, Arquivo do Partido Democrático; *Correio Paulistano*, Jan. 10, 1900, p. 2, and Martinez Corrêa, "História social," p. 333 (illegal registration and voting the dead); A. Ribeiro, *Falsa democracia*, p. 130, Santos Abreu, *Formação*, p. 217, and Nogueira, "Movimentos," p. 241 (vote buying); and Martinez Corrêa, "História social," p. 332, Santos

Abreu, *Formação*, p. 212, Cobra, pp. 114ff, 259–60, and Lage de Andrade, pp. 131–44 (murder and other political violence). For an official attempt to refute charges of violence, see Moraes Filho.

130. Santos Abreu, *Formação*, p. 282; Walker, p. 158.

131. Ferreira Lima, p. 492.

132. Campos Sales to Prudente de Morais, São Paulo, Aug. 25, 1897, Arquivo Prudente de Morais.

133. Soares Júnior, 2: 473.

134. *Ibid.*, pp. 473–75. In 1907 and 1909 the Assis Brasil two-stage voting system was adopted for município and state elections, respectively.

135. *OESP*, Jan. 13, 1912, p. 10.

136. Vasconcellos, pp. 21–29.

137. In the 1890 Constituent Assembly elections, 35,000 of the 42,000 voters supported the official Republican (and anticlerical) slate. Soares, 1: 260.

138. Ralliement was implemented in 1892, though its earliest indications had come in November 1890.

139. On the Catholic Electoral League and Leme's involvement, see Williams, "Politicization" and "Integralism."

140. Arruda Dantas, pp. 58–64; Silveira Camargo, 2: 68.

141. Margaret Williams notes that the chief opponent of Leme's tacit alliance between the Church and the Integralists was Bishop Gastão Liberal Pinto of São Carlos, São Paulo. Since the bishop was a personal friend of Archbishop Leopoldo e Silva, the archbishop may have used the bishop as his surrogate to oppose the Cardinal on the matter. See Williams, "Integralism," pp. 433, 448; and Silveira Camargo, p. 70. In a letter to the Catholic clergy of São Paulo on the 1934 elections, Dom Duarte instructed them not to take a position in favor of any political party. Leopoldo, pp. 134–38. Nonetheless, *O Operário*, a Catholic labor newspaper in São Paulo, occasionally printed articles implicitly favorable to Integralism. For example, in 1934 it ran an unsigned commentary denouncing liberalism, democracy, and "international Jewish capitalism," and supporting a "wholesome nationalism." *O Operário*, Sept. 23, 1934, p. 6, Arquivo Leuenroth.

142. Carone, *República Velha (Instituições)*, pp. 381–82, 189–92.

143. Jaguaribe, "The Dynamics," p. 182.

144. On Salgado's early career, see Trindade, *Integralismo*, pp. 13–133. The term Integralismo had already been adopted in 1914 by a reactionary group in Portugal modeled on the Action Française, but it seems to have had no direct influence on Salgado. In a broader sense, Brazil had had an authoritarian tradition of sorts since the beginning of the Republic in *florianismo* and *jacobinismo*, and the positivist ideology that accompanied them.

145. Dulles, *Anarchists*, p. 11. On radical groups in Brazil down to 1922, see also Moniz Bandeira et al., and Leuenroth.

146. Dulles, *Anarchists*, p. 514.

147. In a 1912 survey of 31 textile factories by the São Paulo Department of Labor, 59% of the work force was Italian-born, and only 18% Brazilian-born. Carone, *República Velha (Instituições)*, p. 190. See also Chap. 1, above.

148. The Adolfo Gordo laws were passed by Congress in 1907 and 1921; Azevedo's bill was also approved in 1921. On the legislation and its uses, see Dulles, *Anarchists*, pp. 20, 60, 116, 139; and Carone, *República Velha (Instituições)*, p. 238.

149. Dulles, *Anarchists*, pp. 489, 494–95; Carone, *República Nova*, p. 251; Basbaum, pp. 121–23, 140, 164–65, 173, 191 (source of quotation). A chronology of PCB history is found in Chilcote, pp. 333–39.

150. Consul Foster to Ambassador Gibson, "Political Report no. 2," Oct. 22, 1934, United States, Decimal File 1930–39, 832.00/916, p. 10; Carone, *República Nova*, pp. 251, 271.

151. Carone, *República Nova*, p. 332.

152. Only 3,919 foreigners were naturalized in the whole country between 1889 and 1905, according to Wileman, p. 37.

153. DGE, *Recenseamento*, 1920, pp. x–xi; Brazil, VI *Recenseamento*, p. 257. In the 1950 census São Paulo passed Rio Grande in literacy (59.4% to 58.6% of the population age five and older), and thus took first place among the states.

154. In all cases, data employed in these calculations are those counted as the final verified (*apurada*) vote. See Brazil, *Diario: 1894–1906, 1914–1930* (for precise references, see Love, "Autonomia," p. 56); DGE, *Annuario*, 1: 66; and Brazil, *Boletim eleitoral*, March 26, 1934, p. 388, Feb. 22, 1936, p. 498. For the 1933 and 1934 elections, Minas's voter registration was larger than São Paulo's, though São Paulo led in votes cast and validated. The gap between São Paulo and the other states in vote totals has progressively widened since the Second World War. In the 1970 congressional elections, São Paulo accounted for twice as many votes as Minas, still in second place. IBGE, *Anuário estatístico*, 1971, p. 816.

155. For sources on voting data in 1892 and 1936, and population data in 1890 and 1934, see Table 4.2. Although a comparison of the adult (voting age) population and turnout would be more meaningful, data by age groups are not available in these censuses. Registration figures for federal elections show a similar albeit less dramatic increase. Though registration, like participation, rose and fell, the long-term trend was a steep upward climb—a sharp increase with the institution of the Republic, slower and irregular rises till the rapid movement upward in 1930, a lower rate in 1933, and then an increase again in 1936. The rise in registration thus was a little more than half as much as actual voter turnout, i.e., 8.3 times between 1893 and 1936. But as we see in the table below, by 1945

Voter Registration in Select Contests
in São Paulo, 1886–1945

Year	Registration	Year	Registration
1886	19,440	1930	516,651
1893	79,943	1933	299,074
1902	105,534	1934	534,487
1905	76,220	1936	662,004
1912	179,700	1945	1,688,598
1922	164,234		

SOURCE: SP, *Relatorio* (Commissão Central), p. 178; SP, *Relatorio* (Repartição), foldout opposite p. 12; SP, *Annuario estatistico*, 1902, p. 39, 1905, p. 29; Brazil, *Estatistica eleitoral*, p. 234; Brazil, Diario, July 8, 1922, p. 795, May 21, 1930, p. 545; IBGE, *Anuário estatistico*, 1960, p. 411; Brazil, *Brasil: Estatísticas*, p. 370.

registration had shot up again, this time to more than two and a half times the 1936 figure. Registration rose 507% between 1934 and 1945 in Brazil as a whole, and 565% in São Paulo. Brazil, *Dados*, p. 7.

Federal and state registrations differed. In 1902, the electorate for federal contests was 105,534, but only 92,717 for state elections. SP, *Annuario estatístico*, 1902, pp. 32, 39.

156. SP, *Relatorio* (Commissão Central), p. 178; SP, *Relatorio* (Repartição), foldout opposite p. 12; SP, *Annuario estatístico*, 1905, 1: 29.

157. Note that the wild-and-woolly Alta Sorocabana zone registered a large share of the 1892 vote relative to its 1890 population (10% and 7%, respectively), and a disproportionately small share in 1936 (8%, compared with its 1934 population share of 9%). This change may reflect a diminution of the power of regional bosses in the zone, the stronghold of Ataliba Leonel in the Old Republic.

158. The percentage of PRP dues assigned to each zone in 1895 was as follows: Capital, 6; Paraíba Valley, 19; Central, 19; Mogiana, 21; Baixa Paulista, 12; Araraquarense, 7; Alta Paulista, 0; Alta Sorocabana, 8; Baixa Sorocabana, 4; Southern Coast, 4. Derived from Carone and Arantes Junqueira, pp. 151-55. In 1886 the Central, Mogiana, and Baixa Paulista zones accounted for 78% of the coffee output; in 1905, they still possessed 68% of the coffee trees. Camargo, 2: table 62; 3: table 107.

159. Derived from Table 4.2, above; SP, *Annaes* (Camara), 1927, pp. 19-20, 40; *OESP*, April 4, 1936, p. 4; and Camargo, 2: table 22 (on 1934 census). By 1945 the capital accounted for 39% of the state's registered voters. Brazil, *Dados*, p. 8.

160. Levine, *Pernambuco*, Table 4.2, p. 92; Wirth, *Minas Gerais*, Table 4.2, p. 138.

161. Voting data from Brazil, *Diario*, June 9, 1926, p. 437; *OESP*, April 16, 1936, p. 2. Population data from SP, *São Paulo*, p. 7.

Chapter Five

1. For a full definition of the elite and the conventions used in the coding, see Appendix A; a complete list of elite members, with their tenure in office, is found in Appendix B. It should be borne in mind that the information presented here in many respects represents only minimal findings. For example, many foreign ties were probably not discovered, and the same is true, one assumes, for kinship links. The list of variables and values in Appendix A gives definitions, a list of scores for the three state elites and a composite group, and the number (*n*) on which adjusted frequencies were based. Unless otherwise noted, the figures cited in this chapter refer to these tables or the computer printouts from which they were derived.

2. Camargo, 2: table 54.

3. It is true that Brazilians choose surnames among their ancestors almost at will. But the Minas group had only one English surname, and the principal point is the low frequency of Italian surnames in São Paulo, since the vast majority of first- and second-generation Italo-Brazilians would have had no Luso-Brazilian names to adopt among their forebears.

4. Compare similar arguments for the imperial elite: Pang and Seckinger, p. 218; and Barman and Barman, p. 426.

5. IBGE, *Recenseamento*, 1940. *Série nacional*, 2: 67, 89.

6. São Paulo Law School graduates: Prudente de Morais, Manuel Campos Sales, Francisco Rodrigues Alves, Afonso Pena, Wenceslau Braz, Artur Bernardes, and Washington Luís. Another graduate, Delfim Moreira, was acting President in 1918–19. Nilo Peçanha began his studies at São Paulo, but completed his law degree at Recife. (Júlio Prestes, the President-elect in 1930, whose inauguration was blocked by the Vargas revolution, was also a São Paulo Law graduate.) On the imperial Ministers, see J. M. de Carvalho, p. 90.

In absolute terms, access to legal education in São Paulo expanded dramatically under the Republic. From 1867 to 1886, 1,075 persons graduated from the São Paulo Law School, of whom only 333 were Paulistas. In the 20 years from 1907 to 1926, 1,816 students reached the final year of law school, of whom at least 1,234 were Paulistas—three and a half times as many as in 1867–86. Yet there were almost three times as many graduates in 1867–86 relative to the 1886 population as there were in 1907–26 relative to the 1926 population, though the share of Paulista graduates seems to have decreased only slightly. In the Republic, of course, the law school in São Paulo had less of an "obligation" to non-Paulistas and Paulistas alike, since new law schools opened their doors in most of the southern states, and São Paulo gained other professional schools to educate its youth.

For the population figures, see Camargo, 2: tables 1 and 2. (The 1926 population estimate probably has an upward bias, since it is based on the 1920 census, whose nationwide estimates are known to be too high.) For the number of law school graduates from 1867 to 1886, see SP, *Relatorio* (Commissão Central), pp. 118–19. For the period after 1900 there are no published lists of law-school graduates, only annual lists of students by class year. Though using the data for fifth-year students biases the figure upward, this is probably more than offset by the fact that the lists state only where the students' fathers were born—obviously a more restrictive criterion. See *Lista geral*, 1907–26.

In the Recife Law School, the total enrollment declined absolutely, from 1,657 in 1867–86 to 1,339 in 1907–26, but the number of Pernambucano graduates rose both absolutely and relatively—from 575 and 35% of the graduates to 658 and 49%. Data supplied by Robert Levine from H. Martins, *Lista*.

7. These variables and the others discussed in this chapter are fully defined in the six-page table in Appendix A.

8. Except for a 100% rate in the Alta Paulista, but this was for only two members of the elite, compared with 17 in the Central zone. (The relationship is statistically significant at the 0.0433 level for the chi-square test. All subsequent statements of significance refer to this test. The 0.05 level indicates that chances are 19 out of 20 that the relationship is not random.)

9. Statistical significance: 0.0200.

10. The diagram on the following page shows how 97 political elite members were linked to one another by kinship or business ties.

11. Luís Pereira Barreto, Jorge Tibiriçá, and José Levy Sobrinho, respectively. (Pereira Barreto was the most prominent and consistent Positivist among the elite members, but was not a member of the Positivist Church in Rio.)

12. Tibiriçá's fondness for Arantes dated from 1906, when at the age of 29 Arantes made a brilliant speech in Congress in favor of the Exchange Bank (linked with coffee valorization). Soares Júnior, 2: 553–54.

13. See Appendix A, convention 8, for our reasons for locating the justices in the capital city.

São Paulo's Elite Networks
Diagram for Note 10

Key

- b   brother
- bl   brother-in-law
- c   (first) cousin
- cl   (first) cousin-in-law
- g   grandson
- gn   grandnephew
- n   nephew
- nl   nephew-in-law
- s   son
- sl   son-in-law

The dotted lines link directors of the same firm.

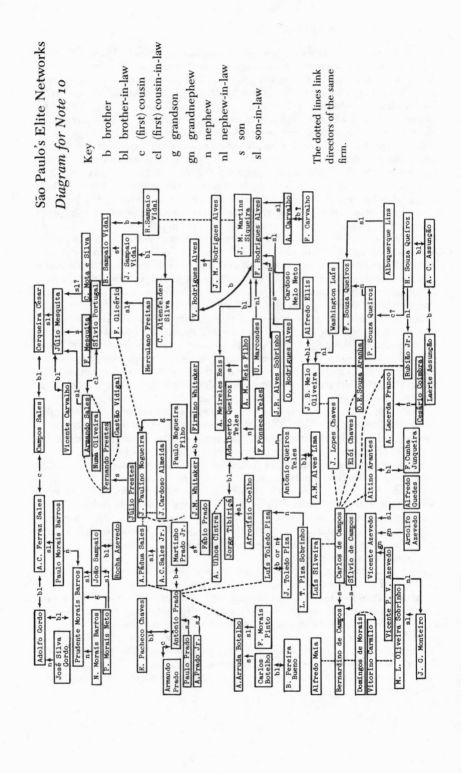

14. But the significance of this relationship was only 0.0922.

15. Significance: 0.0045; significance for Minas: 0.0020.

16. Castilho Cabral, pp. 3–6.

17. Data are available for a slightly smaller number than the interior-based group in Table 5.1, where $n = 75$.

18. Walker, pp. 86, 211.

19. This was Edmundo Navarro de Andrade. (Note that the variable "other university degree," item 47 in the table in Appendix A, includes foreign degrees. Thus São Paulo's relatively high score—10%—is largely accounted for by the group that studied abroad.)

20. One of the groups in this composite variable—investor in mining, item 65 —was not represented in the São Paulo elite.

21. In contrast, 49% of the Paulista elite had served in the state legislature, the highest share of the three state groups.

22. Neither of these relationships, however, reaches significance at the 0.05 level.

23. He was governor of Paraíba in 1866–67 and of Rio de Janeiro Province in 1868. Data for São Paulo's imperial governors from Marcus, pp. 198–203.

24. Barman and Barman, pp. 446–47n.

25. Shirley, "Judicial System," chart 1, following p. 63.

26. Paulistas on the state supreme court: Empire, 21%; Old Republic, 58%; Vargas era, 79%. São Paulo Law School graduates on the court: Empire, 63%; Old Republic, 80%; Vargas era, 98%. Ibid.

27. McGann, pp. 6, 288. (McGann's judgment is not presented as an explicit quantitative statement.)

28. The rise in the numbers of educators is explained in part, of course, by the increase in the number of professional schools in the last two-thirds of our period.

29. The figure is probably exaggerated, however, since no one of that generation was older than 49 by the end of our period.

30. Significance: 0.0007.

31. J. M. de Carvalho, p. 177.

32. The PRR of Rio Grande do Sul also had a bureaucratized dues-collecting system.

33. In Appendix A, items 5–7 refer only to the incumbent parties, i.e., in São Paulo, the PRP.

34. The largest split in the São Paulo elite was the dissidência of Prudente, Júlio Mesquita, and Cerqueira César in 1901, when 17% of the elite of the time opposed the PRP leadership. But unlike Pernambuco in 1910 and 1930, São Paulo in 1901 risked little chance of federal intervention with Campos Sales, a Paulista, as President.

35. Historicals (including "eleventh-hour" Republicans): São Paulo, 51%; Minas, 49%; Pernambuco, 23%. Abolitionists: São Paulo, 20% plus 7% who declared for abolition in the last 16 months of the dying slave regime; Minas, 9%; Pernambuco, 17%.

36. Yet the "outlying" West in the late imperial era, consisting of the Mogiana and Baixa Paulista zones, contributed 14% of the Historicals. Significance: 0.0550.

37. Historical Republicans supplied 63% of the committeemen and 68% of the man-years of service.

38. This change was due in part to the exclusion of many older PRP leaders from political activity by the revolutionary government.

39. Export trade, significance: 0.0000. Businessmen, significance: 0.0196.

40. Significance: 0.0005.

41. Significance: 0.0135.

42. For Fausto's thesis, see his *Revolução*, pp. 32–38. (Fausto was contesting the analysis of Nogueira Filho's *Ideais . . . O Partido Democrático*.) For the entire group of 601 signers of the PD manifesto, Levi has computed that 43% were middle-class professionals, 23% were white-collar workers, 16% were "planters or other property owners," and 15% were engaged in commerce, banking, or industry; the remainder were not identified (p. 320). His computation does not take into account multiple careers, however.

43. See data for Pernambuco and Minas in the companion volumes by Levine (p. 114) and Wirth (p. 151).

44. Tacito, pp. 84, 119, 133.

45. Information on Tibiriçá from Soares Júnior; and Arquivo *OESP*, pasta 858.

46. Information on Azevedo from Aroldo Azevedo, *Arnolfo*; Arquivo *OESP*, pasta 4,860; and Abranches, *Governos*, 2: 164.

47. Information on Miranda from Arquivo *OESP*, pasta 2,407; Abranches, *Governos*, 1: 180–81; British Chamber, *Personalidades*, p. 488; and Ellis Júnior, *Parlamentar*, p. 371.

48. Fonseca Filho, pp. 170–71.

49. Carone, *República Nova*, p. 318.

50. Mantua, 1: 200; *OESP*, Nov. 14, 1891 (source of quotation).

51. Information on Leonel from Arquivo *OESP*, pasta 4,566; *OESP*, Oct. 30, 1934, p. 5; British Chamber, *Personalidades*, p. 404; E. Silva, *Precursores*, p. 207.

52. Santos Abreu, *Formação*, p. 210. Fernando Prestes was also influential in the far West. *Ibid.*, p. 211.

53. Ayres de Camargo, p. 65.

54. Information on Sales from A. M. Araújo, "Chefes," pp. 418–20; and Pacheco e Silva.

55. I.e., the five clubs designated in the Code Book: Atlético, Hípica, Jockey, Automóvel, and Comercial. British Chamber, *Personalidades*, p. 537.

56. H. W. Brown, "São Paulo dissidence renewed," Nov. 16, 1931, United States, Decimal File 1930–39, 832.00/770, p. 2. Other information on Oliveira from Arquivo *OESP*, pasta 29,770.

57. Information on Ráo from Arquivo *OESP*, pasta 7,349; Hilton, p. 210; and British Chamber, *Personalidades*, p. 742.

58. A large research team, however, could undoubtedly obtain many data on ritual kinship by an examination of parish archives.

59. Speech in Chamber, Aug. 28, 1891, in Brazil, *Annaes . . . 1 a 3 de novembro de 1891* (Camara), Appendix [containing September speeches], p. 70.

Chapter Six

1. Furtado, p. 197.

2. Schulz, p. 208.

3. Campello de Souza, p. 198, Schulz, p. 233 (on the PRP's influence among northeastern congressmen); Abranches, *Golpe*, pp. 84–91.

4. Hahner. See also Schultz, p. 255.

5. Partido Republicano Federal, pp. 35, 52.

6. During Prudente's illness, Finance Minister Bernardino de Campos was the President's watchdog on acting President (and Vice-President) Manuel Vitorino. See Prudente de Morais to Bernardino de Campos, Teresópolis, Jan. 6 and Jan. 8, 1897, Arquivo Prudente de Morais.

7. Campello de Souza, p. 205; Melo Franco, 1: 177; Campos Salles, pp. 161–62.

8. Faoro, 2: 566. Campos Sales's notion of the presidency was to govern above "national" parties, as his official apologist makes clear. Guanabara, pp. 29–35, 51–56, 81–86, 101–14.

9. Campos Salles, pp. 236–78 *passim*, especially p. 250.

10. Melo Franco, 1: 96, 101, 104, 245.

11. *Ibid.*, 2: 441; Love, *Rio Grande do Sul*, pp. 139–41.

12. U.S. Ambassador Dudley to Secretary of State Knox, April 27, 1909, United States, Numerical File, 1906–10, case 2372/26, p. 1; José Vieira, p. 145.

13. José Vieira, pp. 153–54.

14. Campello de Souza, p. 219.

15. UK Ambassador Haggard to Foreign Secretary Grey, Jan. 7, 1910, FO 371/831 3991.

16. See Rui Barbosa to Bernardino de Campos, Aug. 21, 1909 (copy), Arquivo Rui Barbosa.

17. Brunn, p. 84; UK Ambassador Haggard to Foreign Secretary Grey, Jan. 7, 1910, FO 371/831 3991. In the same dispatch the British ambassador also stated his low regard for Rui Barbosa.

18. Gov. Albuquerque Lins telegraphed Rui that Nilo's insistence on having the PRP supply him with a cabinet member was a sign of neutrality. Albuquerque Lins to Barbosa, São Paulo, June 18 (two messages), 1909, Arquivo Rui Barbosa.

19. Love, *Rio Grande do Sul*, pp. 165–67; Melo Franco, 2: 727.

20. Dep. Vespúcio de Abreu to Protásio Alves, Rio, Feb. 20, 1919, ABM; Campello de Souza, p. 240.

21. Fausto, "Expansão," p. 233; Love, *Rio Grande do Sul*, p. 186.

22. Schurig Vieira, pp. 105, 121, 134, 137–38.

23. Fausto, *Pequenos ensaios*, p. 55.

24. Valdomiro Lima to Vargas, São Paulo, April 23, 1933, AP, pasta 2, lata 4; Carone, *República Nova*, p. 34; Zimmermann, p. 151.

25. Dean, *Industrialization*, p. 200. But see Chap. 2, note 109.

26. *Ibid.*, pp. 188, 190.

27. Werneck Vianna, pp. 172–78, 206–11.

28. See Wirth, *Minas Gerais*, Table 6.1, p. 174; and Love, *Rio Grande do Sul*, Table 3, p. 123, for some details on 1889–1930.

29. José Maria Whitaker was president of the bank from December 1920 to December 1922, Cincinato Braga, from February 1923 to January 1925. As early as November 1918, the Paulista congressman Sampaio Vidal had introduced a bill to make the Bank of Brazil a bank of issue. But the executive branch, led by Vice-President (and acting President) Delfim Moreira and Finance Minister João Moreira, blocked the measure. Sampaio Vidal was Minister of Finance in 1922, when the bank finally received its monopoly. Bouças, *História*, p. 265.

30. Data from Lago.

31. In the 1933 Constituent Assembly, there were 40 delegates of corporations

in addition to the 212 representatives from geographical units. The corporate representatives supported Vargas, except for Paulista industrialists and a few representatives of the liberal professions. Leal, p. 476. For a list of delegations by state and corporation, see INE, *Anuário estatístico*, 1937, p. 832.

32. For a list of chairmanships of the principal committees by state, see Wirth, *Minas Gerais*, Table 6.2, p. 176.

33. *Ibid.*, p. 173.

34. São Paulo was also represented on the Tariffs Committee during its brief existence (1901-3).

35. Antonio Azeredo to Borges de Medeiros, Rio, Sept. 19, 1915, and March 22, 1916, V. Abreu to Borges, Rio, June 29, 1921, ABM.

36. In 1920, for example, São Paulo and Minas competed to determine the governor of Espírito Santo in a disputed election; with Rio Grande's support, Minas won. Love, *Rio Grande do Sul*, p. 188.

37. Dep. Carlos Maximiliano Pereira dos Santos to Borges de Medeiros, Rio, Sept. 27, 1914 (on bribes by Paulistas), Sen. Soares dos Santos to Borges, Rio, March 15, 1917, and Dep. Carlos Penafiel to Borges, Rio, May 4, 1921 (on newspaper subsidies), ABM.

38. Sen. Alfredo Ellis, speech of July 1, 1903, in Brazil, *Política*, 1: 114.

39. Denis, p. 261.

40. Delfim Netto, pp. 43-44.

41. Brazil, *Política*, 1: 38, 81, 96-97.

42. Melo Franco, 2: 455, 463. Conceivably, his opposition might also have been based on the fear that valorization would reduce his profits as an exporter.

43. Brazil, *Política*, 1: 408-9, 428.   44. *Ibid.*, 2: 20, 186.

45. *Ibid.*, pp. 182, 214-15, 249-50.   46. *Ibid.*, pp. 270, 428.

47. *Ibid.*, pp. 431, 433, 436, 437. Braga's point on federal revenues was made explicit in the Chamber in 1920. See his *Problemas brasileiros*, p. 292.

48. Brazil, *Política*, 2: 435, 442.

49. See the excellent discussion of the origin of the Exchange Bank idea in Holloway, *Brazilian Coffee*, pp. 50-52.

50. Brazil, *Política*, 1: 424.   51. Melo Franco, 2: 469, 471.

52. Brazil, *Caixa*, 1: 69-70.   53. *Ibid.*, pp. 128-29.

54. *Ibid.*, pp. 133, 142, 283, 480.

55. *Ibid.*, pp. 345, 564; Melo Franco, 2: 473.

56. Brazil, *Caixa*, 2: 32, 56, 163, 165, 231, 266-72, 298-99, 304, 311, 322, 401-7. The bill became law on Dec. 31, 1910. Earlier in the year, the Paulista power structure was so sensitive to rises in the exchange rate that *O Estado de S. Paulo* charged that friends of President-elect Hermes were trying to force the acceptance of his victory by threatening to raise the rate. Cited in Carone, *República Velha (Evolução)*, p. 252.

57. Dallari, "Estados," p. 33.

58. Brazil, *Impostos*, pp. 174-75, 199, 411-12.

59. Valladares, p. 305; Dallari, "Estados," p. 36 (citing Minas decree 4,400 of June 16, 1915); Supreme Court decision of Jan. 18, 1919 (on São Paulo's tax on Minas's coffee) in *Revista Forense*, 32 (July-Dec. 1919): 274-76; Egas, *Impostos*, p. 13.

60. Hugon, p. 189. But see Chap. 8, below.

61. M. Ribeiro, "Revisão," p. 78 (on the British financial mission); H. G. James, p. 73 (on the partial veto).

62. M. Ribeiro, "Revisão," p. 94. For the full debates, see Brazil, *Revisão constitucional*.

63. Romeiro, pp. 22, 23, 30. The federally owned lines in São Paulo were the Central, the Oeste de Minas, the Noroeste, and the Rede Sul Mineira.

64. Duncan, pp. 139, 149, 152.

65. P. E. James, p. 795.

66. Melo Franco, 2: 459–60, 529.

67. Brazil, *Annaes* (Congresso), 1: 781; Macedo Soares, p. 12.

68. Wirth, *Minas Gerais*, p. 41; Denis, p. 259.

69. Soares Júnior, 2: 539–45; Pinheiro Machado, speech in Senate of July 12, 1915, in Brazil, *Annaes* (Senado), 4: 153–54.

70. Dep. Evaristo Amaral to Borges de Medeiros, Rio, May 10, 1916, Sen. Vitorino Monteiro to Borges, Rio, March 19, 1916, ABM. Following Pinheiro Machado's assassination, Rio Grande temporarily returned to a position of isolation in national politics.

71. Love, *Rio Grande do Sul*, especially p. 123.

72. João Neves to Borges de Medeiros et al., Rio, June 7, 1932 (copy), ABM.

73. Mesquita Filho, p. 238. The railroad was also important in securing Paulista domination of Goiás's cattle industry after 1900, according to Wirth (*Minas Gerais*, p. 46).

74. Corrêa Filho, pp. 592–93, 603.

75. Partido Republicano, *Scisão*, p. 105.

76. Westphalen et al., pp. 2, 32; Margolis, pp. 1–41 *passim*. One of the early investors who sold land to the British company was Col. José Soares Marcondes, of the Alta Sorocabana zone, one of the most notorious of São Paulo's coronéis. Alceu Barroso, p. 99.

77. Fontoura was born in São Paulo in 1842, but only because Paraná formed part of São Paulo province till 1853. On his career, see F. Monteiro, *Figuras*, pp. 24–28.

78. For a theoretical statement on the role of foreign factors in domestic politics, see Chalmers.

79. Monbeig, *Pionniers*, p. 98; Carone, *República Velha (Instituições)*, pp. 37–38.

80. Zimmermann, p. 154; Holloway, *Brazilian Coffee*, p. 13; Peláez, "State," p. 23.

81. Gauld, pp. 72, 169, 176. See the denunciation of Farquhar, and by implication of the São Paulo government, in Toledo, p. 64. (Toledo made his speech as an opposition deputy in the state legislature in 1907.)

82. Holloway, "Migration," p. 427; Wileman, p. 770; Lloyd et al., p. 632; Zimmermann, p. 150; Monbeig, *Pionniers*, pp. 183–84; Margolis, p. 21. Wille also owned land in the Alta Sorocabana region. Schmidt, p. 449.

83. UK Ambassador Alston, "Annual Report," 1927, Feb. 16, 1928, FO 371/12744 3724, pp. 5, 17; J. W., "Situation in São Paulo," July 27, 1932, United States, Decimal File 1930–39, 832.00/293. A few American banks had foreign branches before World War I, but the Federal Reserve Act of 1913 greatly facilitated the development of their overseas operations.

84. Ribeiro and Guimarães, pp. 363, 365; Lipkau, especially p. 81; Brazil, *Sinopse*, pp. 130, 223.

85. Holloway, *Brazilian Coffee*, pp. 56, 58; Zimmermann, pp. 132, 141.

86. Zimmermann, p. 150. Such estates were sold off in smaller lots through a colonization company, the Retalhadora de Terras.

87. *Ibid.*, pp. 121, 128, 146, 148, 157, 186.

88. Delgado de Carvalho, pp. 173-74; Zimmermann, p. 135; "Corrected minutes of the meeting of the interdepartmental committee appointed to consider Secret E.O.C. No. 80," June 10, 1918, FO 371/3167 4119, especially pp. 4-5.

89. Gifun, p. 95; Uebele, pp. 61-62.

90. Alceu Barroso, p. 29; Oberacker, pp. 360, 362; Santos Abreu, "Comunicações," pp. 203-12.

91. Subiroff, pp. 16, 35-36; Zimmermann, p. 112; Schompré, p. 251.

92. Wileman, p. 775 (on Prado); Cerqueira César's dealings with Wille inferred from Schmidt, p. 449. On Prado's links, see note 10, Chap. 5.

93. Richard Graham, *Britain*, p. 80; Wileman, p. 774; G. E. H., "City of Santos Improvement Company," July 31, 1918, FO 371/3168 4119, p. 3 (on Prado and the British blacklist). When Farquhar briefly gained control of the Paulista Railroad, he wisely left Antônio Prado as its president. Gauld, p. 176.

94. Ellis Júnior, *Parlamentar*, p. 333. Simonsen, unlike Ellis, was not a member of the Paulista political elite as defined in this study.

95. UK Consul General Abbott to Chargé, July 28, 1934, FO 371/17486 3884. The 23 were Macedo Soares, Sousa Aranha, Elói Chaves, José Martiniano Rodrigues Alves, Virgílio Rodrigues Alves, Cardoso Melo Neto, Martins de Siqueira, Luís Silveira, Altino Arantes, Bernardino de Campos, Carlos de Campos, Júlio Prestes, Alvaro Carvalho, Sílvio de Campos, Gastão Vidigal, José Silva Gordo, Antônio Lacerda Franco, Alfredo Maia, Numa de Oliveira, Paulo Prado, Antônio Prado, João Sampaio, and Marcos Sousa Dantas. On Sousa Aranha, Chaves, the Rodrigues Alveses, Cardoso Melo Neto, Martins de Siqueira, and Silveira, see sources cited in note 91; on Arantes, Bernardino and Carlos de Campos, Prestes, and Carvalho, see Subiroff, pp. 13, 119; on Sílvio de Campos and Vidigal, see Ronald Hilton, pp. 49, 262; on Silva Gordo, see Araújo, *Chefes*, p. 69; on Lacerda Franco, see *Eles construíram*, p. 15; on Oliveira, see H. W. Brown, "São Paulo Dissidence Renewed," Nov. 16, 1931, United States, Decimal File 1930-39, 832.00/770, p. 2; on the Prados, see note 93 sources; on Sampaio, see British Chamber, *Personalidades*, p. 656; and on Sousa Dantas, see Arquivo *OESP*, pasta 2,780.

96. Wileman, p. 432.

97. Lefevre, p. 8; IBGE, *Anuário estatístico*, 1939/1940, pp. 1424-25. In addition, the municípios of São Paulo and Santos had contracted foreign loans worth several million pounds. Since municípios were legal subdivisions of the state, the state was ultimately responsible for the debt incurred. (For details, see Chap. 8.)

98. *A ação da bancada paulista*, p. v.

99. Tobias Monteiro, p. 224. Monteiro cites Vice-President Charles Johnston of the London and Brazilian Bank, on the occasion of a banquet for Campos Sales during the President-elect's financial mission to London in 1898.

100. Campos Salles, p. 186.

101. Wirth, *Minas Gerais*, pp. 179, 288.

102. Campos Sales to Prudente de Morais, São Paulo, March 5, 1897 (copy), Arquivo Prudente de Morais; Campos Salles, pp. 283–85.

103. SP, *Annaes* (Camara), 1891, p. 891. On this occasion, the anti-Deodoro faction lost, after having won a close vote on a related issue the previous day. The opponents of the dictator then withdrew from the assembly, and after Deodoro's fall, his supporters were purged from the new legislature.

104. Francisco Glicério to Jorge?, Rio, June 5, 1893, cited in Witter, p. 174.

105. For example, see *Correio de Manhã* (Rio), Oct. 1, 1909.

106. *The Economist*, June 5, 19, 26, 1909, pp. 1178–79, 1283, 1314, 1359.

107. Barbosa, *Escritos*, pp. 310–11; Barbosa, *Contra o militarismo*, p. 108, cited in Faoro, 2: 598. At the Hague Peace Conference in 1907, Rui had not supported the (Argentine) Drago Doctrine, which denied that debt collection was a legitimate reason for foreign intervention. Brazil's Foreign Minister, Rio Branco, also rejected the doctrine because Brazil paid its debts, and was a creditor to Uruguay and Paraguay. Burns, p. 121.

108. Rodrigues Alves in Egas, *Galeria*, 2: 416.

109. The English word natives was used in the original. Percival de Oliveira, p. 34. (Article originally in *O Diario de S. Paulo*, Sept. 3, 1929.)

110. UK Consul General Abbott to Foreign Secretary Simon, Oct. 12, 1932, FO 371/15809, p. 5.

111. Salgado, *O Esperado*, pp. 107, 188; G. Barroso, *Sinagoga* and *Brasil*.

112. Carone, *República Nova*, pp. 364–65.

113. For São Paulo's role in national politics after 1945, see Schwartzman, pp. 136–75.

Chapter Seven

1. Compare Weiner, p. 253.

2. Galtung, especially pp. 378–80.

3. For the theory, see Lemarchand and Legg.

4. Haas, pp. xv, 16. See also the useful collection edited by Lindberg and Scheingold, *Regional Integration*; and Deutsch's classic *Nationalism and Social Communication*.

5. Lara, pp. 207–8.

6. Joaquim Floriano de Godoy celebrated São Paulo's "hybrid race," as he called it, as early as 1882. See his *Provincia*, p. 66. Later, the modernist Cassiano Ricardo wrote that "in descending order, the Indian, the Spaniard, the Portuguese, and the Negro were those who contributed most to the bandeirante's ethnic and cultural makeup." *Marcha para oeste*, 1: 21. But the credit given to blacks was primarily for physical rather than intellectual achievements. Thus an implicit racism occurs to today's reader that would probably have escaped Ricardo's contemporaries.

7. Ricardo, 2: 246.

8. Carone, *República Velha (Evolução)*, p. 135.

9. In November 1904, several military officers took advantage of popular riots against compulsory smallpox vaccination in the Federal District, and led a short-lived rebellion of cadets against the government of Rodrigues Alves. See Partido Republicano, *Scisão*, p. 105 (on Mato Grosso); and Dias de Campos, p. 153 (on the rebellion in Rio).

10. Dallari, *Pequeno exército*, pp. 63-64. But Mineiro and Gaúcho troops also came to São Paulo during the 1924 uprising.

11. Heloísa Fernandes, p. 161.

12. Evaristo Amaral to Borges de Medeiros, April 12, 1917, Rio, ABM.

13. Carone, *República Nova*, p. 373.

14. Federal troops in other states, of course, experienced similar divisions in this period. There were some 20 army risings across Brazil in 1931, and repeated revolts in 1932 and beyond. *Ibid.*, pp. 293-94, 373.

15. Andrade and Câmara, p. 136.

16. Arquivo *OESP*, pastas 27,747 (on Oliveira) and 46,788 (on Almeida); Leite, *Páginas*, p. 115.

17. U.S. Vice Consul Flournoy to Ambassador Caffery, "São Paulo Political Report no. 113," Feb. 9, 1938, United States, Decimal File 1930-39, 832.00/1169, p. 2.

18. Love, *Rio Grande do Sul*, p. 117; Brazil, *Almanack*, pp. 7-14; Amaral Peixoto, pp. 268-69. Compare São Paulo's situation to the analogous position of industrial Catalonia in the Spanish military hierarchy, in Linz and Miguel, p. 303.

19. Martinez Corrêa, *Rebelião*, p. 27 (citing figures of José Murilo de Carvalho); Alfred Stepan, p. 17.

20. Souza Ferraz; Dias de Campos.

21. See Wirth, *Minas Gerais*, pp. 186-92.

22. On "warlord" coronéis, see Pang, especially chaps. 3 and 4.

23. Union des Associations, p. 11.

24. Twenty-five were created in the 1870's, 40 in the 1880's, 68 in the 1890's, and 300 from 1900 to 1914. Schröder, p. 169.

25. DGE, *Annuario*, 3: 453.

26. Representatives from all regions of Brazil were present, as well as a representative from the Ministry of the Interior in Rio. *OESP*, Feb. 18, 1911, p. 6. The second Congress took place in Belo Horizonte in 1912. Wirth, *Minas Gerais*, p. 197.

27. Data on meetings in São Paulo from Leite, *História*, pp. 156-212 *passim*.

28. The 1903 law was Legislative Decree 979 of Jan. 6. See the brief discussion in Schmitter, p. 110.

29. The manufacturers, slow to follow the fazendeiros' lead (a growers' association was already powerful by 1902), did not have a group of their own (outside textiles) until 1928, and it was not until 1944 that the country's industrialists assembled for a national congress. As early as 1917, however, manufacturers got the government of São Paulo city to sponsor an industrial fair, based on models in Lyon and Leipzig. Ortigão, pp. 397-98.

30. The following is necessarily only a sketch of planters' organizations in São Paulo. This topic, including relations between these groups and state and federal governments, deserves a book-length study.

31. Gov. Bernardino de Campos, message to state legislature, March 5, 1903, in Egas, *Galeria*, 2: 144.

32. *OESP*, page one stories on March 26, March 27, and March 28, 1899; Rodrigues, especially p. 25.

33. Instituto Historico, *Diccionario*, 1: 495-96.

34. *OESP*, Feb. 22, 1902, p. 1, Feb. 23, p. 2. The organizing group for the SPA was called the Centro Agrícola Paulista.

35. *Revista Agricola*, 1903, pp. 93–96. (Information courtesy of Thomas H. Holloway.)

36. E.g., at the Saint Louis World's Fair in 1904 and the National Exposition in Rio in 1908. (Information supplied by Thomas H. Holloway from Sociedade Paulista de Agricultura "Relatorios.")

37. *O Fazendeiro*, 8 (Aug. 1913): 267; and information supplied by Thomas H. Holloway from Sociedade Paulista, "Relatorio," 1913, pp. 60–75.

38. Information supplied by Thomas H. Holloway from *O Fazendeiro*, 1911, pp. 538–40, and 1912, pp. 181, 284; and from Sociedade Paulista, "Relatorio," 1913, pp. 20, 35.

39. *O Fazendeiro*, 9, no. 4 (April 1, 1916); *OESP*, March 29, 1916, p. 6.

40. "Sociedade Rural Brasileira," Arquivo *OESP*, pasta 5,272.

41. Annaes da Sociedade Rural Brasileira, April 1920, p. 2.

42. Revista da Sociedade Rural Brasileira, April 1931, p. 161.

43. *OESP*, March 31, 1922, p. 8; and information supplied by Thomas H. Holloway from *Revista dos Fazendeiros*, 5, nos. 58/59 (March 31, 1922). Georgism was also receiving attention in Rio Grande do Sul, where Gov. Borges de Medeiros for a time made the rural land tax the state's main source of revenue. Love, *Rio Grande do Sul*, p. 102.

44. On Magalhães's speech, see "O Imposto Territorial" in *Revista da Sociedade Rural Brasileira*, June 1922, pp. 303ff; and July 1922, pp. 365ff, especially p. 372.

45. *OESP*, Oct. 24, 1922, p. 2.

46. Sociedade Paulista, *Relatorio da Directoria*, p. 3, and "Sociedade Rural Brasileira," Arquivo *OESP*, pasta 5,272 (on Diedrichsen); *OESP*, April 19, 1938, p. 4 (on Ribeiro dos Santos).

47. *OESP*, Dec. 24, 1921, p. 3, Jan. 17, 1930, p. 4.

48. U.S. Consul General Cameron, "Fusion of Agricultural Societies," Dec. 13, 1930, in United States, American Consulate General, São Paulo: correspondence, 1930, v. 12, 843/861.33, no. 339, pp. 2–3. One estimate in 1925 put the SRB's membership at about 2,000. *Almanak Agricola*, p. 163.

49. *OESP*, Dec. 1, 1929, p. 2; Cameron (see preceding note), p. 2.

50. Fausto, *Pequenos ensaios*, p. 56.

51. *OESP*, Aug. 23, 1931, p. 5.

52. Nogueira Filho, *Guerra*, 1: 278–79; Carone, *República Nova*, p. 52.

53. Nogueira Filho, *Guerra*, 1: 296. The Federação das Associações de Lavradores de Café was finally absorbed by the SRB in 1951.

54. The three associations together in 1930 had 2,400 members, but there was an overlap. For the 1934 report on agricultural syndicates, see SP, *Diário oficial*, Feb. 16, 1934, pp. 1–4.

55. Denis, p. 205.

56. Santos dockers frequently had knowledge of strike activity in Rio, and possibly knew of such activities in Buenos Aires as well, since the stevedores in Rio were in contact with their Argentine counterparts on at least one occasion. Fausto, *Trabalho*, p. 124.

57. *Ibid.*, pp. 129–32 (citing Sheldon Maram).

58. Swings in the trade cycle should perhaps be added to the list. According to Fausto, *Trabalho*, pp. 133–34, labor organization and strikes tended to increase during times of prosperity. (See also Simão, p. 109). But this was not so

true after the First World War, possibly because of the sterner measures taken to repress the labor movement after 1919.

59. Hall, "Immigration," p. 404; Simão, pp. 106–7; Fausto, *Trabalho*, pp. 129–30; Pinheiro, p. 97. The eight-hour day, however, did not become conventional until the 1930's. Simão, p. 72.

60. Carone, *República Velha (Instituições)*, p. 227; Fausto, *Trabalho*, pp. 165, 167.

61. Salgado, *O extrangeiro* [sic], p. 129; Hall, "Immigration," pp. 399, 403.

62. Simão, pp. 167–70.

63. However, textile factories also employed large numbers of women and children, who were generally difficult to organize. For data, see *ibid.*, pp. 104, 106, 108, 145, 148, 151, 154.

64. *Ibid.*, pp. 161, 163.

65. Fausto, *Trabalho*, pp. 120, 158; Carone, *República Velha (Instituições)*, p. 204.

66. In 1917, the Federação Operária was briefly replaced by the Comité de Defesa Proletária. Simão, pp. 168–69, 171; Fausto, *Trabalho*, p. 175.

67. The Confederação Brasileira do Trabalho, the political party Mário Hermes established in Rio in 1912, had no influence in São Paulo. Simão, p. 169; Fausto, *Trabalho*, p. 55.

68. Simão, pp. 171, 215.

69. *Ibid.*, pp. 112, 116.

70. *Ibid.*, pp. 116–17.

71. But the final working out of the 1919 law involved concessions to Gaúcho legislators. Love, *Rio Grande do Sul*, p. 179.

72. Malloy, p. 5.

73. *Ibid.*, pp. 1, 10, 33n.

74. Simão, p. 184.

75. INE, *Anuário estatístico*, 1937, p. 536, and 1938, p. 474; IBGE, 1939/1940, pp. 698–99; 1941/1945, p. 377, and 1946, p. 413.

76. Simão, pp. 86–87.

77. *Ibid.*, pp. 85–86, 97–98.

78. Text of the bishops' statement in Vasconcellos, pp. 21–30. The prelates were led by Archbishop Antônio Macedo Costa of Bahia, one of the two bishops imprisoned in the Religious Question of 1872–75.

79. Another southern bishops' congress convened in São Paulo in 1910.

80. *OESP*, Nov. 17, 1901, p. 2; Vasconcellos, p. 30.

81. "O nosso programma," *São Paulo*, Oct. 28, 1905, p. 1.

82. Vasconcellos, p. 96; Gabaglia, p. 38.

83. Fausto, *Trabalho*, p. 72n.

84. On Leopoldo e Silva's life, see *Esboço biographico*; Arruda Dantas; and Silveira Camargo.

85. *OESP*, Nov. 20, 1938, p. 8.   86. *OESP*, Sept. 7, 1928, p. 10.

87. *New Catholic Encyclopedia*, 1: 652.   88. Gabaglia, p. 39.

89. Williams, "Politicization," p. 302; Gabaglia, p. 39.

90. *Esboço biographico*, p. 149.

91. Leopoldo, pp. 135–38.

92. Gontijo de Carvalho, preface to Arantes; Silveira Camargo, p. 54; Ronald Hilton, p. 16.

93. The burcha was supposedly introduced in the law school in the 1830's by a mysterious immigrant from Saxony named Júlio Frank. Morse, p. 67. A brief description of the burcha's significance in the politics of the Republic is found in Melo Franco, 1: 24–35.

94. Information supplied by Professor Dalmo de Abreu Dallari, of the São Paulo Law School.

95. Melo Franco, 1: 34 (on burcha and PD). Former XI de Agosto officers who helped found the PD included Antônio Carlos de Abreu Sodré, Paulo Nogueira Filho, and César Vergueiro.

96. Evolución, p. 7. Other delegates included two future South American presidents, Manuel Prado Ugarteche of Peru and Baltasar Brum of Uruguay, and a future Peruvian diplomat and scholar, Víctor Andrés Belaúnde. Ibid., pp. 7–8.

97. Polyanthea, pp. 3–4. Brazilian students were perhaps influenced by the rise of universities in France. There, the revolution had suppressed universities in the 1790's, and the government only reconstituted them (by grouping professional schools) in 1896. Zeldin, 2: 316.

98. Arquivo OESP, pasta 1,063. Another future elite member, Oscar Stevenson, attended a student meeting in Uruguay in 1924.

99. Seganfreddo, pp. 26–29.

100. More than half the PD executive committee members for whom any data were found had been Liga members (12 of 23).

101. "Liga Nacionalista," OESP, July 27, 1917, p. 4.

102. Manor, pp. 11, 16, 19. Paulo Nogueira Filho, a member of the Liga, later commented on its elitism in Partido, 1: 76.

103. Vergueiro Steidel and Bishop Leopoldo e Silva jointly issued a request to President Bernardes to stop the bombing of the city. Martinez Corrêa, Rebelião, p. 141. On Macedo Soares's role, see his memoir, Justiça.

104. O'Neil, "Search," pp. 75, 77.

105. João G. de Oliveira, pp. 250–51.

106. Law 199 of Jan. 23, 1936.

Chapter Eight

1. See Appendix C for definitions and tables on the São Paulo budget. Where a source is not provided for data in this chapter, they are found in, or derived from, these tables or the analogous tables in the companion volumes by Wirth and Levine.

2. Figures exclude the Federal District. IBGE, Anuário estatístico, 1939/1940, p. 1416. (These data differ in a few years from my own. See the next note.)

3. Ibid., pp. 1415–16. In the IBGE figures, 1920 is counted as a surplus year, but since the state already owned the Sorocabana Railroad, the "expropriation" of the line should be classed as an expenditure, not as an investment, and with this change we find that expenditures in 1920 outran income by almost 48,000 contos.

4. See Chap. 2 for a discussion of the positions of Furtado, Peláez, Fishlow, and Silber. For federal deficits, see IBGE, Anuário estatístico, 1939/1940, p. 1409.

5. Deveza, pp. 75, 76, 83.

6. IBGE, Anuário estatístico, 1939/1940, p. 1410; price index in Appendix C, col. C-1; IBGE, Brasil em números, p. 5.

7. These findings contradict Richard Graham's recent judgment that "the creation of a *federal* republic and the allocation of certain tax revenues to the states and municípios [had a] minimal effect . . . on the overall structure of the [federal] budget." "Government Expenditures," p. 343. (Italics in original.) In other respects, his conclusions are consonant with my own, especially his finding that federal budgets in the early years of the Republic responded to coffee planters' needs.

8. Brazil, *Imperio do Brazil*, p. 442 (unfortunately, it is not clear in these data how the Corte, later the Federal District, is classified); IBGE, *Anuário estatístico*, 1939/1940, pp. 1409–10, 1412, 1418, 1420.

9. Argentina, p. 633; IBGE, *Anuário estatístico*, 1939/1940, p. 1422.

10. Data from Holloway, "Migration," p. 204; SP, *São Paulo*, p. 22; Appendix C, col. A-1; and Wirth, *Minas Gerais*, p. 208.

11. Lefevre, p. 61; Egas, *Impostos*, p. 13.

12. The surcharge was supplemented by a stipulation in the loan agreement of 1908 that all coffee sold above fixed quotas would be subject to an additional ad valorem rate. Krasner, p. 500.

13. SP, *Revista*, 7, no. 72 (Dec. 1932), p. 24.

14. Villela and Suzigan, p. 196, citing Fishlow. On coffee's price inelasticity of demand, see Delfim Netto, p. 76.

15. Love, *Rio Grande do Sul*, pp. 140–41.

16. Peláez and Suzigan, p. 175.

17. Lefevre, p. 31.

18. SP, *Annaes* (Camara), 1904, p. 386; Egas, *Impostos*, p. 87; SP, *São Paulo*, pp. 21–22. The *imposto territorial* was introduced between 1901 and 1905 in Rio Grande do Sul, Minas Gerais, and São Paulo. Only in Rio Grande did it become a major revenue producer during the Old Republic.

19. Holloway, "Migration," p. 204; Appendix C, col. A-1; Egas, *Galeria*, 2: 576–78 (Arantes), 3: 31, 36 (Washington Luís); Walle, p. 114.

20. SP, *Finanças*, especially pp. 40–41, 58; British Chamber, *Facts*, p. 30; Hugon, pp. 260–61. By 1949 the sales-and-consignments rate had been raised to 2.5 percent ad valorem.

21. IBGE, *Anuário estatístico*, 1939/1940, p. 523.

22. Deveza, p. 66.

23. On this point, see Miranda Guimarães, p. 41; and *Revista dos Tribunais*, 42, v. 215 (Sept. 1953): 198–99. On the Vargas government's efforts to abolish interstate taxes in the 1930's and 1940's, see Hugon, pp. 183–85, 189.

24. For data, see Bouças, *Finanças*, 19: 481; Wileman, p. 432; Brazil, *Discurso*, first foldout after p. 24; and Appendix C, D series, in all three volumes.

25. Brazil, *Discurso*, first foldout after p. 24.

26. Krasner, p. 498.

27. But the loan also involved Baring Brothers, Rothschild, and Speyer.

28. Foreign Bondholders, *Annual Report*, 1937, p. 108.

29. United Nations, *External Financing*, p. 25. Argentina did default on some nonfederal foreign debts.

30. Brazil, *Discurso*, first foldout after p. 24 and p. 53. For an excellent analysis of Brazilian debt management in the 1930's and early 1940's, see Paiva Abreu, "Dívida," and for background, his "Missão Niemeyer."

31. Brazil, *Discurso*, p. 39.

32. For a description of the Aranha Plan, see Foreign Bondholders, *Annual Report*, 1941/44, pp. 156–57. Paiva Abreu argues that Brazil got a much better deal from its creditors in 1940–43, when it had a greater capacity to pay (because of exports), than it did in the early 1930's. He also asserts that dollar loans on the whole got considerably better treatment in the 1943 grading system than in the Aranha Plan (presumably because of the relative shifts in economic and military power of the United States and Britain by 1943). "Dívida," pp. 66, 76.

33. Guastini, *Café*, pp. 174–75, 185–86.

34. Egas, *Galeria*, 2: 96; Rippy, pp. 152–53.

35. Melo Franco, 1: 155.

36. On São Paulo, see Bouças, *Finanças*, 19: 481–95, 567–79 *passim*; on Latin America, see United Nations, *External Financing*, p. 27; on real interest rates of 9–10 percent, compare Baklanoff, p. 24. Krasner (p. 500) estimates an effective interest rate of 10 percent on the two valorization loans of 1906 and 1908.

37. *Moody's Manual*, 1931, p. 146; Appendix C, col. A-1.

38. See the statement on methodology in Appendix C for the calculation of debt servicing.

39. Delfim Netto, p. 144.

40. Souza Lobo, p. 152.

41. According to Carone, the state of São Paulo was assisted by private organizations in recruiting migrants from other states in the 1930's. *República Nova*, p. 10.

42. Figures are available only from 1894 for Pernambuco, and data for 1897 are missing for São Paulo. Excluding the 1897 data for both states, São Paulo spent 17,100 (current) contos on immigration and Pernambuco 8,900 on public works in the years 1894–99.

43. According to official figures, the Sorocabana earned a modest profit each year, but such accounting must exclude more than capital costs. SP, *São Paulo*, p. 33.

44. Egas, *Impostos*, p. 9; Levi, p. 266. Percival Farquhar, the American capitalist, opened a meat-packing plant later in 1915.

45. IBGE, *Anuário estatístico*, 1939/1940, p. 1411; SP, *Relatório* (Fazenda), 1943, p. 81. Figures for São Paulo in earlier decades are not comparable because of the impossibility of factoring out overhead costs when "security" was included in the Secretariat of the Interior or the Secretariat of Justice.

46. Bouças, *Finanças*, 1: 253.

47. IBGE, *Anuário estatístico*, 1939/1940, p. 1422. By 1971, São Paulo's municípios collected 49 percent of all municipal revenues and made 50 percent of the outlays. *Ibid.*, 1974, pp. 908, 915.

48. SP, *São Paulo*, pp. 71–99 *passim*; IBGE, *Anuário estatístico*, 1939/1940, p. 1420.

49. SP, *São Paulo*, pp. 71, 73, 95, 99.

50. SP, *Boletim estatistico* (1912), pp. 27–28.

51. Walker, p. 78.

52. Dean, *Rio Claro*, Table 6.6, p. 166. Undercounting the weight presumably meant fewer trees would be taxed.

53. Egas, *Galeria*, 2: 279.

54. SP, *Boletim estatistico* (1912), pp. 27–28; Walker, p. 75. This situation is especially interesting considering that the state constitution limited a município's interest and amortization payments to a quarter of its annual revenues.

55. Derived from data in *Moody's Manual*, 1932, p. 149, and 1933, p. 144, 146. The rate of U.S. $70.30 to one conto in 1931 was used in this calculation.

56. Figures exclude the Federal District. São Paulo city and Santos owed 219,566 contos in foreign obligations in 1931. Bouças, *Finanças*, 3: 83.

57. Orlando de Carvalho, pp. 110–11.

58. Brazil, *78 anos*. In 1973, São Paulo accounted for 48 percent of federal revenues. IBGE, *Anuário estatístico*, 1974, pp. 853, 857.

59. Villela and Suzigan, p. 141.

60. For federal collections in São Paulo, see Brazil, *78 anos*. São Paulo's contributions to federal receipts for 1925–43 are found in Quadros A-18, B-18, C-18, and D-18.

61. *Ação da bancada paulista*, p. 33.

62. Minas did make some direct contributions to tariff receipts at the port of Rio, though no records of the amounts were kept.

63. Brazil, *78 anos*, Quadros A-10, A-14, B-10, B-14.

64. To arrive at this ratio, I have divided the two states' gross domestic products for 1939, the first year that state breakdowns are available, by their population in 1940, the closest census year. This yields a per-capita ratio of 2.9 for São Paulo to 1 for Minas. Then, in order to exclude import tariffs and factor out per-capita income differences, I have divided this ratio into the ratio for the federal non-import receipts collected in the two states—8.3 : 1—arriving at a figure of 2.86, or 2.9 in round figures. For sources, see the next note.

65. Under these assumptions, the ratio of federal non-import receipts collected in São Paulo and Minas Gerais becomes 5.4 : 1. Correcting for per-capita income differences between the states (2.9 : 1) yields the 1.9 : 1 ratio in taxes paid. Based on data in Brazil, *78 anos*, Quadros A-14, A-18, B-14, B-18; IBGE, *Anuário estatístico*, 1971, p. 41; *Conjuntura Econômica*, Portuguese edition, 24, no. 6 (June 1970): 95. For the case that Minas Gerais was underrated as a taxpayer, see Daniel de Carvalho, pp. 169–70. For the contrary view that São Paulo was overtaxed even in non-import duties compared with Minas, see Romeiro, pp. 77–79. For a list of goods taxed at the factory during the Old Republic, see Vieira Machado, pp. 67–70.

66. L. Silva, "No limiar," p. 63.

67. As noted above, the treasury received 13% of its revenues from São Paulo in the years 1890–99, a period in which the state got only 1% of the federal outlays. The ratio, however, was lower than 13 : 1 because the absolute federal expenditures were greater than the revenues. In the decade 1928–37, the respective percentages were 30% and 4%. Brazil, *Contas*, 1931, p. 266 (foldout); INE, *Anuário estatístico*, 1936, pp. 397–98, and 1937, p. 797; IBGE, *Anuário estatístico*, 1939/1940, pp. 1269, 1410; Marc, 2: 178; SP, *Relatório* (Fazenda), 1915, p. 12; Brazil, *Balanço*, p. 42.

68. IBGE, *Anuário estatístico*, 1939/1940, p. 1269. The four states with net gains in federal fiscal operations were, not surprisingly, among the lowest producers of import duties. *Ibid.*, p. 510.

69. Brazil, *Relatório* (Banco), 1934, p. 19.

70. In 1931 Juarez Távora charged in a press interview that the bulk of the

Bank of Brazil's total assets (700,000 contos of 1,000,000) had already been pledged to coffee support in São Paulo, and that the remainder would soon be committed for the same purpose. This is surely an exaggeration, but I am unable to determine to what extent. See *OESP*, Jan. 7, 1931, p. 1.

71. Brazil, *Relatório* (Banco), 1937, pp. 67-68. Private borrowers received more in the Federal District than in São Paulo.

72. "Banco do Brasil: empréstimos a estados e municipais—situação em 31 de janeiro de 1938": Section I: "empréstimos ao governo federal: situação em 31 de outubro de 1937," pp. 1-3; Section II: empréstimos concedidos a estados e municipais com garantia do Tesouro Nacional," pp. 5-6; Section III: empréstimos . . . sem garantia . . . ," pp. 2-3, in AP, 14/14006. Federal coffee-related loans consisted of monies lent to the National Coffee Department (DNC) and to the Ministry of Finance for purchase of DNC bonds and for "operações de café" with two private companies.

73. Getúlio Vargas to Gov. Olegário Maciel, [Oct. 1932], Rio, AP 3/19.

74. Katzman, *Cities*, p. 211. Katzman gives data on direct federal outlays in São Paulo for the 1930's and 1960's (p. 97).

75. SP, *Relatório* (Fazenda), 1940, p. 5; *Moody's Manual*, 1933, p. 137.

76. Villela and Suzigan, pp. 202-3; *Moody's Manual*, 1932, p. 141.

77. São Paulo's state revenues amounted to 18% of the value of the (overseas) exports from Santos in 1892-99, 17% in 1920-29, and 29% in 1930-37. The per-capita state revenue in constant 1912 contos was 11.1 milréis in 1890, 30.6 milréis in 1892, 24.9 milréis in 1928, and 29.2 milréis in 1937, though the figure exceeded 30 milréis in several earlier depression years. Data for population and exports from SP, *São Paulo*, pp. 7, 8.

78. The figures for São Paulo in the retrospective comparative data are those of the IBGE, not my own. Similar trends are found for expenditures in the same sources. Both ordinary and extraordinary revenues and outlays are included in these data for the states and the Union, but extrabudgetary items for São Paulo are not. I therefore assume the same is true for the Union and the other states, where such accounts were probably much smaller for lack of a coffee-support program. But the validity of this assumption can be determined only by an examination of all Fazenda reports for the Union and all states in this period—a task that would require a team of researchers.

79. IBGE, *Anuário estatístico*, 1974, pp. 877, 884. The percentages were 35 and 37, respectively. It is unclear, however, whether the 1973 figures for the federal government include the budgets of semiautonomous and quasi-state enterprises; if not, then the federal budget is considerably underestimated. Though the corporatist state was essentially organized in the 1930's, most important semiautonomous corporations (such as Petrobrás) had not yet come into being; and however these were accounted for in the budgets up to 1945, they were far less important than they were to be by the 1970's. In any case, it needs to be proven, rather than assumed, that such enterprises are part of the "centralization" of government. On the 1930's as the formative era for the corporatist state, see L. Martins, "Politique," pp. 69-138. For a brief statement of the argument that federal government enterprises are not under central control, see Baer, Newfarmer, and Trebat, pp. 89-90.

80. U.S. data for 1938 from Elazar, p. 65; Brazilian data from IBGE, *Anuário estatístico*, 1939/1940, p. 1409. However, there is one more level of government

in the United States than in Brazil, where county and municipal budgets are combined. For data on Canada and Brazil in 1940, see Hugon, fig. 2, opposite p. 224.

81. In Brazil and Mexico, during the two phases of Vargas's 15-year government, the state revenues as a percent of federal revenues were as follows:

Period	Brazil	Mexico
1931–37	57.9%	22.7%
1938–45	55.7%	17.3%

The Brazilian figures are from sources cited in Table 8.2. See Mexico, *Anuario estadístico*, 1939, pp. 666–67, 678–79; 1942, pp. 1234, 1238; and 1943/45, pp. 762, 766–67 for the Mexican data. In neither case did I count the Federal District as a state, though it is grouped with the states in the Mexican sources. For the 1939 Mexican revenues I used the revised figures published in the 1942 volume.

Conclusion

1. Veríssimo; Skidmore, p. 323.

2. Cardoso to Vargas, n.p., June 16, 1932, Arquivo Getúlio Vargas; Shirley, *End*, p. 108; Carone, *Estado Novo*, p. 71. On regionalism in the historiography of Latin America, see Love, "Approach."

3. Edward Johnston and Co., pp. 17, 26; Tobias Monteiro, p. 224.

4. Edward Johnston and Co., pp. 29, 32.

5. Pereira de Sousa, pp. 6, 53.

6. "Madeira Gets Autonomy but Assesses It Warily," *New York Times*, May 9, 1976, p. 12.

7. Williamson, p. 112; Baer, Geiger, et al., p. 12. Compare Katzman: "The degree of disparity in 1970 was about equivalent to 1940, when Brazil was one of the most regionally unequal nations in the world." *Cities*, p. 211. Another study, by Merrick and Graham, shows that São Paulo's per capita income lead over the national average may have decreased slightly from 1960 to 1970. But the authors caution that data are weakest in the sector where the greatest convergent gains have occurred (services), and note that overall divergence in regional incomes may have occurred between 1960 and 1974. Their data also show that the per capita income gap widened between São Paulo and the Northeast between 1960 and 1970. See pp. 134, 144.

8. Cano, 1: 44, 47; 2: 264.

9. On the metropolis-satellite chain, see Frank. On comprador regimes, see Baran, pp. 205–18. For a theoretical statement on "associated-dependent" development, see Cardoso.

10. Cano, 1: 68; 2: 118.

11. Over half the federal government's foreign loans during the years 1889–1937 were subscribed by Rothschild. Bouças, *História, passim*.

12. Simonsen, *A margem*, pp. 250–51; Werneck Vianna, p. 173; Manoïlesco, pp. 281, 296–97. A Portuguese edition of Manoïlesco's work, first published in French in 1929, was published by the São Paulo industrialists' association (CIESP) in 1931.

13. Weffort, especially p. 73.

14. Brazil, *Politica*, 1: 132–33.

Bibliography

Archival Sources, Diplomatic Correspondence, and Unpublished Documents and Collections

Arquivo Borges de Medeiros. Instituto Histórico e Geográfico do Rio Grande do Sul, Pôrto Alegre.

Arquivo Edgard Leuenroth. Universidade Estadual de Campinas, Campinas, São Paulo. (A collection of rare newspapers and pamphlets concerning working-class activities and parties.)

Arquivo de *O Estado de S. Paulo*. São Paulo. (The central source of biographical information for this study.)

Arquivo Getúlio Vargas. Rio. Private collection.

Arquivo Osvaldo Aranha. Rio. Private collection.

Arquivo do Partido Democrático. Instituto Histórico e Geográfico de São Paulo, São Paulo.

Arquivo da Presidência. "Banco do Brasil; empréstimos a Estados e Municipais —situação em 31 de janeiro de 1938"; "Interventor: São Paulo." Arquivo Nacional, Rio.

Arquivo Prudente de Morais. Instituto Histórico e Geográfico Brasileiro, Rio. (This archive was being organized at the time I used it, and my access was limited.)

Arquivo Rui Barbosa. Casa Rui Barbosa, Rio.

Great Britain, Foreign Office. Annual reports from the Embassy in Rio de Janeiro, 1906–38; and selected reports, dispatches, and telegrams, 1906–39. Public Record Office, London.

United States, Department of State. American Consulate General, São Paulo: correspondence, 1920–32; Decimal File, 1930–39: Brazil, Internal Affairs (record group 59: 832.00); Numerical File, 1906–10, sections 842, 1251, 2372 (Brazil). National Archives, Washington, D.C.

———. Decimal File, 1910–29: Brazil, Internal Affairs (832.00), microcopy 519; dispatches from U.S. Consuls in Santos, 1831–1906, microcopy T-351. National Archives Microfilm Publications.

(Two other manuscripts, by Alceu Barroso and Eugene V. Davenport, are listed under "Other Sources.")

Newspapers

O Combate, São Paulo, 1915. Reformist and anti-PRP.
Correio da Manhã, Rio, 1909.
Correio Paulistano, São Paulo, 1874–1937, 1949–50, 1953. The PRP organ in the Republic.
Diário Nacional, São Paulo, 1930. The organ of the Partido Democrático.
Diário Popular, São Paulo, 1889–91.
O Estado [during the Empire, *A Província*] *de S. Paulo*, São Paulo, 1875–1938, 1977. Owned by the Mesquita family; favorable to the Partido Democrático and its successor, the Partido Constitucionalista.
O Federalista, São Paulo, 1889. Briefly the organ of the provincial Liberal Party.
O Operário, São Paulo, 1934. Catholic tabloid directed toward workers.
A Plateia, São Paulo, 1932. Generally favorable to labor.
A Plebe, São Paulo, 1933. Anarchist publication.
São Paulo, São Paulo, 1905. Catholic organ.

Other Sources

(The following list consists of works cited in the text, plus two dozen other items used in preparing the biographical data for Chapter 5. Unless otherwise noted, all books listed were published in the city of São Paulo.)

Abranches, Dunshee de. O golpe de estado; atos e atas do govêrno Lucena. Rio, 1954.

———. Governos e congressos da Republica dos Estados Unidos do Brasil. 2 v., 1918.

Ab' Sáber, Aziz Nacib, "São Paulo; o chão, o clima e as águas," pp. 13–27 in J. V. Freitas Marcondes and Osmar Pimentel, eds., São Paulo; espírito povo instituições. 1968.

A ação da bancada paulista "Por São Paulo Unido" na Assembléa Constituinte: O programa da 'Chapa Unica' e a nova constituição. 1935.

Almanak agricola brasileiro: 1925. 1925.

Almanak-Laemmert de São Paulo e indicador para 1903–1904. N.d.

Almeida, Tácito de. O movimento de 1887. 1934.

Alves Motta Sobrinho. A civilização de café (1820–1920). 2d ed. N.d.

Amado, Gilberto. Depois da política. Rio, 1960.

Amaral Peixoto, Alzira Vargas do. Getúlio Vargas, meu pai. Pôrto Alegre, 1960.

Andrade, Euclides, and Hely F. da Câmara. A Força Pública de São Paulo; esboço histórico, 1831–1931. 1931.

Andrade, Mário de. O movimento modernista. Rio, 1942.

Andrade, Oswald de. Memórias sentimentais de João Miramar. 1964. (Originally published in 1924.)

Annuario administrativo, agricola, profissional, mercantil e industrial da Republica dos Estados Unidos do Brasil para 1913, v. 3: Estado de S. Paulo. Rio, 1913.

Annuario commercial do Estado de São Paulo para 1904 abrangendo o Triangulo Mineiro (Estado de Minas Gerais). 1904.

Arantes, Altino. Passos do meu caminho. Rio, 1958.

Araújo, Alceu Maynard. "Achegas á 'Galeria dos Presidentes de S. Paulo,'" 2 parts, Revista de Administração (1961), nos. 175 (tomo I) and 178 (tomo II).

————. "Chefes do Governo Paulista de 24 de outubro de 1930 a 14 de março de 1947," Revista do Instituto Histórico e Geográfico de São Paulo, 58 (1960): 325–476.

Araújo Filho, José Ribeiro. Santos, o pôrto do café. Rio, 1969.

Argentina, Presidencia de la Nación, Ministerio de Asuntos Técnicos. Anuario estadístico de la República Argentina, v. 1: Compendio 1948. Buenos Aires, [1951].

Arruda Dantas, [Antônio]. Dom Duarte Leopoldo. 1974.

Assis Cintra. Bernardino de Campos e seu tempo. 1953.

————. "Bernardino expulsa da Convenção de Itu um 'comboeiro' e Quirino liberta uma mulata, 'quase branca,'" Correio Paulistano, Dec. 9, 1949.

————. "A dissolução do congresso de S. Paulo e a reorganização do P.R.P.," Correio Paulistano, June 17, 1950.

————. "Nos alicerces do P.R.P.," Correio Paulistano, Nov. 18, 1949.

————. "O P.R.P. na primeira campanha presidencial da República," Correio Paulistano, Jan. 30, 1953.

Associação Commercial de Santos. Boletim; edição especial dedicada ao 2º centenario do café. Santos, São Paulo, 1927.

Ayres de Camargo, [João]. Patriotas paulistas na columna sul. N.d.

Azevedo, Aroldo de. Arnolfo Azevedo; parlementar da Primeira República, 1868–1942. 1968.

————. "José Vicente de Azevedo; sua vida e sua obra (1859–1950)," Revista do Instituto Histórico e Geográfico de São Paulo, 59: 111–27.

————, ed. Brasil, a terra e o homem. 2 v. 1964.

Azevedo, Augusto Cezar de Miranda. Factos historicos da politica republicana brasileira e a scisão do Partido Republicano Federal. Lisbon, 1897.

————. Mortos illustres (1900–1901). 1902.

Azevedo, Fernando de. Brazilian Culture: An Introduction to the Study of Culture in Brazil. Tr. William Rex Crawford. New York, 1950.

Baer, Werner. "The Brazilian Boom, 1968–72: An Explanation and Interpretation," World Development, 1, no. 8 (1973): 1–16.

————. Industrialization and Economic Development in Brazil. Homewood, Ill., 1965.

Baer, Werner, Richard Newfarmer, and Thomas Trebat. "On State Capitalism in Brazil: Some New Issues and Questions," Inter-American Economic Affairs, 30, no. 3 (Winter 1976): 69–91.

Baer, Werner, Pedro Pinchas Geiger, et al. "Industrialização, urbanização e a persistência das desigualdades regionais do Brasil," Revista Brasileira de Geografia, 38, no. 2 (April–June 1976): 3–99.

Baer, Werner, and Annibal V. Villela. "Industrial Growth and Industrialization: Revisions in the Stages of Brazil's Economic Development," Journal of Developing Areas, 7, no. 2 (Jan. 1973): 217–34.

Baklanoff, Eric N. "External Factors in the Economic Development of Brazil's Heartland: The Center-South, 1850–1930," pp. 19–35 in Baklanoff, ed., The Shaping of Modern Brazil. Baton Rouge, La., 1969.

Bananére, Juó [pseud. for Alexandre Ribeiro Marcondes Machado]. La divina increnca. 1924.

Baran, Paul A. The Political Economy of Growth. New York, 1957.

Barbosa, Rui. Escritos e discursos seletos. Ed. Virgínia Côrtes de Lacerda. Rio, 1960.

Bardi, P. M. Profile of the New Brazilian Art. Rio, 1970.

Barman, Roderick, and Jean Barman. "The Role of the Law Graduate in the Political Elite of Imperial Brazil," *Journal of Inter-American Studies and World Affairs*, 18, no. 4 (Nov. 1976): 423–50.

Barros Brotero, Frederico de. Tribunal de Relação e Tribunal de Justiça de São Paulo; sob o ponto de vista genealógico. 1944.

Barroso, Alceu. "A civilização rural no sertão paulista e a revisão dos valores venais das propriedades agrícolas na Alta Sorocabana; relatório apresentado ao Tribunal de Impôstos e Taxas do Estado de São Paulo." Manuscript dated November 1936. Library, Secretaria da Fazenda, São Paulo.

Barroso, Gustavo. Brasil: Colônia de banqueiros. (História dos empréstimos de 1824 a 1934). 4th ed. Rio, 1935.

———. A sinagoga paulista. Rio, 1937.

Bartolotti, Dominico. Il Brasile meridionale. Rome, 1930.

Basbaum, Leôncio. Uma vida em seis tempos (Memórias). 1976.

Bassanezi, Maria Sílvia Beozzo. "Absorção e mobilidade da força de trabalho numa propriedade rural paulista (1895–1930)," pp. 241–64 in Carone, ed., O café, cited below.

Batista, Marta Rosetti, Telê Porto Ancona Lopez, and Yone Soares de Lima. Brasil: 1º tempo modernista—1917/29. Documentação. 1972.

Beiguelman, Paula. A formação do povo no complexo cafeeiro; aspectos políticos. 1968.

Berlinck, Manoel Tosta. "The Structure of the Brazilian Family in the City of São Paulo." Ph.D. dissertation, Cornell University. Ithaca, N.Y., 1969. (Latin American Studies dissertation series, 12.)

Blount, John Allen, III. The Public Health Movement in São Paulo, Brazil: A History of the Sanitary Service, 1892–1918." Ph.D. dissertation, Tulane University. New Orleans, 1971.

Boehrer, George C. A. Da monarquia à Republica: História do Partido Republicano do Brasil (1870–1889). Tr. Bernice Xavier. [Rio], n.d.

Bonilla, Frank. The Failure of Elites. Cambridge, Mass., 1970.

Bouças, Valentim F. Finanças do Brasil. v. 1, 2d ed.; v. 3 (Iª Parte); v. 19. Rio, 1934, 1955. (Title varies slightly. Commissioned by the Ministério da Fazenda.)

———. História da dívida externa. 2d ed. Rio, 1950.

Boxer, C. R. The Golden Age of Brazil, 1695–1750: Growing Pains of a Colonial Society. Berkeley, Calif., 1962.

Braga, Cincinato. Problemas brasileiros: Magnos problemas econômicos de São Paulo. 3d ed. Rio, 1948.

Brandão Sobrinho, Julio. A lavoura de canna e a industria assucareira dos Estados paulista e fluminense: Campos e Macahé em confronto com S. Paulo. 1912.

Brasiliense, A. "A correspondência de Américo Brasiliense (1889–1892) com notas de J.M.C.A. [J. Mariano de Camargo]," *Revista do Arquivo Municipal*, 57 (May 1939): 203–43.

———. Os programas dos partidos e o 2º Imperio. São Paulo, 1878.

Braudel, Fernand. The Mediterranean and the Mediterranean World in the Age of Philip II. 2 v. Tr. Sian Reynolds. New York, 1972–73.

Brazil, Almanak, 1937. Ministério da Guerra. Rio.

——, Annaes, 1891–1928. Camara dos Deputados. Rio.

——, Annaes, 1890–91. Congresso Constituinte da Republica. 3 v. 2d ed., rev. Rio, 1924–26.

——, Annaes, 1915. Senado. Rio, 1918.

——, Annuario estatistico do Brazil, 1908–12. Directoria Geral de Estatistica. 3 v. Rio, 1916–27.

——, Anuário estatístico do café, 1939/40. Departamento Nacional do Café. Rio, 1941.

——, Anuário estatístico do Brasil, 1939/1940, 1941/1945, 1946, 1960, 1969, 1971, 1974. Instituto Brasileiro de Geografia e Estatística. Rio.

——, Anuário estatístico do Brasil, 1936, 1937, 1938. Instituto Nacional de Estatística. Rio.

——, Balanço geral da União, 1937. Ministério da Fazenda. Rio.

——. Boletim eleitoral, Sept. 9, 1933, March 26, 1934, Feb. 22, 1936. Tribunal Superior de Justiça Eleitoral.

——, O Brasil actual. Instituto de Expansão Commercial. Rio, 1930.

——, O Brasil em números; apêndice do "Anuário estatístico do Brasil—1960." Instituto Brasileiro de Geografia e Estatística. Rio.

——, Brasil: Estatísticas recursos possibilidades. Ministério das Relações Exteriores. Rio, 1936.

——, Caixa de conversão, v. 1: 1906; v. 2; 1910. Documentos parlamentares. Paris, 1914.

——, Contas do exercicio financeiro, 1926, 1931. Ministério da Fazenda. Rio.

——, Dados estatísticos: Eleições federal estadual e municipal realizados no Brasil a partir de 1945, v. 1. Tribunal Superior Eleitoral. Rio, 1950.

——, Diario do Congresso Nacional, 1894–1930 (for election returns). Rio.

——, Discurso pronunciado pelo exmo. Sr. Ministro Dr. Osvaldo Aranha na sessão de 16 de março de 1934. Assembleia Nacional Constituinte. Rio.

——, Estatistica eleitoral da Republica. Ministerio da Agricultura. Rio, 1914.

——, Estatistica da imprensa periódica no Brasil (1929–1930). Departamento Nacional de Estatística. Rio, 1931.

——, O Imperio do Brazil na exposição universal de 1876 em Philadelphia. Rio, 1875.

——, Impostos interestaduaes (1900–1911). Documentos parlamentares. Paris, 1914.

——, Manual bibliográfico da geografia paulista (Junho de 1956). Conselho Nacional de Geografia. 1957.

——, Quarto centenário da fundação da cidade de São Paulo. Banco do Brasil. Rio, 1954.

——, Questionarios sobre as condições da agricultura dos 173 municipios do Estado de S. Paulo . . . de abril de 1910 a janeiro de 1912. Ministerio da Agricultura. Rio, 1913.

——, Questionarios sobre . . . Rio Grande do Norte . . . de 14 de junho de 1910 a 12 de dezembro de 1912. Ministerio da Agricultura. Rio, 1913.

——, Politica economica: Valorisação do café, v. 1: 1895–1906; v. 2: 1908–15. Documentos parlamentares. Rio, 1915.

————, Recenseamento geral do Brasil realizado em 1 de setembro de 1920. Directoria Geral de Estatistica. Rio, 1922–29.

————, Recenseamento geral do Brasil (1º de setembro de 1940). Série nacional, v. 2: Censo demográfico; v. 3: Censos econômicos. Série regional, parte 17, São Paulo, tomos 1–3. Instituto Brasileiro de Geografia e Estatística. Rio, 1950.

————, Relatório, 1934, 1937. Banco do Brasil. Rio.

————, Relatorio, 1909. Ministerio da Guerra. Rio.

————, Relatorio e trabalhos estatisticos, 1871. Directoria Geral de Estatistica. Rio.

————, Revisão constitucional. Documentos parlamentares. 5 v. Rio, 1927–28.

————, "78 anos de receita federal, 1890–1967." Ministério da Fazenda, Direção Geral da Fazenda Nacional, Assessoria de Estudos, Programação, e Avaliação. Mimeo., unpaginated. Rio, 1968.

————, Sexo, raça e estado civil, nacionalidade, filiação, culto e analphabetismo da população recenseada em 31 de dezembro de 1890. Rio, 1898.

————, VI recenseamento geral do Brasil—1950. Série nacional, v. 1: Brasil: Censo demográfico. Instituto Brasileiro de Geografia e Estatística. Rio, 1956.

————, Sinopse estatística do Estado, no. 2. Instituto Nacional de Estatística. 1938.

Bresciani, Maria Stella Martins. "Liberalismo; ideologia e controle social (Um estudo sobre São Paulo de 1850 a 1910)." Ph.D. dissertation, Universidade de São Paulo. 2 v. 1976.

Bresser Pereira, Luís Carlos. "Origens étnicas e sociais do empresário paulista," Revista de Administração de Emprêsas, 4, no. 11 (June 1964): 83–106.

British Chamber of Commerce of São Paulo and Southern Brazil. Facts About the State of São Paulo. 1950 [?].

————. Personalidades no Brasil: Men of Affairs in Brazil. 1933 [?].

————. São Paulo. Official Yearly Handbook. [1930].

Brito, Luiz Tenório de. Memórias de um ajudante de ordens. 1951.

————. "Notas biográficas sobre o Coronel Fernando Prestes de Albuquerque," Revista do Instituto Histórico e Geográfico de São Paulo, 46: 175–88.

Brunn, Gerhard. Deutschland und Brasilien (1889–1914). Cologne, 1971.

Burns, E. Bradford. The Unwritten Alliance: Rio Branco and Brazilian-American Relations. New York, 1966.

Camargo, José Francisco de. Crescimento da população no Estado de São Paulo e seus aspectos econômicos (Ensaio sobre as relações entre a demografia e a economia). 3 v. 1952. (Universidade de São Paulo, Faculdade de Filosofia, Boletim, 153, no. 1.)

Campello de Souza, Maria do Carmo. "O processo político-partidário na Primeira República," pp. 183–282 in Manuel Nunes Dias et al., Brasil em perspectiva. 1968.

Campos Salles, [Manuel Ferraz de]. Da propaganda á presidencia. 1908.

Canabrava, Alice Piffer. O desenvolvimento da cultura do algodão na Província de São Paulo (1861–1875). 1951.

Cândido [de Mello e Souza], Antônio. Literatura e sociedade. 2d ed. 1967.

————. Os parceiros do Rio Bonito; estudo sobre o caipira paulista e a transformação dos seus meios da vida. Rio, 1964.

Cano, Wilson. "Raízes da concentração industrial em São Paulo." Ph.D. dissertation, Universidade Estadual de Campinas. 2 v. Campinas, São Paulo, 1975.

Cardim, Mario. Ensaio de analyse de factores economicos e financeiros do Estado de São Paulo e do Brasil no periodo de 1913–1934 pelo methodo de numeros indices. 1936.

Cardoso, Fernando Henrique. "The Consumption of Dependency Theory in the United States," *Latin American Research Review*, 12, no. 3 (1977): 7–24.

Carneiro, Glauco. "A revolução constitucionalista," pp. 396–413 in Carneiro, História das revoluções brasileiras, v. 2: Da revolução liberal à revolução de 31 de março (1930/1964). Rio, 1965.

———. O revolucionário Siqueira Campos. 2 v. Rio, 1966.

Carone, Edgard. O Estado Novo (1937–1945). Rio, 1976.

———. A Primeira República (1889–1930); texto e contexto. 1969.

———. A República Nova (1930–1937). 1974.

———. A República Velha (Evolução política). 1971.

———. A República Velha (Instituições e classes sociais). 1970.

———, ed. O café: Anais do II Congresso de História de São Paulo. 1975. (Coleção de Revista de História, 59.)

Carone, Edgard, and Maria Sílvia Arantes Junqueira, eds. "Atas do Partido Republicano Paulista," *Estudos Históricos*, 11 (1972): 135–230.

Carvalho, Daniel de. Estudos de economia e finanças. Rio, 1946.

Carvalho, José Murilo de. "Elites and State-Building in Brazil." Ph.D. dissertation, Stanford University. Stanford, Calif., 1974.

Carvalho, Orlando de. Política do município (Ensaio histórico). Rio, 1946.

Carvalho e Silva, Herculano de. A revolução constitucionalista. Rio, 1932.

Castilho Cabral, [Cid]. Tempos de Jânio e outros tempos. Rio, 1962.

Castro Mascarenhas, Gregorio Gonçalves de. Terras devolutas e particulares no Estado de São Paulo, ou colleção das leis, regulamentos e ordens, expedidos a respeito destas materias até o presente. 2d ed., rev. 1912.

Cavalheiro, Edgard. Monteiro Lobato (Vida e obra). 2d ed. 1956.

[Centro dos Industriaes de Fiação e Tecelagem]. Relatorio . . . sobre a crise textil. Suas causas. Seus effeitos. Seus remedios. 1928.

Chalmers, Douglas A. "Developing on the Periphery: External Factors in Latin American Politics," pp. 67–93 in James N. Rosenau, ed., Linkage Politics: Essays on the Convergence of National and International Systems. New York, 1969.

Chilcote, Ronald. The Brazilian Communist Party: Conflict and Integration, 1922–1972. Oxford, 1974.

Clemenceau, G. Notes de voyage dans l'Amérique du Sud: Argentine, Uruguay, Brésil. Paris, 1911.

Club Athletico Paulistano. *Boletim Informativo do CAP*, Sept.–Oct. 1971.

———. Um clube que cresceu com a cidade; edição comemorativa do 70⁰ aniversário. 1970 [?].

Coaracy, Vivaldo. O caso de São Paulo. 1931.

Cobra, Amador Nogueira. Em um recanto do sertão paulista. 1923.

Conniff, Michael L. "Rio de Janeiro During the Great Depression, 1928–1937: Social Reform and the Emergence of Populism in Brazil." Ph.D. dissertation, Stanford University. Stanford, Calif., 1976.

Conrad, Robert. The Destruction of Brazilian Slavery. Berkeley, Calif., 1972.

———. "The Planter Class and the Debates over Chinese Immigration to Brazil, 1850–1893," *International Migration Review*, 9, no. 1 (Spring 1975): 41–55.

Corrêa Filho, Virgílio. História de Mato Grosso. Rio, 1969.
Costa Nogueira, Emília. See Emília Viotti da Costa.
Coutinho, Afrânio, ed. Brasil e brasileiros de hoje. 2 v. Rio, 1961.
Couto de Magalhães, ed. No segundo anniversario do governo Julio Prestes. 1929.
Dallari, Dalmo de Abreu. "Os estados na federação brasileira, de 1891 a 1937." Unpublished manuscript commissioned by author.
———. O pequeno exército paulista. 1977.
Dassin, Joan Rosalie. "The Politics of Art: Mário de Andrade and the Case of Brazilian Modernism, 1922–1945." Ph.D. dissertation, Stanford University. Stanford, Calif., 1974.
Davenport, Eugene V. "What One Life Has Seen." Manuscript, record series 8/1/21, Box 4. Archives, University of Illinois, Urbana-Champaign.
Davidson, David M. "How the Brazilian West Was Won: Freelance and State on the Mato Grosso Frontier, 1737–1752," pp. 61–106 in Dauril Alden, ed., Colonial Roots of Modern Brazil. Papers of the Newberry Library Conference. Berkeley, Calif., 1973.
Davis, Horace B., and Marian Rubins Davis. "Scale of Living of the Working Class in São Paulo, Brazil," Monthly Labor Review, 44 (Jan. 1937): 245–53.
Dean, Warren. The Industrialization of São Paulo, 1880–1945. Austin, Tex. 1969.
———. "Latifundia and Land Policy in Nineteenth Century Brazil," The Hispanic American Historical Review, 51, no. 4 (Nov. 1971): 606–25.
———. Review of Andre Gunder Frank's 'Capitalism and Underdevelopment in Latin America,' Hispanic American Historical Review, 48, no. 3 (Aug. 1968): 453–55.
———. Rio Claro: A Brazilian Plantation System, 1820–1920. Stanford, Calif., 1976.
Debes, Célio. O Partido Republicano na propaganda (1872–1889). 1975.
Deffontaines, Pierre. "Pays et paysages de l'Etat de Saint-Paul (Brésil)," Annales de Geographie, 45 (1936): 50–71, 160–74.
Delfim Netto, Antônio. O problema do café no Brasil. 1959. (Universidade de São Paulo, Faculdade de Ciências Econômicas, Boletim, no. 5, cadeira 3, no. 1.)
Delgado de Carvalho, C. M. Le Brésil meridional: Etude économique sur les états du sud: S. Paulo, Paraná, Santa-Catharina et Rio-Grande-do-Sul. Rio, 1910.
Denis, Pierre. Brazil. Tr. Bernard Miall. London, 1911. (Originally published in 1909.)
Denslow, David. "As origens de desigualdade regional no Brasil," Estudos Econômicos, 3, no. 1 (April 1973): 65–88.
Os deputados republicanos na assembléa provincial de São Paulo: Sessão de 1888. 1888.
Deutsch, Karl W. Nationalism and Social Communication. Cambridge, Mass., 1953.
Deveza, Guilherme. "Política tributária no período imperial," pp. 60–85 in Sérgio Buarque de Holanda and Pedro Moacyr Campos, eds., História geral da civilização brasileira, 2, no. 4. 1971.
Dias de Campos, Pedro. O espirito militar paulista; na colonia, no Imperio, na Republica. 1923.

Dulles, John W. F. Anarchists and Communists in Brazil, 1900–1935. Austin, Tex., 1973.
———. Vargas of Brazil: A Political Biography. Austin, Tex., 1967.
Duncan, Julian Smith. Public and Private Operation of Railways in Brazil. New York, 1932.
Edward Johnston and Co. Um século de café. Rio, 1942.
Egas, Eugenio. Galeria dos presidentes de São Paulo. 3 v. 1926–27.
———. Impostos e taxas de São Paulo (Synthese historica de sua evolução). 1926.
Eisenberg, Peter L. The Sugar Industry in Pernambuco: Modernization Without Change, 1840–1910. Berkeley, Calif., 1973.
Eisenberg, Peter L., and Michael M. Hall. "Labor Supply and Immigration in Brazil: A Comparison of Pernambuco and São Paulo." Paper presented at the Latin American Studies Association annual meeting, Madison, Wis., May 3–5, 1973.
Elazar, Daniel J. American Federalism: A View from the States. New York, 1966.
Eles construiram a grandeza de São Paulo (In Memoriam). 1954.
Ellis Júnior, Alfredo. A lenda da lealdade de Amador Bueno e a evolução da psicologia planaltina. 1967.
———. Um parlamentar paulista da República; subsídios para a história da República em São Paulo e subsídios para a história econômica de São Paulo. 1949.
Ensaios paulistas. 1958.
Esboço biographico: D. Duarte Leopoldo e Silva. Arcebispo de São Paulo. 1929.
Evolución: Revista mensual de ciencias y letras: Relación oficial del primer congreso internacional de estudiantes americanos celebrado en Montevideo de 26 de enero a 2 de febrero de 1908. Montevideo, n.d.
Faoro, Raymundo. Os donos do poder; formação do patronato político brasileiro. 2 v. 2d ed. 1975.
Fausto, Boris. "Expansão do café e política cafeeira," pp. 195–248 in Fausto, ed., História geral da civilização brasileira, 3, no. 1. 1975.
———. "Pequenos ensaios de história da República: 1889–1945." Mimeo. Cadernos CEBRAP [Centro Brasileiro de Análise e Planejamento]. 1972.
———. A revolução de 1930; historiografia e história. 1970.
———. "A revolução de 1930," pp. 253–84 in Manuel Nunes Dias et al., Brasil em perspectiva. 1968.
———. Trabalho urbano e conflito social (1889–1930). 1976.
Fernandes, Florestan. A integração do negro na sociedade de classes. 2 v. 1965.
———. The Negro in Brazilian Society. Tr. J. Skiles, A. Brunel, and A. Rothwell; ed. Phyllis B. Eveleth. New York, 1969.
Fernandes, Heloísa Rodrigues. Política e segurança: Força Pública do Estado de São Paulo; fundamentos histórico-sociais. 1974.
Ferreira, Tito Lívio. História de São Paulo. 2 v. N.d.
Ferreira Lima, Heitor. "Roberto Simonsen e os problemas econômicos nacionais," pp. 451–95 in Aureliano Leite et al., Homens de São Paulo. 1955.
Figueiredo, Adherbal Oliveira. Tenente Galinha. 1965.
Fishlow, Albert. "Algumas observações adicionais sôbre a discussão," Estudos Econômicos, 3, no. 1 (1973): 148–55.
———. "Origens e consequências da substituição de importações no Brasil," Estudos Econômicos, 2, no. 6 (Dec. 1972): 7–75.

Flynn, Peter. "The Revolutionary Legion and the Brazilian Revolution of 1930," pp. 63–105 in *St. Antony's Papers*, no. 22: Latin American Affairs. London, 1970.

Foerster, Robert F. The Italian Emigration of Our Times. Cambridge, Mass., 1919.

Fonseca, Antonio Carlos da. Camara dos deputados do Estado de São Paulo no antigo e no novo regimen. 2 v. 1924.

————. Senado de São Paulo, 1891–1930. N.p., n.d.

Fonseca Filho, Hermes da. Marechal Hermes; dados para uma biografia. Rio, 1961.

Foreign Bondholders Protective Council, Inc. Annual Report, 1937, 1941/44. New York, 1938, 1945. (Title varies slightly.)

Frank, Andre Gunder. Capitalism and Underdevelopment in Latin America: Historical Studies of Chile and Brazil. Rev. ed. New York, 1969.

Frey, Frederick W. The Turkish Political Elite. Cambridge, Mass., 1965.

Furtado, Celso. The Economic Growth of Brazil: A Survey from Colonial to Modern Times. Tr. Ricardo W. de Aguiar and Eric Charles Drysdale. Berkeley, Calif., 1965.

Gabaglia, Laurita Pessôa Raja. O Cardeal Leme (1882–1942). Rio, 1962.

Galante de Sousa, J. Indice de biobibliografia brasileira. 1963.

Galtung, Johan. "A Structural Theory of Integration," *Journal of Peace Research*, no. 4 (1968): 375–95.

Gardner, James A. Urbanization in Brazil: International Urbanization Survey. [A Ford Foundation project.] New York, 1972.

Gauld, Charles A. The Last Titan. Percival Farquhar: American Entrepreneur in Latin America. Stanford, Calif., 1964.

Gauthier, Howard L. "Transportation and the Growth of the São Paulo Economy," *Journal of Regional Science*, 8, no. 1 (1968): 77–94.

Gifun, Frederick Vincent. "Ribeirão Preto, 1880–1914: The Rise of a Coffee County, or the Transition to Coffee in São Paulo as Seen Through the Development of Its Leading Producer." Ph.D. dissertation, University of Florida. Gainesville, 1972.

Godinho, Wanor R., and Oswaldo S. Andrade. Constituintes brasileiros de 1934. N.p., n.d.

Godoy, Joaquim Floriano de. Projecto de lei para creação da Provincia do Rio Sapucahy. Rio, 1888.

————. Provincia de São Paulo; tentativas centralisadoras do governo liberal. Rio, 1882.

Gonçalves, Francisco de Paula Lazaro. Relatorio apresentado á Associação Promotora de Immigração em Minas. Juiz de Fora, Minas Gerais, 1888.

Gonçalves de Oliveira, Eden. "Areas homogêneas no território do Estado de São Paulo sob o ponto de vista da organização agrária," *Revista Brasileira de Economia*, 27, no. 1 (Jan.–March 1973): 115–64.

Gonçalves Maia, Julio Joaquim. "Lista geral. Bachareis e doutores formados pela Faculdade de Direito de São Paulo e dos lentes e diretores effectivos até 1900," *Revista da Faculdade de Direito de São Paulo*, 7 (1900).

Goulart, Maurício. "Júlio Mesquita," pp. 305–65 in Aureliano Leite et al., Homens de São Paulo, 1955.

Graham, Douglas H. "Internal and Foreign Migration and the Question of Labor

Supply in the Early Economic Growth of Brazil." Paper presented at the Latin American Studies Association annual meeting, Madison, Wis., May 3–5, 1973.

———. "Migração estrangeira e a questão da oferta de mão de obra no crescimento econômico brasileiro, 1880–1930," Estudos Econômicos, 3, no. 1 (April 1973): 7–64.

Graham, Douglas H., and Sérgio Buarque de Hollanda Fº. "Migration, Regional and Urban Growth and Development in Brazil: A Selective Analysis of the Historical Record, 1872–1970." Mimeo. Instituto de Pesquisas Econômicas, Universidade de São Paulo. 1971.

Graham, Richard. Britain and the Onset of Modernization in Brazil: 1850–1914. Cambridge, Eng., 1968.

———. "Government Expenditure and Political Change in Brazil, 1880–1899: Who Got What," Journal of Inter-American Studies and World Affairs, 19, no. 3 (Aug. 1977): 339–67.

Greenfield, Gerald Michael. "The Challenge of Growth: The Growth of Urban Public Services in São Paulo, 1885–1913." Ph.D. dissertation, Indiana University. Bloomington, 1975.

Guanabara, Alcindo. A presidencia Campos Salles. Rio, 1902.

Guastini, Mário. Café e outros assuntos. 1946.

———. Politica em torno de uma cadeira. Rio, 1924.

Gurgel, Leoncio A. Genealogia do Snr. Dr. Manoel Ferraz de Campos Salles. 1906.

Haas, Ernst B. The Uniting of Europe: Political, Social, and Economic Forces, 1950–1957. Stanford, Calif., 1958.

Hagen, Everett E. On the Theory of Social Change: How Economic Growth Begins. Homewood, Ill., 1962.

Hahner, June E. "The Paulistas' Rise to Power: A Civilian Group Ends Military Rule," Hispanic American Historical Review, 47, no. 2 (May 1967): 149–65.

Hall, Michael M. "Emigrazione italiana a San Paolo tra 1880 e 1920," Quaderni Storici, 25 (Jan.–April 1974): 138–59.

———. "Immigration and the Early São Paulo Working Class," Jahrbuch für Geschichte von Staat, Wirtschaft und Gesellschaft Lateinamerikas, 12 (1975): 393–407.

———. "The Origins of Mass Immigration in Brazil, 1871–1914." Ph.D. dissertation, Columbia University. New York, 1969.

Hilton, Ronald, ed. Who's Who in Latin America, Part 6: Brazil. 3d ed. Stanford, Calif. 1948.

Hilton, Stanley E. "Vargas and Brazilian Economic Development, 1930–1945: A Reappraisal of His Attitude Toward Industrialization and Planning," Journal of Economic History, 35, no. 4 (Dec. 1975): 754–78.

Holloway, Thomas H. The Brazilian Coffee Valorization of 1906: Regional Politics and Economic Dependence. Madison, Wis., 1975.

———. "Condições do mercado de trabalho e organização do trabalho nas plantações na economia cafeeira de São Paulo, 1885–1915—uma análise preliminar," Estudos Econômicos, 2, no. 6 (Dec. 1972): 145–80.

———. "Immigration and Abolition: The Transition from Slave to Free Labor in the São Paulo Coffee Zone," pp. 150–77 in Dauril Alden and Warren Dean, eds., Essays Concerning the Socioeconomic History of Brazil and Portuguese India. Gainesville, Fla., 1977.

————. "Migration and Mobility: Immigrants as Laborers and Landowners in the Coffee Zone of São Paulo, Brazil, 1886–1934." Ph.D. dissertation, University of Wisconsin. Madison, 1974.

Hugon, Paul. O imposto; teoria moderna e principais sistemas: O sistema tributário brasileiro. 2d ed., rev. Rio, 1955 [?].

Hutchinson, Bertram, et al. Mobilidade e trabalho; um estudo na cidade de São Paulo. Rio, 1960.

Hutter, Lucy Maffei. Imigração italiana em São Paulo (1880–1889); os primeiros contactos do imigrante com o Brasil. 1972.

In memoriam: Martinho Prado Júnior, 1843–1943. 1944.

Instituto Historico e Geographico Brasileiro. Diccionario historico, geographico e ethnographico do Brasil (Commemorativo do primeiro centenario da independencia), v. 1. Rio, 1922.

Instituto Histórico e Geográfico de São Paulo. São Paulo em quatro séculos. 2 v. 1954.

International Coffee Organization. "Le Café au Brésil." Mimeo. London, 1972.

Jaguaribe, Hélio. "The Dynamics of Brazilian Nationalism," pp. 162–87 in Claudio Véliz, ed., Obstacles to Change in Latin America. London, 1965.

James, Herman G. The Constitutional System of Brazil. Washington, D.C., 1923.

James, Preston E. Latin America. 4th ed. New York, 1969.

Jardim, Renato. Reminiscências (de Resende, Estado do Rio, às plagas paulistas: S. Simão, Batatais, Altinópolis e Ribeirão Preto). Rio, 1946.

Joslin, David. A Century of Banking in Latin America. London, 1963.

Katzman, Martin T. "The Brazilian Frontier in Comparative Perspective," Comparative Studies in Society and History, 17, no. 3 (July 1975): 266–85.

————. Cities and Frontiers in Brazil: Regional Dimensions of Economic Development. Cambridge, Mass., 1977.

Kern, Robert, ed. The Caciques. Albuquerque, N.M., 1973.

Klinger, [Bertoldo]. Narrativas aotobiográficos, v. 6, 7. Rio, 1951, 1953.

Knowlton, Clark S. "Spatial and Social Mobility of the Syrians and Lebanese in the City of São Paulo, Brazil." Ph.D. dissertation, Vanderbilt University. Nashville, 1955.

Krasner, Stephen D. "Manipulating International Commodity Markets: Brazilian Coffee Policy 1906 to 1962," Public Policy, 21, no. 4 (Fall 1973): 493–523.

Laërne, C. F. van Delden. Brazil and Java: Report on Coffee-Culture in America, Asia and Africa, to H. E. the Minister of the Colonies. London, 1885.

Laffitte Junior. Pela patria. Casa Branca, São Paulo, 1888.

Lage de Andrade, Edgard. Sertões do noroeste: 1850–1945. N.d.

Lago, Laurênio. Supremo Tribunal de Justiça e Supremo Tribunal Federal; dados biográficos (1828–1939). Rio, 1940.

Lalière, A. Le Café dans l'Etat de Saint-Paul (Brésil). Paris, 1909.

Lampedusa, Giuseppe di. The Leopard. Tr. Archibald Colquhoun. New York, 1960.

Lara, Cecília de. 'Klaxon' e 'Terra Roxa e Outras Terras'; dois periódicos modernistas de São Paulo. 1972.

Leal, Hamilton. História das instituições políticas do Brasil. Rio, 1962.

Lefevre, Eugênio. A administração do Estado de São Paulo na República Velha. 1937.

Leff, Nathaniel H. "Economic Development and Regional Inequality: Origins of the Brazilian Case," *Quarterly Journal of Economics*, 86, no. 2 (May 1972): 243–62.

———. "Long-term Brazilian Economic Development," *Journal of Economic History*, 29, no. 3 (Sept. 1969): 473–93.

Leite, Aureliano. "Causas e objetivos da revolução de 1932," *Revista de História*, 25, no. 51 (July–Sept. 1962): 139–66.

———. História da civilização paulista. N.d.

———. Páginas de uma longa vida. N.d.

Lemarchand, René, and Keith Legg. "Political Clientelism and Development: A Preliminary Analysis," *Comparative Politics*, 4, no. 2 (Jan. 1972): 149–78.

Leme, Marisa Sáenz. "Café e indústria de sacaria," pp. 341–61 in Edgard Carone, ed., O café, cited above.

Leopoldo [e Silva], Duarte. Illuminuras. 1937.

Leuenroth, Edgard, ed. Anarquismo—Roteiro da libertação social. Rio, 1963.

Levi, Darrell E. "The Prados of São Paulo: An Elite Brazilian Family in a Changing Society, 1840–1930." Ph.D. dissertation, Yale University. New Haven, Conn., 1974.

Lévi-Strauss, Claude. Tristes tropiques. Tr. John Russell. New York, 1967.

Levine, Robert M. Pernambuco in the Brazilian Federation, 1889–1937. Stanford, Calif., 1978.

———. "Some Views on Race and Immigration During the Old Republic," *The Americas*, 27, no. 4 (April 1971): 373–80.

Lewis, W. Arthur. Aspects of Tropical Trade, 1883–1965. Stockholm, 1969.

———, ed. Tropical Development, 1880–1913. Evanston, Ill., 1970.

Lindberg, Leon N., and Stuart A. Scheingold, eds. Regional Integration: Theory and Research. Cambridge, Mass., 1971.

Lins, Ivan. História do positivismo no Brasil. 1964.

Linz, Juan J., and Amando de Miguel. "Within-Nation Differences and Comparisons: The Eight Spains," pp. 267–319 in Richard L. Merritt and Stein Rokkan, eds., Comparing Nations: The Use of Quantitative Data in Cross-National Research. New Haven, Conn., 1966.

Lipkau, Ernst Günther. "Deutsche auslandbanken in Brasilien," *Staden-Jahrbuch*, 17 (1969): 73–99.

Lista geral dos estudantes matriculados nas aulas da Faculdade de Direito de S. Paulo, 1901–1930. 1902–31. (Title varies.)

Little, George F. G. "Fazenda Cambuhy: A Case History of Social and Economic Development in the Interior of São Paulo, Brazil." Ph.D. dissertation, University of Florida. Gainesville, 1960.

Lloyd, Reginald, et al. Impressões do Brazil no seculo vinte. London, 1913.

Lobo, Eulália Maria Lahmeyer, et al. "Evolução dos preços e do padrão de vida no Rio de Janeiro, 1820–1930—resultados preliminares," *Revista Brasileira de Economia*, 25, no. 4 (1971): 235–65.

Lopes, Betralda. "Comércio de café através do Porto de Santos (1810–1974)," pp. 57–74 in Edgard Carone, ed., O café: Annais do II Congresso de História de São Paulo. 1975.

López Toro, Alvaro. Migración y cambio social en Antioquia durante el siglo diez y nueve. Bogotá, 1968.

Love, Joseph L. "An Approach to Regionalism," pp. 137–55 in Richard Graham and Peter H. Smith, eds., New Approaches to Latin American History. Austin, Tex., 1974.

———. "Autonomia e interdependência: São Paulo e a Federação Brasileira, 1889–1937," pp. 53–76 in Boris Fausto, ed., História geral da civilização brasileira, 3, no. 1. 1975.

———. "Political Participation in Brazil, 1881–1969," Luso-Brazilian Review, 7, no. 2 (Dec. 1970): 3–24.

———. Rio Grande do Sul and Brazilian Regionalism, 1882–1930. Stanford, Calif., 1971.

Lowrie, Samuel H. Imigração e crescimento da população no Estado de São Paulo. 1938.

Luz, Nícia Vilela. "A administração provincial de São Paulo em face do movimento abolicionista," Revista de Administração, 2, no. 8 (Dec. 1948): 80–100.

———. A luta pela industrialização do Brasil (1808 a 1930). 1961.

Lyra, João. Cifras e notas (Economia e finanças do Brasil). Rio, 1925.

McCreery, Walter Gay, and Mary L. Bynum. The Coffee Industry in Brazil. Washington, D.C., 1930 (U.S. Department of Commerce Trade Promotion Series, no. 92.)

McGann, Thomas F. Argentina, the United States, and the Inter-American System, 1880–1914. Cambridge, Mass., 1957.

McGreevey, William Paul. An Economic History of Colombia, 1845–1930. Cambridge, Eng., 1971.

Macedo Soares, José Carlos de. Justiça; a revolta militar em São Paulo. Paris, 1925.

Machado de Assis, Joaquim Maria. Memórias póstumas de Brás Cubas. 1960. (Originally published in 1880.)

Maeyama, Takashi. "Familialization of the Unfamiliar World: The Família, Networks and Groups in a Brazilian City." Ph.D. dissertation, Cornell University. Ithaca, N.Y., 1975 (Latin American Studies Dissertation series, no. 59.)

Malloy, James M. "The Evolution of Social Security Policy in Brazil: Policy Making and Income Distribution." Paper presented at the American Political Science Association Meeting, San Francisco, Calif., Sept. 2–5, 1975.

Manoïlesco, Mihaïl. Théorie du protectionnisme et de l'échange international. Paris, 1929.

Manor, Paul. "The Liga Nacionalista de S. Paulo and Its Weight in Paulista Politics, 1917–1924." Unpublished manuscript, n.d.

Mantua, Simão de [pseud. for Antônio Gomes Carmo]. Figurões vistos por dentro (Estudo de psychologia social brasileira). 2 v. 1921.

Maram, Sheldon Leslie. "Anarchists, Immigrants, and the Brazilian Labor Movement, 1890–1920." Ph.D. diss., University of California. Santa Barbara, 1972.

Marc, Alfred. Le Brésil: Excursion à travers ses 20 provinces. 2 v. Paris, 1890.

Marcílio, Maria Luiza. "Tendence et structures des ménages dans la capitainerie de São Paulo (1765–1868) selon les listes nominatives d'habitants," pp. 157–65 in Colloques Internationaux du Centre National de la Recherche Scientifique, no. 543: L'Histoire quantitative du Brésil de 1800 a 1930. Paris, 1973.

Marcus, Howard. "Provincial Government in São Paulo: The Administration of João Teodoro Xavier (1872–1875)." Ph.D. dissertation, Yale University. New Haven, Conn., 1973.

Margolis, Maxine L. The Moving Frontier: Social and Economic Change in a Southern Brazilian Community. Gainesville, Fla., 1973.

Marson, Adalberto. "Dimensões políticos do modernismo na década de 20," Ciência e Cultura, 25, no. 11 (Nov. 1973): 1030–37.

Martin, Percy Alvin, ed. Who's Who in Latin America. 2d ed. Stanford, Calif., 1940.

Martin du Gard, Roger. Jean Barois. Tr. Stuart Gilbert. New York, 1949. (Originally published in 1913.)

Martinez Corrêa, Ana Maria. "História social de Araraquara (1817 a 1930)." M.A. thesis, Universidade de São Paulo. 1967.

———. A rebelião de 1924 em São Paulo. 1976.

Martins, Henrique. Lista geral dos bacharéis . . . na Faculdade de Direito de Recife desde . . . 1828 até o anno de 1931. Recife, 1931.

Martins, João Candido. Necessidades do Brasil. 1887.

Martins, Luciano. "Politique et développement économique: Structures de pouvoir et système de décisions au Brésil (1930–1964)." Ph.D. dissertation, Université René Descartes. Paris, 1973.

Martins, Wilson. The Modernist Idea: A Critical Survey of Brazilian Writing in the Twentieth Century. Tr. Jack E. Tomlins. New York, 1970.

Martins Filho, Amílcar Vianna. "Minas e São Paulo na Primeira República Brasileira: A 'política café com leite' (1900–1930)." M.A. thesis, Universidade Federal de Minas Gerais. Belo Horizonte, 1978.

Mattoon, Robert Howard, Jr. "The Companhia Paulista de Estradas de Ferro, 1868–1900: A Local Railway Enterprise in São Paulo, Brazil." Ph.D. dissertation, Yale University. New Haven, Conn., 1971.

Mauro, José Eduardo Marques. "Os primórdios do desenvolvimento econômico brasileiro, 1850–1929; o Brasil e os fundamentos de seu processo de crescimento econômico." Ph.D. dissertation, Universidade de São Paulo. 2 v. 1972.

Meio século de progresso paulista. 1938.

Melo, Luís Correia de. Dicionário de autores paulistas. 1954.

Melo Franco, Afonso Arinos de. Rodrigues Alves; apogeu e declínio do presidencialismo. 2 v. Rio, 1973.

Mendes de Almeida, Candido. Atlas do Imperio do Brazil; comprehendo as respectivas divisões administrativas . . . Rio, 1868.

Menezes, Raimundo de. Dicionário literário brasileiro—ilustrado. 5 v. 1969.

Mennucci, Sud. O precursor do abolicionismo no Brasil: Luiz Gama. 1938.

Merrick, Thomas W., and Douglas H. Graham. Population and Economic Development in Brazil: 1800 to the Present. Baltimore, 1979.

Mesquita Filho, Júlio. "A comunhão paulista," pp. 236–39 in Edgard Carone, ed., A Primeira República, cited above.

Mexico, Secretaría de Economía, Dirección General de Estadística. Anuario estadístico, 1939, 1942, 1943/45. Mexico City, 1941–50.

Milliet, Sérgio. Roteiro do café e outros ensaios. 1946.

Miranda Guimarães, Ylves de. Comentários ao código de impostos e taxas do Estado de São Paulo, v. 1. 2d ed. 1960.

Monbeig, Pierre. Pionniers et planteurs de São Paulo. Paris, 1952.

———. "Os problemas da divisão regional de São Paulo," pp. 181–207 in Instituto Brasileiro de Geografia e Estatística, Aspectos geográficos da terra bandeirante. Rio, 1954.

Moniz Bandeira, Clovis Melo, and A. T. Andrade. O ano vermelho. Rio, 1967.
Monteiro, F. Figuras do Banco do Brasil. Rio, 1955.
Monteiro, Tobias. O Presidente Campos Salles na Europa. Rio, 1928.
Monteiro Lobato, [José Bento]. Cidades mortas. 1959. (Originally published in 1919.)
————. A onda verde. 2d ed. 1922.
Moody's Manual of Investments, 1928–33. New York.
Moraes Filho, M. J. Vieira de. A lenda dos assassinatos politicos em São Paulo; simples e documentada narrativa dos factos occorridos no Estado de São Paulo, aos quaes a paixão partidaria denominou assassinatos politicos. 1911.
Moreira Alves, Márcio. A Grain of Mustard Seed: The Awakening of the Brazilian Revolution. New York, 1973.
Morse, Richard M. From Community to Metropolis. 2d. ed. New York, 1974.
Motta, Cássio. Cesário Motta e seu tempo. 1947.
Motta Filho, [Cândido]. Uma grande vida; biografia de Bernardino de Campos. 1941.
Mouralis, Louis. Un Séjour aux Etats-Unis du Brésil. Paris, 1934.
Nagle, Jorge. "A educação na Primeira República," pp. 259–91 in Boris Fausto, ed., História geral da civilização brasileira, 3, no. 2. 1977.
New Catholic Encyclopedia. 15 v. New York, 1967.
Nogueira, Oracy. "Indices do desenvolvimento de São Paulo," Revista Brasileira de Ciências Sociais, 2, no. 2 (July 1962): 143–96.
————. "Os movimentos e os partidos políticos em Itapetininga," Revista Brasileira de Estudos Políticos, 11 (June 1961): 222–47.
Nogueira de Matos, Odilon. "O desenvolvimento da rêde ferroviária e a expansão da cultura do café em São Paulo," Boletim Geográfico, 14, no. 133 (July–Aug. 1956): 371–81.
Nogueira Filho, Paulo. O Partido Democrático e a revolução de 1930. (Part 1 of Ideais e lutas de um burguês progressista.) 2d ed. 2 v. Rio, 1965.
————. A guerra cívica 1932. (Part 2 of Ideais e lutas de um burguês progressista.) 4 v. Rio, 1965–67.
Noronha, Abilio de. Narrando a verdade; contribuição para a historia da revolta em São Paulo. 1924.
Nunes, Aristides. "História do Banco do Estado de São Paulo, S.A." Mimeo. Banco do Estado de São Paulo. N.d.
Nunes Leal, Victor. Coronelismo, enxada e voto: O município e o regime representativo no Brasil. Rio, 1948.
Oberacker, Karl Heinrich, Jr. Der deutsche Beitrag zum Aufbau der brasilianischen Nation. 1955.
Oliveira, Clovis de. A indústria e o movimento constitucionalista de 1932. 1936.
Oliveira, João Gualberto de. "55 anos de fundação do Instituto dos Advogados de São Paulo," Revista do Instituto Histórico e Geográfico de São Paulo, 68 (1970): 247–54.
Oliveira, Percival de. O ponto de vista do P.R.P. (Uma campanha politica). 1930.
[Oliveira Carvalho], Paulo Egydio de. A Provincia de São Paulo em 1888 (Ensaio historico-politico). 1888.
Oliveira Mello. Revolta de São Paulo; acontecimentos dos dias 14 e 15 de dezembro de 1891. 1892.

Oliveira Torres, João Camillo de. A democracia coroada; teoria política do Império do Brasil. 2d ed. Petrópolis, Rio de Janeiro, 1964.

Oliveira Vianna, [Francisco]. Populações meridionais do Brasil; história-organização-psicologia, v. 1: Populações rurais do centro-sul; paulistas-fluminenses-mineiros. 5th ed. Rio, 1952. (Originally published in 1922.)

O'Neil, Charles F. "Educational Innovation and Politics in São Paulo, 1933–34." Luso-Brazilian Review, 8, no. 1 (June 1971): 56–68.

————. "The Search for Order and Progress: Brazilian Mass Education, 1915–1935." Ph.D. dissertation, University of Texas. Austin, 1975.

Ortigão, Ramalho. O anno commercial economico e financeiro de 1917. Rio, 1918.

Osório, Manoel. O Brasil unido ou o separatismo paulista. 1934.

Pacheco e Silva, A. C. Armando de Salles Oliveira. 1966.

Paiva Abreu, Marcelo de. "A dívida pública externa do Brasil, 1931–1943," Pesquisa e Planejamento Econômico, 5, no. 1 (June 1975): 37–87.

————. "A missão Niemeyer," Revista de Administração de Empresa, 14, no. 4 (July–Aug. 1974): 7–28.

Palmer, Thomas W., Jr. "São Paulo in the Brazilian Federation: A State Out of Balance." Ph.D. dissertation, Columbia University. New York, 1950.

Pang, Eul-Soo. "The Politics of Coronelismo in Brazil: The Case of Bahia, 1889–1930." Ph.D. dissertation, University of California. Berkeley, 1969.

Pang, Eul-Soo, and Ron L. Seckinger. "The Mandarins of Imperial Brazil," Comparative Studies in Society and History, 14, no. 2 (March 1972): 215–44.

Partido Republicano [of São Paulo]. Programma dos candidatos; eleição na Provincia de São Paulo. 1881.

————. A scisão 1901. 1901.

Partido Republicano Dissidente de São Paulo. Manifestos politicos de 7 de setembro e 5 de novembro de 1901. 1901.

Partido Republicano Federal. Preliminares de organisação, discussão de programma, installação e deliberação da convenção provisoria, apresentação das candidaturas presidenciaes, apurações e proclamação da eleição presidencial, instrucções. Rio, 1895.

Paula, Lafayette Soares de. São Paulo, um ano após a guerra, 1932–1933. Rio, 1934.

Peláez, Carlos Manuel. "Análise econômica do programa brasileiro de sustentação do café—1906–1945; teoria, política e medição," Revista Brasileira de Economia, 26, no. 4 (Oct.–Dec. 1971): 5–211.

————. "A balança comercial, a grande depressão e a industrialização brasileira," Revista Brasileira de Economia, 22, no. 1 (March 1968): 15–48.

————. História da industrialização brasileira: Crítica à teoria estruturalista no Brasil. Rio, 1972.

————. "The State, the Great Depression and the Industrialization of Brazil." Ph.D. dissertation, Columbia University. New York, 1968.

Peláez, Carlos Manuel, and Wilson Suzigan. História monetária do Brasil; análise da política, comportamento, e instituições monetárias. Rio, 1976.

Penteado, Jacob. Belenzinho, 1910; retrato de uma época. 1962.

Pereira de Sousa, Pedro Luís. Meus cinquenta anos na Companhia Prado Chaves. 1950.

Pierson, Donald. Cruz das Almas: A Brazilian Village. Washington, D.C., 1951.

Pinheiro, Paulo Sérgio de M. S. Política e trabalho no Brasil (dos anos vinte a 1930). Rio, 1975.

Piza, Moacyr. Vespeira. 1923.

Polyanthéa: Commemorativa do 1º congresso brasileiro de estudantes. Rio, 1909.

Prado, Paulo. Retrato do Brasil; ensaio sôbre a tristeza brasileira. 6th ed. Rio, 1962. (Originally published in 1928.)

Prado Júnior, Caio. The Colonial Background of Modern Brazil. Tr. Suzette Macedo. Berkeley, Calif., 1971.

————. "Distribuição da propriedade fundiária rural no Estado de São Paulo," Boletim Geográfico, 3, no. 29 (Aug. 1945): 692–700.

————. História econômica do Brasil. 1945.

Pupo Nogueira, O. Em torno da tarifa aduaneira. 1931.

————. "Super-producção textil," Observador Econômico e Financeiro, 4, no. 20 (Sept. 1937): 54–58.

Quem é quem no Brasil; biografias contemporâneas, v. 1, 5, 8. N.d.

Ramos, Augusto. O café no Brasil e no estrangeiro. Rio, 1923.

Rawick, George P., ed. The American Slave: A Composite. 2d ed. 19 v. Westport, Conn., 1972.

Rebelo Horta, Cid. "Famílias governamentais de Minas Gerais," pp. 45–91 in Segundo Seminário de Estudos Mineiros, Universidade de Minas Gerais. Belo Horizonte, 1956.

Renard, Antoine. São Paulo é isto! A riqueza econômica de São Paulo. A alma cívica paulista. A epopeia das bandeiras. 1933.

Ribeiro, Alvaro. Falsa democracia; a revolta de São Paulo em 1924. Rio, 1927.

Ribeiro, Benedito, and Mário Mazzei Guimarães. História dos bancos e do desenvolvimento financeiro do Brasil. 1967.

Ribeiro, José Jacintho. Chronologia paulista. 3 v. 1899–1902.

Ribeiro, Marly Martinez. "Revisão constitucional de 1926," Revista de Ciência Política, 1, no. 4 (Oct.–Dec. 1967): 65–114.

[Ribeiro de Andrada], Martin Francisco. S. Paulo independente. 1887.

Ricardo, Cassiano. Marcha para oeste (A influência da 'bandeira' no formação social e política do Brasil). 2 v. 2d ed. Rio, 1942. (Originally published in 1940.)

Rippy, J. Fred. British Investments in Latin America, 1822–1949: A Case Study in the Operation of Private Enterprise in Retarded Regions. Minneapolis, 1959.

Rocha Nogueira, Arlinda. A imigração japonesa para a lavoura cafeeira paulista (1908–1922). 1973.

Rodrigues, Duarte. Discurso pronunciado no congresso dos lavradores paulista reunido em Campinas a 26 de março de 1899. 1899.

Romeiro, Manoel Olympio. São Paulo e Minas na economia nacional (Contribuição ao estudo das relações financeiras destes dous estados com o governo da União). 1930.

Saes, Décio Azevedo Marques de. "O civilismo das camadas médias urbanas na Primeira República brasileira (1889–1930)." M.A. thesis, Universidade de Campinas. 1971.

Safford, Frank. "Significación de los antioqueños en el desarrollo económico colombiano; un examen crítico de la tesis de Everett Hagen," Anuario Colombiano de Historia Social y de la Cultura, 1967, pp. 49–69.

Saint-Hilaire, Auguste de. Viagem a Província de São Paulo e resumo das viagens ao Brasil, Província Cisplatina e missões do Paraguai. Tr. Rubens Borba de Moraes. 1940. (Originally published in 1851.)

Salgado, Plínio. O esperado. 4th ed. 1949. (Originally published in 1927.)

———. O extrangeiro. 4th ed. Rio, 1937. (Originally published in 1926.)

Salles, Alberto. A patria paulista. Campinas, São Paulo, 1887.

Salles Júnior, A. C. de. O idealismo republicano de Campos Salles. Rio, n.d.

Salles Oliveira, Armando de. Jornada democrática (Discursos políticos). Rio, 1937.

Sampaio, João. "Adolfo Gordo," Digesto Econômico, 143 (Sept.–Oct. 1958): 77–90.

Sampaio Vidal, Bento A. O café na economia brasileira. 1943.

Santo Rosário, Maria Regina do. See Laurita Pessoa Gabaglia.

Santos, José Maria dos. Bernardino de Campos e o Partido Republicano Paulista; subsídios para a história da República. Rio, 1960.

———. A política geral do Brasil. 1930.

———. Os republicanos paulistas e a abolição. 1942.

Santos Abreu, Diores. "Comunicações entre o sul de Mato Grosso e o sudoeste de São Paulo; o comércio de gado," Revista de História, 53, no. 105 (Jan.–March 1976): 191–214.

———. Formação histórica de uma cidade pioneira paulista: Presidente Prudente. Presidente Prudente, São Paulo, 1972.

São Paulo, Annaes, 1891–1927. Camara dos Deputados.

———, Annaes, 1929. Senado.

———, Annaes da Assembléa constituinte de 1935. Assembléa Legislativa.

———, Annuario estatistico de S. Paulo, 1898, 1900–1905, 1911, 1920, 1921. Repartição de Estatistica.

———, Boletim, Dec. 1938, Aug. 1940 (Anexo). Departamento Estadual de Estatística.

———, Boletim estatistico, no. 1 (Oct. 1912). Repartição de Estatistica.

———, Colleção das leis e decretos do Estado de São Paulo, 1888–1937.

———, Contas. Secretaria da Fazenda, 1930–37.

———, Diário oficial, Jan. 25, 1934, Feb. 16, 1934.

———, Estatística agrícola e zootécnica, 1934–1935. Secretaria da Agricultura, Directoria da Estatística.

———, Estatística agrícola e zootécnica, 1939–1940. Departamento Estadual de Estatística.

———, Estatística escolar de 1930. Directoria Geral do Ensino.

———, As finanças de S. Paulo no governo Armando de Salles Oliveira. 1937.

———, Relatorio. Commissão Central de Estatistica. 1888.

———, Relatorio, 1879–80, 1884–85. Inspector do Thesouro Provincial.

———, Relatorio, 1894. Repartição de Estatistica.

———, Relatório, 1894–1929, 1940, 1943, 1949. Secretaria da Fazenda.

———, Revista, 6, no. 63 (Dec. 1931); 7, no. 72 (Dec. 1932). Instituto de Café.

———, Quadro demonstrativo do desmembramento dos municípios: Qüinqüênio 1954–1958. Departamento de Estatística. 6th ed. 1954.

———, São Paulo, 1889–1939. Departamento Estadual de Estatística. [1940].

São Paulo e seus homens no centenario. 1922.

Schmidt, Cornélio. "Diário de uma viagem pelo sertão de São Paulo, realizada em 1904," Anais do Museu Paulista, 15 (1961): 337–458.

Schmitter, Philippe C. Interest Conflict and Political Change in Brazil. Stanford, Calif., 1971.
Schompré, Emile Quoniam de. La Bourse de São Paulo, 1911. N.d.
Schorer Petrone, Maria Thereza. A lavoura canavieira em São Paulo; expansão e declínio (1765–1851). 1968.
Schröder, Brigitte. "Caractéristiques des relations scientifiques internationales, 1870–1914," Cahiers d'Histoire Mondiale, 10, no. 1 (1966): 161–77.
Schulz, John Henry. "The Brazilian Army and Politics, 1850–1894." Ph.D. dissertation, Princeton University. Princeton, N.J., 1973.
Schurig Vieira, Francisca Isabel. "O pensamento político-administrativo e a política financeira de Washington Luís," Revista de História, 11, no. 41 (Jan.– March 1960): 105–46.
Schwartzman, Simon. São Paulo e o estado nacional. 1975.
Seganfreddo, Sônia. UNE: Instrumento de subversão. Rio, 1963.
Sensabaugh, Leon F. "The Coffee-Trust Question in United States–Brazilian Relations, 1912–1913," Hispanic American Historical Review, 26 (Nov. 1946): 480–96.
Shirley, Robert W. The End of a Tradition: Culture Change and Development in the Município of Cunha, São Paulo, Brazil. New York, 1971.
———. "The Judicial System of São Paulo State, Brazil. An Historical Survey." Unpublished manuscript, 1973.
———. "Notes on Kinship of the Members of the Tribunal of Justice, S.P." Unpublished manuscript, n.d.
Silber, Simão Davi. "Política econômica; defesa do nível de renda e industrialização no período 1929/1939." M.A. thesis, Instituto Brasileiro de Economia, Fundação Getúlio Vargas. Rio, 1973.
Silone, Ignazio. Bread and Wine. Tr. G. David and E. Mosbacher. New York, 1937.
Silva, Eddie Augusto da. Os precursores do progresso no Brasil (In memoriam). 1957.
Silva, Hélio. 1932: A guerra paulista. (v. 5 of O ciclo de Vargas.) Rio, 1967.
———. 1931: os tenentes no poder. (v. 4 of O ciclo de Vargas.) Rio, 1966.
Silva, Liana Maria Lafayette Aureliano da. "No limiar da industrialização; estado e acumulação de capital, 1919–1937." Ph.D. dissertation, Universidade Estadual de Campinas. Campinas, São Paulo, 1976.
Silva, Moacir. "Tentativa de classificação das cidades brasileiras," Revista Brasileira de Geografia, 8, no. 3 (July–Sept. 1946): 283–316.
Silva, Sérgio. Expansão cafeeira e origens da indústria no Brasil. 1976.
Silva Brito, Mário da. História do modernismo brasileiro, v. 1: Antecedentes da semana de arte moderna. 2d ed. Rio, 1964.
Silva Bruno, Ernani. "Esboço da história do povoamento de São Paulo," pp. 1–17 in Silva Bruno, ed., São Paulo; terra e povo. Pôrto Alegre, 1967.
———, ed. O planalto e os cafèzais; São Paulo. 1959.
Silveira, Joel. Grã-finos em São Paulo e outras notícias do Brasil. 1945.
Silveira Camargo, Paulo Florêncio da. "Dom Duarte Leopoldo e Silva," Revista do Instituto Histórico e Geográfico de São Paulo, part 1: 65 (1968): 22–43; part 2: 66 (1969): 46–78.
Simão, Azis. Sindicato e estado; suas relações na formação do proletariado de São Paulo. 1966.

Simonsen, Roberto. A margem da profissão. Discursos. Conferências. Publicações. N.d.

———. Brazil's Industrial Revolution. 1939.

Singer, Paul. Desenvolvimento econômico e evolução urbana; análise da evolução econômica de São Paulo, Blumenau, Pôrto Alegre, Belo Horizonte e Recife. 1968.

Skidmore, Thomas E. Politics in Brazil, 1930–1964: An Experiment in Democracy. New York, 1967.

Slenes, Robert Wayne. "The Demography and Economics of Brazilian Slavery, 1850–1888." Ph.D. dissertation, Stanford University. Stanford, Calif., 1976.

Smith, Gordon Whitford. "Agricultural Marketing and Economic Development: A Brazilian Case Study." Ph.D. dissertation, Harvard University. Cambridge, Mass., 1965.

Smith, T. Lynn. Brazil: People and Institutions. 4th ed. Baton Rouge, La., 1972.

Soares Júnior, Rodrigo. Jorge Tibiriçá e sua época. 2 v. 1958.

Sociedade Paulista de Agricultura. Estatutos. 1902.

———. Relatorio da diretoria (Exercicio de 1922). 1923.

Sociedade Rural Brasileira. Annaes, 1, no. 1 (April 1920).

———. Revista, 1922, 1931. (Numbering varies.)

Société de Publicité Sud-Americaine. O Estado de São Paulo. Barcelona, 1918.

Sousa, Alberto. Memoria historica sobre o Correio Paulistano. N.d.

Souza Ferraz, Arrisson de. Grandes soldados de São Paulo. 1960.

Souza Keller, Elza Coelho de. "Notas sobre a evolução da população do Estado de São Paulo de 1920 a 1950," pp. 209–36 in Instituto Brasileiro de Geografia e Estatística, Aspectos geográficos da terra bandeirante. Rio, 1954.

Souza Lobo, T. de. São Paulo na Federação. 1924.

Souza Martins, José de. Empresário e empresa na biografia do Conde Matarazzo. Rio, 1967.

———. "Frente pioneira; contribuição para uma caracterização sociológica," Estudos Históricos, 10 (1971): 33–41.

Stein, Stanley J. The Brazilian Cotton Manufacture: Textile Enterprise in an Underdeveloped Area, 1850–1950. Cambridge, Mass., 1957.

———. Vassouras: A Brazilian Coffee County, 1850–1900. Cambridge, Mass., 1957.

Stepan, Alfred. The Military in Politics: Changing Patterns in Brazil. Princeton, N.J., 1971.

Stepan, Nancy. Beginnings of Brazilian Science: Oswaldo Cruz, Medical Research and Policy, 1890–1920. New York, 1976.

Strassmann, W. Paul. "The Industrialist," pp. 161–85 in John J. Johnson, ed., Continuity and Change in Latin America. Stanford, Calif., 1964.

Subiroff, Ivan [pseud. for Nereu Rangel Pestana]. A oligarchia paulista, v. 1. 1919.

Suzigan, Wilson. "A industrialização de São Paulo, 1930–1945," Revista Brasileira de Economia, 25, no. 2 (April–June 1971): 89–111.

Tacito, Hilario [pseud. for José Maria de Toledo Malta]. Madame Pommery; chronica muito veridica e memoria philosophica da sua vida; feitos e gestos mais notaveis nesta cidade de São Paulo. 2d ed. N.d.

Tarrow, Sidney G. Peasant Communism in Southern Italy. New Haven, Conn., 1967.

Taunay, Affonso de Escragnolle. História geral das bandeiras paulistas. 11 v. 1924–50.
———. Pequena história do café no Brasil (1727–1937). Rio, 1945.
Tavares Bastos, [Aureliano Candido]. A provincia; estudo sobre a descentralização no Brazil. Rio, 1870.
Tavares de Almeida, A. Oeste paulista; a experiência etnográfica e cultural. Rio, 1943.
Thistlethwaite, Frank. "Migration from Europe Overseas in the Nineteenth and Twentieth Centuries," Comité International des Sciences Historiques, XIᵉ Congrès International, Rapports, v. 5: Histoire contemporaine (1960): 32–60.
Thorman, Canuto. Almanak administrativo, commercial e profissional do Estado de São Paulo para 1897 incluindo indicador da capital. 1897.
———. Completo almanak administrativo, commercial e profissional do Estado de São Paulo para 1896. 1896.
Todaro, Margaret Patrice. "Pastors, Prophets and Politicians: A Study of the Brazilian Catholic Church, 1916–1945." Ph.D. dissertation, Columbia University. New York, 1971.
Toledo, Pedro de. Discursos proferidos no parlamento de São Paulo. 1910.
Topik, Steven C. "Economic Nationalism and the State in an Underdeveloped Country: Brazil, 1889–1930." Ph.D. dissertation, University of Texas. Austin, 1978.
Toplin, Robert Brent. The Abolition of Slavery in Brazil. New York, 1972.
Trindade, Hélgio. Integralismo (O fascismo brasileiro na década de 30). 1974.
[Uebele, Otto]. Cem anos da Casa Theodor Wille & Cia. no Brasil. 1946.
Ukers, William H. All About Coffee. 2d ed. New York, 1935.
Union des Associations Internationales. Les Congrès internationaux. Liste complète. 2 v. Brussels, 1964.
United Nations. Coffee in Latin America, v. 2: Brazil, State of São Paulo, part 1: The State and Prospects of Production. Mexico City, 1960. Published by the Economic Commission for Latin America and the Food and Agriculture Organization.
———. External Financing in Latin America. New York, 1965. Published by the Department of Economic and Social Affairs: Economic Commission for Latin America.
United States. Historical Statistics of the United States: Colonial Times to 1957. A Statistical Abstract Supplement. Department of Commerce. Washington, D.C., 1961.
Universidade de São Paulo, Faculdade de Direito. Revista, 60 (1965).
Valladares, Francisco. "Questões debatidas sobre competencia tributaria. Impostos interestadoaes," pp. 281–307 in Livro do centenario da Camara dos Deputados (1826–1926), v. 2. Rio, 1926.
Vasconcellos, Vasco Joaquim Smith de. História da província eclesiástica de São Paulo. 1957.
Velho Sobrinho, J. F. Diciónario bio-bibliográfico brasileiro. 2 v. Rio, 1937–40.
Venâncio Filho, Alberto. A intervenção do estado no domínio econômico; o direito público econômico no Brasil. Rio, 1968.
Veríssimo, Erico. O arquipélago. 3 v. Pôrto Alegre, 1961–62. (Part 3 of O tempo e o vento.)
Versiani, F. R. "Resenha bibliográfica; história da industrialização brasileira;

crítica à teoria estruturalista no Brasil," *Pesquisa e Planejamento Econômico*, 4, no. 1 (Feb. 1974): 181–88.

Viana, Victor. O Banco do Brasil. Sua formação, seu engrandecimento, sua missão nacional. Rio, 1926.

Vieira, Hermes, and Osvaldo Silva. História da polícia civil de São Paulo. 1955.

Vieira, José. A Cadeia Velha (Memoria da camara dos deputados). Rio, n.d.

Vieira Machado, Carlos. O imposto de consumo no Brasil. Apontamentos: 1772–1922. N.p., n.d.

Villela, Annibal Villanova, and Wilson Suzigan. Política do governo e crescimento da economia brasileira, 1889–1945. Rio, 1973.

Viotti da Costa, Emília. Da senzala à colônia. 1966.

———. "O movimento republicano em Itu," *Revista de História*, 20 (1954): 379–405.

———. "A proclamação da República," *Anais do Museu Paulista*, 19 (1965): 169–207.

Walker, Thomas W. "From Coronelismo to Populism: The Evolution of Politics in a Brazilian Municipality; Ribeirão Preto, São Paulo, 1910–1960." Ph.D. dissertation, University of New Mexico. Albuquerque, 1974.

Walle, Paul. Au pays de l'or rouge, l'Etat de São Paulo (Brésil): Ses resources—ses progrès—son avenir. Etude generale économique et descriptive. Paris, 1921.

Weffort, Francisco C. "Classes populares e política (Contribuição ao estudo do 'populismo')." Ph.D. dissertation, Universidade de São Paulo. 1968.

Weiner, Myron. "National Integration vs. Nationalism," *Comparative Studies in Society and History*, 15, no. 2 (March 1973): 248–54.

Werneck Vianna, Luiz. Liberalismo e sindicato no Brasil. Rio, 1976.

Westphalen, Cecília Maria, Brasil Pinheiro Machado, and Altiva Pilatti Balhana. "Nota prévia ao estudo da ocupação da terra no Paraná moderno," *Boletim da Universidade Federal do Paraná*, no. 7 (1968): 1–52.

Wileman, J. P. The Brazilian Year Book . . . 1908. Rio, n.d.

Williams, Margaret Todaro. "Integralism and the Brazilian Catholic Church," *Hispanic American Historical Review*, 54, no. 3 (Aug. 1974): 431–52.

———. "The Politicization of the Brazilian Catholic Church: The Catholic Electoral League," *Journal of Inter-American Studies and World Affairs*, 16, no. 3 (Aug. 1974): 301–25.

Williamson, J. G. "Regional Inequality and the Process of National Development: A Description of the Patterns," pp. 99–158 in L. Needleman, ed., Regional Analysis: Selected Readings. Baltimore, 1968.

Wirth, John D. Minas Gerais in the Brazilian Federation, 1889–1937. Stanford, Calif., 1977.

———. The Politics of Brazilian Development, 1930–1954. Stanford, Calif., 1970.

Witter, José Sebastião. "A primeira tentativa de organização partidária na República—o Partido Republicano Federal—(1893/1897)." Ph.D. dissertation, Universidade de São Paulo. 1971.

Zeldin, Theodore. France, 1848–1945, v. 1: Ambition, Love and Politics; v. 2: Intellect, Taste and Anxiety. Oxford, 1973. 1977.

Zimmermann, Siegfried. Theodor Wille, 1844–1969. Hamburg, 1969.

Index